Keep your
brain
healthy
for life

Keep your brain healthy for life

Reader's Digest

Keep Your Brain Healthy for Life is published by Reader's Digest (Australia) Pty Limited, 80 Bay Street, Ultimo, NSW, 2007
www.readersdigest.com.au
www.readersdigest.co.nz
www.readersdigest.co.za
www.rdasia.co.in

This book is based on *Un cerveau tonique pour la vie,* which was published by Reader's Digest, France, in 2009

This edition first published 2011

National Library of Australia Cataloguing-in-Publication entry

Title: Keep Your Brain Healthy for Life: proven ways to boost your memory, sharpen your mind and stay mentally fit at any age.

    ISBN: 9781921743627 (hbk.)
    Notes: Includes index.
    Subjects: Intellect. Mental work.
    Thought and thinking. Memory.
    Brain—Popular works.
    Dewey Number: 153

Prepress by Sinnott Bros, Sydney
Printed and bound by Leo Paper Products, China

We are interested in receiving your comments on the content of this book. Write to: The Editor, General Books Editorial, Reader's Digest (Australia) Pty Limited, GPO Box 4353, Sydney, NSW 2001, or email us at: bookeditors.au@readersdigest.com

To order additional copies of *Keep Your Brain Healthy For Life,* contact us at: 1300 300 030 (Australia), 0800 400 060 (New Zealand) or 0800 980 572 (South Africa), or email us at: customerservice@au.readersdigest.com

Keep Your Brain Healthy for Life

Chief Consultants for Australia and New Zealand

Associate Professor Dr Sharon Naismith, Senior Clinical Neuropsychologist, Brain and Mind Institute, The University of Sydney,

Dr Sara Lucas, clinical neuropsychologist

Other Consultants and Contributors

For the Australian and New Zealand edition: Allan Bolton (exercise), Susan Butler (language), Anne Dodd (mathematics), Suzie Ferrie (nutrition), Colin Groves (anthropology), Karen McGhee (nature), Phillip Staines (logic). For the original French edition: Gauthier Andujar, Dr Sébastien Bohler (neuroscience), Marie Borrel, Christophe Boujon (teacher and researcher in cognitive psychology – attention), Fabrice Bouvier, Valérie Buron (science journalist), Françoise Caille, Liliane Charrier, Dr Nicolas Chevassus-au-Louis (biology), Dr Serge Ciccotti (psychology), Professor Laurent Cohen (Professor of Neurology), Matthieu Crocq, Frédéric Denhez (science journalist), Dr Michel Galobardès, Christophe Hardy, Dominique Imbert, Patrick Lemoine (psychiatrist, sleep disorder specialist, Director of *La Recherche*), Véronique Liégeois (dietitian and nutritionist), Marielle Mayo (science journalist), Tomaz Mezou (sports coach), Dr Patrick Philipon (biology), Éditions Pole, Laurent Raval, Laure Schalchli (science journalist), Catherine Vidal (neurobiologist, Research Director, Institut Pasteur).

Consultant Editor for South Africa Judy Beyer
Project and Rewrite Editor Carol Natsis
Puzzles Editor Margaret McPhee
Cover Design Sally Kinging
Project Designers Amy Laker, Sally Kinging
Translators Shan Benson, Narelle Fletcher
Proofreader Kevin Diletti
Index Diane Harriman
Senior Production Controller Monique Tesoriero

READER'S DIGEST GENERAL BOOKS
Editorial Director Elaine Russell
Managing Editor Rosemary McDonald
Art Director Carole Orbell

Alternative food names

capsicum ...... sweet pepper
eggplant .... brinjal
karela .... bitter melon
rockmelon ...... spanspek, sweetmelon
silverbeet .... Swiss chard
witlof .... chicory, endive
zucchini .... courgette

In South Africa, ostrich is a lean meat comparable to kangaroo. It has approximately the same omega-3 content (depending on the cut) and the same zinc content. Its copper and iron content is different: 100 g cooked ostrich meat contains 0.1 mg copper and 2 mg iron.

Foreword

The human brain is fascinating – highly developed and individualised – and is unique among mammals. Its interconnected circuits contain a lifetime's worth of human experiences, emotions, skills, knowledge and memories. Our childhood memories, understanding of history or the arts, ability to dance the tango, and love for our family and friends all reside in the labyrinth of the human brain. Even though modern medicine has made rapid advances in organ transplants, replacing the brain is unthinkable.

Diseases of the brain and mind highlight just how precious our brain is. From mental illnesses such as depression and schizophrenia, to degenerative conditions such as Alzheimer's and Parkinson's diseases, we have discovered just how sensitive our brain is to developmental, genetic, environmental and disease-specific insults. Most importantly, we have learned a great deal about what contributes to these diseases, giving new hope for treatments and disease prevention.

Increasingly, we are recognising how important it is to protect our brain from the harmful effects of many lifestyle and medical risks. At the same time, we understand more about what we can do to protect our brain. Being empowered with this knowledge is important for us as an ageing society. Since we are now living longer than ever before, we also have a greater chance of having a stroke or developing dementia. Of course, healthy ageing is not just about our physical state. Instead, the secrets of ageing successfully lie equally in our sense of wellbeing and satisfaction with life.

Keep Your Brain Healthy for Life provides a comprehensive insight into how the brain works, including intelligence, memory, emotions, senses, creativity and movement. It also incorporates the latest medical advances and enables us to understand the critical role that sleep, diet, lifestyle and exercise have for maintaining a healthy brain. Perhaps one of the most exciting lessons we have learned is that the brain is actually malleable or 'plastic'; it continues to evolve with new emotions, knowledge and experiences, which in turn produce physical changes in the brain's neurons, synapses and connections. If you keep your brain active intellectually and socially earlier in life, it also seems to create a 'buffer' against the harmful effects of brain disease. This means that if you want to keep your brain healthy for life, it is never too early to start!

Together with facts, figures and diagrams to help your brain absorb as much as possible, this book is packed with a range of practical tips and exercises for promoting your physical and emotional wellbeing. The fun and challenging quizzes and games in each chapter are guaranteed to keep your most precious organ active! Be good to your brain and it will return the favour.

Associate Professor Sharon Naismith

Senior Clinical Neuropsychologist and Director,
Ageing Brain Centre, Brain and Mind Research Institute,
The University of Sydney

Contents

Anatomy of the brain

1

Looking inside the brain

Until relatively recent times, it was not possible for scientists to see inside the human brain or to begin to understand how it works.

Parts that make the whole

Protected by the skull and enclosed by three membranes called meninges, the brain consists of three main parts:
● the cerebrum, which contains the thinking parts of the brain, including high-level skills, memory, personality, feelings and control of movement
● the brainstem, which links the spinal cord to the brain and controls breathing and heart rate
● the cerebellum, which controls balance and physical coordination.

Revealing techniques

Concealed inside the skull, the brain couldn't be observed properly until the eighteenth century, when alcohol was first used to preserve organs – a technique that paved the way for examining body tissues under the microscope. By the early twentieth century, it was possible to make recordings of electrical activity in the brain using the electroencephalogram, which is still used to this day to diagnose epilepsy. But it was not until the 1970s, when increasingly sophisticated medical imaging techniques such as computed tomography (CT) were developed, that extensive scientific exploration of brain function and studies of brain activity began. Used to detect tumours and serious lesions, a CT scan is produced by taking X-ray images of an organ in a series of slices, which a computer then reconstructs into a cross-sectional image by interpreting the level of X-rays absorbed by the tissue.

Magnetic resonance imaging (MRI) uses the energy from the hydrogen electrons in brain tissue to produce a three-dimensional detailed 'map' of the brain and detect any anomalies that might be present. Functional MRI provides a real-time record of activity in the different areas of the brain, analysing the amount of oxygen used by various brain regions at rest or while completing tasks.

PARTS OF THE BRAIN

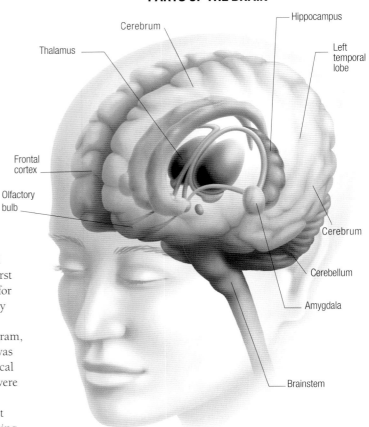

Cerebrum

Thalamus

Hippocampus

Left temporal lobe

Frontal cortex

Olfactory bulb

Cerebrum

Cerebellum

Amygdala

Brainstem

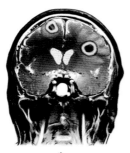
1

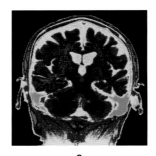
2

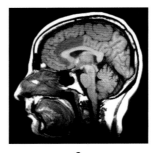
3

Mapping the brain Magnetic resonance imaging (MRI) allows the brain to be viewed in precise detail.
1 Two tumours, outlined in yellow, are revealed in this section across the back of the brain.
2 The two small purple masses at centre left and right of this frontal cross-section are the regions containing the amygdalae – important in processing emotion.
3 This section across the side of the head illustrates a theory that people with schizophrenia have fewer receptors for the neurotransmitter dopamine (the coloured areas), which is involved in cognition and movement and is linked to behavioural problems.

Positron emission tomography

Positron emission tomography (PET) is a comparatively old technology, but is still used today. When a PET scan is taken, the person is given an injection of a small amount of a radioactive drug, or tracer. A commonly used tracer is fluorine 18, a radioactive form of glucose. This emits positively charged particles, or positrons, to produce three-dimensional images that show how much of the tracer has been taken up by different parts of the brain. Cancer cells are extremely active, absorbing more glucose than healthy cells, and their level of metabolic activity is represented by specific colours in the scan.

SPECT scans

Single photon emission computed tomography (SPECT) is a three-dimensional imaging technique that uses gamma rays to examine the brain. A patient is injected with a gamma-emitting radioisotope, often combined with a special radioactive substance that binds to a specific kind of tissue. A gamma camera then takes a series of images as it is rotated around the patient. SPECT scans have been used to compare brain blood flow in different brain diseases. They are also used to diagnose early dementia such as Alzheimer's disease and can sometimes help to differentiate early dementia from depression and other conditions.

Scanning the brain After being injected with a radioactive drug, the subject is moved into the tunnel of the PET scanner, which is fitted with detectors. The data recorded is processed by a computer to generate a three-dimensional image.

Cerebrospinal fluid

A colourless substance called cerebrospinal fluid (CSF) circulates between the inner and outer meninges. Made up of 99 per cent water and containing glucose and proteins, this fluid buffers the brain from impact by providing a cushioning, 'airbag' effect. CSF flows through brain cavities, known as ventricles, before reaching the spinal cord and ultimately being reabsorbed into the blood. The body contains an average of 1 litre of CSF, constantly secreting and absorbing it and replacing the entire volume three or four times every 24 hours. As well as acting as a shock absorber, CSF protects the brain against attacks from germs and provides it with nutrients. Infection of the CSF can lead to meningitis, while any disruption to normal CSF circulation (for example, after a head injury) can cause a condition called hydrocephalus, or water on the brain, in which an abnormal accumulation of fluid puts pressure on brain structures and impairs functions.

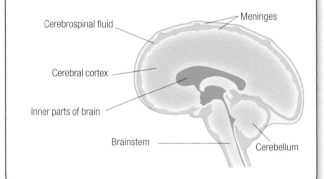

Cerebrospinal fluid

Meninges

Cerebral cortex

Inner parts of brain

Brainstem

Cerebellum

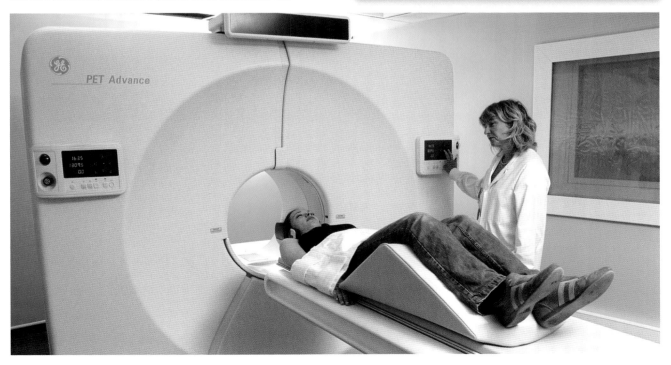

How the brain developed

The surface area of the outer layer (cortex) of the human brain has an impressive number of folds. This feature emerged with the evolution of mammals as the primitive brain increased spectacularly in size. Because the skull couldn't expand at the same rate, the brain had to roll back on itself, forming the many deep, wavy folds of the cortex. In fact, if we were able to spread the tightly convoluted tissue out flat, it would cover an area of more than 1 square metre. This folding phenomenon, which is found in the most highly evolved species, led to the development of a new cortex, or neocortex, which gradually became the larger part of the brain. The neocortex doesn't exist in fish, but accounts for 15 per cent of total brain volume in a hedgehog, 60 per cent in a dolphin, 68 per cent in a gorilla, 72 per cent in a chimpanzee and 80 per cent in a human.

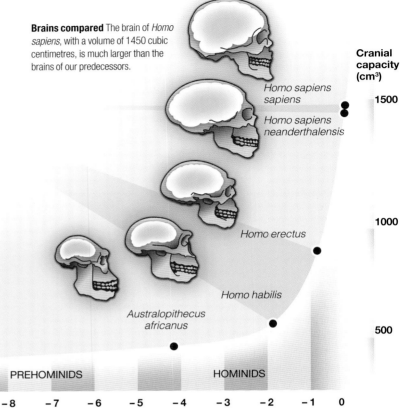

Brains compared The brain of *Homo sapiens*, with a volume of 1450 cubic centimetres, is much larger than the brains of our predecessors.

Cranial capacity (cm³)

1500

1000

500

Homo sapiens sapiens

Homo sapiens neanderthalensis

Homo erectus

Homo habilis

Australopithecus africanus

Anthropoid monkey

PRIMATES   PREHOMINIDS   HOMINIDS

Years (millions) − 10 − 9 − 8 − 7 − 6 − 5 − 4 − 3 − 2 − 1 0

A high energy consumer

In adult humans, the brain weighs an average of 1.4 kilograms and makes up approximately 2 per cent of total body mass, yet it consumes 20 per cent of all the glucose in the body, which shows just how great the brain's energy requirements are. As brain cells can't store energy, they need to have a constant supply from the bloodstream; two-thirds of brain glucose is replaced every minute. With this high level of activity, the brain absorbs large quantities of oxygen – approximately 20 per cent of all the oxygen consumed by the body at rest – and so the slightest disruption of the oxygen supply to the brain can have extremely serious consequences.

Blood travels to the brain through two sets of arteries, the internal carotid arteries and the vertebral arteries, which then branch into a series of vessels that make it possible for the brain to receive more than 10 per cent of the body's blood flow. These major vascular pathways form an interconnected network, including an arterial intersection at the base of the brain, known as the Circle of Willis. This operates as a kind of back-up system that can, to a certain extent, maintain the blood supply to the brain if arteries are damaged.

The two hemispheres and their roles

The brain is divided from front to back into two halves, or hemispheres – one on either side of a deep fissure – and these are linked by a band of tissue called the corpus callosum. Made of the same substance, each hemisphere has four separate lobes and is in constant communication with the other through bundles of nerve fibres.

Mirror images, but not the same

The two hemispheres may be anatomically similar, but their functions are quite different. By observing patients with damage to the brain, specifically to the corpus callosum, and by using functional imaging techniques, it has been shown that each hemisphere controls different tasks. For most people, the left hemisphere is associated with language, rational thought and logical analysis, while the right hemisphere is the centre for emotion, creativity, intuition and spatial analysis.

The first person to establish a link between an area of the brain and language was the French neurologist Paul Broca. One of Broca's patients couldn't say anything clearly except 'tan', which he would often repeat – and so earned himself the nickname Tan-Tan, according to medical records. But his ability to understand speech was not affected and his speech organs functioned normally. When Tan-Tan died in 1861, Broca performed an autopsy of his brain and discovered an egg-sized growth in the left frontal lobe, in the area now called Broca's area. Today it is widely accepted that Broca's area is critical for producing fluent speech. Another area that controls speech comprehension is called Wernicke's area.

Right brain, left brain

The side of the brain responsible for specific functions, known as lateralisation, can vary from one individual to another. For example, 70 per cent of left-handed people have the language centre in the left hemisphere, the same side as for the vast majority of right-handers, but in 15 per cent of left-handed people the right hemisphere is dominant for speech, while the remaining 15 per cent have language centres in both hemispheres. What's more, functions may not reside permanently in one side of the brain, but may change sides in certain circumstances – for example, after trauma to the brain. In young children, the undamaged hemisphere spontaneously takes over from the damaged one, but adults need the stimulation provided by speech, physical and occupational therapists to make this happen.

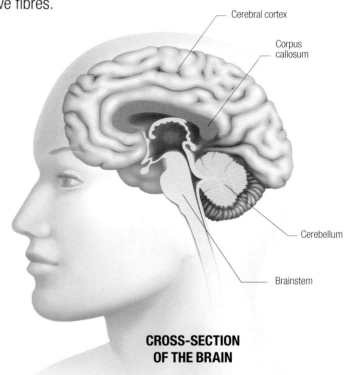

Cerebral cortex

Corpus callosum

Cerebellum

Brainstem

CROSS-SECTION OF THE BRAIN

The corpus callosum

Most of the information that passes from one hemisphere to the other is relayed by the corpus callosum, a white band 8 centimetres long that contains some 200 million nerve fibres and has branches extending into the cortex. When the corpus callosum is missing, the separate roles of the two hemispheres, as well as how they interact, become obvious; its absence can lead to problems affecting memory and coordination of movement, causing loss of balance, learning difficulties or epileptic fits.

Crossed wires

Most motor skills and senses on one side of the body are controlled by the opposite, or contralateral, side of the brain. For example, nerve pathways starting in the left hemisphere cross to the right side at the lower brainstem, near the spinal cord and vice versa. This explains why the left hand is controlled by the right hemisphere, why signals coming from the right visual field are processed by the left hemisphere, and why brain damage to the left hemisphere affects the right side of the body – and vice versa.

Ambidexterity

People are said to be ambidextrous when they can use either hand equally well, but in practice this ability is rarely found for the same action or activity. An ambidextrous person usually uses one hand for certain actions or movements and the other hand for different movements. This is because most ambidextrous people are naturally left-handed but have learned to develop some right-handed skills, either deliberately or influenced by society's emphasis on right-handed habits. True ambidexterity – existing from birth – is found in only 3 per cent of the population.

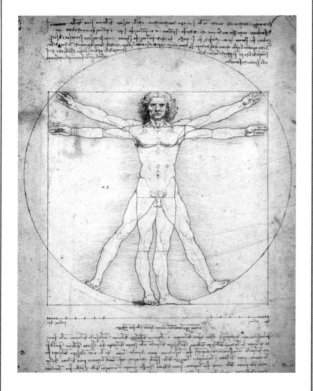

Back to front Leonardo da Vinci was ambidextrous, but the notes he wrote with his left hand were written backwards, from right to left – that is, in mirror writing – as shown in his comments accompanying the *Vitruvian Man*, a drawing he created in about 1487.

Which is your dominant side?

1. Dominant hand

The most reliable test for both children and adults is to sharpen a pencil. Which hand holds the pencil and which hand holds the sharpener?

A left-handed person holds the sharpener in the right hand and rotates the pencil with the left.

Deal a pack of cards or unscrew a bottle cap and watch your hands. Your non-dominant hand holds the cards or bottle, while your dominant hand deals or turns.

2. Dominant foot

If you push someone from behind (warn them first to avoid accidents), they will recover their balance on the dominant foot first.

3. Dominant eye

With both eyes open, focus on a point a few metres away. Then, without moving, close or cover one eye. What happens? If the alignment suddenly shifts, the eye you have covered or closed is the dominant one.

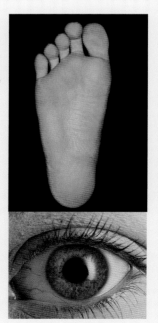

Brain topography

The cortex in each of the brain's hemispheres is made up of four lobes, which are separated by deep fissures known as sulci. Each lobe, named after the overlying cranial bone, has distinct tasks. The frontal lobes, which comprise 86 per cent of the cortex, are the centres for coordination, movement, thought, reasoning and language. The occipital lobes control vision, the parietal lobes process sensory information about touch and spatial orientation, and the temporal lobes are concerned with the senses of hearing, smell and taste.

The cortex is divided into 52 smaller areas belonging to three broad categories that have been defined by medical imaging or by observing brain damage caused by accidents. These are the primary sensory areas, the primary motor areas and the association areas. The primary sensory areas, found in the temporal, occipital and parietal lobes, receive information from the sense organs and play a key role in perception. The primary motor areas send information required for voluntary movement to the muscles via the spinal cord; these areas are located in the frontal lobes and include Broca's area, which is involved in speech production. The association areas, covering more than 75 per cent of the surface area of the cortex, are connected to many brain regions and provide appropriate responses to the sensory information from the primary areas.

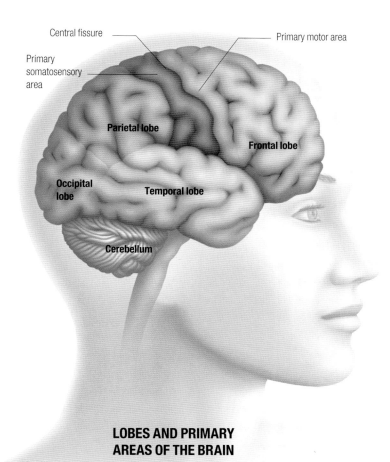

LOBES AND PRIMARY AREAS OF THE BRAIN

Brain teaser

Unscramble the words below to find a list of terms related to the brain that all appear in Chapter 1.

1. **XORTEC** ....
2. **NIGEMSEN** ....
3. **MALASUTH** ....
4. **SHOPPUPIMAC** ....
5. **PICONCOTER** ....
6. **PANSSEY** ....
7. **REBULLCEEM** ....
8. **UNORNER** ....
9. **NOXA** ....
10. **TUGAMALTE** ....
11. **TRINEDED** ....
12. **BUREMIXOSTAD** ....
13. **NILMEY** ....

Answers: **1.** cortex; **2.** meninges; **3.** thalamus; **4.** hippocampus; **5.** nociceptor; **6.** synapse; **7.** cerebellum; **8.** neuron; **9.** axon; **10.** glutamate; **11.** dendrite; **12.** ambidextrous; **13.** myelin.

Sharing the work

The most complex functions can be shared by different specialised areas, which are activated simultaneously. For example, hearing a word will stimulate one of the primary auditory areas in the temporal lobe. If the word is also onomatopoeic – a word that sounds like the object or action it describes – hearing it will also stimulate a neighbouring area in the same lobe. Saying a word out loud will activate Broca's area in the frontal lobe, while reading it at the same time will simultaneously activate not only Broca's area but also the primary visual areas in the occipital lobe and the association areas in the same lobe that are involved in reading.

Information superhighways

To collect and transmit information, the brain employs some 100 billion nerve cells, or neurons, and it is these that give the cortex its grey colour.

Our little grey cells

Each neuron is wrapped in a membrane that is able to conduct electrical impulses. Each has a cell body from which many branching projections, called dendrites, reach out to receive a mass of signals that arrive from other neurons. After processing, this bundle of electrical information – called the nerve impulse – is transmitted to a fibre, or axon, that extends from the cell body. Dendrites are short, but axons can range in length from a few millimetres inside the brain, to tens of centimetres when transmitting a nerve impulse from the brain to the spinal cord, and up to 1 metre when sending it from the spinal cord to the toe muscles.

The speed of a nerve impulse depends on the diameter of the axon: the wider the diameter, the faster the impulse travels. When the impulse moves along an axon in a myelin sheath – an outer coating of lipids that can increase the axon's diameter 100 times – it can reach speeds of almost 120 metres per second. If the axon is not myelinated, the impulse travels at only 50 metres per second.

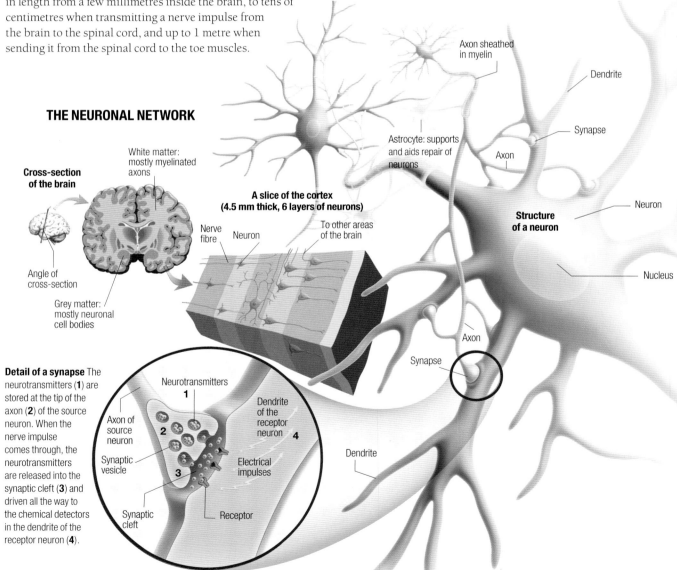

THE NEURONAL NETWORK

Cross-section of the brain

White matter: mostly myelinated axons

Angle of cross-section

Grey matter: mostly neuronal cell bodies

A slice of the cortex (4.5 mm thick, 6 layers of neurons)

Nerve fibre

Neuron

To other areas of the brain

Axon sheathed in myelin

Dendrite

Synapse

Astrocyte: supports and aids repair of neurons

Axon

Structure of a neuron

Neuron

Nucleus

Axon

Synapse

Dendrite

Detail of a synapse The neurotransmitters (**1**) are stored at the tip of the axon (**2**) of the source neuron. When the nerve impulse comes through, the neurotransmitters are released into the synaptic cleft (**3**) and driven all the way to the chemical detectors in the dendrite of the receptor neuron (**4**).

Neurotransmitters

1

Axon of source neuron

2

Synaptic vesicle

3

Synaptic cleft

Receptor

Dendrite of the receptor neuron

4

Electrical impulses

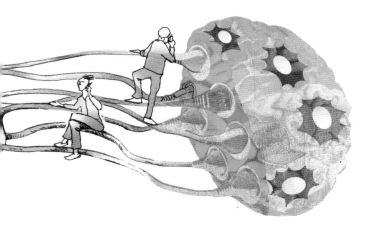

Communication experts

When a nerve impulse travels from the axon of one neuron to the dendrite of another neuron, it has to cross the gap between them, called the synapse. Each neuron has between 1000 and 10,000 billion synapses that link it to other neurons. The neurons are not in direct contact with one another but make use of go-betweens – chemical compounds known as neurotransmitters – to pass the nerve impulse on to neighbouring neurons.

Each to its own

Each neuron has a specialised site called a receptor, which responds to a certain type of neurotransmitter that will either transmit or block the nerve impulse. To date some 50 neurotransmitters have been identified, and two of them – glutamate and GABA (gamma-aminobutyric acid) – are used by nearly 80 per cent of neurons. Glutamate stimulates communication between neurons and in this way contributes to learning and memorisation, as well as to efficient motor skills and sensory function. A glutamate deficiency will cause cognitive systems to decline, with brain damage in some cases, but too much glutamate will also have negative effects. Excess glutamate destroys neurons, which then release their own glutamate, and this in turn kills off other neurons. This kind of chain reaction may be found in some psychiatric disorders and in neurodegenerative conditions like Alzheimer's disease, Huntington's disease and motor neuron disease, in which motor neurons are gradually destroyed. Unlike glutamate, GABA inhibits neuronal activity in the brain, helping to control movement and regulate anxiety. A GABA deficiency may lead to depression and anxiety, while a surfeit may cause severe migraines and reduce muscle tone. A number of anxiety-relieving and anti-seizure drugs act by raising GABA levels in the brain.

Alzheimer's disease

Approximately 70 per cent of all cases of senile dementia are Alzheimer's disease, which in Australia and New Zealand affects about one person in four over the age of 80, particularly women. In addition to advancing age, there are a number of risk factors, including genetics, type 2 diabetes, stroke, depression, high blood pressure, brain damage, obesity, smoking and an unhealthy lifestyle.

In its early stages, Alzheimer's disease manifests mainly as lapses of memory and problems with language, progressing later to difficulties with visual and spatial tasks, problem-solving and complex movements, then behavioural and sleep problems, personality change, gradual loss of autonomy and finally dementia. As these symptoms develop, between 10 and 20 per cent of the brain's weight is lost. This is because neurons die off, often starting in the hippocampus – a primitive part of the brain that plays a key role in memory function. At the same time an abnormal number of protein deposits – known as senile plaques – appear, gradually altering how neurons function, while nerve fibres become dense and tangled inside

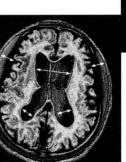

Diagnosing Alzheimer's MRI scans are commonly used to help to diagnose Alzheimer's disease. *Above:* A side view of the head, produced by magnetic resonance imaging. *Left:* The brain of a person with Alzheimer's disease is seen from the top in this scan. The outer white arrows show a moderate degree of atrophy, or shrinkage, around the brain's surface, which in a healthy person sits closely against the skull. The centre arrows indicate enlarged ventricles.

neurons, eventually destroying them. In addition to these changes, blood flow in the brain slows down and the production of neurotransmitters is impaired. While treatments that are currently available cannot slow the progression of the disease, they do succeed in regulating the number of neurotransmitters and how they work, so alleviating some symptoms and improving a person's ability to function.

Self-renewal

By the age of 25 our neuron pool has begun to shrink, and by the time we reach 50 we are losing tens of thousands of neurons every day. This is no cause for concern, as our original pool of neurons is huge and we never use all of them. But, like all body cells, neurons do age and their performance declines: they communicate less efficiently with one another as nerve endings are lost, fewer neurotransmitters are produced and networks become disorganised. Yet, contrary to the theory widely accepted only two decades ago, even though neurons can't reproduce, they are able to generate new neurons and create new connections. This process, known as neurogenesis, is possible because stem cells inside the hippocampus can differentiate to become new neurons.

There are a number of ways that you can help this process of renewal and keep your neurons and synapses functioning efficiently: take physical exercise, stimulate your brain regularly with varied activities, train your memory, lead an active social life, have a diet rich in antioxidants with a moderate intake of alcohol, and adopt good sleeping habits. The absence of medical conditions such as high blood pressure, high cholesterol and diabetes, plus a stress-free, smoke-free lifestyle are also important. Some drugs, such as antidepressants, also promote neurogenesis, while a range of dietary supplements may also be helpful.

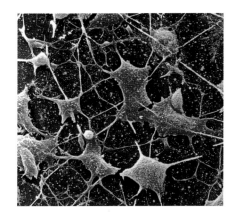

A mesh of neurons This image shows how neurons (coloured pink, orange and red), the basic components of the nervous system, are linked together by countless connections in a complex network. On average, each neuron constantly emits or receives around 1000 impulses.

Parkinson's disease

After Alzheimer's, Parkinson's disease is the most common neurodegenerative disease. In Australia and New Zealand it affects approximately 1–2 per cent of the population over the age of 65, mainly men. While the cause is unknown, a combination of genetic and environmental factors may be relevant, and repeated contact with substances such as some insecticides can also destroy the neurons associated with the disease.

Symptoms include tremor when at rest, slow movements, muscular stiffness, loss of balance and falls. Around 40 per cent of people with Parkinson's experience depression, over 50 per cent have sleep disturbances, and dementia occurs in 20 per cent of sufferers. What causes these symptoms is a deficiency of dopamine, a neurotransmitter that is involved in motor control and produced by neurons in a tiny region of the brainstem called the substantia nigra. By the time the first signs of the condition appear, 70 per cent of these neurons have already been destroyed, suggesting that the disease starts very early. Good results can be obtained with drugs that treat the dopamine deficiency, but after a few years side effects are common – mostly abnormal and involuntary movements – while the effect of the medication can wear off during the day. For severe cases, some 10 per cent of patients may be helped by brain surgery, in which a pacemaker is implanted in the brain to relieve certain symptoms by deep electrical stimulation. Currently, gene therapy trials are attempting to restore the production of dopamine in the brain. Other trials are testing chemical compounds that might be able to protect and regenerate neurons.

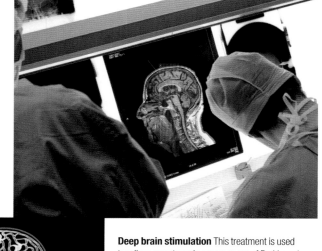

Deep brain stimulation This treatment is used to relieve symptoms in severe cases of Parkinson's disease. *Above:* An MRI image is used to guide the implantation of a mini-electrode in a precisely targeted area of the brain that is associated with symptoms. *Left:* A pacemaker, implanted in the chest and connected to the brain electrodes, provides electrical stimulation, which reduces the activity of the neurons at the targeted site.

The nervous system

The nervous system is a complex network that manages nerve impulses, controls sensations and movements, and regulates the emotions and the mind. Its anatomy has two complementary parts: the central nervous system and the peripheral nervous system.

Central nervous system

The central nervous system (CNS) is made up of the brain and the spinal cord. Running inside the spinal column, which protects it, the spinal cord is 45 centimetres long and is joined to the brain by the lower part of the brainstem. It is made up of grey matter formed by the cell bodies of its neurons and can transmit a nerve impulse from the brain to the rest of the body and vice versa. The role of the CNS is to decipher and process information that arrives from the sense organs and the body's internal receptors, and then to issue an appropriate response.

Peripheral nervous system

The peripheral nervous system (PNS) is a network consisting of all the body's nerves. These are carried throughout the body by bundles of axons sheathed in conjunctive tissue and linked to the central nervous system. There are two kinds of peripheral nerves: cranial nerves, which originate in the brainstem, and spinal nerves coming from the spinal cord. Depending on the sort of information they transmit, nerves are classified as either sensory (when the nerve message comes from a sense organ and goes to the CNS) or motor (when the connection is between the CNS and muscles). Some nerves can serve both purposes. For example, the sciatic nerve, the longest nerve in the body, has a motor function when it enables the knee to bend and a sensory function when it transmits feeling in the leg. When the sciatic nerve is ruptured, the leg is paralysed and all feeling is lost. Surgical repair can make it possible for nerve impulses to be transmitted again, either by restoring continuous connective tissue or by grafting another, less important nerve. These procedures rely on the fact that axons in the PNS are able to regenerate. When damage occurs, the ends of axons sprout buds, which then grow at a rate of approximately 1 millimetre a day. This means that it can take up to two years for a patient to recover full use of the affected leg.

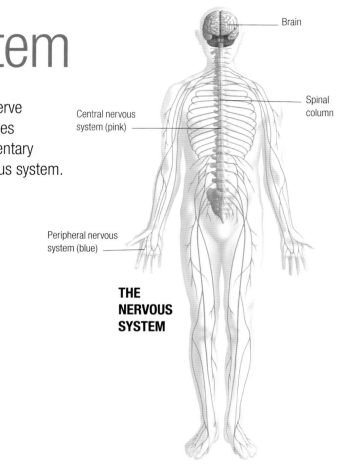

Brain

Spinal column

Central nervous system (pink)

Peripheral nervous system (blue)

THE NERVOUS SYSTEM

CROSS-SECTION OF THE SPINAL CORD

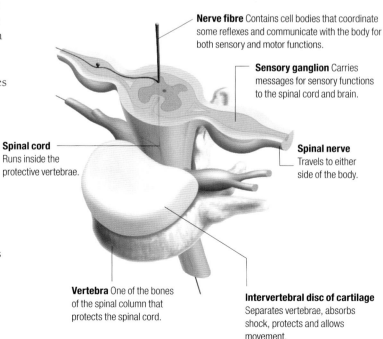

Nerve fibre Contains cell bodies that coordinate some reflexes and communicate with the body for both sensory and motor functions.

Sensory ganglion Carries messages for sensory functions to the spinal cord and brain.

Spinal cord Runs inside the protective vertebrae.

Spinal nerve Travels to either side of the body.

Vertebra One of the bones of the spinal column that protects the spinal cord.

Intervertebral disc of cartilage Separates vertebrae, absorbs shock, protects and allows movement.

Programming movement

The motor areas are responsible for directing voluntary movement. To do this, they use information provided by the parietal cortex on the position of the body and location of the target, together with a known motor program – such as standing, jumping, running or grasping an article – that is specifically intended to carry out the movement. The program selects the muscles that will be needed as well as the power and speed of their contraction. This information is then sent via the motor cortex and the spinal cord to the muscles so that they can carry out the appropriate instructions. The cerebellum, which stores records of sequences of movements already learnt, factors in the information it receives, so ensuring that the motor program is suited to the position of the body and that there is no loss of balance. Sportspeople or those who need special manual expertise for their jobs have a muscle memory that contains highly sophisticated motor programs. These are developed over time in a complex learning process that involves training and repeating the same movements over and over again.

Data processing

Our eyes, ears, skin, taste buds and nasal mucous membranes process different kinds of information – mechanical, thermal, electromagnetic and chemical – to produce an electric signal, which then travels to the appropriate primary sensory areas for each sense organ. On arrival, the message is then transformed 'in real time' into a sensation or feeling of sound, light, colour or temperature. This group of basic sensations is then processed, sorted and interpreted in the association areas to create a complete image in the mind. Billions of neurons in the prefrontal cortex can simultaneously process data involving more than one sense, assessing whether it is pleasant or unpleasant and finding words related to the information. The result of all this activity by neurons is an organised, coherent picture of our environment. For the senses alone, the exercise of identifying an object and deciding on a movement to pick it up takes approximately 130 thousandths of a second. Another 100 thousandths of a second are needed to carry out the action.

One action, many players When you carry out a complex movement such as a tennis serve, a large number of muscles need to be contracted in coordination. Determining the direction of the movement involves processing information that is received both visually and from many different detectors of strength, extension, angle and gravity.

Involuntary movement: the knee-jerk reflex

A reflex is a swift, involuntary movement triggered by a stimulus. How promptly you react to the stimulus is a good indication of the health of your nervous system. When a doctor takes a small hammer and taps the tendon beneath your kneecap, sensitive nerves are stimulated. The nerve impulse travels to the spinal cord, which then sends it straight to the motor nerves, without passing through the brain. The motor nerves cause a muscle in your thigh, called the quadriceps, to contract suddenly, so that your foot jerks forward. It takes less than 40 thousandths of a second for the nerve message to complete its course. An exaggerated reflex could indicate that the motor nerves are damaged, while the lack of a reflex is a sign that something is wrong.

The sensation of pain

Pain lets you know that there has been an attack on your body, either internally or from the outside, and that something has to be done. The pain may be caused by physical damage but may also relate to the mind or indicate that pain mechanisms are not functioning normally.

How we feel pain

Pain starts with the release of substances that activate specific nerve receptors, called nociceptors. These are found all through the body – in the skin, muscles, joints, blood vessels, mucous membranes and walls of internal organs – with the exception of the brain. The nerve message then travels along the peripheral nerves to the spinal cord, where it is eased by local neurons that produce a form of natural morphine, known as endorphins or endomorphins. When the message reaches the brain, it is processed and becomes the sensation of pain. The brain responds by triggering an appropriate motor program – when you move away from a source of heat, for example. This usually happens straight after the initial reflex reaction, such as when you draw your hand away from a sharp object after feeling pain.

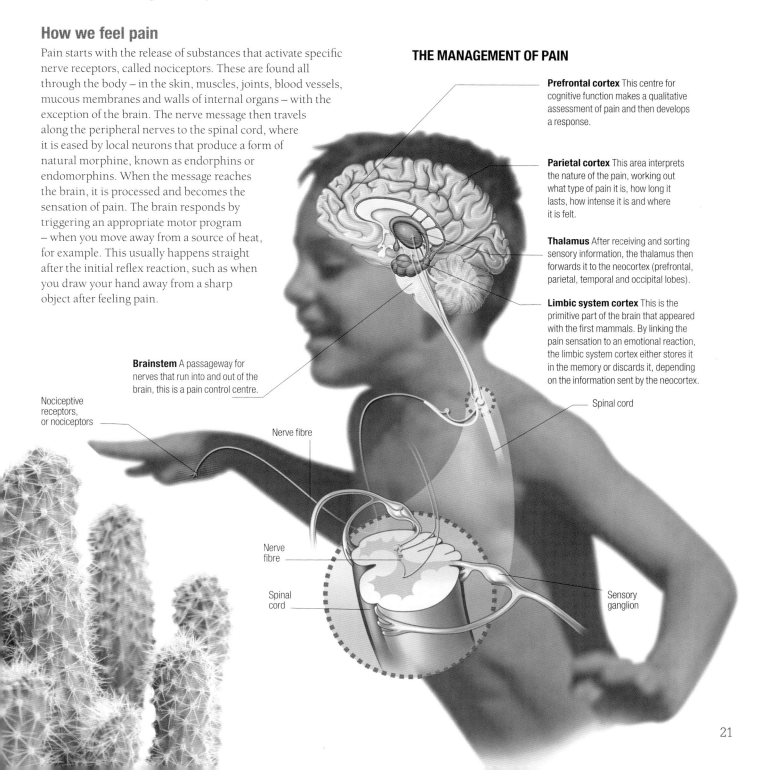

THE MANAGEMENT OF PAIN

Prefrontal cortex This centre for cognitive function makes a qualitative assessment of pain and then develops a response.

Parietal cortex This area interprets the nature of the pain, working out what type of pain it is, how long it lasts, how intense it is and where it is felt.

Thalamus After receiving and sorting sensory information, the thalamus then forwards it to the neocortex (prefrontal, parietal, temporal and occipital lobes).

Limbic system cortex This is the primitive part of the brain that appeared with the first mammals. By linking the pain sensation to an emotional reaction, the limbic system cortex either stores it in the memory or discards it, depending on the information sent by the neocortex.

Brainstem A passageway for nerves that run into and out of the brain, this is a pain control centre.

Nociceptive receptors, or nociceptors

Nerve fibre

Nerve fibre

Spinal cord

Spinal cord

Sensory ganglion

Fighting pain

The perception of pain is, by definition, subjective, and in a bid to measure it health professionals have developed pain scales, from zero to ten. Other secondary factors are also taken into account – for example, the site of the pain, the duration and type described, plus any aggravating or alleviating factors. These pain assessment tools are designed to help to provide the appropriate treatment.

One remedy is acetylsalicylic acid, more commonly known as aspirin, which acts on the injured tissues to block the production of prostaglandins – substances that increase the sensitivity of nociceptors and therefore contribute to the level of pain felt. Local anaesthetics stop the nerve message from being conducted locally, making the painful area numb. Very strong painkillers affect the central nervous system, activating morphine receptors in the spinal cord, brainstem, thalamus and limbic system. Other drugs inhibit the release of substance P (see *Dangerous malfunctions*, below), which stops the pain message from being transmitted.

Which pain?

The terms *-alge-* and *-algia* mean 'pain'. Look at the list below, then match each word with its meaning.

a. Neuralgia	**1.** Joint pain
b. Fibromyalgia	**2.** Heartburn
c. Analgesic	**3.** Kidney pain
d. Dorsalgia	**4.** Earache
e. Nephralgia	**5.** Nerve pain
f. Arthralgia	**6.** Pain reliever
g. Otalgia	**7.** Stomach ache
h. Gastralgia	**8.** Continuous pain of the muscles, tendons and ligaments
i. Cardialgia	**9.** Back pain

Answers: **a.** 5 ; **b.** 8 ; **c.** 6 ; **d.** 9 ; **e.** 3 ; **f.** 1 ; **g.** 4 ; **h.** 7 ; **i.** 2.

Dangerous malfunctions

When pain mechanisms go wrong, this can lead to serious conditions. In industrialised countries, between 2 and 6 per cent of the population (particularly women) suffer from fibromyalgia, in which continuous pain affects the muscles, tendons and ligaments, yet with no identifiable organic cause. The symptoms are incapacitating and sufferers also experience sleep disorders and chronic fatigue. Examinations and analyses have shown that patients with fibromyalgia have abnormally high levels of substance P, a neurotransmitter that acts on nociceptive neurons in the spinal cord. A high level of substance P may trigger an abnormal number of pain signals. Low levels of other neurotransmitters such as serotonin, which is involved in controlling pain, may also play a role. Conversely, certain individuals have little or no response to painful stimuli, even though their nerve circuitry is undamaged – this condition is known as pain asymbolia (asymbolia means 'the loss of symbols needed for identification'). It may be caused by poor connections in some of the brain's neuronal networks, damage to the parietal lobe or gene mutation. For those who suffer from fibromyalgia and pain asymbolia, the disruption of the normal function of pain as a warning can have dangerous consequences.

When the brain takes charge

There are a number of important aspects of the body's operation that need to be monitored constantly for stability. A healthy body temperature, for example, must always be in the region of 37°C, and blood sugar level should be about 1 gram per litre.

Keeping the body in balance

The body's ability to keep its inner environment stable is known as homeostasis. This state is maintained both by conscious control through our behaviour – for example, we eat when feelings of hunger indicate a drop in blood sugar – and by unconscious control through metabolic action, such as when the pancreas secretes insulin to release glucose stored in the liver. These two types of regulation are coordinated by a part of the limbic system called the hypothalamus, a cluster of nerve cells occupying less than 1 per cent of the brain and connected to almost all the other areas of the brain. The hypothalamus receives nerve signals from the body and sends back appropriate behavioural and/or metabolic responses. It also helps to regulate a variety of functions such as hunger, thirst, sleep, stress, mood, blood pressure and libido. To control all these functions, it works with the pituitary gland using hormones, and with the autonomic nervous system using the nerves.

Conducting the endocrine orchestra

The tiny pituitary gland, weighing less than 1 gram, controls the other glands in the endocrine system (the thyroid, pancreas, ovaries, testicles and adrenal glands) and is responsible for secreting hormones into the bloodstream. In particular, it releases the hormones produced by the hypothalamus. These are vasopressin, an antidiuretic hormone that acts on the kidneys to regulate the excretion of liquids from the body in the form of urine, and oxytocin, which helps to trigger childbirth and produce breast milk. Under the control of the hypothalamus, the pituitary gland also secretes its own hormones. Of these, some have a direct effect, such as follicle-stimulating hormone (FSH) and luteinising hormone (LH), both of which act on the reproductive glands. Others exert an indirect influence, such as thyroid-stimulating hormone (TSH) and corticotrophic hormone, which acts on the adrenal glands. To achieve a proper balance, the amount that is produced of each of these hormones is regulated by their target organs through a kind of self-checking process.

Sympathetic systems

The hypothalamus also controls another key player whose participation is needed to maintain homeostasis – the vegetative, or autonomic, nervous system, so named because it operates independently, without any conscious will or decision. It comprises the sensory and motor nerve networks to the heart, the glands and smooth muscles (muscular fibres in the skin that contract without any conscious order being given), the blood vessels and the organs (such as the lungs, intestine, liver, uterus and bladder).

The body's organs are regulated by two opposing and complementary subsystems: the sympathetic nervous system and the parasympathetic nervous system. The sympathetic nervous system uses stimulation to prepare the body to deal with emergency situations. For example, when the sympathetic nervous system takes over in a high-stress situation, it makes the body sweat, the heart beat faster, the airways expand and blood pressure rise. These reactions occur when the sympathetic system's neurons release stimulating neurotransmitters, mainly adrenaline and noradrenaline. In contrast, the parasympathetic system has an inhibitory effect, slowing down the way organs function. It takes over during periods of recovery and rest, reducing the heart rate and blood pressure and constricting the airways.

On the go 24/7

While our body has rest periods and we often sleep very deeply, the brain never stops working. During sleep the brain continues to control all of our vital organs. It also assists with body repair and maintenance, and during periods of dreaming sleep it plays a vital role in memory consolidation, as well as neuronal growth, survival and maintenance. This is why getting a good night's sleep is so important for mood, physical energy and levels of mental alertness during the day.

The senses and perception

2

A new view of the senses

At school we learned that we have five senses – sight, hearing, taste, smell and touch – and that each of these is a distinct sensory system that gives us a particular perception of the world around us. But in more recent times this view has been replaced by the concept of unity of the senses. What this means, in brief, is that while each of the peripheral receptor organs – eyes, ears, nose, tongue and skin – responds to a specific type of physical or chemical stimulus, the brain combines these to produce a single, overall impression.

Five senses, one code

While external sources of stimulation can be very different – for example, light, soundwaves or heat – all sensory channels are similar in structure and work in similar ways. By implanting microelectrodes in neurons, scientists have been able to decipher the electrical signals that the brain uses to decode sensory information. The signals provide data not only on the intensity of a given sensation – the strength or weakness of light seen, or the loudness of sound heard – but also on qualitative aspects, such as the shape and colour of an object or the pitch of a sound.

What these experiments tell us is that all five channels use an identical code. This is the fundamental prerequisite for messages coming from the different senses to be integrated by the brain. Using this one code, the cerebral cortex – where conscious perception develops – simultaneously interprets visual, auditory, olfactory or other sensory signals and builds up one single multidimensional image of what is around us.

Prefrontal cortex

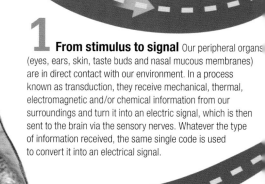

SENSORY CHANNEL AND THE BRAIN

1 **From stimulus to signal** Our peripheral organs (eyes, ears, skin, taste buds and nasal mucous membranes) are in direct contact with our environment. In a process known as transduction, they receive mechanical, thermal, electromagnetic and/or chemical information from our surroundings and turn it into an electric signal, which is then sent to the brain via the sensory nerves. Whatever the type of information received, the same single code is used to convert it into an electrical signal.

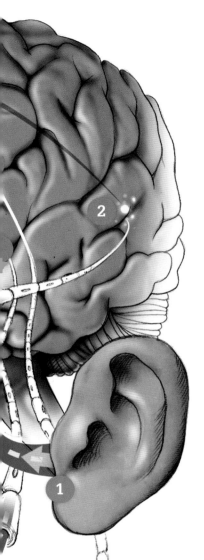

2 From signal to image

The electrical signal is transmitted to the primary sensory areas that correspond to each relevant sensory channel, where it is transformed to produce a sensation of sound, light, colour or temperature. These basic sensations are then processed, sorted and interpreted in the association areas to produce an image in the mind.

3 Integrating the messages

Integration occurs in the prefrontal and other parts of the cortex, where billions of neurons form a vast, interconnected network. The messages exchanged in the cortex are all coded in the same way, so the neurons can receive and combine information from all the different senses, as well as semantic information (words associated with the relevant sensation) and hedonic information (whether we consider it pleasant or unpleasant). The result is a multidimensional image of what has been perceived in the world around us.

A measured approach

Conscious perception of an object is not simply a matter of making sense of an objective physical signal. It also involves a multidimensional interpretation that takes account of the past (our memories), the present (the combined message from the different senses) and even the immediate future. Brain imaging has shown that the neurons providing us with information about the outside world are also those that devise actions and/or responses so that we can adapt to our environment. Our perception of an object develops by combining information from all our sensory systems and then comparing and associating aspects of it with our background and experience. Would it be possible to set standards that would allow everyone to have exactly the same perceptions? To answer that question, we first need to distinguish between two major sense groups, those that react to physical stimuli and those that rely on a chemical stimulus.

Unity of the senses in daily life

● **Sound with pictures – movies**
Going to see a movie is a good example of how the brain builds up a single impression using different types of stimuli from different sources. When actors in the movie speak, we have the impression that their voices are coming from their mouths, but in fact the sound is coming from loudspeakers in the auditorium. What has happened is that the brain has integrated the auditory and visual information it has received, so bringing what we see and what we hear together as one experience.

● **Appearance, taste, aroma – the experience of food**
When official comparative tastings of food are conducted, specific levels of lighting and background noise are stipulated, so that the results are not flawed. This shows just how much outside elements can influence the perceived flavour of food. What's more, when professional wine tasters are not shown the wine they are tasting, they often can't tell whether it's white or rosé! And it's common knowledge that taste and smell interact; just try eating while holding your nose and you'll see how important it is to smell food to appreciate its flavour.

Physical stimuli The senses of sight, hearing and touch react to physical stimuli, which can be mechanical (for hearing and touch), temperature-related (for touch) or electromagnetic (for sight). The stimuli create a direct sensory imprint on a sensitive area of the body, such as on the retina for sight. Each individual perceives these stimuli through the same sensory imprints, and the same words can convey the same categories of objects to all observers. A colour, for instance, can be defined by three universal properties – hue, brightness and saturation. So this means that a 'standard' visual observer does exist in this case. Similarly, it is possible to read and write music because the sounds and notes correspond to elements of objective reality: everybody hears middle C as the same note.

Chemical stimuli The process is not the same for the senses of taste and smell, which rely on the detection of a chemical signal – that is, a certain molecule in the air or food. These molecules are so small and their paths so random that they can't leave an impression on the surface of the mucous membranes. In addition, the types of chemoreceptors and the way they are implanted in the mucous membranes vary from person to person, so that it's not possible for a standard perceiver to exist. This explains why descriptions of taste and smell rely mainly on comparisons and evocations. A savoury flavour tastes salty, but no one knows if everyone experiences salt in the same way. And lemon is the quintessence of acidity, while a strawberry flavour can be defined only by reference to a strawberry.

Do you have good eyesight?

Sight is essential for moving and carrying out most actions, but what does having 'good eyesight' really mean? Is it simply a matter of correctly seeing what is around us as we perceive it through light, or is the process much more complex?

What is sight?

Like the other senses, sight consists of the perception of an outside stimulus – in this case electromagnetic waves – and the brain's interpretation of what has been perceived. Being able to see doesn't mean just seeing ambient light, but also – and perhaps most importantly – recognising objects and movements. Optical illusions, which could be described as errors in interpretation, provide tangible evidence of the role the brain plays in producing sight.

An eagle eye

Ophthalmologists define visual acuity as the ability to distinguish an object placed as far away as possible or to see the smallest possible object. This means that visual acuity is related to the minimum angle required for the rays of light emitted by an object to reach the retina at the back of the eye. Ophthalmologists calculate the angle using standardised charts that have letters and figures of different sizes. The result is expressed as a score between 1 and 20, with 20 representing normal eyesight; it is even possible to have a visual acuity score above 20.

Keen observation

All that is involved in telling the difference between two small Australian birds, the brown thornbill and the inland thornbill, is spotting slight variations in colour and tail length. Yet keen birdwatchers can tell them apart at a glance, sometimes with only a fleeting glimpse of the birds in flight. Such an outstanding ability is not the result of exceptional eyesight, but of a skill learned through observing and recognising specific characteristics – such as the colour of certain parts of the body, the trajectory of flight and the wingbeat frequency – making it possible to distinguish species that are very similar. In fact, identifying as many birds as possible in their natural habitat is in itself an objective for such enthusiasts.

Brown thornbill   Inland thornbill

Powers of observation

Visual acuity is essential, but it's not enough. To see well, you also have to grasp what is important in what you have seen, without missing anything, and you should also remember what has just been observed. These are abilities that correspond to two kinds of question:

● 'What are you looking at?' or 'Have you noticed this?' Questions like these demand the ability to recognise objects, as well as good observation skills.

● 'What did you just see?' This calls on the visual memory. In an ever-changing world, someone with excellent eyes but no visual memory would effectively see nothing.

Where's Elvis?

How quickly can you find Elvis Presley in this crowd? This will exercise your visual acuity, powers of observation and speed of recognition, whether you search randomly or scan systematically.

Spot the seven differences

This child's game will put your powers of observation and visual discrimination to the test. It also requires perseverance, and many give up before finding all seven differences.

Answers

Train your visual memory

Study the pictures and then answer the questions. These visual memory tests will check and help to improve your powers of observation, while also exercising your concentration skills and reaction speed, as you must complete each test in the given time.

The birthday party

1. Look at the picture for one minute and then cover it.

2. Answer the following questions:

a. Where is the party?

....

b. How many children are there?

....

c. How many are wearing hats?

....

d. How many are wearing glasses?

....

e. What is the youngest one doing?

....

f. What objects did you see behind the people?

....

Time to eat!

1. Look at these ten objects for one minute and then cover the picture.

2. List all ten objects.

....
....
....
....
....
....
....
....
....
....

Shapes

For each puzzle, look at the picture on the left, then cover it and follow the instructions on the right.

1.

1. Circle the pattern that has been added.

2.

2. Add the missing shape.

3.

3. Mark the shape that has been added.

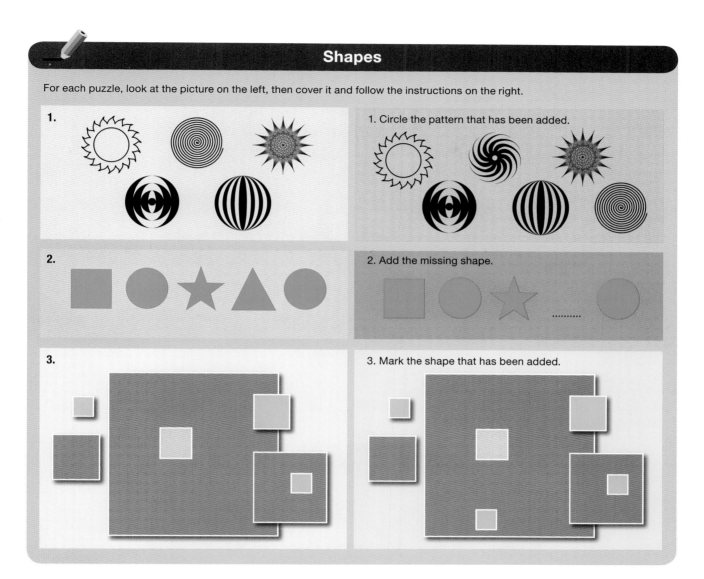

---

1. Study this picture for one minute and then cover it.

2. In this picture, which cyclists have changed positions?

How we see the world

Seeing — being able to detect objects in an undifferentiated moving mass of light waves — is the result of a complex sequence of operations that take place at different levels.

Perceiving light

The sequence begins when light enters the eye and reaches the retina, where there are two types of light-sensitive cells, or photoreceptors, called cones and rods. The five million cones are found mainly in the centre of the retina, in a high-density area named the fovea. Their task is to distinguish colour and detail, but they need a great deal of light to do so. There are three kinds of cones — sensitive to red, green or blue depending on the pigment of the cone. Cones are used for daytime vision, which determines visual acuity.

The peripheral part of the retina mostly contains rods (approximately 100 million). These cells are not sensitive to colour, but they can detect very low levels of light (as in night vision) and are involved in discerning movement.

1 **Crossover point** The optic nerves start from the retina in each eye and cross over at the optic chiasm, but they do so in a very particular way. At this point, the fibres (or axons) from the inner half-retinas intersect, but those from the outer half-retinas do not. As a result, the axons processing the right half of the surrounding environment — no matter which eye was originally involved — are routed towards the left hemisphere, and vice versa.

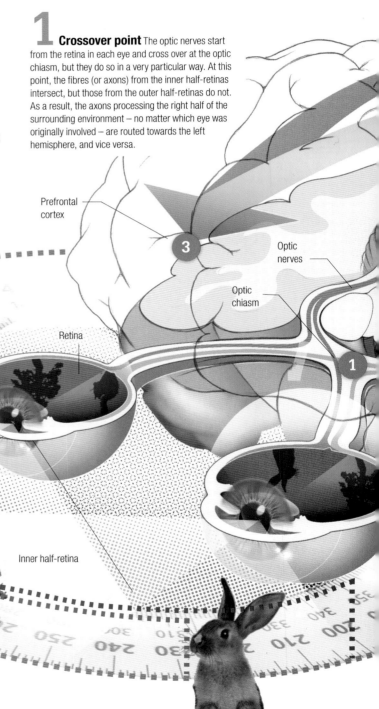

Prefrontal cortex

Optic nerves

Optic chiasm

Retina

THE MECHANISM OF SIGHT

Outer half-retina

Inner half-retina

■ ■ ■ ■ ■ Right field of vision

■ ■ ■ ■ ■ Left field of vision

Seeing in three dimensions

The visual message becomes an electrical signal in the retina and travels to the brain along the optic nerve, which brings together some one million axons, each extending from a light-sensitive cell. Once the message leaves the eye, neurons carry out some initial processing to enhance contrasts and reduce flatness. The retinal image becomes more graphic than photographic.

As we have two eyes, every object in our field of vision is detected by two retinas, or rather by two half-retinas, because the left half of a retina sees the right half of our environment and vice versa. The vertical dividing line runs through the fovea in the centre of the retina, where there is a very narrow overlap of the two half-images. Before the brain processes the information to make it three-dimensional, the four half-images pass across the optic chiasm – the name given to the area of the brain where some of the fibres of the two optic nerves intersect.

Over to the brain

Nerve bundles from the optic nerves connect to the right and left parts of the visual cortex in the occipital lobe. The image is detected by the primary visual areas and is then processed by a series of interconnected association areas. These areas discern constant patterns – that is, the shape of objects – and give objects colours, which are also constant, despite any differences in lighting. The association areas also introduce a link with time so that movement is detected. Finally, because the images from each eye are slightly different, the visual areas analyse the differences to detect dimension and depth. This is the principle of three-dimensional vision, which is mainly effective up to only a few metres away from the observer; images that are farther away do not include information on depth. If we do see a three-dimensional scene in the distance, it means that the brain is interpreting differences in distance by means of perspective – the farther away an object is, the smaller it seems.

Information is then sent to the prefrontal cortex, where the visual message is combined with information from other senses, as well as with knowledge and recollections that are stored in areas controlling memory, language and emotion.

Right visual cortex

Left visual cortex

Optic nerves

2 Processing the message The paths from the two sides meet at the visual cortices. These are composed of areas with complementary functions, which work together to extract shape, colour and movement from the initial message.

Cerebellum

3 Producing a visual image The prefrontal cortex receives information sent by the visual cortex and by the other senses. Other information from the memory (personal experience and language) plus emotional content are then added and integrated. All this information is then processed simultaneously to produce a picture of our environment.

The human field of vision

● The human field of vision – between 170 and 190 degrees – is relatively small compared to the range of a goat or rabbit, which extends to over 300 degrees. The main difference is the position of the eyes – on the front of the head for humans, but on the side of the head for goats and rabbits.

170°   300°

● In the central field of vision, we have a clear perception of colour and detail.
● In the peripheral field of vision, we are more sensitive to movement: our perception of stationary objects is poor, but we can see what is moving. This feature was no doubt useful for our ancestors, who needed to spot any potential danger in plenty of time.

Our eyes are not the same as cameras

Because the brain plays a key role in how we see the world, it is hardly surprising that what we actually see is sometimes quite different from the physical reality perceived by our eyes.

Building an image

We don't have to see all of an object to be able to recognise it. The brain can reconstruct a missing part or create a complete image by using knowledge already acquired and experience, as well as images and emotions stored from the past. So visual perception is the brain's interpretation of what we see, rather than a kind of photographic image cast on the retina. Visual input is only one of the elements the brain uses to put together this interpretation – our knowledge, experience and feelings also contribute.

Optical illusions

We can understand how much the brain contributes to our view of the world by considering the phenomenon of optical illusion, which occurs when images we perceive are different from reality.

The brain loves symmetry The photo on the left is real, but the two pictures to its right are not. They are symmetrical compositions – in the centre photo, the left side of the face has been flipped to form the right side, and in the photo on the right the right side of the face has been flipped to form the left side. The difference between the two photos on the right shows that no face is truly symmetrical. The brain has a preference for symmetry, and so 'sees' a face as symmetrical, distorting the perception of what is real. Try this experiment for yourself, using photocopies of a close-up of your own face.

Not what it seems The fresco on the wall of the Place Royale in the city of Quebec, Canada, is more than just a decoration. It is painted in a style known as trompe l'oeil – French for 'tricks the eye'. Although it is a flat painting, the depiction of Quebec, its people and famous historical personalities over four centuries creates the optical illusion of being in three dimensions.

Completing the picture In the illustration below, you can see a triangle, yet its sides have not been drawn. This phenomenon can be explained by the brain's tendency to find meaning in random shapes or to complete partial shapes when they match parts of known objects. This is an essential skill for survival – for example, when prey and predators are not completely visible in thick, dense vegetation, it is crucial to be able to identify them immediately from the few parts that can be seen.

Facial recognition Look at these two pictures of Margaret Thatcher, one the right way up and the other upside down. Now turn the book around. You may not have noticed the changes in the picture that you previously saw upside down, even though they are quite obvious now. What happened was that your brain projected Margaret Thatcher's face as you know it onto the picture, which prevented you from noticing the changes. (Example from research by British psychologist Peter Thompson.)

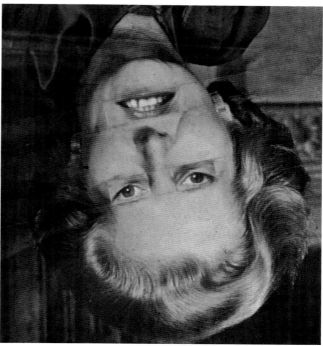

Is sight the dominant sense?

Rightly or wrongly, sight is often considered to be the most important sense, the one that opens the world for us, making it possible to establish a point of view and to see whether things are real (for example, a common saying is 'seeing is believing'). Sight is also considered to be the first sense involved in falling in love (we talk about 'love at first sight').

Use the words listed here to make as many well-known expressions as possible containing references to sight (a total of 20). Definite and indefinite articles ('a', 'an' and 'the') may be added and words can be used more than once.

at · catch · evil · love · feast · turn · sight · before · is · look · make · blind · for · one's · through · eyes · put · rose · on · give · eye · daggers · see · glad · peeled · only · in · coloured · out · mind · to · glasses · of · leap · you · keep · have · someone

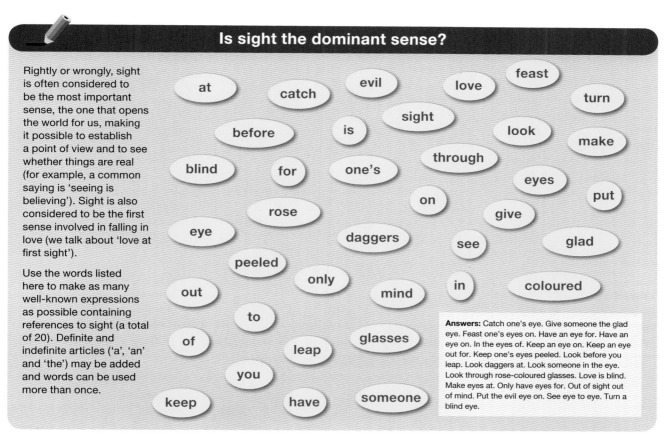

Answers: Catch one's eye. Give someone the glad eye. Feast one's eyes on. Have an eye for. Have an eye on. In the eyes of. Keep an eye on. Keep an eye out for. Keep one's eyes peeled. Look before you leap. Look daggers at. Look someone in the eye. Look through rose-coloured glasses. Love is blind. Make eyes at. Only have eyes for. Out of sight out of mind. Put the evil eye on. See eye to eye. Turn a blind eye.

When the brain plays tricks on us

Optical effects and illusions, mirages and other kinds of visual deception clearly prove that the brain reconstructs images.

Illusions

The brain can mislead us when it makes us believe that we have seen something that is not there. This happens because it has misinterpreted the message received from the light rays. Such illusions show that there are limits to the brain's ability to interpret reality. They also help to explain what happens when the visual cortex compares what is seen with images stored in its memory banks. Learning, then, can trigger many illusions when the brain interprets what is seen as something learnt.

A sense of proportion The red circle in the pattern on the left seems bigger than the one on the right, yet their diameters are the same. This is just one of many illusions based on the juxtaposition of  scales. The error occurs when the brain assesses size by comparing objects rather than by interpreting measurements. When an object is placed next to one or more similar but larger objects, the former looks small, and vice versa.

The horizon as reference. The vertical line of a capital T looks longer than its horizontal line, yet they are the same length. The vertical line is overestimated because it is easier for the eyes to scan from side to side than up and down.

No good at geometry In the two drawings on the right, the horizontal lines seem to be curved, but they are perfectly straight. This effect is created by the angles. The brain tends to underestimate obtuse angles (those over 90 degrees) and overestimate acute angles (those under 90 degrees). In the drawings below, on the other hand, the brain overestimates the length of the sides of an obtuse angle and underestimates the sides of an acute angle, so that the top horizontal line seems shorter than the bottom one, yet they are both the same length.

Very real phenomena

Our brain can also fool us when it correctly perceives something that is physically real but fails to interpret it, as happens with mirages.

● Mirages
Driving along the road in summer, you may think you can see a puddle in the middle of a perfectly dry road. This shiny patch that reflects the sky is a mirage and occurs because the refractive index of the air changes with its temperature. Usually, air is colder at higher altitudes than it is near the ground. As the light rays pass from the colder to the warmer air, the angle at which they are bent changes, so that they follow a curved path. As a result, the image of objects in the air appears to come from the ground. In the desert, the reflection of the sky on the ground looks like a puddle. In polar regions, where the ground is very cold, the light rays curve in the opposite direction and objects on the ground appear to be floating in the sky. Mirages can be photographed, proving that they are not hallucinations.

● The broken stick
Do you know why a stick dipped in water suddenly appears to break? The explanation is simple: water does not have the same refractive index as air, and so when the light rays enter the water they move in a slightly different direction. Your eyes perceive the difference but your brain doesn't compensate, even though you know that the stick is not broken.

Undecided The shape on the right is a cube drawn in isometric projection – a view that presents three-dimensional objects in two dimensions. The brain can't work out which side is the front and which is the back; its interpretation of the cube can switch from one to the other at any moment. It wavers between two possible and quite valid interpretations of the drawing, and is unable to make a final choice.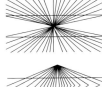

An impossible object The drawing on the right, known as the Penrose triangle, appears at first glance to depict a three-dimensional object. On closer examination, it is clear that such an object cannot possibly be real. In this case, the brain follows its usual interpretation of volume through perspective and tries to see a three-dimensional object, even though no such object exists.

When the brain can't see

Different kinds of brain damage can have quite different effects on our vision, depending on the part of the brain affected, sometimes even causing blindness.

Perception of dimension

If one optic nerve is ruptured just in front of the optic chiasm – the place where the optic nerves cross – sight is lost in the affected eye. This alters how the remaining eye perceives dimension. To understand what this is like, try closing one eye. On the other hand, rupture of the same nerve beyond the chiasm affects both eyes, but only half of the field of vision. This means that only half of what is seen will be in three dimensions.

Partial losses

The effects of damage to the visual cortex will depend on the specialised areas involved. If the damaged areas are used to identify shape and colour, it will be difficult to recognise objects. If areas required for movement are affected, the person will be unable to watch and follow moving objects, or may be disoriented. When the area specialising in facial recognition is damaged, it may not be possible to recognise well-known faces, but as the remaining sight and memory are spared it is still possible to identify others by their voice or clothing.

Blindsight

Damage to one complete side of the cortex may lead to a condition known as blindsight. In the early 1970s, a patient in a British hospital whose right visual cortex had been surgically removed was able to reach out his hand towards an object in his left field of vision, while saying that he could not see it! This was the first formally investigated case of blindsight. The eyes are functional, but because the message can go no farther than the damaged area it can't reach the prefrontal cortex, where awareness of the object observed develops. Nearly all of the axons from the retina go through the visual cortex, but a small number (10 per cent) go around it and send the visual information to the midbrain – the upper part of the brainstem. This is sufficient to produce motor responses (extending a hand, or following with the eyes), but is not enough to see.

Hallucinations

Hallucinations are perceptions that we experience without the involvement of the relevant sensory organs. They can be as varied as a sudden impression of falling into a chasm when dropping off to sleep, the threatening voices heard by people with schizophrenia or the visions triggered by certain drugs or neurodegenerative diseases.

People hallucinate for many different reasons. Some who have become deaf can hear pieces of music that they learned in the past. Hallucinations can occur with schizophrenia, post-traumatic stress syndrome, alcoholism, or certain medicines or recreational drugs. They can also be triggered by migraine, epileptic fits, a brain tumour, multiple sclerosis, or Parkinson's or Alzheimer's disease. Extended fasting, fatigue, extreme stress and even states of hypnosis or trance are other causes.

How do hallucinations happen? Hallucinogenic drugs interfere with the chemical communication between neurons by acting on neurotransmitters such as dopamine and serotonin. These same substances could also be involved in hallucinations that are triggered by other factors. Researchers using brain-imaging techniques have reported that hallucinations activate the sensory areas for sight, hearing, touch, smell and taste, according to the type of hallucination. The perception that a bell can be heard ringing, for example, is linked to abnormal stimulation of neurons in the auditory cortex. When people with schizophrenia hear voices, it is thought that they are misinterpreting their own internal language, believing it to be coming from someone else.

Lazy eye Also known as amblyopia, lazy eye is the loss of sight in a functioning eye, even though there is no brain damage. It occurs when the brain doesn't process information coming from a healthy eye. This may be because one eye is stronger than the other, and the brain overlooks or rejects information from the weaker eye as it is not good enough to produce a coherent three-dimensional image.

Similarly, strabismus (squint) is a condition that is often caused by poor coordination of the eye muscles, which causes misalignment of the gaze of each eye. As a result of this discrepancy, the brain rejects one of the images and this may lead to poor depth perception. If strabismus persists for an extended period, in particular into later childhood, it may result in permanent loss of vision in the affected eye. To avoid this, the good eye is covered with a patch to force the brain to process the information coming from the weaker eye until vision improves and equalises.

Staying tuned

Hearing is often considered to be a less important sense than sight, yet hearing is essential for alerting us to unseen dangers. Our hearing is tuned in to every direction simultaneously and is never turned off.

Warning and communication

Sound, unlike light, can travel around obstacles and alert us to unseen dangers, as long as they're not too far away. Because sound weakens as it passes through the air, our hearing range is limited. Hearing is also a key factor in communication. When you consider the role that language plays in social contact, hearing is of critical importance and hearing loss is a serious disability. Poor hearing is not a minor problem, and someone who can no longer rely on their hearing to warn them is in very real danger – crossing a road, for example, becomes a highly risky exercise when you can't hear a car approaching. Most importantly, a person unable to hear what others are saying is effectively cut off from human contact in society. Even mild hearing loss can be distressing, and a person who misunderstands what others are saying will find it difficult to interact with others.

How good is your hearing?

Loss of hearing, unless caused by an accident, develops insidiously during adult life. A child or teenager can detect sounds at frequencies between 20 and 20,000 hertz. The perception of higher-pitched sounds declines first, and around the age of 60 it is impossible to hear anything above 12,000 hertz. Similarly, the hearing threshold – the minimum level of loudness for perceiving a sound – goes up with age. This very gradual loss of hearing is scarcely noticed and we get used to it unconsciously, modifying our lifestyle to suit a lower level of perception. So watch out for any indications of hearing loss, such as difficulty following the conversation when you're talking with a number of people or in noisy places. If you find yourself turning the volume up too high on the TV or radio, it's time to consult a specialist. In any case, it's advisable for everyone over the age of 60 to have a hearing test.

Be kind to your ears

Looking after your hearing is mainly a question of avoiding excessive noise. Loss of hearing occurs earlier for people who have given their ears a rough time, because the sensory cells for hearing are very fragile and do not regenerate. Everyone should use protective gear (ear plugs and headsets) whenever the noise level is high, as well as when swimming in the sea or a pool. And high doses of some medications – such as antibiotics, aspirin and anti-inflammatory drugs – can affect hearing, so you should discuss this with the doctor who is prescribing them.

In many cases, hearing loss can be treated. Hearing aids, which take over sound-processing from the ears, have their limitations, such as their inability to locate the source of a sound, but they do help people to maintain all-important social interaction.

Hearing more than you'd like

Some people suffer from a condition known as hyperacusis, in which everyday noises and sounds seem excessively loud. Hearing for such people can become extremely painful, causing constant distress and becoming a genuine obstacle to social contact – even a simple conversation can be intolerable. A more frequent phenomenon is tinnitus, in which buzzing, whistling, clicking and other noises are heard when there is no such external noise source. Tinnitus is caused by changes to the auditory pathways, often in the inner ear. It may be temporary, occurring after exposure to extreme noise, or it may be permanent.

How we hear sound

Because sound is produced by the vibration of air, it is a mechanical signal.
What the ear does is to transform all the vibrations it detects into an electrical signal.

Transmitting and locating

The outer and middle parts of the ear are mainly responsible for transmitting and amplifying vibrations. The inner ear then turns them into a nerve impulse, which travels along the auditory nerve to the brain. As sound is processed by two ears, the brain can locate the source of the sound by analysing the differences between the two incoming nerve impulses, especially lapses in time. This ability is particularly important for the role hearing plays in warning or alerting us.

The selective brain

The ear is in constant use. This means that the brain has to work full-time as a filter, dismissing background noise and selecting only meaningful sounds – for example, a car moving away or a person speaking. You only have to listen to a recording of a conversation that took place against a great deal of background noise to fully appreciate this selectivity and how amazing it is that we can hear one another in such a hubbub. Yet the brain's ability to select doesn't mean that the other noises are completely eliminated. The 'cocktail party effect' refers not just to being able to focus your auditory perception in a very noisy environment, but also to being able to react to a sound that has special meaning, such as your own name, when it is all but drowned out by background noise. Your brain takes in all the sound stimuli, even though you are not consciously aware of this, but provides you with information only when words or sounds are relevant to you.

A similar process explains why we are able to sleep with background noise, but are woken by a warning sound, even a tiny one such as a child whimpering. Continuous background noise may not be noticed at all until it stops; it's only the conscious awareness of silence that makes us realise how noisy it was previously.

Noises, speech and music

Hearing involves many different areas of the brain, depending on the type of sound detected. The auditory nerve transmits sound information to the auditory cortex in the temporal lobe. After complex processing, the sounds are sorted by category: speech, music or noise. Words are channelled to language areas, while tunes activate different brain circuits. Specific changes in the brain that have been observed when a person listens to music are evidence that these different kinds of processing exist, because the perception of language or noise in the environment remains unaltered.

THE MECHANISM OF HEARING

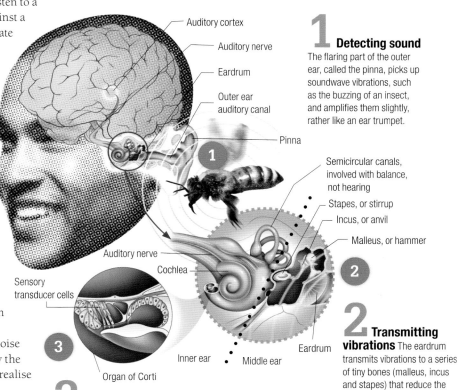

Auditory cortex

Auditory nerve

Eardrum

Outer ear auditory canal

Pinna

1 Detecting sound The flaring part of the outer ear, called the pinna, picks up soundwave vibrations, such as the buzzing of an insect, and amplifies them slightly, rather like an ear trumpet.

Semicircular canals, involved with balance, not hearing

Stapes, or stirrup

Incus, or anvil

Malleus, or hammer

Auditory nerve

Cochlea

Sensory transducer cells

Inner ear

Middle ear

Eardrum

Organ of Corti

2 Transmitting vibrations The eardrum transmits vibrations to a series of tiny bones (malleus, incus and stapes) that reduce the amplitude of the mechanical soundwaves, but make them stronger, adapting them so that they can pass into the liquid environment of the inner ear.

3 Generating the nerve impulse Located in the centre of the cochlea, the organ of Corti contains thousands of receptor cells. These have hairs that react to vibrations of the cochlea via movements in the liquid surrounding them. This generates electrical impulses that the auditory nerve transmits to the brainstem and auditory cortex of the brain, where sound is perceived.

The art of listening

Listening and hearing differ in just the same way as watching and seeing, touching and feeling, or sniffing and smelling. These subtle distinctions in the terms we use show how important being actively attentive is to the process of perception.

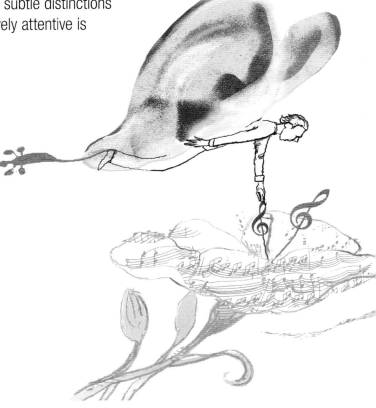

Listen and learn

Listening is an active, voluntary, conscious process involving areas of the brain that are not the same as those we use just for hearing. Listening is essential for learning, especially for learning a language. But listening is an art that can also be learnt, and musicians provide the best proof of this. They can, for example, pick out the sound of a single instrument in an orchestra, disregarding the others, while their ears can still hear the entire orchestra. Listening regularly to music, even without playing or learning an instrument, helps to develop listening skills. A recent Canadian study showed that learning to play music when young changes the way a child's brain develops and seems to increase memory and attention skills.

Perfect pitch

Perfect pitch is found in one in every ten thousand people. It is the ability to identify a note – that is, the pitch of the sound – without having to compare it to a reference note. A person with relative pitch, on the other hand, needs to refer to a tuning fork or middle C on the piano. Perfect pitch is not determined by the ear, which hears all notes, but by the brain, which can identify a single note.

Are we born with perfect pitch or is it something we learn? The jury is still out, but either way it is obvious that training helps to develop the skill.

Musical brain Music is a specialised area in neuroscience research. Just like language, music involves many different areas of the brain, depending on whether the person is listening, performing or composing. The Canadian pianist Glenn Gould was well known for his ability to hum at the same time as playing the piano.

Active listening

When you listen to a play or a documentary on the radio, you create your own images based on what you hear. Your brain conjures up a face for each voice. It also colours in settings and atmospheres, and produces emotional responses to different noises. With no visual interpretation, radio dramas and documentaries give the imagination greater scope than film and television, just as reading does. Listening to radio broadcasts and creative radio programs involves a special kind of attention, a paradoxically calm state of mind and a sense of closeness to speakers or actors – all experiences that never occur with television. Try it for yourself: rediscover the pleasure of listening to the radio. Let yourself be carried away by voices that seem to be speaking to you and you alone. It's as though listening creates a greater sense of intimacy than when sound is accompanied by visual images.

Words and music

When we listen to a song, we hear and can remember the lyrics, but may not pay much attention to their meaning. The way we listen to a song is different from how we listen to speech. We can focus on the tune rather than the words, or the other way around. Can you remember the words or the themes of these songs?

First names

In which songs do these names occur?

1. John, Bill, Paul, Davy

....

2. Lil, Nancy, Dan, Danny, Daniel

....

3. Louis, Suki, Jenny, Lotte, Lucy

....

4. Abraham, Martin, John, Bobby

....

Themes

Give the song title that matches each theme.

1. A place that provides accommodation for lovers who are grief-stricken.

....

2. A young man's desire for revenge on the absent parent whose only legacy was to give him an inappropriate name.

....

3. The bartender boyfriend of a showgirl is murdered by a rich rival; years later, the faded showgirl drinks alone at the bar.

....

From real life

Which real-life people or true stories inspired these songs?

1. And I would have liked to have known you/But I was just a kid./Your candle burned out long before/Your legend ever did

....

2. Walk right in, it's around the back/Just a half a mile from the railroad track

....

3. Starry starry night, paint your palette blue and grey/Look out on a summer's day with eyes that know the darkness in my soul.

....

Lyrics

Here are the opening lines of four songs, and the name of the performers most associated with each. Which is the correct next line?

1. Frank Sinatra Fly me to the moon/Let me play among the stars

- [ ] **a.** Let me see what spring is like
- [ ] **b.** Let me fill my heart with joy
- [ ] **c.** And let me take you with me

2. ABBA You can dance/you can jive

- [ ] **a.** The night is young and the music's fine
- [ ] **b.** Having the time of your life
- [ ] **c.** Young and sweet, feel the beat

3. Bob Dylan How many roads must a man walk down/Before you can call him a man?

- [ ] **a.** How many seas must the white dove sail
- [ ] **b.** How many years must a mountain exist
- [ ] **c.** How many times must a man look up

4. Gene Kelly I'm singing in the rain/Just singing in the rain

- [ ] **a.** I've a smile on my face
- [ ] **b.** I'm laughing at clouds
- [ ] **c.** What a glorious feelin'

Answers: First names 1. *Piano Man* (words and music: Billy Joel; performed by Billy Joel and others). **2.** *Rocky Raccoon* (words and music: Lennon and McCartney; performed by The Beatles and others). **3.** *Mack the Knife* (words: Bertholt Brecht; music: Kurt Weill; performed by Lotte Lenya; later performed by Louis Armstrong, Frank Sinatra, Bobby Darin and others). **4.** *Abraham, Martin and John* (words: Dick Holler; performed by Dion and others). **Themes 1.** *Heartbreak Hotel* (words and music: Mae Axton, Tommy Durden, Elvis Presley; performed by Elvis Presley and others). **2.** *A Boy Named Sue* (words and music: Sheldon Silverstein; performed by Johnny Cash and others). **3.** *Copacabana* (words and music: Jack Feldman, Barry Manilow and Bruce Sussman; performed by Barry Manilow and others). **From real life 1.** *Candle in the Wind* (words: Bernie Taupin; music: Elton John), about the death of Marilyn Monroe. **2.** *Alice's Restaurant* (words and music: Arlo Guthrie), a Vietnam protest song that tells how a conviction for littering prevented Guthrie from being conscripted. **3.** *Vincent* (words and music: Don McLean), a tribute to the life and work of artist Vincent van Gogh. **Lyrics 1. a.** (*Fly Me to the Moon*, also known as *In Other Words*. Words and music: Bart Howard.) **2. b.** (*Dancing Queen*. Words and music: Benny Andersson, Björn Ulvaeus and Stig Anderson.) **3. a.** (*Blowin' in the Wind*. Words and music: Bob Dylan.) **4. c.** (*Singin' in the Rain*. Words: Arthur Freed. Music: Nacio Herb Brown.)

Inseparable senses

For a long time taste and smell were considered to be quite distinct, but these two senses have a great deal in common. They are linked anatomically and functionally, they both react to chemical stimuli and they both trigger strong emotional responses.

Why taste and smell are alike

Much of what we call the taste of food comes from the aroma that reaches the nostrils from the back of the mouth, a phenomenon known as retro-olfaction. This is why food seems flavourless when you have a cold.

Unlike sight, hearing and touch, the senses of taste and smell respond to chemical stimuli that are triggered by molecules in the food we eat (taste) and in the air we breathe (smell). Hundreds of thousands of different molecules exist, and, even though we can't perceive them all, these two senses can recognise a huge number of them.

Taste and smell have another feature in common that distinguishes them from the other senses. As we have seen earlier in this chapter, we can say that there is a standard observer for the physical senses – that is, the experience of sight, hearing and touch is the same for everybody. But this is not the case for taste and smell. We each have our own way of perceiving an odour or a taste. This is why there are no specialised terms for describing a smell or taste, whereas, for example, something we perceive visually can be described as 'green', a sound we hear can be defined as 'high-pitched', or an object we touch can be felt to be 'warm'.

Tastes and odours can trigger very strong reactions, ranging from delight to repulsion or even nausea. There's obviously a link between our ability to remember smells and flavours and our emotional response. It is this aspect of the sense of smell that is targeted by marketers when they develop the image of a brand or product. For example, real estate agents suggest that the aroma of freshly brewed coffee or home-baked bread wafting through a house elicits feelings of warmth and contentment that may make it appeal to potential buyers.

Are we born with these responses?

A rabbit that has never seen a fox will, if it smells one, immediately freeze and display signs of stress. Other examples show that most animals appear to have an instinctive response to certain odours. What about humans? Do we have instinctive responses to certain smells or flavours? Do our genes determine which odours or flavours will be attractive or unpleasant? If a newborn baby is given a few drops of a sweet or bitter liquid, the baby's facial expressions show a clear and

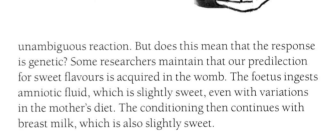

unambiguous reaction. But does this mean that the response is genetic? Some researchers maintain that our predilection for sweet flavours is acquired in the womb. The foetus ingests amniotic fluid, which is slightly sweet, even with variations in the mother's diet. The conditioning then continues with breast milk, which is also slightly sweet.

Or are they learned?

Leaving aside very simple flavours such as sweet and bitter, our preferences for food and olfactory phenomena develop through learning and change with age. Children usually find complex or very strong flavours as unappealing as bitter tastes. It's not until we reach adulthood that we begin to enjoy sophisticated dishes and bitter drinks, such as coffee or beer. The learning process can't rely on words, as there are none to describe these tastes, but on experience: food has to be tasted.

Adults' flavour preferences are mainly the result of experience and cultural background. In one part of the world, certain types of food may be considered unpalatable while elsewhere they are a delicacy – for example, insects, seafood, snails or karela (a bitter melon eaten in Asia). Odours and flavours associated with rotting and decomposition appear to be the only ones that are universally rejected, no doubt because they indicate that the food is not fit for human consumption.

The ability to detect and recognise a smell or flavour is an acquired skill. In the food industry, any attempt to measure aromas by investigating only physical and chemical processes, without factoring in their emotional force, produces unsatisfactory results. The people who participate in such investigations are chosen not for their outstanding olfactory skills but for their ability, acquired through learning, to identify smells and gauge their strength.

The vocabulary of taste and smell

Find the words that match these definitions. All the answers have to do with taste or smell.

Across

2. A stale, stuffy smell.

6. Describes water that is not salty.

7. Having an intense, penetrating smell.

9. Can describe both a sweet baked food and a food that is sharp to the taste.

12. Describes a flavour such as lemon juice or vinegar.

14. Highly pleasing in taste; palatable.

15. Harsh or biting in taste.

17. Can describe soup or fabric.

18. Agreeably sharp in taste.

19. Of a thick consistency.

20. Having little or no distinguishing flavour.

Down

1. Having or producing a pleasant odour; fragrant.

3. Describes a flavour that some researchers say we first encountered in the womb.

4. A dog can sniff and follow this.

5. Is used as a seasoning and as a preservative.

8. Sickening.

10. The smell or taste of a spoiled fatty food, such as butter.

11. Enhances the flavour of food.

12. Can be triggered by the thought, sight or smell of food about to be served.

13. Food loses this when you have a cold.

15. Sour; bitter.

16. Can describe both a person's status and an offensive smell or taste.

Answers

Across: 2. Mustiness. **6.** Fresh. **7.** Pungent. **9.** Tart. **12.** Sour. **14.** Delectable. **15.** Acrid. **17.** Velvety. **18.** Piquant. **19.** Creamy. **20.** Bland.
Down: 1. Perfumed. **3.** Sweet. **4.** Scent. **5.** Salt. **8.** Nauseating. **10.** Rancid. **11.** Seasoning. **12.** Salivation. **13.** Flavour. **15.** Acidic. **16.** Rank.

Speaking of food

Food appears in a variety of English expressions. Bread, as a staple representing the bare necessities of life, features in many examples, such as 'daily bread', 'breadwinner' and 'to earn a crust'. Can you find the food idioms that match the following definitions?

All about money

1. To provide for a family.
....

2. To have the best of both worlds.
....

3. To know where one's money or favours come from.
....

4. To obtain access to an easy source of financial benefits.
....

Character and personality

5. Crazy or eccentric.
....

6. Calm when under pressure.
....

7. An unhealthy or destructive influence.
....

8. To pretend innocence.
....

Fortune and misfortune

9. An additional enhancement to an already good situation.
....

10. To cause trouble or spoil another's plans.
....

11. To suffer the consequences of one's own actions.
....

12. To risk losing everything by putting all one's resources into a single undertaking.
....

Answers

1. To bring home the bacon. **2.** To have one's cake and eat it too. **3.** To know on which side one's bread is buttered. **4.** To get on the gravy train. **5.** Nutty as a fruitcake; nuts. **6.** Cool as a cucumber. **7.** A bad apple. **8.** To look like butter wouldn't melt in one's mouth. **9.** The icing on the cake. **10.** To upset the apple cart. **11.** To stew in one's own juices. **12.** To put all one's eggs in one basket.

How we detect odours

The sense of smell is the most ancient of all the senses. In higher-order animals, it provides information about the environment and guides social interaction – initiating sexual encounters, marking territory and repelling others. Humans consciously use it in relation to food and sometimes for detecting threats such as fire, a toxic substance or rotten food.

1 Olfactory receptors Located in a tiny area (just 5 cm²) of the nasal mucous membranes are the olfactory receptor cells – distinctive neurons with minuscule, hair-like cilia containing the receptor proteins. The axons extending from these millions of neurons all converge at the olfactory bulb.

THE MECHANISM OF SMELL

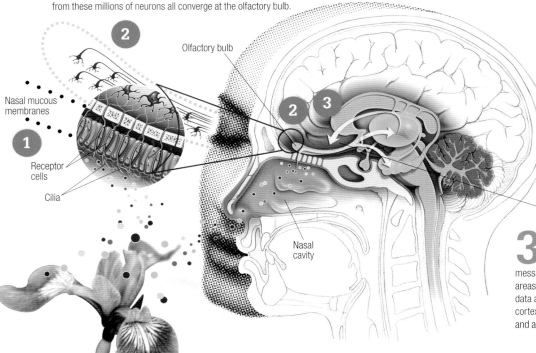

Olfactory bulb

Nasal mucous membranes

Receptor cells

Cilia

Nasal cavity

Olfactory cortex

2 The olfactory bulb This is a highly organised nerve relay node, where axons are grouped according to the type of 'odorant' message they are carrying. The olfactory bulb also receives information from the brain (attention, interest, hunger and desire) that influences the response to the olfactory message. Thousands of nerve fibres pass from the olfactory bulb to the olfactory cortex.

3 The olfactory cortex The messages are first analysed in the olfactory areas and then pooled with other sensory data and processed by different areas of the cortex. The brain can then identify the odour and also produce an emotional response.

Ten thousand different odours

An odour is usually a blend of dozens or even hundreds of odour molecules – a rose, for example, has nearly 400. On average, humans can distinguish some 10,000 different odours. To achieve this, we have hundreds of different protein receptors – many more than the receptors for the other senses (sight has only a few types), but not many compared to the vast number and range of molecules that need to be identified. Each protein reacts to several kinds of molecules, which vary in similarity and strength, and each receptor cell has a specific combination of proteins. A single odour stimulates only some of these cells and to varying degrees.

Why we can't smell our own body odours

The olfactory threshold is the minimum concentration at which an individual can detect an odour and has two levels. The first is the level at which an individual can notice an odorant molecule but not identify it; the second is the higher concentration needed to identify the odour. When odours are persistent, the olfactory threshold eventually increases to the point where they are no longer perceived. This phenomenon of familiarisation allows the olfactory system to be available once more, so that it can be receptive to new odours. This explains why we can't (or can only just) perceive our own body odour.

The complexity of taste

The sense of taste, often regarded as the fifth sense, is used to appreciate the flavour of food. It involves the interpretation of complex information and requires the interaction of several senses.

A combined response

Our impression of food is the combined effect of its aroma (detected through retro-olfaction at the back of the nose), its flavour (distinguished by the tongue) and sensory input related to temperature and texture. Even the sight and sound of a dish can have an effect on our enjoyment of food. The sense traditionally referred to as taste, meaning the processing of information about flavour provided by the tongue, is now called gustation, but this is only one aspect of taste.

How many flavours?

What happens inside the mouth? Traditionally we have four types of taste buds in different parts of the tongue, and these are sensitive to the four basic flavours: sweet, salty, bitter and sour. The thousands of different taste sensations we experience are said to be a combination of these flavours. To these four basic flavours the Japanese add a fifth, called umami, which is sometimes described as the 'savoury taste'. It is triggered by chemicals called glutamates, found naturally in foods like mushrooms, cheese and tomato, and also used as a food additive.

Today controversy surrounds the idea that all flavours are nothing more than a combination of a few basic flavours. Experts maintain that there are not just five (or six) groups of highly specialised taste buds. On the contrary, they propose that each receptor cell in our taste buds reacts to a number of molecules and to different degrees. Each flavour-producing molecule then acts on a certain combination of taste receptor cells in a process similar to the mechanism involved in the sense of smell.

Protective role

Taste is essential for survival, because it provides information about the food to the person eating it. Vestiges of this protective role can be seen with children, and a number of adults, who display spontaneous food preferences and dislikes. We usually find fatty or sweet foods to be quite tasty – and these foods are our greatest sources of energy. But bitterness is often judged unpleasant – and bitterness is a characteristic of alkaloids and tannins, toxic substances secreted by plants in self-defence. So when children refuse to eat food with unfamiliar flavours (just as animals do), taste is fulfilling its protective function, for unknown food is potentially dangerous.

THE MECHANISM OF TASTE

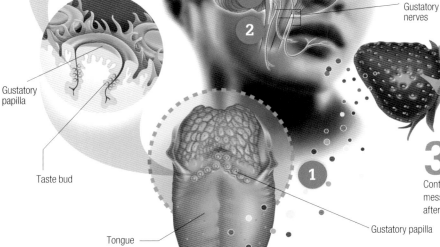

Taste bud

Nerve fibre

Gustatory papilla

Taste bud

Tongue

Prefrontal cortex

Lower brainstem

Gustatory nerves

Gustatory papilla

1 Flavour molecules When a flavour molecule is dissolved in saliva, it comes into contact with a gustatory papilla. The mouth has thousands of papillae, mostly on the tongue, but also on the soft palate, epiglottis and pharynx. Each papilla contains dozens of taste buds with taste-sensitive receptor cells.

2 The three gustatory nerves At the base of each receptor cell, a nerve fibre takes over the task of relaying the message. The fibres form three distinct gustatory nerves that converge in a nucleus in the lower brainstem.

3 The lower brainstem, or medulla oblongata Contrasts between flavours are amplified here and the processed message is then sent on, via the thalamus, to the gustatory area and afterwards to the prefrontal cortex.

The sense of touch

The sense of touch is made up of two parallel systems, each with its own receptors and anatomical pathways. One of these systems deals with temperature and pain and the other processes mechanical information such as pressure, light contact and vibrations.

Tactile matters

The skin puts us in direct contact with our environment. It can warn us of dangers such as potential burns, and through its sensors all over the body it can compensate for any deficiencies in the other senses. The skin is also a means of conveying messages and emotions to others. It has several kinds of mechanical receptors, each of which responds in a different way. Some receptors trigger only a transient response on initial contact, such as when you feel the pressure and texture of a piece of clothing as you are putting it on, but then disregard it. Other receptors keep the information in the foreground for as long as the stimulation lasts.

Temperature and pain are not detected by receptors, but by free nerve endings found in the skin for temperature and throughout the body for pain. These nerve endings respond directly to temperature or, in the case of pain, to specific substances released by the injured tissue. Again, the response can be rapid, such as the reflex action of pulling away from something dangerously hot, or it can be ongoing, as with chronic pain.

The pathway to the brain

A message sometimes has to travel a long way before reaching the brain. Nerves that carry sensory messages to the central nervous system run from all the peripheral parts of the body to the spinal cord and then up to the brainstem. The right hemisphere manages the left part of the body, and the left hemisphere the right part, as the nerve pathways cross over from one side of the spinal cord to the other. Nerves dealing with mechanical information cross over in the medulla oblongata, while nerves relaying pain and temperature messages cross over as soon as they reach the spinal cord.

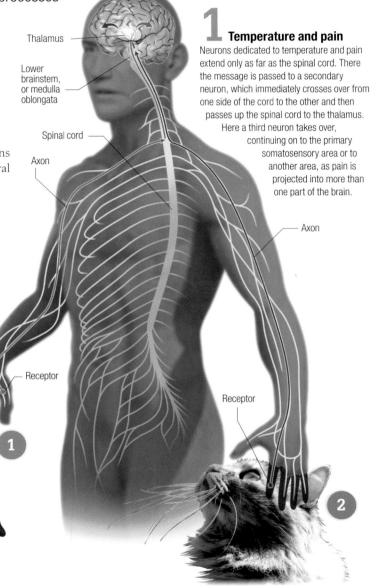

Thalamus

Lower brainstem, or medulla oblongata

Spinal cord

Axon

Receptor

Axon

Receptor

THE TWO SYSTEMS OF TOUCH

1 Temperature and pain
Neurons dedicated to temperature and pain extend only as far as the spinal cord. There the message is passed to a secondary neuron, which immediately crosses over from one side of the cord to the other and then passes up the spinal cord to the thalamus. Here a third neuron takes over, continuing on to the primary somatosensory area or to another area, as pain is projected into more than one part of the brain.

2 Mechanical sensation The axons that make up the peripheral nerves start from the receptor in the part of the body where pressure is felt and extend via the spinal cord as far as the lower brainstem, or medulla oblongata. This means that these axons cover the whole distance. In the medulla, each axon hands over to a second neuron, which extends up to the thalamus. Then a third neuron continues to the primary somatosensory area.

NERVE PATHWAYS FOR TOUCH

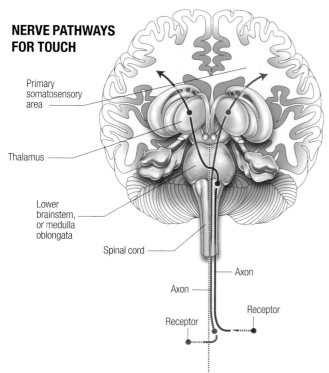

Primary somatosensory area

Thalamus

Lower brainstem, or medulla oblongata

Spinal cord

Axon

Axon

Receptor

Receptor

Receptor

The brain's body map

Neurons that transmit the sense of touch are projected onto the surface of the somatosensory cortex, following a kind of map for different parts of the body, but not all parts of the body have the same amount of coverage. The hands and face, which convey essential information (and have to obey complex orders for movements), occupy a large part of the somatosensory cortex. By comparison, the areas devoted to the legs and trunk seem much smaller.

The hands

Because the hands play such a major role in relation to touch, the nerve projections from them occupy a disproportionately large part of the somatosensory cortex. The skin of the fingers or palm of the hand has up to 200 mechanical receptors per square centimetre, whereas the legs have only five receptors per square centimetre. The tip of the tongue is the only other part of the body that has as many receptors.

THE SOMATOSENSORY CORTEX

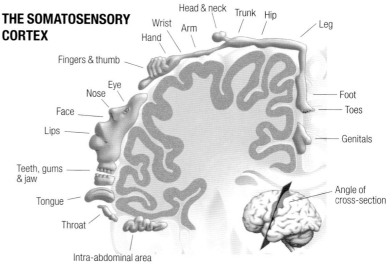

Head & neck
Trunk
Hip
Wrist
Arm
Hand
Leg
Fingers & thumb
Eye
Nose
Foot
Face
Toes
Lips
Genitals
Teeth, gums & jaw
Tongue
Angle of cross-section
Throat
Intra-abdominal area

The face – a special case

For obvious anatomical reasons, the sensory nerves coming from the face, the trigeminal nerves, do not go through the spinal cord before reaching the brain. Instead they pass directly to the brainstem and then follow the same pathway to the thalamus as the other nerves. The trigeminal nerves transmit standard information on touch (mechanical, temperature and pain data), as well as information from taste and olfactory sensors about specific chemical components – for example, the hot spiciness of capsaicin (found in hot peppers), the 'cool' effect of menthol or the acrid effect of ammonia.

Phantom limbs

Most people who have lost an arm or a leg feel sensations from their missing limb. Usually this sensation disappears after a relatively short period of time, but a small number of patients have persistent pain for years afterwards, or even forever. The source of the pain can be at various levels of the sensory or motor systems, often making treatment difficult.

Phantom pain may come from a tangle of nerve fibres at the end of the nerve that has been severed, with the injured nerves continuing to send pain messages after the limb has been amputated. The illusion that the limb is still there may also be because the brain misinterprets the sensations.

Someone whose arm has been amputated may think the arm is being touched, when in fact the contact is with the cheek. This confusion between the missing limb and the face may occur because after amputation the body map in the primary somatosensory cortex is rearranged. Connections that were once silent may sometimes become active, linking a part of the cortex that was previously assigned to the limb to an adjacent part such as the face. These sensations are proof of the brain's plasticity – its ability to adapt and reorganise. Usually this process aids the recovery (at least in part) of functions that were damaged, but with severed limbs it has a negative effect.

10 WAYS TO EXPERIENCE TOUCH

1 Walk barefoot

Each kind of surface you walk on will give you a different sensation, whether it's smooth, warm floorboards, cold, hard marble or soft, plush carpet. Try walking outside on grass, sand or soil. Each will stimulate the touch receptors on the soles of your feet in a different way.

2 Have a massage, or give one to somebody else

The hand has a large number of sensory receptors. When you give someone a massage, you can feel the slightest variations in that person's body, such as tension in muscles and differences in temperature. On the other hand, when you are the one being massaged, you experience your own body quite differently as you discover it through the hands of the person giving the massage.

3 Test your awareness of touch

Take two sharp pencils. Place the two points 1 centimetre apart on the soft pad at the top of one of your fingers. Then do the same on your thigh. You will clearly feel two distinct points of contact on your finger, but will feel only one pressure point on your thigh. For the two pressure points on your thigh to be felt separately, the distance between them would have to be at least 5 centimetres. This demonstrates how the perception of touch changes in different parts of the body; the smaller the space needed for the brain to discern two distinct sources of pressure, the more accurate your awareness of them.

4 Touching with hands and lips

All over your skin there are receptors and nerve endings that are sensitive to heat or cold, soft or rough textures, and wet or dry surfaces. These receptors are not evenly distributed – the highest density of receptors is found in the face and hands. If we were to sketch the outline of a human body in proportion to the density of its sensory receptors, the hands would be huge, the face would be large with an enormous mouth, while the limbs and feet would be tiny, and the back would be smaller than the trunk. The way these sensors are distributed means that we perceive sensations differently in different parts of the body, depending on whether contact is with the hands, feet or lips. Try touching your lips and then your bare foot with something rough, such as a coarse piece of fabric, and feel the difference.

5 Try tickling yourself

Laughing when you're tickled is a reflex reaction that is triggered by surprise. Two experiments, one conducted at the University of California and the other at the Institute of Neurology in London, showed that we can bear being tickled when an area of the brain in the cerebellum is activated. If you try to tickle yourself, this area is automatically activated, so that you don't react to something you initiate yourself. This inhibitory mechanism allows us to ignore some sensations, while leaving us more susceptible to others to which we need to adapt because we can't anticipate them.

6 Touch with your eyes closed

When you can see an object before touching it, you know what feeling to expect. To develop your awareness of touch, try touching things with your eyes closed. Place some items made of different materials in a large box: a damp tea towel, a cup that has been in the freezer for ten minutes, a piece of silk, a sheet of sandpaper, a hot stone that has been out in the sun, a dried leaf, a piece of corrugated cardboard and a ball of wool. Cover the box with a towel, slip your hands underneath and let your fingers move randomly over the contents. The effect of surprise, combined with touching objects without seeing them, will heighten your sensitivity and a give you a better appreciation of the wide range of touch sensations that are possible.

7 Test how you feel temperature

How we feel heat or cold is relative – we are not so much aware of temperature itself as of variations in temperature. A simple experiment can show that this is true. Put one hand in cold water and the other in hot water, and then dip both hands in warm water. The warm water will feel hot or cold according to the temperature of the water in which each hand was first immersed. The faster the temperature change and the larger the surface area of skin exposed, the greater our sensitivity to temperature. Take, for example, what happens when you immerse your whole body in the cold water of a swimming pool or in a bathtub of hot water. For temperatures in the middle range, a process of adaptation ensues in which the swimming pool no longer feels cold, or the bathwater no longer feels hot.

8 Touch as therapy

The effectiveness of manual therapy relies on the tactile contact between therapist and patient. Some types of therapy focus on relieving tension in muscles, joints or posture (osteopathy or chiropractic, for example), while others also include a more psychological approach. Unhappy emotions can be expressed physically in the tension and tightness of the body. By releasing the physical symptoms using touch, a therapist can help to relieve the underlying cause.

9 Be creative with your hands

Kneading clay and shaping it into an object, using fingers to spread paints on a canvas – these are just two of many creative activities that make use of the sense of touch. Such pursuits help to expand our range of sensations and to develop artistic skills and manual dexterity. Sensitivity to touch is a somewhat passive characteristic of the skin's whole surface area, but touching is a voluntary action that we mostly do with our hands. The hand can both inform us (by touching) and carry out actions (by grasping and moving objects), but its links to intelligence, memory and creativity also make it a very special sensory organ.

10 'Touch me – wrinkles aren't contagious'

This slogan was coined by Maggie Kuhn (1905–95), a US activist who founded the Gray Panthers Movement to fight discrimination against the elderly. Touch, unlike the senses of sight or hearing, brings us into direct contact with others. It is the first sense to develop and is no doubt the most important, because we couldn't live without any tactile stimulation. Communication in relationships involves not only sight and speech, but also the sense of touch, which is a wonderful way of expressing affection and tenderness.

Between perception and action: the sense of movement

Sight, hearing, touch, taste and smell provide us with essential information about the world around us, but in order to survive we also need to find our place in our environment, to navigate our way through it and to take action. This is the function of kinaesthesia, the sense of movement.

Is this sense new?

Strangely, it is only in recent years that our ability to assess the movements of the body in space has been considered as a sixth sense, yet it is probably the oldest of all the senses. Without it we couldn't control our actions or respond to those of others – as, for example, in catching prey or avoiding a predator.

Unlike the traditional senses, kinaesthesia relies on several kinds of sensors. Our perception of movement requires external information about what is happening around us, as well as internal information about the different positions of the body. The brain integrates all the data and builds up a single, consistent image of the movements of the body in space.

An original mechanism

Kinaesthesia, like the other senses, uses peripheral sensors that code information as electrical signals, which are then sent to the brain along neuronal pathways. But in kinaesthesia the brain also performs two special and essential functions.

First, many types of sensors take part in the process, supplying many different kinds of information that need to be constantly coordinated, sorted and selected. But even though it's generally necessary for the different data sources to work together, some of the data received may be irrelevant or even detrimental. The brain is constantly selecting relevant data and ignoring other information – for example, it cuts off visual input when we spin around very fast, as in a pirouette.

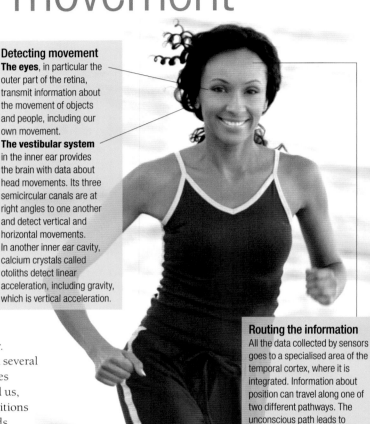

Detecting movement
The eyes, in particular the outer part of the retina, transmit information about the movement of objects and people, including our own movement.
The vestibular system in the inner ear provides the brain with data about head movements. Its three semicircular canals are at right angles to one another and detect vertical and horizontal movements. In another inner ear cavity, calcium crystals called otoliths detect linear acceleration, including gravity, which is vertical acceleration.

Routing the information
All the data collected by sensors goes to a specialised area of the temporal cortex, where it is integrated. Information about position can travel along one of two different pathways. The unconscious path leads to the cerebellum, which controls posture and basic movements, in particular locomotion. The conscious path passes through the thalamus before reaching the temporal cortex. The frontal cortex then integrates the image of movement, adding other sensory information, plus data from individual experience and knowledge.

Sensing position
Stretch sensors in the muscle fibres, angle sensors in the joints and touch sensors in the skin provide information on the position and movement of the different parts of the body in relation to one another.

Ultimate test Slalom skiing, as demonstrated here by Austria's Elisabeth Görgi, involves speed, using gravity, making sudden changes of direction and avoiding gates – it is a formidable test of movement control. Everything happens so fast that it is impossible for the skier to make conscious decisions about movements to be made. The skier's brain appraises a trajectory and from time to time the skier uses a number of senses to check that the path travelled is in line with the plan. One miscalculation and the skier will miss the gate.

Second, responses involving movement need to be swift for survival. This means that the brain can't construct the image of a movement after it has happened, whereas for the other senses it can interpret sensations after they have been perceived. The brain must anticipate the movements of the body and also of people and objects nearby. It develops hypotheses about movements, which will then be either confirmed or invalidated by what actually happens – for example, falls, collisions or crashes. This is the skill you use to catch a ball, positioning your hand according to the trajectory calculated by the brain and starting to grasp even before the ball has reached you. In fact, simulation of the movement activates the same areas of the brain as carrying out the action itself.

Head and legs

Why does your view of the environment remain steady even when you are running or jumping? The answer is simple – it's because your head follows a perfectly even path. Unconsciously the muscles in your neck, your eyes and ultimately your whole body offset your movements, so that the retinas of your eyes and vestibular systems of your ears can operate efficiently from a steady base. In fact, the head could be described as an inertial navigation platform. This is one of the most outstanding features of kinaesthesia and is a skill that is acquired in the first year of life.

Travel sickness: an internal conflict

Travel sickness is caused by a conflict between the fast-moving landscape seen by the eyes and the vestibular sensors of the ears, which normally detect acceleration but are not activated when a person is comfortably seated in a car or train that is moving at a steady speed. What's more, the body is at rest. Position sensors give no information on movement. Mechanisms used for solving any conflict between kinaesthetic sensors, which are designed for running and natural movements, can then be overtaxed, causing travel sickness.

The changing brain

3

Champion of evolution

The brain of *Homo sapiens* is unique among primates, thanks to its highly developed cerebral cortex. This is the centre for sophisticated cognitive functions – language, reasoning, consciousness, imagination and the ability to envision the future.

A unique feature

As humans evolved, the brain's expanding cortex had to fold back on itself to fit inside the skull, forming deep convolutions. If we could unfold the cortex, it would be about 3 millimetres thick and cover an area of 1–2 square metres. The human cortex is ten times larger than the cortex of the most highly evolved apes.

A thinking animal

This large surface area of the human cortex is what has allowed us to develop the ability to choose what we do, whereas the behaviour of the simplest animals is strictly controlled by their genes. In the course of evolution, the increasing complexity of the human nervous system has been accompanied by the decreasing influence of genes in determining our actions. Primates such as the great apes have an extraordinary capacity to learn – in their brains a range of options are made possible by neuroplasticity – that is, the ability of neurons to change. Of all the primates, humans especially have been able to develop an exceptional capacity for adapting to new situations. Unlike most other animals, we can question our habits as we are exposed to new experiences and we can do this far better even than chimpanzees, our closest living primate relatives. It's thanks to the size of our brains that we humans have been able to break free from the laws dictated by genetics and acquire the freedom to think, to envision the future, to imagine and to dream.

Freedom to think Lost in deep reflection, *The Thinker*, executed by French sculptor Auguste Rodin in 1902, epitomises the specifically human ability to enjoy freedom of thought and free will.

4 CRITICAL

1 Walking on two legs

There are two conflicting hypotheses about when our ancestors began to walk on two legs. According to one of these, upright posture evolved from four-legged locomotion and was a stage in the evolution of hominids. The second and more recent idea is that upright posture, not the four-legged one, is a very ancient, primitive phenomenon. A hominid living some six million years ago, *Orrorin tugenensis*, was already standing on two legs, and the knuckle-walking gait of chimpanzees and gorillas may have derived from its upright posture. No matter which hypothesis is correct, walking upright was accompanied by two other developments: the size of the brain increased (the upright spinal column was able to support a larger skull) and the hands were freed.

2 Freeing the hands

With permanently upright posture, the hands could function independently of the legs. Not only were the hands now available for other uses, but the opposable thumb (also found in a rudimentary form in the great apes) made it possible to develop

manual dexterity. This required a high level of sensorimotor coordination (between the brain, the hands and the senses, especially sight). The hand both sends information to the brain and makes great demands on it, especially on the frontal cortex and the cerebellum. Intellectual skills and manual dexterity are thus closely related.

STAGES

3 Making tools with tools

Many animals make tools from natural materials, some keep them for later use, and there are some chimpanzees that use stone tools, but without modifying them. Only humans, it seems, are able to craft a tool by using another one, and have been doing so for at least 2.7 million years. Tool making probably appeared at about the same time as primitive languages began to be used and both these activities required substantial input from the brain.

4 Speech

No one knows why language appeared. It was most likely preceded by an elaborate sign language that our earliest ancestors developed for greater safety in a world of predators. In all probability, primitive language was first used some two million years ago – simple words juxtaposed without grammar, but sufficient to build social bonds. Complex symbolic languages and art have been part of the culture of the indigenous people of Australia and New Guinea since they arrived as much as 50,000 years ago, so language must have emerged well before that. It appears to have adapted as life and the human mind became more complex.

What makes humans different?

Laughter is no longer viewed as a uniquely human activity, since chimpanzees have been caught smiling at their own reflection in a mirror. And sex for the sake of sex is not uniquely human either: bonobos (pygmy chimpanzees), the primates closest to humans, also indulge in sexual activity for pleasure. As for being aware of others and being able to guess what someone else intends to do, there are plenty of mammals and even some birds that possess these abilities. What's more, intelligence, speech and the use of tools are not considered to be distinguishing features either. Our uniqueness does not even reside in the complexity of the human genome, for 90 per cent of our genes are found in the mouse genome, and there is only a 2 per cent difference between humans and bonobos. Of course, genes themselves aren't everything – gene expression, gene regulation and the cellular environment are just as important.

So just what *is* unique about humans? In the end, it may be the fact that humans think about that very question. They try to describe the world around them and understand their role in it. Apes have only a limited ability for abstract and conceptual thought; as far as we know, religion, art, stories and legends belong only to the human realm, while only a human could have invented cooking. Machines can calculate much faster than we can, but no computer has the human brain's plasticity – its ability to adapt: no computer can learn, unlearn and relearn. This is why we still need pilots to fly aeroplanes: only human beings can react and respond instantly to the unforeseen.

We were born to evolve

The brain of a newborn baby contains 100 billion neurons. While the number of neurons doesn't increase after birth, the development of the brain is far from complete, for the synapses, the connections between the neurons, are only just beginning to form.

Neuronal networks

At birth only 10 per cent of the brain's synapses are present – the remaining 90 per cent are formed later. For the brain to continue to develop, it needs to be stimulated so that it can set up networks of neurons to manage the major functions – sensory, motor and cognitive. This process is influenced by the environment – the body's internal environment created by factors such as hormones, nutrition and disease, and the external environment shaped by the family, society and knowledge. External influences such as these will affect a child's development of certain skills and help to forge personality traits.

Neuroplasticity is the term used to describe the brain's ability to adapt to new conditions. With magnetic resonance imaging (MRI) we can now observe how the brain changes with different learning experiences. MRI images of pianists' brains, for example, show that those specialised parts of the brain that control finger movement, hearing and sight are thicker. The extent of these changes is proportional to the length of time spent studying the piano as a child.

It's not all over by the age of 3!

The brain continues to adapt throughout adult life, making it possible to learn new skills, change habits or even choose different paths in life. A good example of this adaptability was observed when researchers asked study participants to learn to juggle three balls. After two months of practice, MRI images of their brains showed that the areas for sight and for hand and arm coordination had grown thicker. A second MRI image taken a few months later revealed regression in these same areas for those participants who had not kept up their practice. These findings show how past events can change the way the brain works. This is why children need to be stimulated by their surroundings, and a lack of stimulation can often cause problems in personality development. For adults, neuroplasticity means that we can learn, reason and make plans. Nothing is ever permanently fixed in the brain, no matter what our time of life. The best way for us to maintain this adaptability is to interact with the environment, be open to new experiences, exchange ideas with others and learn from one another. In fact, all we need to do is to enjoy life.

Herbert von Karajan conducted his last concert with the Vienna Philharmonic Orchestra at the age of 81, just a few months before he died.

In 1973, at the age of 92, Picasso held an exhibition featuring 156 etchings, which he had executed between late 1970 and March 1972.

In 2004, the Seattle Art Museum commissioned a fountain from the sculptor, Louise Bourgeois, who was 93 at the time.

The mind knows no bounds, and neither does creativity

Mental skills and creativity improve with proficiency and experience. We may not learn as fast as we grow older, and we may take more time to solve problems, but we tackle them in a more holistic way, combining ideas and knowledge that we have acquired over the years. This ability contributes both to creativity and to a better understanding of the world.

What gives the brain its plasticity?

Our brain cells contribute to neuroplasticity in a number of ways. The best known of these processes is the way that the connections between the neurons, or synapses, strengthen with use. The more often we put them to work, the more neurotransmitters they produce (see pages 16–17) and the stronger the electrical signal conducted by dendrites (the parts of the neuron that receive nerve impulses). On the other hand, synapses that are never used gradually wither and eventually disappear.

Another way the brain adapts is through the formation of new synapses. As we learn something new, the ends of the axons sprout new branches, which then come into contact with the dendrites of the next neuron. New networks are formed and will remain for as long as they are used. The more the brain is stimulated, the greater the number of new connections formed.

Lastly, recent discoveries have shown that new neurons can be formed in the adult brain, invalidating a long-held theory that our lifetime stock of neurons is present in the embryo and that numbers decline from birth onwards. Today, we know this older theory to be incorrect, because certain areas of the brain – such as the hippocampus, which plays a role in memory – can produce new neurons until we are quite old, in a process called neurogenesis. These new neurons are then wired into existing networks, forming new connections.

An amazing feat of adaptation

In 2007, doctors in Marseille, France, examined a man who had been leading a perfectly normal life even though his skull was filled with liquid and his brain was flattened against the bones of the cranium. His condition was a type of hydrocephalus (in which the brain's chambers contain an abnormally large amount of cerebrospinal fluid) and had developed since childhood. The pressure of the intracranial fluid had gradually pushed his brain mass towards the outer edges of the cranium, yet this anomaly had not affected the social, personal or professional life of this 44-year-old father of two.

This is a striking example of neuroplasticity, showing how the human brain is able to adapt and rearrange itself. It is also proof that, contrary to common belief, mental skills are not directly dependent on the shape of the brain.

STRUCTURE OF A NEURON

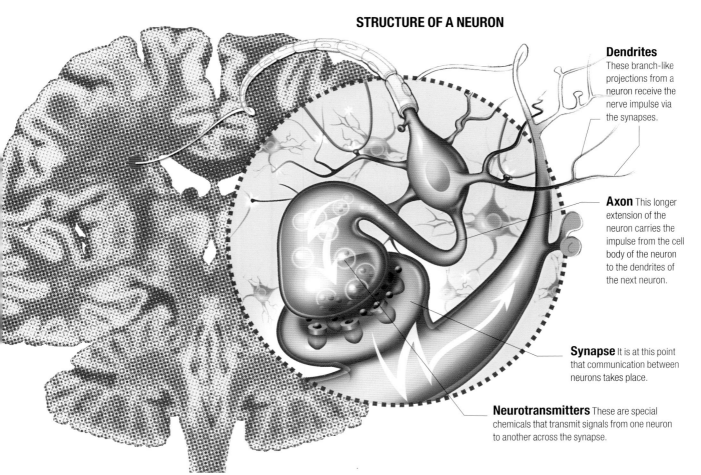

Dendrites These branch-like projections from a neuron receive the nerve impulse via the synapses.

Axon This longer extension of the neuron carries the impulse from the cell body of the neuron to the dendrites of the next neuron.

Synapse It is at this point that communication between neurons takes place.

Neurotransmitters These are special chemicals that transmit signals from one neuron to another across the synapse.

6 WAYS TO STIMULATE YOUR NEURONS

1 Lead an active social life

A stimulating environment is a basic requirement for keeping your brain in good working order. Social contact is one way of remaining alert and is bound to place a range of demands on the brain. Group leisure activities offer many opportunities not only for learning but also for discussing and observing. When different generations get together, it opens up new horizons and leads to interesting discoveries. Having good friends and satisfying personal and family relationships also contributes to the sense of wellbeing that is essential to keep the brain functioning efficiently.

2 Control your emotions

For a long time we have known that extreme stress has negative effects on learning and memory. Fear and anxiety, for example, interfere with judgment and the ability to think clearly. Medical imaging has shown that stress and depression damage neurons and change the way the brain functions. These negative effects can be countered by learning to control your emotions.

3 Take pleasure in what you do

Motivation is a key factor in learning and intellectual pleasure. Each new experience we have establishes a new but temporary circuit for information to travel through the brain. It can be consolidated and stabilised only when you pursue things you enjoy.

4 Train your brain

Lifelong learning can slow down the deterioration of the brain and the appearance of neuro-degenerative diseases, so grasp every opportunity to exercise your memory and acquire new knowledge and skills. Any skills that you don't use are gradually lost – an obvious example of this is the ability to speak a foreign language, which needs to be practised to be remembered. In general, tasks requiring problem solving, organisation and planning improve brain function. And the many brain-training programs available in books and magazines, on the internet or as video games will all help to keep your brain fit. You'll find some good examples in the games section of this book (see page 294).

5 Get a good night's sleep

Lack of sleep has a direct impact on many cognitive functions, including concentration, memory and the ability to solve problems. An increasing number of studies have shown that sleep plays a critical role in laying down new memories and also seems to contribute to neurogenesis. These findings suggest that sleep is very important for neuroplasticity and that new neuronal connections grow stronger while we are asleep.

6 Exercise and eat well

See the sections of this book about eating (page 232) and physical exercise (page 272).

---

5 keys to brain fitness

● **Difficulty**
To develop new skills, set stretch targets that are slightly beyond your ability – but don't make them too unattainable, as failure is a source of stress.

● **Speed**
Doing easy exercises fast is sometimes more stimulating for the brain than the satisfaction of solving a complicated problem. Set a time limit and gradually shorten it as you improve.

● **Novelty**
This is the number one brain stimulant. It is important to adapt your brain exercises gradually so that they remain novel and challenging to the brain.

● **Practice**
Regular practice is the only way to consolidate newly acquired knowledge and skills in any area, whether in sport, learning, hobbies or other pursuits.

● **Reward**
This is the tangible result of an effort or personal commitment. It may be perfecting your golf swing, conversing fluently in a foreign language, setting up a blog or creating a vegetable garden.

Can the brain repair itself?

If people who have suffered brain damage after a stroke or head injury undergo rehabilitation, they can recover all or part of their brain function.

Self-repair

MRI images of patients with brain damage show that during rehabilitation sessions the brain excludes the damaged parts of the neural network that are normally used for that activity. Functions previously managed by these areas are then taken over, in full or in part, by the neurons in adjacent areas, establishing new neuronal connections to do so.

The ability of a connection to change, called synaptic plasticity, is a natural process, but it still requires considerable stimulation. By starting to do specific exercises as soon as possible, the patient utilises the maximal amount of healthy brain tissue, including the areas of the brain surrounding the injured region.

Researchers have also been working with neuroplasticity mechanisms in an effort to find new treatments for neuro-degenerative diseases, such as drugs that stimulate neurons, promote neurogenesis and help neuron or stem-cell grafts. In many cases, techniques that promote neuro-plasticity can also be non-pharmacological, such as cognitive exercises.

> ## Build your cognitive capital
>
> A number of studies have shown that connecting with others socially and keeping an active mind throughout life may delay the onset of Alzheimer's disease, or alleviate its symptoms by restoring an affected area of the brain or by using a different area.
>
> A US study initiated in 1986 reported a lower incidence of Alzheimer's disease in a community of 678 nuns with an average age of 85 than in the general population. Various suggestions were made to explain the phenomenon, including the level of education of the women and the fact that they were engaging in social and mental activities at an advanced age. Another study, conducted in Canada in 2007, found a link between speaking two languages on a regular basis and the delayed emergence of signs of dementia – on average, 4 years later.
>
> These studies, together with many other observations, have shown that mental activity (whether games, reading, social interaction or leisure activities) – and particularly more complex or challenging activities – builds a kind of cognitive reserve that can delay dementia-related decline.

Rehabilitation techniques

Speech therapy is the most common method used in brain rehabilitation. Speech therapists treat language and reading disorders by giving speaking and writing exercises and by asking questions about the meanings of words and the structure of sentences. The aim is to develop neuroplasticity by stimulating one particular brain function.

Occupational therapy employs similar resources but applies them to a physical disability. The exercises introduced by the occupational therapist aim to improve the patient's motor skills and orientation by handling various objects and practising the movements needed for everyday activities. Occupational therapy is a key stage in recovering autonomy and independence after the loss of neuromotor function.

Physiotherapy is another type of rehabilitation that helps patients to recover any lost or altered function as quickly as possible. Massage, repetition of movements plus strengthening and stretching exercises all help to develop the neuroplasticity that is needed to recover the use of an affected limb.

In the case of major injuries, the brain can't fully compensate for the damaged neuronal connections, leaving the patient with serious permanent effects. Neuroplasticity may even make a problem worse – for example, the rearrangement of brain functions could explain why pain is felt in a limb that is no longer there (see page 47).

Nature and nurture

The question of whether humans are born with certain abilities or whether these are acquired through experience is no longer a subject of debate. Our understanding of how certain factors influence gene expression and of the brain's capacity to regenerate has shown that these two approaches, once believed to be mutually exclusive, are in fact two parts of the same whole.

Genetically modified

Researchers who studied a number of generations of families in Sweden found a link between the grandparents' diet and certain physiological features of the grandchildren. There appeared to be a lower prevalence of cardiovascular disease and diabetes in the descendants of people who had suffered from malnutrition in their childhood, but no genetic alteration could be found to account for the difference.

This suggests that a response to an external factor can be passed on without being handed down in our genes. Environmental factors such as pollutants, smoking, stress and – as in this example – diet, create a kind of imprint that influences later generations by modifying the expression of their genes. The fact that acquired features can be transmitted in this way shows that innate and external elements combine in a complex gene–environment interaction and that our genes (with which we are born) are modified by an environmental imprint.

And what's more, since the wiring of the brain is coded by our genes, it's clear that intelligence has a genetic component. Intelligence, then, can be altered by hereditary changes to the transcription of the genome as well as by the influence of social, economic and cultural factors on neuroplasticity.

Like genes, neurons form a network and the connections between them (synapses) are shaped by experience and learning. In addition to genes – which determine the number of neurons, their distribution in the areas of the brain, and each person's abilities – the lessons of life also play a role. In the end, what shapes an adult are characteristics that are inherited at birth and gradually modified during childhood and adolescence.

Is intelligence inherited or acquired?

A good way to explore the hereditary aspect of intelligence is to study identical twins who have been raised separately. If intelligence is solely hereditary, then identical twins must have the same intelligence. A British psychologist named Cyril Burt set out to prove this theory in the 1940s and 1950s, and the findings of his research were unequivocal: the correlation between IQ scores for identical twins raised separately was 0.77, but it was only 0.54 for non-identical twins. For Cyril Burt, therefore, intelligence was clearly hereditary. But in the 1970s evidence was produced showing that he had faked the data to make the figures match his view of intelligence.

Even though many studies have been undertaken, so far none have been able to prove that intelligence is purely hereditary. The reasons for this are mainly to do with methodology, because identical twins are rarely raised separately and, even if they are, they usually live with close relatives. Studies of twins and siblings raised by their biological parents are not really convincing, so how can inherited abilities be distinguished from those that are due to the influence of family?

Neurogenetics

Neurogenetics is a recent discipline that uses genome analysis to investigate diseases affecting the nervous system, especially neurodegenerative and neuromuscular conditions. The aim is to find genes that are anomalous or that could predispose an individual to a disease, such as cancer or diabetes, as well as to detect hereditary risks or more specific causes of disease. Research focuses not only on genes and protein coding, but also on environmental influences: the objective is to see how and why an outside factor can cause a predisposing gene to be expressed or, on the other hand, why this factor affects the genes needed for certain neurons.

In fact, there is no proof that intelligence is solely hereditary, and nothing to prove the opposite either. It may simply be by chance that a father and his daughter have the same level of intelligence, but can chance also explain that a father, mother and all their children are equally intelligent? There is no doubt that heredity plays a role in intelligence. A person is born with potential, and this will be recognised, fostered and enhanced by social contacts, family background and a good education. If a child with limited abilities is adopted by a family that is keen on social and cultural activities, that child will develop those abilities to the maximum. By contrast, a child raised by a family that has little intellectual curiosity will develop at a modest rate, unless outside elements, such as school, reveal that child's potential.

Education sparks curiosity

Being intelligent is not just a matter of acquiring knowledge, but also of learning how to organise and use it. By developing our knowledge in various subject areas, we end up – almost without realising it – creating links between them so that we also acquire a transdisciplinary understanding of our world. By learning and relearning in different ways, we can collate and organise the mass of information that we read, see and hear.

This level of intellectual maturity means that the mind is always on stand-by. Even unknown words or pictures will trigger a familiar feeling because the mind has found approximate matches in its stock of general knowledge. In this way, a basic knowledge of ancient languages can help us to understand unknown words, past events can cast light on current geopolitical situations, and a basic knowledge of science can lead to an understanding of the universe.

The feeling of being empowered that comes with knowledge stirs curiosity and is an incentive to find out more. Those who are knowledgeable will have a better understanding of the world because they are more likely to have a sense of belonging.

Famous families

The following families and groups of family members are known for their shared intellectual or artistic ability. Who are they?

1. An English poet and her painter brother.
....

2. Three English sisters, all authors.
....

3. English sisters known for their outspoken, and opposing, political views.
....

4. Family active in journalism and the mass media over three generations.
....

5. Family of English actors spanning three generations.
....

6. Four American brothers, all film actors.
....

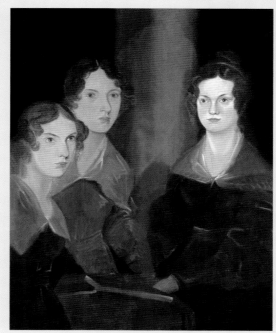

This family portrait of the three literary Brontë sisters, (from left to right) Anne, Emily and Charlotte, is the work of their brother, Branwell, whose image was originally in the background .

Answers

1. Christina and Dante Gabriel Rossetti.
2. Charlotte, Emily and Anne Brontë. **3.** The Mitford sisters: Jessica (a communist sympathiser), Unity and Diana (fascist supporters). **4.** The Murdoch family: Keith; his son, Rupert; and Rupert's children, Elisabeth, Lachlan and James.
5. The Redgraves: Michael; his children, Vanessa, Corin and Lynn; and Vanessa's daughters, Natasha and Joely Richardson.
6. Alec, Daniel, William and Stephen Baldwin.

A lifetime of learning

It is partly the plasticity of the brain that makes it possible for us to continue to learn new skills – both mental and manual – throughout life.

Learning and necessity

Learning is not a uniquely human activity. Lion cubs, for example, learn to hunt with their mothers. And when apes learn to do tasks like picking leaves from a branch, each group of apes has a different way of doing it, which shows that the young are definitely taught by the adults in the group, a typical trait of a tribal culture. Humans, on the other hand, are born in a state of much greater dependency than monkeys, so learning inevitably takes much longer.

For all animals, as for humans, the key to learning is neuroplasticity – that is, the ability of neurons, when stimulated, to modify synaptic connections. This means that for effective learning we don't need a huge brain or a greater number of neurons. What is important is the number of synaptic connections between the neurons and how often they change. For learning, a malleable brain is needed, and the human brain – probably because of its large number of mirror neurons (specialised neurons involved in observing and imitating) – has a remarkable capacity for memorisation, imitation, empathy and understanding others.

I repeat, therefore I know

Learning can't happen without memory, and repetition helps us to absorb new information and commit it to memory. Then, to establish what we have learnt firmly in our memory, we need to come back to it and to revise it on a regular basis.

The only way to remember some sorts of information is to learn it by heart. Rote learning may be criticised as a teaching method, but it gets the memory working and, most importantly, it helps us to acquire automatic skills, which gives the brain a rest. Just think how much time and energy we would need to do calculations if we had never learnt our multiplication tables, to write without having a basic knowledge of grammar and spelling, or to solve a mathematical problem if first we had to prove all the relevant theorems. Similarly, actors who have rehearsed and repeated

their lines enough times are free to devote themselves to interpreting a role, because they no longer have to make an effort to remember their part.

But there is more to repetition than just learning things off by heart. We are more likely to remember something if we use visual, auditory and emotional prompts. Hearing, writing, reading, visualising or linking the information to an emotion can help to record memories and, more importantly, can lead to a better understanding of complex data. Knowledge is not simply stockpiled in the memory, but is broken down and then linked or related to other data. You can see this when you recall a fact or an event – it's never quite the same from one time to the next; it comes to mind with other memories, and each time they are different. By increasing the number of associations, repetition reinforces both memorisation and understanding.

Comprehension first and foremost

Memorising a text, an explanation or facts needs to be done slowly so that the information can gradually permeate, giving the brain time to encode the memory and to reach the point of fully understanding a complex subject. If you want to know how something works – like a car, an aeroplane or a complex piece of machinery – or to understand what is meant by an accounting balance, a black hole, existentialism or photosynthesis – then an explanation that breaks down the information and leads you step by step through the different stages will ensure that you can understand, even when it involves highly specialised technical data.

In addition, continuous learning and training play important roles: the more we are exposed to learning and the more we use our mental faculties – whether through enrolling in continuing education or distance learning, or through social activities – the easier and faster it is to learn and the better we perform.

Practice makes perfect At the age of 86, British actor Sir John Gielgud played Prospero in *Prospero's Books* (the film version of Shakespeare's *The Tempest*), a role he played many times and first interpreted on stage 60 years earlier. Gielgud (centre) is seen here with actors Mark Rylance, as Ferdinand, and Isabelle Pasco, as Prospero's daughter, Miranda.

The beauty of movement

The dexterity and control of movement that characterise people who excel in the arts, crafts and sport are acquired through practice and repetition. This kind of learning requires patience and perseverance, but the rewards are tangible: the novice will gradually gain skills and may even become an expert.

● **The golf swing**
The subtlety and effectiveness of this stroke is mastered only after hours and hours of practice.

● **Manual dexterity**
Cooking, an art that we practise every day, combines culinary traditions handed down from the past with skill and creativity.

● **Nautical knots**
Like any other manual skill, tying these sailors' knots is a traditional craft with a practical application. The special combination of know-how and movements is handed on through imitation and practice.

● **Dancing**
This is a good example of the body's intelligence, involving the perfection of technique, expressive interpretation and memorising a series of movements.

● **Shuffling cards...**
...or playing the piano, woodworking, sewing and many other activities for which we use our hands: all of these skills are acquired through practice.

● **Drawing and painting**
We learn to draw and paint by first copying an image exactly. Then we progress to imitating a style and eventually developing our own original style.

● **Origami**
The Japanese art of paper folding requires very precise, controlled movements and great care. First you copy a design, and then, with practice, you can move on to creating your own original work.

Learning by imitation

Primates and some birds, such as parrots, are imitators. They mimic one another or humans, because they know how to observe behaviour and replicate it. Humans start imitating in the first few weeks of life – a baby responds with a smile upon seeing a person smile, or squeals after hearing a loud voice. It is thought that by the age of 12 months a baby already consciously copies others. Young children are eager to learn and want to absorb as much as possible of their everyday world. That's how they learn to speak, by reproducing the sounds and tones they hear.

Imitation through patient and attentive observation is essential for learning and development. The techniques that we need for manual activities, art or sport can never be standardised and explained only orally or in writing. They must be learnt through practice, by making mistakes and correcting them – and this trial-and-error process is in itself educational and contributes to learning, whether it's a question of theoretical knowledge or practical skills. It's a process that obliges learners to play an active role, to be committed and involved, and that ultimately helps them to fully understand why a particular approach is the best one. Learning by trial and error also allows incorrect or inefficient strategies, behaviour or actions to be rejected, and leads eventually to the satisfaction of mastering a new skill.

When it comes to the intellect, imitation occurs in a social context. If we admire somebody, we unconsciously aspire to match that person's achievements. In this case, imitation is an incentive that stimulates the brain during the learning process, keeps us focused on the objective and boosts our ability to memorise – all because we associate positive outcomes with gaining knowledge.

Clever pets During World War II, Winston Churchill's parrot, Charlie, learned to swear and curse Hitler and the Nazis, imitating exactly his owner's tone of voice and expression. More recently in Tokyo, a lost parrot was taken home after giving the name and address of its owner to the vet who found it.

Do you remember?

These quizzes will test your general knowledge, particularly what you learned at school. You've probably forgotten some of the things you learned then, but you'll find that you do recall much of what you once learned by heart.

Poetry

Try to remember the next lines of these poems.

1. I wander'd lonely as a cloud/That ....
2. Half a league, half a league,/Half ....
3. The Owl and the Pussy-Cat went to sea/In ....
4. I remember, I remember,/The ....
5. The wind was a torrent of darkness among the gusty trees,/The ....
6. Tyger! Tyger! Burning bright/In ....
7. Shall I compare thee to a summer's day? /Thou ....
8. Two roads diverged in a yellow wood,/And ....
9. I must go down to the seas again, to the lonely sea and the sky,/And ....
10. Let us go then, you and I,/When ....

Who said this?

Who said…?

	a. Benjamin Franklin	b. Pablo Picasso	c. Confucius	d. Gandhi	e. Winston Churchill
1. 'Live as if you were to die tomorrow. Learn as if you were to live forever.'	☐	☐	☐	☐	☐
2. 'Tell me and I forget. Teach me and I remember. Involve me and I learn.'	☐	☐	☐	☐	☐
3. 'I am always ready to learn, but I do not always like being taught.'	☐	☐	☐	☐	☐
4. 'I am always doing that which I cannot do, in order that I may learn how to do it.'	☐	☐	☐	☐	☐
5. 'If you think in terms of a year, plant a seed; if in terms of ten years, plant trees; if in terms of 100 years, teach the people.'	☐	☐	☐	☐	☐

Maths and geometry

Match each of these terms with its correct definition.

a. Product

b. Parallelogram

c. Perimeter

d. Hypotenuse

e. Quotient

f. Radius

1. In a right-angled triangle, the side opposite the right angle

2. The distance from the centre to the circumference of a circle

3. The result of multiplication

4. Quadrilateral with diagonals intersecting at the centre

5. Measurement of length

6. The result of division

Geography

1. Which statement is false?

- **a.** The Strait of Gibraltar is located between Europe and Africa.
- **b.** The Cape of Good Hope is the southernmost point of South America.
- **c.** The Bay of Pigs is on the coast of Cuba.

2. After China and India, the three next most highly populated countries in the world are:

- **a.** Indonesia, the USA and Pakistan
- **b.** The USA, Indonesia and Russia
- **c.** The USA, Indonesia and Brazil

3. The third longest river or river system in the world is the:

- **a.** Mississippi–Missouri (USA)
- **b.** Yangtze (China)
- **c.** Volga (Russia)

4. The smallest country in the world is:

- **a.** Vatican City
- **b.** Andorra
- **c.** Liechtenstein

5. Which pair of countries both have an Indian Ocean coastline?

- **a.** Sri Lanka and Japan
- **b.** Australia and Kenya
- **c.** India and Angola

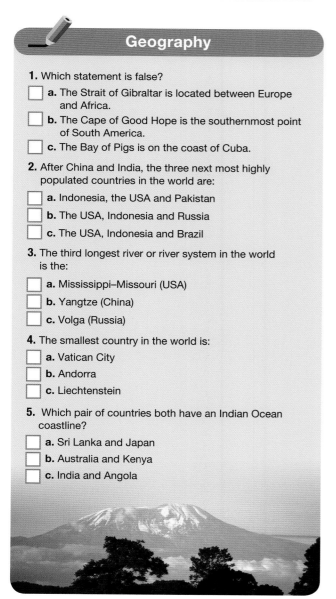

Kings and queens

Who was on the English throne when the following events happened?

a. William the Conqueror b. Elizabeth I c. George III d. Victoria

1. Abraham Lincoln was assassinated.

2. Navigators George Bass and Matthew Flinders established that Tasmania is an island.

3. The Indian Rebellion began.

4. The Normans took control of England.

5. The Duke of Wellington defeated Napoleon in the Battle of Waterloo.

6. Sir Francis Drake became the first Englishman to circumnavigate the globe.

7. French revolutionaries stormed the Bastille.

8. The world's first national census, the Domesday Book, was compiled.

9. Catherine the Great became Empress of Russia.

10. James Watt invented the steam engine.

11. The First Boer War began.

12. Shakespeare's *Hamlet* was staged at the original Globe Theatre.

13. Australian bushranger Ned Kelly was executed.

14. The potato was introduced into Europe.

15. Henry Morton Stanley found the explorer and missionary Dr David Livingstone.

16. The American Congress passed the Declaration of Independence.

17. James Cook made the first charts of New Zealand.

18. The English navy defeated the Spanish Armada.

Answers: **Poetry 1.** …floats on high o'er vales and hills,/When all at once I saw a crowd,/A host of golden daffodils… (*William Wordsworth*). **2.** …a league onward,/All in the valley of Death/Rode the six hundred… (*Alfred, Lord Tennyson*). **3.** …a beautiful pea-green boat./They took some honey, and plenty of money/Wrapped up in a five-pound note… (*Edward Lear*). **4.** …house where I was born,/The little window where the sun/Came creeping in at morn… (*Thomas Hood*). **5.** …moon was a ghostly galleon tossed upon cloudy seas,/The road was a ribbon of moonlight over the purple moor,/And the highwayman came riding – … (*Alfred Noyes*). **6.** …the forests of the night,/What immortal hand or eye/Could frame thy fearful symmetry?… (*William Blake*). **7.** …art more lovely and more temperate:/Rough winds do shake the darling buds of May,/And summer's lease hath all too short a date… (*William Shakespeare*). **8.** …sorry that I could not travel both/And be one traveller, long I stood/And looked down one as far as I could… (*Robert Frost*). **9.** …all I ask is a tall ship and a star to steer her by… (*John Masefield*). **10.** … the evening is spread out against the sky/Like a patient etherised upon a table… (*T.S. Eliot*). **Who said this? 1.** d. **2.** a. **3.** e. **4.** b. **5** c. **Maths and geometry 1.** d. **2.** f. **3.** a. **4.** b. **5.** c; **6.** e. **Geography 1.** b (it's in South Africa and is not the southernmost point). **2.** c. **3.** b **4.** a **5.** b. **Kings and queens 1.** d. **2.** c. **3.** d. **4.** a. **5.** c. **6.** b. **7.** c. **8.** a. **9.** c. **10.** c. **11.** d. **12.** b. **13.** d. **14.** b. **15.** d. **16.** c. **17.** c. **18.** b.

Intelligence

4

The intelligence debate

Philosophers, psychologists and neurobiologists are still trying to unravel the mystery of human intelligence. It is indeed a difficult concept to grasp. And in any case, can it really be defined in any way other than in terms of what it allows us to do – such as to understand, to reason and to adapt to new situations?

One or many?

The very concept of intelligence is the subject of debate. Some argue that it is a single, general cognitive ability underpinning all thinking processes. Others distinguish a number of forms of intelligence that vary in their degree of specialisation and operate independently of one another. Researchers have also investigated the biological foundations of intelligence. Is there one gene for intelligence or are there several genes? Can the speed with which we understand something be attributed to the efficiency of connections between neurons? Can the reasoning process be linked to certain areas of the brain?

These questions remain unanswered and have led to substantial debates about education, learning and ageing. What can we learn from neuroscience that we could apply to developing, expanding and maintaining our potential at every stage of life? Is academic intelligence, as measured by the intelligence quotient (IQ), the most important aspect, or should creativity and emotional intelligence be given equal consideration? Should intelligence be restricted to the purely intellectual realms of the mind, or does it need to be defined in broader terms, encompassing such aspects as capacity for happiness, individual achievement and the ability to act effectively in the face of new situations?

Theories of intelligence

Since the early twentieth century and the first attempts to measure intelligence, many scientists have developed theories about this major function, but none of these theories can claim to deliver an absolute truth. Each casts a different light on a number of different faculties that are considered together, rightly or wrongly, under the umbrella of intelligence.

The g factor According to the English psychologist Charles Spearman (1863–1945), all our abilities are part of a general intelligence called the 'g factor', which determines our aptitude for reasoning and problem solving, use of language, spatial perception and new learning. With this approach, tests covering a wide range of skills produced quite similar scores; whether they performed well or badly, individuals tended to achieve a similar performance level in each subject area.

Fluid versus crystallised intelligence After Spearman, psychologists set about determining subgroups of general intelligence. Raymond Cattell (1905–98) made a distinction between fluid and crystallised intelligence. He theorised that fluid intelligence is unrelated to cultural background and is the ability to think logically, adapt and learn. Crystallised intelligence, on the other hand, is the ability to use skills, knowledge and experience, and to remember and implement acquired knowledge. Crystallised intelligence improves with age, while fluid intelligence tends to decline.

Quick thinking Intelligence is often considered to be the ability to adapt to new situations, to develop relevant strategies to cope with the unknown. The ingenious response of those who have been shipwrecked, such as the fictional Robinson Crusoe, provides an extreme example. In everyday life, we use this ability when we are faced with a problem for the first time.

Howard Gardner's 8 types of intelligence

● **Verbal-linguistic** intelligence is the ability to express ideas and feelings through language. It is one of the skills assessed in IQ tests and encompasses richness of vocabulary, mastery of grammatical rules, stylistic quality and the ability to communicate and be understood.

● **Logical-mathematical intelligence** makes it possible for us to reason, calculate and solve problems and is also an important aspect of IQ testing.

● **Spatial intelligence** is the ability to perceive and visualise the world in three dimensions. This is the kind of intelligence that architects and engineers need: an aptitude for self-orientation, the ability to quickly understand assembly diagrams, operating instructions and the mechanisms of technical devices, or to come up with plans for land use and transportation networks.

● **Kinaesthetic intelligence** is the ability to understand how the body moves, to imitate and remember movements and actions. People who have this kind of intelligence are good at sports and are suited to activities that demand manual dexterity such as crafts, sculpture or surgery. It can be described as an intelligence of action.

● **Interpersonal intelligence** determines the quality of the relationships we have with others, as well as our ability to understand them and to adapt to different social environments. It could be compared to emotional intelligence (see page 200).

● **Intrapersonal intelligence** is another aspect of emotional intelligence. It is the ability to understand yourself, and to assess your own strengths and weaknesses accurately – qualities that are needed to lead a harmonious and balanced life.

● **Musical intelligence** is the ability to recognise and analyse sounds, rhythms and melodies.

● **Naturalistic intelligence** is an aptitude for understanding our natural environment: being able to identify different species of plants and animals, to grasp the causes of natural phenomena (such as tides, the water cycle or winds), and having an interest in minerals, astronomy and ecology. Geologists, farmers, landscape gardeners, biologists or others who work with the natural environment possess this kind of intelligence.

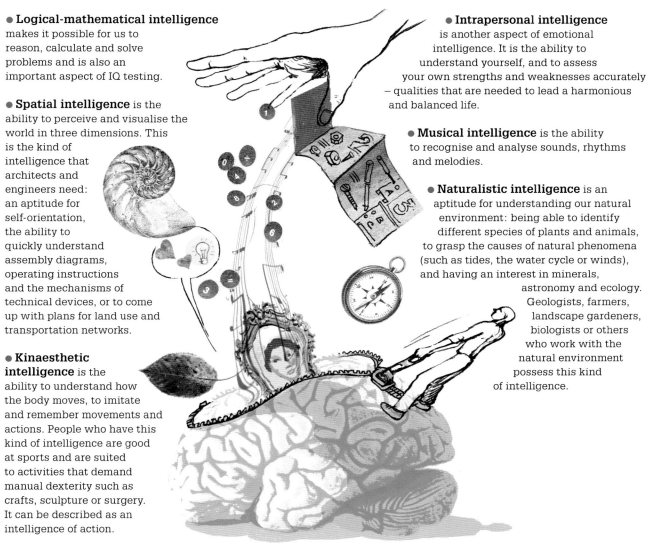

Successful intelligence The American psychologist Robert Sternberg maintains that there are three forms of intelligence: analytical intelligence (measured with an IQ score), creative intelligence and practical intelligence. Successful intelligence is the combination of all three. According to Sternberg, a good leader must have all three abilities: creativity to come up with ideas, analytical intelligence to make sure that the ideas are good, and practical intelligence to have them accepted and implemented. He also adds to these a fourth prerequisite for leadership: wisdom.

Multiple intelligences In the 1980s, another American psychologist named Howard Gardner proposed a different classification consisting of eight basic types of intelligence. He argued that we each have them all to varying degrees and that they are developed to a different level in each individual to form an 'intelligence profile'. This profile can develop further through learning, experience, practice and motivation.

What is IQ?

In 1905, the French psychologist Alfred Binet and his colleague, Théodore Simon, were asked to devise a tool for measuring intelligence that could be used in education. The aim was to evaluate those students who appeared to be lacking in intelligence to see whether they could cope with a normal education.

The rules of IQ

The tool invented by Binet, known as the intelligence scale, has since been developed and adapted by other psychologists to become the IQ tests we know today. The scale that is most widely used was initially devised by the American David Wechsler in 1939 and has different versions for different age groups. IQ tests have been adapted for use with people of different cultural backgrounds, and have been updated and rescaled over the years. They don't measure intelligence as such, but the results of intelligence at work in various areas (verbal skills, reasoning and logic, visual and spatial skills, speed of processing and working memory). They can be used to rank an individual in relation to an average value set at 100. So-called 'average' intelligence is defined statistically by scores between 90 and 110, a range that covers about 50 per cent of the population. But IQ tests don't include every aspect of intelligence and can't claim to be an absolute measurement. Combined with other factors, they simply help psychologists to appraise cognitive performance to help people to overcome difficulties or to choose a course of study or a career. They are also used to assess the impact of a disease or injury of the brain, which can have varying effects on different areas of ability.

Gifted people

A person with an IQ score above 130 is said to be gifted or advanced, or to have 'very superior IQ'. Scores are standardised so that just over 2 per cent of the population would be in this category. Gifted people are not necessarily geniuses or walking encyclopaedias, but the way they reason and use their thinking skills and memory means that they understand faster and so can learn more. This may be because in gifted people the connections between the neurons are faster and are triggered simultaneously in the whole of the brain. At the same time, such people tend to absorb all perceived information at the same level, leading to intense brain activity. They reason intuitively and in images, processing data through associations of ideas – sometimes so rapidly that they may have difficulty in structuring or expressing their thoughts.

Gifted people may have an unusual emotional profile that makes them quite fragile. They constantly evaluate the risks of failure or error and have great difficulty coping with them. Such extreme sensitivity can become excruciating when their ability is vastly different from that of their peers, which explains why they may have trouble fitting in. Some develop a false personality that corresponds with what others expect of them rather than with who they really are. The stress they experience from trying to fit in can make it hard for them to cope. They may need psychological support to help them to manage this difference between themselves and others, to develop a positive attitude towards the effort they need to make to adapt, and to tackle life with the right degree of maturity. To help them, associations for gifted people, such as Mensa, can put them in touch with others who are 'different' in the same way.

Paradoxical skills

Sometimes a person may have a mental development disorder but at the same time exhibit outstanding skills in certain areas of ability. The best-known example of this paradox was the American Kim Peek (1951–2009), who inspired the character Raymond Babbitt, played by Dustin Hoffman, in the film *Rain Man*. Unlike Babbitt, Peek was not autistic – his social and developmental difficulties were probably related to congenital brain abnormalities – but like Babbitt he had a phenomenal memory.

With exceptional talents such as these, a prodigious memory is often accompanied by specific expertise or detailed knowledge of specialised subjects: for example, the calculation of dates, musical ability, mathematics, drawing or spatial skills (as in estimating distances or building models). This syndrome, known as savant syndrome, is often, but not exclusively, found with some types of autism, including Asperger's syndrome. Experts have also noted the same ability in people with other developmental disorders or brain damage, most often in the left hemisphere. It is thought that savant syndrome might be triggered by a mechanism in the right hemisphere that compensates for the brain damage. Some even suggest that these abilities are pre-existing skills that are actually controlled by the right hemisphere but that have been stifled by the dominance of the left hemisphere.

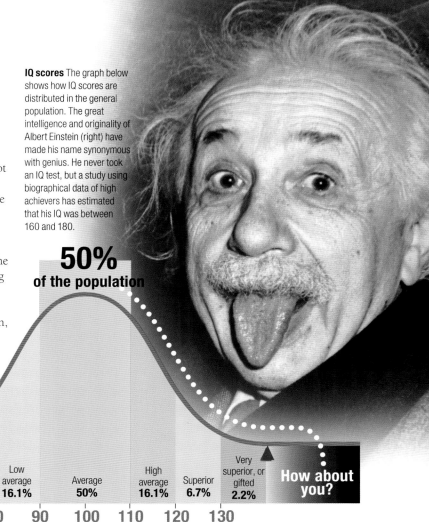

IQ scores The graph below shows how IQ scores are distributed in the general population. The great intelligence and originality of Albert Einstein (right) have made his name synonymous with genius. He never took an IQ test, but a study using biographical data of high achievers has estimated that his IQ was between 160 and 180.

50%
of the population

How about you?

| | Extremely low 2.2% | Borderline 6.7% | Low average 16.1% | Average 50% | High average 16.1% | Superior 6.7% | Very superior, or gifted 2.2% |

IQ 70 80 90 100 110 120 130

All about IQ

1. What is the minimum IQ required to be a member of Mensa (one of the organisations for gifted people)?

☐ **a.** 121
☐ **b.** 131
☐ **c.** 141

2. Which American actor is a member of Mensa?

☐ **a.** Sharon Stone
☐ **b.** Jodie Foster
☐ **c.** Julia Roberts

3. How old was the youngest person to join Mensa, in 2009, with an estimated IQ of 156?

☐ **a.** 2 years
☐ **b.** 8 years
☐ **c.** 12 years

4. In 1926 the psychologist Catherine Morris Cox devised a method for posthumous measurement of IQ, assessing authors on the basis of their written texts. Which author scored highest using this method?

☐ **a.** Dickens
☐ **b.** Goethe
☐ **c.** Tennyson

5. According to an Ulster University study published in 2006, which of the following European countries has the highest average IQ?

☐ **a.** Netherlands
☐ **b.** Sweden
☐ **c.** United Kingdom

6. William James Sidis (1898–1944) was renowned for having the highest IQ in the world. What was he doing at the age of 11?

☐ **a.** Studying at Harvard
☐ **b.** Reading Homer in the original Greek
☐ **c.** Speaking fluent Russian, German, Hebrew, Turkish and Armenian

Answers: 1. b. **2.** b. In April 2002, Sharon Stone confessed to having lied about her membership of this organisation. **3.** a. **4.** b. Tennyson is estimated to have had an IQ of 170, Dickens 180 and Goethe 210. **5.** a. The Netherlands scored 107, Sweden 104, and the United Kingdom 100. **6.** a.

Test your intelligence

These questions will help to reveal your comfort zones as well as the areas that need to be improved. If you don't find the answer within a minute, move on to the next question. When you have finished the quiz, score your answers in the bottom right square of each question (see page 75, 'How to interpret your score').

Skills tested

A colour code will help you to recognise which skill is being tested.

- Logic and reasoning
- Language
- Calculation and mathematics
- Memory
- Visual and spatial perception

1

1. Look closely at these two sets of geometric shapes, then cover them.

2. Which shape is missing from the picture below?

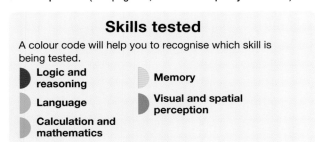

2

What word can be added either before or after each of these three words to produce a recognised term?

absolute

silent

verdict

....

3

If you take two steps to the right, two steps forward and one step to the left, where are you in relation to the starting point?

- **a.** One step forward
- **b.** Two steps back and one step to the right
- **c.** Two steps forward and one step to the right
- **d.** One step forward and one step to the left

4

1. Study the picture carefully, then cover it.

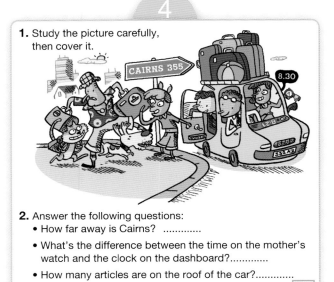

2. Answer the following questions:
- How far away is Cairns?   ....
- What's the difference between the time on the mother's watch and the clock on the dashboard?.............
- How many articles are on the roof of the car?.............

5

Study this logical sequence. What number has to be added to complete the sequence?

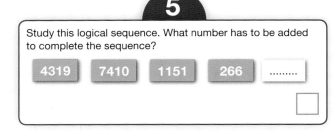

4319   7410   1151   266   ....

6

Using the numbers provided, what calculation is needed to get the answer of 92.5?

You can add, subtract, multiply or divide.

NB: Each number can be used only once and not all numbers are used.

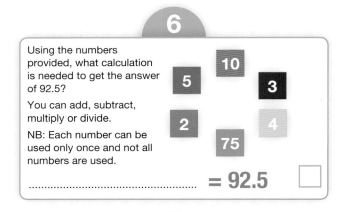

10   5   3   2   4   75

.... = 92.5

7

Which is the odd one out?

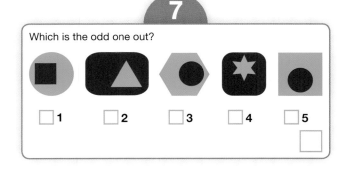

1   2   3   4   5

8

1. Look carefully at these groups of symbols for 30 seconds, then cover them.

2. Answer the following questions
- Which symbol is always on the bottom line? ....
- How many different symbols for weather are there? ....
- Did you see a flower? ....

9

Place these words in the right order to find a well-known quote from Shakespeare's *Romeo and Juliet*.

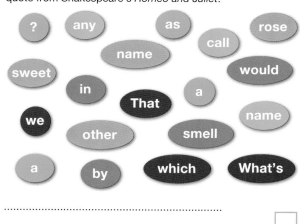

....

....

10

Are these two figures identical?

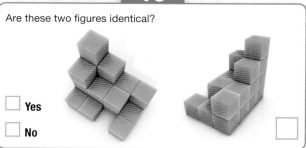

- ☐ **Yes**
- ☐ **No**

11

Which is the odd one out?

☐ vase ☐ cupboard ☐ milk bottle ☐ painting ☐ backpack ☐ box

12

1. The first picture is of four objects on a round table. Study it carefully.

2. On the second picture, mark the position of the person observing the scene shown in the first picture.

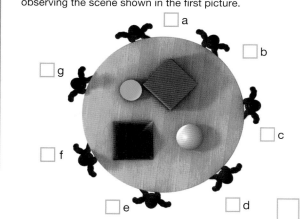

☐ a
☐ b
☐ g
☐ c
☐ f
☐ e ☐ d

13

Which word in the list is closest in meaning to **obsequious**.

- ☐ **obscene**
- ☐ **clever**
- ☐ **misogynist**
- ☐ **subtle**
- ☐ **servile**
- ☐ **biased**

14

If Tanya is the daughter of the brother of Dan's father, Dan is

- ☐ **a.** Tanya's uncle
- ☐ **c.** Tanya's brother
- ☐ **b.** Tanya's nephew
- ☐ **d.** Tanya's cousin

15

I am wearing at least one piece of clothing which is blue, my hair is not loose, I never wear jewellery and I have at least one of the following: glasses, a belt, high-heeled shoes. What number am I?

Concert Tonight

....

16

1. Study the list of words for one minute, then cover it.

advance	dim	large
hunger	democracy	fusion
illuminate	obey	altruism

2. The words below are the opposites of the words in the first list (in the same order), except for one. Which one is not an opposite?

☐ retreat ☐ brighten ☐ small

☐ satiety ☐ dictatorship ☐ fission

☐ darken ☐ order ☐ generosity

17

What is this person's age, given that her age multiplied by 3, minus 7 makes 98?

(......... x 3) − 7 = 98

18

Complete this logical sequence by adding the last number.

400 404 412 419 433 443 ....

19

The three winning lottery tickets have consecutive numbers that add up to 2007. What are the numbers?

.... + ... + ... = 2007

20

Which word is closest in meaning to 'empirical'?

☐ **pyramidal** ☐ **irrational**

☐ **scientific** ☐ **deductive**

☐ **pragmatic** ☐ **dictatorial**

21

Josh has $3 more than Omar. If Omar had three times more money than he has, he would have $12 more than both Omar and Josh together. How much does Josh have?
$.................

22

1. Memorise the combination of letters and figures below, then cover them.

A L I G N E D
7 4 8 3 9 1 2

2. Write the word LEADING in figures using the same code.

L E A D I N G
. . . .

23

1. Look closely at the words then cover them up.

green **BOLD** blue

underlined crossed out

black capitals

SHADOW purple **green**

ITALICS red

lower case CAPITALS

2. Answer the following questions.

• How many words were written in the style or colour they described? ....

• Which colour appeared twice? ....

24

Every row in the cinema is full. There are five people to my right and three to my left. In all, there are two rows in front of me and four rows behind. How many people are there in the audience? ....

25

1. Study the dominos below.

2. Which of these dominos will complete the sequence?

☐ a ☐ b ☐ c ☐ d ☐

Interpreting the results

Score 1 point for every correct answer and half a point if you have at least one correct answer for questions 4, 8 and 19.

● Your score is out of a total of 25. The test is not designed to measure IQ and cannot be used to calculate a set quotient. We can simply estimate that a result between 10 and 16 means that you are in the average range with a large majority of the general population.

● It is more interesting to calculate the score for each type of skill (scored out of 5) to see what your favourite areas are and where you can make improvements.

Skills	Questions	Points	To improve, see:
Logic and reasoning	5, 14, 15, 18, 25	☐ 5	Chapter 8, page 158
Language	2, 9, 11, 13, 20	☐ 5	Chapter 6, page 124
Calculation and mathematics	6, 17, 19, 21, 24	☐ 5	Chapter 8, page 170
Memory	4, 8, 16, 22, 23	☐ 5	Chapter 5, page 82
Visual and spatial perception	1, 3, 7, 10, 12	☐ 5	Chapter 7, page 144
	total		
	25		

Answers
1. The triangle is missing.
2. The word is 'majority'.
3. c.
4. 355 km; the watch is nine minutes ahead of the time displayed on the dashboard; six articles.
5. 812; each number in the sequence is the result of adding together the pairs of numbers in the number preceding it; for example, (4 + 3 =) 7, (3 + 1=) 4 and (1 + 9 =) 10, making 7410, so (2 + 6 =) 8 and (6 + 6 =) 12, making 812.
6. (3 × 10 + 5) divided by 2 = 17.5, then add 75.
7. Diagram number 2 cannot be divided into two identical halves, unlike the other four.
8. The snowflake; three weather symbols; there is no flower.
9. What's in a name? That which we call a rose by any other name would smell as sweet.
10. Yes.
11. The word 'painting' is the odd one out; the other words all describe containers.
12. g.
13. Servile
14. d. Tanya's cousin.
15. 6.
16. Generosity.
17. 35 years old.
18. 454. Take the preceding number and add to it the sum of the individual digits comprising it: 454 = 443 + 11 (4 + 4 + 3).
19. 668 + 669 + 670.
20. Pragmatic.
21. $18.
22. 4172893.
23. Nine words; green appears twice.
24. 63 people.
25. b. The top and the bottom are alternately black and green. The green part loses a dot each time, while the black part gains one.

Knowing how to use your intelligence

It's not your intellectual faculties that determine your ability to succeed or the type of life you lead. Your personality, how you use your abilities, as well as your general approach to life can all be either powerful driving forces or obstacles that prevent you from reaching your potential.

Are you a specialist or a generalist?

Some people appear to be extremely knowledgeable and competent in a field to which they devote all their energy, but they can be at a complete loss when it comes to areas that are regarded as general knowledge. An expert might be able to solve a legal problem requiring highly specialised knowledge or to do a detailed historical analysis, yet be quite ignorant of other issues such as sport, the economy or art.

Generalists, on the other hand, explore a number of different fields to satisfy their curiosity, acquiring a wide range of knowledge. This can help them to develop an overview of issues and to assess all the parameters in a given situation. But sometimes, generalists run the risk of acquiring a lot of superficial information that is of little practical use. And in today's world, where we are bombarded with ever-increasing amounts of information, it's just not possible to have an in-depth knowledge of a wide range of subjects.

Of course, the two personalities described above are clearly caricatures. While no-one is completely one or the other, each of us probably tends towards one of the two. What society needs today are 'general specialists', who can solve complex problems that require an overview of a large number of parameters – people, for example, who can develop a new product while at the same time taking into account its ecological impact or planning its marketing in different countries. So the ideal, as is often the case, would be to strike the right balance between the two tendencies.

Perfectionists

Striving for perfection is a powerful driver of success, provided that the desire to do better doesn't become counterproductive. Successful perfectionists accept the idea of progressing gradually and will experience genuine pleasure in a job well done. They learn from their mistakes without allowing them to be a source of stress. Neurotic perfectionists, on the other hand, may stubbornly persist for hours in a bid to achieve an unattainable or pointless level of perfection. They are never pleased with what they do, are incapable of delegating, always put obligations before pleasure and will never admit to being wrong. Only our emotions can tell us when we've done as much as we can, when it is time to let go before frustration and inertia make it impossible to move ahead.

Motivation and perseverance

When we are obliged to do something that we don't want to do or that seems pointless, we have little motivation to do it. Yet when there is a good reason for making an effort, the pleasure and satisfaction we experience gives us the incentive to persevere, to discover more and to excel. This is what happens when we decide to learn a foreign language, climb a mountain, research a favourite author, or spend hours practising a piece of music to enjoy a brief moment of satisfaction. The keys to success, then, even more than IQ, are motivation, ambition and the desire for self-improvement.

Ingenuity

The fairytale in which Hansel and Gretel find their way out of the woods by leaving a trail of white pebbles to follow is a good example of what is meant by ingenuity, even though the second time they make the mistake of using breadcrumbs. When human beings find themselves driven into a corner, they can come up with all kinds of original ways to make the best use of whatever is available, no matter how little, and find a clever solution. Ingenuity – the efficient management of problems in everyday life – is born of creative thinking combined with technical expertise. When it is used to achieve a goal or to complete a project, it is an essential resource for inventors and innovators.

How ingenious are you?

Read the instructions several times to take note of all the clues. Take time to study the pictures and diagrams carefully. Then use your ingenuity and a clever trick or two and solving these apparently complex games will seem like child's play.

Connect the dots

Connect all nine dots by drawing four straight, continuous lines.

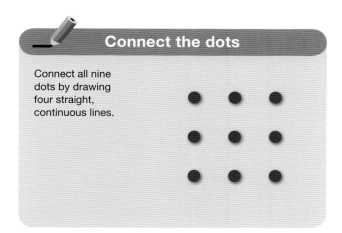

Racing numbers

There are three blue racing numbers and two red racing numbers. Three of them are on the back of the three cyclists who are one behind the other. The leading cyclist wears no. 1, the next wears no. 2 and the third cyclist wears no. 3. The cyclists don't know the colour of the numbers on their own backs, nor do they know the colour of the numbers on the cyclists behind them.

Cyclist no. 3 is asked if he knows the colour of his number and says 'no'. The same question to cyclist no. 2 gets the same answer. But when cyclist no. 1 is then asked the question he answers 'yes'. Each cyclist has heard the answers of the others.

What colour is the number on the back of cyclist no. 1?

....

Water, water

You have to put exactly 5 litres of water in a bucket. You have a tap and two plastic containers, one with a capacity of 3 litres and the other 4 litres.

What will you do?

Matches

Move just one match to make six squares instead of five.

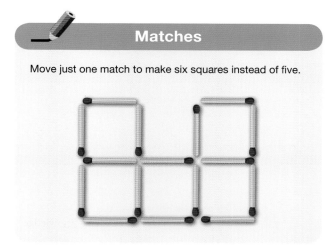

Coins

Ten coins are arranged as shown.

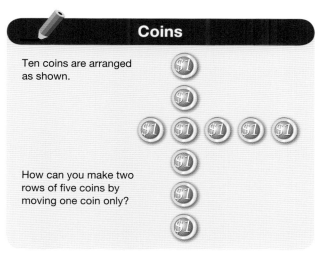

How can you make two rows of five coins by moving one coin only?

Answers

Connect the dots

Racing numbers If either of the first two cyclists was wearing a red number, then no. 3, who is following, would have known that his was blue. So the numbers of the first two are either both blue or one blue and one red. If cyclist no. 1 had a red number, cyclist no. 2 would have known that his was blue (see above). As he doesn't know what colour his number is, that means he can see a blue number on cyclist no. 1. And although cyclist no. 1 can't see any numbers, using this information, he can say that he is wearing a blue number.

Water, water Fill the 4-litre container and pour the water into the bucket. Fill the same container again and pour the water into the 3-litre container until it is full. One litre of water is then left in the 4-litre container, and this can then be poured into the bucket to make 5 litres.

Matches Although one square has been lost, another two, each made up of two squares and a rectangle, have been added (formed by the left and right two-thirds of the diagram).

Coins Place one coin from the six-coin line on top of the intersecting coin.

The mystery of intuition

Why do we say first impressions are often right? How is it that we sometimes feel we know something, without knowing exactly why? In addition to logical thought and reasoning, part of the brain seems to be able to draw relevant conclusions from a minimum of information.

Researchers refer to the 'adaptive unconscious' when referring to the brain's ability to operate on the surface of consciousness without using the mechanism of reasoning. It's as though the brain records and uses data from past experiences to develop patterns of behaviour, which it then reactivates in certain circumstances. In this way, at certain moments our 'unconscious' may sort and reject excess information so that it can respond efficiently in a split second. The brain goes straight to the objective, without informing us how it got there. While some people may pay more attention to their intuition than others, the best decisions are probably based on the right balance between conscious thought and instinctive response.

Curiosity

According to an African proverb, 'Not to know is bad. Not wishing to know is worse.' Curiosity, when properly channelled, is a driving force for intelligence and knowledge. By observing, reading and asking questions, we can develop our ability to solve problems, devise strategies, find solutions and check them against other possibilities.

Curiosity is acquired and is self-generating: the keener our curiosity and the more satisfying it is to increase our knowledge, the greater our curiosity and the number of subjects that interest us. Reading a newspaper each day may initially seem tedious, but after a few weeks keeping up to date with the news becomes a pleasure, a special time that puts us in touch with the world. An open mind and a genuine thirst for knowledge also form the basis of our social relations and friendships, not just because of the depth and range of interaction that are made possible, but also because it is essential to be interested in other people in order to form mutual attachments.

Conversely, indifference or a lack of curiosity can lead to boredom, isolation, narrow-mindedness, or even to a general decline overall because of a lack of mental stimulation.

 Test your curiosity

What's been happening in the world? It is not easy to keep up to date on everything. How many of the following questions about current affairs can you answer?

 World health

The 2009 influenza pandemic was caused by an H1N1 strain of flu commonly known as:

a. Hong Kong flu

b. Bird flu

c. Swine flu

 Olympic gold

Who won two individual events in this stadium?

a. Cathy Freeman

b. Usain Bolt

c. Michael Johnson

 Skyscrapers

When it opened in 2010, this was the world's tallest building. Where is it?

☐ **a.** Kuala Lumpur

☐ **b.** Dubai

☐ **c.** Shanghai

High cost

In April 2010, ash from the eruption of Iceland's Eyjafjallajökull volcano closed airspace in Europe for more than seven days. According to IATA, the estimated cost to the aviation industry was:

- [ ] **a.** $950 million
- [ ] **b.** $1.7 billion
- [ ] **c.** $2.4 billion

TV audiences

Which of the following methods are used to calculate audience figures for television programs?

- [ ] **a.** An analysis is done of the electromagnetic waves emitted by every television set that is switched on.
- [ ] **b.** A people meter is fitted to the television sets in a panel of households selected as a representative sample of the population.
- [ ] **c.** Every channel organises daily surveys, which are paid for by advertisers and validated by an official body.

Obama

On 4 November 2008, the American people elected Barack Obama president by universal suffrage.

- [ ] **True**
- [ ] **False**

BMI

Can you calculate your BMI?

....

....

....

Maastricht

The Maastricht Treaty, signed in 1992, lead to the creation of the European Union. Where is the city of Maastricht?

- [ ] **a.** Switzerland
- [ ] **b.** The Netherlands
- [ ] **c.** Austria

Oil spill

What caused the 2010 oil spill in the Gulf of Mexico?

- [ ] **a.** The grounding of the oil tanker Exxon Valdez
- [ ] **b.** A blowout of the Ixtoc I exploratory well
- [ ] **c.** The explosion of the *Deepwater Horizon* oil-drilling rig

Nobel Peace Prize

Who won the Nobel Peace Prize in 2009?

....

Answers: World health c. swine flu. **Olympic gold b.** In 2008 Jamaican Usain Bolt won three gold medals at the Beijing Olympic Games – the 100 metres, 200 metres and the 4 × 100 metres relay; Australian Cathy Freeman won gold in the 400 metres in Sydney in 2000, and US sprinter Michael Johnson won gold in the 200 metres and 400 metres in Atlanta in 1996 and in the 4 × 400 metres relay in Barcelona in 1992. **Skyscrapers b.** The Burj Khalifa building in Dubai is 828 metres high, the Shanghai World Financial Centre is 429 metres and the Petronas Towers in Kuala Lumpur, 452 metres. **High cost b.** This estimate includes costs saved on fuel. **TV audiences b. Obama** False. In the United States, the president is elected by indirect suffrage. Voters vote for electors, who in turn vote for the president. **BMI** Body mass index is calculated by dividing your weight in kilograms by your height in centimetres squared. The healthy range for adults is between 20 and 25. Anyone below 20 is underweight and those 25 to 30 are overweight, and above 30 are obese. **Maastricht b. Oil spill c.** Following the explosion of the drilling rig on 20 April 2010, the underwater well gushed up to an estimated 60,000 barrels of oil a day into the Gulf of Mexico until it was eventually stemmed on 15 July 2010. **Nobel Peace Prize** Barack Obama, for his efforts to strengthen international diplomacy and cooperation between peoples.

Issues of gender

As the brain develops, it is influenced by aspects of the external environment – a person's family, social and cultural background. As a result, men and women have different kinds of brains and, similarly, the brains of two women – one an opera singer and the other a champion swimmer – can also be quite different.

Brain size

The average weight of the human brain is 1.35 kilograms for men and 1.2 kilograms for women. In the nineteenth century, this difference was cited to justify the claim that women were less intelligent. When differences in the build of men and women are taken into account, neither has a larger brain than the other. Nor is there a correlation between the weight of the brain and mental faculties; it is not quantity, but quality, that is important – the quality of the connections between neurons. On average, men and women have the same intelligence quotient. Where their brains differ is in the areas that control sexual reproduction. For higher functions such as memory, reasoning, attention and language, there is great diversity in ability but it is largely unrelated to gender.

Men on the right, women on the left

It has been claimed that men use the right half of the brain more than women do – that is, the hemisphere specialising in spatial functions – whereas women are thought to make greater use of the left hemisphere, where language functions are located. This theory, dating back to 1968, was refuted after the invention of magnetic resonance imaging (MRI), which has shown that there are no gender-related differences in the areas of the brain used for spatial and language functions. We also know now that there is constant communication between the two hemispheres and that a single function is never located entirely in a single region.

In fact, neuropsychological tests have shown that men perform better in tasks involving spatial skills in three dimensions but not in two dimensions, which is surprising. What could explain this? The difference can't be detected at birth and appears only in adolescence. In any case, all that is needed for men and women to achieve the same scores is a week's training doing the same kind of tests. This shows that it is education or training that makes the difference. Football can be cited as convincing evidence of this, as the sport is played mainly by boys and is an excellent way to learn spatial orientation.

Are women more emotional than men? No, men and women feel the same emotions, but they don't express them in the same way. Women usually talk about their feelings more readily, while men are more inclined to take action, but these differences in behaviour are easily attributed to upbringing and to social and cultural stereotypes.

These findings have been reported in comparative brain-function studies, in which men and women have been observed while speaking or doing mathematical calculations and memory exercises. When these studies include a sufficiently large number of subjects, any differences between individuals of the same sex are greater than the differences between men and women, which in the end are minimal.

In animals, hormones act on the brain to trigger mating behaviour, which coincides with the time when the females are on heat during ovulation. Sexuality and reproduction go together in the animal kingdom, but human beings are not pre-programmed in this way. While it's true that hormones are linked to the functioning of sex organs in humans, they don't determine the timing of the encounter or the choice of partner. No scientific study has found a correlation between the level of sex hormones and variations in our feelings, except at times of major physiological changes, such as pregnancy or menopause, or as a result of hormonal disorders.

Train the brain

The fact that humans are not controlled by sex hormones can be explained by the extraordinary development of the cerebral cortex, which supervises all our behaviour, including the basic instincts of hunger, thirst and reproduction. Sex hormones may contribute, but they certainly don't play a major role. Male and female behaviour patterns are primarily determined by mental constructs that are related to each person's background and to the influence of the culture that has shaped that individual's identity as a man or woman. Besides, if biological factors did play a key role in determining individual behaviour, we would expect to see common traits across all populations, regardless of cultural background, but this is clearly not the case. Whether at the individual or the community level, there is no evidence of a universal law guiding human behaviour. The general rule is that of cultural diversity, which is made possible by neuroplasticity – the human brain's amazing capacity to adapt and change.

An example of a stereotype

A simple test can show just how strong male–female prejudices are. 'Susie is reserved, very shy, likes to help others but has very little interest in social life and the real world. She is gentle, neat and meticulous. What does she do for a living? Is she a lawyer, sales representative, librarian or pilot?' Most people answer 'librarian', even when they are told that the sample surveyed had ten times as many sales representatives as librarians. Why? Because the description fits the stereotype of the female librarian.

© KFS TM HEARST

Memory

5

A very useful resource

Whether it's a question of recalling a phone number, remembering where we put our keys or recognising the faces of those dear to us, we are constantly calling on our memory – the brain's amazing ability to record information, retain it for varying amounts of time and recall it at a given moment.

Storing memories

Memory depends on the brain's extraordinary capacity to constantly reconfigure its circuits. Today we know that storing memories not only brings about long-lasting changes in the efficiency of the links between neurons (called synaptic plasticity), but also creates new connections – it even makes new neurons appear in some areas of the brain, such as the hippocampus.

Without memory, our brain would be like a library with empty shelves. Most of our knowledge is actually acquired through experience. A vocabulary composed of thousands of words, the rudiments of algebra, a crowd of faces, a long succession of lived memories – we accumulate and retain so much information that our brain's capacity seems unlimited. This store of knowledge and memories is essential for constructing the personality, as is demonstrated by the example of patients who suffer from amnesia following brain damage – by forgetting their own history, they also forget their identity.

A working tool

Memory is not only a store of information: it is also a working tool. How can we follow a conversation if we keep forgetting what has been said? How can we develop an argument without basing it on prior knowledge? What's more, our memory of events allows us to predict the consequences of our actions and to adapt our behaviour to the circumstances and to the expected results. This means it allows us to envision and influence our future. People with severe amnesia, on the other hand, live locked in the present with little recall of the past, and so find it very difficult to plan their future actions.

An independent function

While memory is central to our mental life, it appears to be independent of the other cognitive functions. This is what studies of people suffering from severe amnesia seem to indicate. Even when these people have become incapable of storing new memories or remembering important episodes in their life, or sometimes can't even recognise their partner, they can still speak normally, have no loss of perception, can carry out the activities of daily living without any help and achieve normal results in IQ tests. Today we know that memory takes several different forms, and that in people with amnesia not all of these are affected.

Elephants are not the only ones who never forget

Some people have a phenomenal memory. This is the case with prodigies in mental calculation, who can find the square root of a number with a hundred digits in a few seconds or recite off by heart the number pi with its thousands of decimals. So far we have not managed to identify any genetic factor to explain such performances, even though hundreds of genes involved in learning and memory have been listed in laboratory mice.

Aids to memory

People who are endowed with a prodigious memory generally admit that they use various strategies to improve their ability. Some associate numbers with colours or shapes; others create scenes with characters, integrate the information into a story or associate it with specific places. For example, to keep a shopping list in your head, all you have to do to remember what you need to buy is to mentally go through the rooms in your home.

Practice and motivation are also important. A student who is a bad learner at school may still be able to memorise the match results of a favourite sporting team. Mnemonics – devices such as rhymes and acronyms that assign meaning to apparently unrelated details (such as Every Good Boy Deserves Fruit for E, G, B, D, F, the notes represented by the lines on the treble clef in music) – can also be used to improve your performance and help you to remember a certain type of information better. But there is no universal method: the pursuit of intellectual activity, an active social life and a healthy lifestyle are still the best aids to memory.

How memory is influenced

To demonstrate that the quality of memory can be influenced by the information provided, researchers asked some elderly people to read an article on ageing that contained inaccurate information. Some of them received an article that insisted on the inevitable decline of memory, while others were given an article that explained strategies for preserving memory as much as possible.

They were then asked to take a memory test involving a list of words. The results were revealing: those who had read the positive article remembered 30 per cent more words than the others! In the latter group, the negative nature of the information they had read had in fact activated a stereotype according to which loss of memory is inevitable with age. This caused them to react anxiously and to perform less well in the memory test.

Specialisation

Mental gymnastics have targeted effects. The more crosswords we do, the better we become at puzzles involving vocabulary, while actors find it far easier to learn texts by heart than other people do because they practise regularly. Unfortunately, neither doing crosswords nor rehearsing a role will help you to find your keys! Improvement relates only to the type of task involved in the exercise.

Similarly, the prowess of experts – whether they are exceptionally gifted in mathematics, or whether, as is the case with chess champions, they can remember each of their games in detail – doesn't mean that they also have an exceptional memory in every area of knowledge, but rather that their brain has become specialised to process and retain certain types of information. This is logical, since we know today that there is not one single type of memory, but several types, each of which is controlled by a separate brain structure.

Memory expertise can be associated with changes in the brain that are visible. A study of London taxi drivers, who must have a perfect knowledge of many different routes in the European Union's largest city, has shown that the rear part of their right hippocampus is abnormally enlarged. This small area in the brain's limbic system plays an essential role in spatial memory.

Memory decline

From the age of 50, on average, the capacity to temporarily retain information and mentally manipulate it declines. This phenomenon is particularly obvious when several activities have to be carried out at the same time. For example, it becomes more difficult to retain a phone number while following the flow of a conversation, or to remember where you put your keys while focusing on your shopping list. Over time, we also have more trouble remembering proper names or finding the right word quickly. In addition, the memories of recent events leave fewer traces and are more difficult to situate in time, while memories of our youth become comparatively more vivid.

On the other hand, as we get older, we do have one strong advantage, and that is the sum total of the experiences and knowledge we have accumulated throughout our life. This cognitive store can allow us to remain at the top of our game in our areas of expertise. Generally speaking, a good level of education delays memory decline. It actually promotes the development of a vast store of knowledge and strategies, which will allow us to make up for certain failings when the time comes.

Alarm bells

According to research, a good third of the population suffers from this decline in memory, and the proportion increases with age. How can we distinguish between harmless lapses and those that might indicate a more serious disorder – in particular, the early signs of Alzheimer's disease?

The first question that should be asked is: who first noticed the problem? If it was the person in question who noticed it, then there's less need to worry. In actual fact, in the case of people suffering from Alzheimer's disease, it's often those around them who seek help, because the affected individuals misinterpret or minimise their own difficulties. They 'forget that they forget'. They also tend to become withdrawn, to be disoriented (especially in unfamiliar surroundings) and to make up stories (known as confabulation).

The second important question to ask is: what kind of information does the person forget? In the case of harmless lapses, this mostly involves proper names and specific details, and can relate to both the distant past and recent events. In Alzheimer's disease or true amnesia, the lapses are more likely to involve recent information.

Lastly, when faced with simple lapses of memory, often all that is needed is to provide some hints so that the person can remember the information sought. This strategy doesn't work well with Alzheimer's disease, because the process of memorisation itself is affected.

If you are in doubt, only a neuropsychological examination involving specialised tests can allow a diagnosis to be made.

Test your day-to-day memory

Read the following statements about things you do in your daily life and tick the one that best describes you.

The day after watching a program on television

a. You can remember the title or the theme, name the main actors or participants, tell the story or list the topics that were covered.

b. You mostly remember a program if you enjoyed it or found it interesting.

c. You often have trouble remembering what you saw or did the previous evening.

 a.
 b.
c.

After taking a holiday or going on a trip

a. You're able to give a day-by-day account of your holiday and to recall the itinerary you followed. You can remember everything you did in the correct order: places visited, particular events, who you met.

b. You can give a broad outline of your holiday or your trip.

c. You can still recall a few anecdotes or special moments; it's a general impression, but nothing more.

a.
b.
c.

Your car

a. You always remember where you have parked it.

b. You sometimes have to look for it in car parks.

c. You're usually sorry you haven't made a note of the place where you parked your car (street name, location in the car park), because you often waste time trying to find it.

 a.
 b.
 c.

4

People's names

a. You only have to be introduced to people once to remember their names.

b. You sometimes have difficulty, but you have no trouble remembering the names of the people who are important to you or whom you have met at least twice.

c. You have trouble remembering first names and surnames and often have to resort to bluffing your way out of introducing someone to another person. You have even sometimes forgotten the first names of your friends' children.

a. [ ]
b. [ ]
c. [ ]

5

Your appointments

a. You remember the week's or day's appointments and consult your diary only to check the time or the address.

b. You check your diary each morning. This is all you need to do to remember your appointments.

c. Even though you keep a diary, you can sometimes totally forget an appointment or make a mistake with the date.

a. [ ]
b. [ ]
c. [ ]

6

What you ate the previous day

a. You have no problem remembering everything you ate, including snacks.

b. You remember the main meals.

c. You have trouble remembering.

a. [ ]
b. [ ]
c. [ ]

7

The day and the date

a. You always know the day and the date without having to think about it.

b. You sometimes need to think about it.

c. You sometimes have to consult a calendar.

a. [ ]
b. [ ]
c. [ ]

8

What you were wearing yesterday

a. You remember very well without having to think about it.

b. You have to make an effort to see yourself mentally to be able to talk about it.

c. You have forgotten.

a. [ ]
b. [ ]
c. [ ]

9

Passwords and identification numbers (bank and other cards, door or alarm codes, health memberships, car registration)

a. You know ten or more numbers.

b. You remember those you use regularly.

c. You know your bank PIN and maybe one other code, but that's all.

a. [ ]
b. [ ]
c. [ ]

10

Before you leave home

a. You never forget anything (such as mobile phone, diary, glasses and keys)

b. You have to check the contents of your bag or your pockets to make sure you have everything you need. If you happen to have forgotten something, you generally remember in time.

c. You often forget something and you are obliged to go back home to get it, or to make do without it.

a. [ ]
b. [ ]
c. [ ]

11

The price of the milk or bread that you normally buy

a. You know it exactly.

b. You know it approximately.

c. You don't know.

a. [ ]
b. [ ]
c. [ ]

12

Birthdays

a. You know the birthdays of more than 15 people; you remember the birthdays of your childhood friends.

b. You know the birthdays of your very close family (parents, partner, children, grandchildren) and of a few friends.

c. You know the birthdays of your partner and your children, but no others.

a. [ ]
b. [ ]
c. [ ]

13

The exact total of your last purchase

a. You know it.

b. You more or less remember an amount, but it's not necessarily the total of your very last purchase.

c. You don't know what it is.

a. [ ]
b. [ ]
c. [ ]

14

The addresses of those close to you

a. You know them by heart.

b. You know them, but you have to check the street number or the postcode.

c. You always need your address book.

a. ☐
b. ☐
c. ☐

15

Your belongings (such as keys, glasses, handbag, phone or important documents)

a. You always know where they are and you never lose them.

b. You sometimes have to look for them if you haven't put them away in their usual place or if you aren't at home (in a hotel or at a friend's house, for example)

c. You often waste time looking for them. You sometimes lose them or forget them somewhere.

a. ☐
b. ☐
c. ☐

16

Shopping

a. You don't need to make a list. You generally think of everything.

b. You need a list, at least to check that you haven't forgotten anything.

c. You frequently forget something, including your usual purchases. Sometimes you even leave your shopping bag in the shop.

a. ☐
b. ☐
c. ☐

17

The most recent books you have read

a. You know the titles and authors of all the books that you've read in the past 12 months.

b. You can name a few of them.

c. You have trouble naming them, including the latest one (that you've just finished or are still reading).

a. ☐
b. ☐
c. ☐

18

The number of phone numbers that you know by heart

a. More than 20.

b. 10 to 20.

c. Fewer than 10.

a. ☐
b. ☐
c. ☐

19

You are able to recall the exact date you left for your last holiday

a. Yes, spontaneously.

b. More or less, by doing some crosschecking.

c. No.

a. ☐
b. ☐
c. ☐

20

The first question in this test

a. You remember it immediately.

b. You have to make an effort and maybe you are wrong (you name another question).

c. You don't remember.

a. ☐
b. ☐
c. ☐

Total | a. ☐ | b. ☐ | c. ☐

Interpreting the results

● **Mostly a**

You have a good memory for facts and for the details of daily life. This result shows that you are someone who is attentive and organised, and that you are able to concentrate on routine tasks.

● **Mostly b**

You retain what interests you and you eliminate what you regard as insignificant. You probably use your memory more in relation to other aspects of your private and professional life.

● **Mostly c**

If you've always been absent-minded and haven't paid very much attention to the details of daily life, then this test is simply a confirmation of that fact. This can hamper you, but it's the way you operate. The instances of forgetting something stem more from a lack of attention (see page 96) or a lack of organisation and interest than from a poor memory. You can check this very easily. If you answered 'c' to question 11, for example, all you have to do is to pay attention to the prices that are displayed next time you go shopping for you to be able to memorise the amount for an extended period of time. If you have started forgetting things only recently, ask yourself if you are tired or upset. You should also take into consideration that people who really suffer from memory problems are in most cases not aware that they forget things (see page 94). If you're still concerned about forgetting things, you should have a specialist assess your memory.

Different kinds of memory

Nowadays memory is divided into five main modules that interact with one another: working memory, long-term episodic memory, semantic memory, perceptive memory and procedural memory.

Memory in all its forms

● Working memory is a short-term memory. We use it to retain a phone number for a few seconds before dialling it or to remember what we have come into a room to get. It's also this type of memory that allows us to keep in mind the information that we need to speak, calculate or think. This means we use it constantly in daily life.

● Perceptive memory corresponds to the imprint left on the brain by images, sounds and smells that we perceived even before they became significant. It allows the brain to reconstitute complete representations based on fragments and details of analytical elements.

● Episodic memory is for personal memories and memories of events we have experienced that are localised in time and space. It's this memory that allows us to recall scenes from the past with all their emotional intensity. This is the type of memory that is frequently affected in cases of amnesia.

● Procedural memory includes the repertoire of our skills: knowing how to ride a bike, play the flute, recite a poem after learning it by heart, or even walking. This is know-how that we have acquired through practice and that has become automatic.

● Semantic memory corresponds to general knowledge such as vocabulary, concepts or historical facts. It also relates to information about ourselves and our loved ones, such as names and birthdays. This data is not associated with a particular memorisation context: we generally don't know where and when we stored it away.

Explicit and implicit memory

Researchers also subdivide memory into two large categories: explicit memory and implicit memory. These more or less cover the notions of declarative memory and non-declarative memory. In this approach, episodic and semantic memories are explicit because they involve the conscious recall of information, and they are declarative because we can talk about this information (recall our knowledge of the world, relate our personal memories). On the other hand, procedural and perceptive memories are implicit because they are called on automatically, without us being aware of it. Procedural memory is also non-declarative, because automatic functions are difficult to verbalise and are expressed through action.

A threefold process

Three stages are required to make the memory work: acquiring the information, storing it and then retrieving it.

1. Encoding The efficiency of memory initially depends on the first of these stages, encoding. This relates to processing the information that enters the memory and the way in which it is associated with the information already stored there (the word 'mint', for example, could be related to herb, to freshness, to tea or to smell). The encoding may be voluntary – such as when we want to learn a list of words, for example – or automatic, when a fleeting image remains in our memory.

2. Consolidation To stop it being lost, the trace of the memory must be consolidated. To achieve this, the efficiency of some of the synapses is reinforced and connections are created in the brain circuits that are activated during encoding. This begins in the minutes following the moment of learning, and can carry on for years if the memory is reactivated, which explains the value of training sessions spread over time. Sleep also plays a fundamental role in this process of consolidating memories.

3. Recall Once a memory has been stored in the brain, we have to be able to retrieve it. This process largely depends on the way the memory was encoded, because recall operates through the associations made when the encoding took place (the word 'tea', for example, is helpful in remembering the term 'mint'). It is also easier to retrieve a memory in a context that is reminiscent of the one in which it was acquired. This explains why it is easier to learn a speech by standing and saying it out loud than by reading it silently while seated at your desk.

It's on the tip of my tongue!

Who hasn't experienced the frustrating feeling of having a word on the tip of their tongue? Studies confirm it: we are all confronted with this situation once a week on average. This momentary lapse of memory, which is aggravated by age or fatigue, particularly relates to proper names. Yet the information we are seeking hasn't disappeared from our memory: it is simply momentarily inaccessible. To find it, we need some clues. The solution is easy when we are looking for a common term associated with a vast amount of information, but much more difficult when we have to find the name of a person known only to us. We can remember the person's face or profession, even though these are not directly linked to the name. The feeling that the information we are seeking is just about to emerge from our brain and come onto the tip of our tongue comes from the fact that we can't find the name associated with this person, even though the memories she or he evokes are intact.

Handing down memories The association of the words tea and mint can be linked to the North African custom of serving mint tea, which is traditionally prepared by the male head of the household. Passing on such traditions involves encoding, consolidation and recall.

When we're searching for a word, we often try to bring it to mind by thinking of everything we know about it. This is the sort of process that you'll need to employ in this game: using a series of clues, you must identify proper or common names. Take a piece of paper to mask the clues, then uncover them one by one. Try to find the answer using as few clues as possible.

They made their mark on history

Who am I?

1. I was born in India in 1869.
2. I studied law in London.
3. I was involved in the civil rights movement in South Africa in the early twentieth century, where I pioneered the tactic of non-violent protest.
4. After my return to India I became a leader in the movement for Indian independence.
5. In India I am honoured as the Father of the Nation.

a. ....

Who am I?

1. I was born in Sabrosa, in Portugal, in the fifteenth century.
2. I was a navigator, and sailed in the service of Spain.
3. A strait bears my name.
4. I named an ocean.
5. Although I was killed in the Philippines, my expedition was the first one to circumnavigate the globe.

b. ....

Who am I?

1. My statue stands in the Place d'Iéna in Paris.
2. In the United States my image appears on 1 dollar bills and on 25 cent coins.
3. I helped to draw up of the constitution of the United States.
4. An American city bears my name.
5. I was elected president of the United States in 1789.

c. ....

They sing for us

Who are we?

1. Our group was originally called the Quarrymen.
2. Our last album had the name of a London street.
3. We officially separated in 1970.
4. As a group, we are the world's best-selling music artists.
5. We were known as 'the fab four'.

d. ....

Who am I?

1. I was born in Melbourne in 1968.
2. In the late 1980s I gained international recognition in a television soap opera.
3. In 2000 I performed at the opening ceremony of the Sydney Olympics.
4. I was awarded an OBE in 2008 for services to music.
5. My first hit song was 'The Loco-motion'.

e. ....

Who am I?

1. I was born in Belleville, France, in 1915.
2. My father was a street acrobat.
3. My stage name is also a common name for a sparrow in French.
4. In 2007 Marion Cotillard played me in a film of my life.
5. My signature song is 'La vie en rose'.

f. ....

Everyday essentials

What am I?

1. You may have a table especially for me.
2. I am found as beans or powder.
3 I can be short, long or flat.
4. I can also be black or white.
5. I often appear at the end of a meal.

g. ....

What am I?

1. I am one of a pair.
2. I can be lent if you need help.
3. I am a unit of measurement.
4. In cards, I am dealt to each player.
5. I am on the face of a clock.

h. ....

What am I?

1. When hot, I am a fast food.
2. If you are in my house, you are probably in trouble.
3. If I am asleep, it's best not to disturb me.
4. I am sometimes used as a term for a contemptible person.
5. I am man's best friend.

i. ....

Answers: a. Mahatma Gandhi. **b.** Ferdinand Magellan. **c.** George Washington. **d.** The Beatles. **e.** Kylie Minogue. **f.** Edith Piaf. **g.** Coffee. **h.** Hand. **i.** Dog.

Where memories are stored

There is no single memory centre in the brain where all of our memories and knowledge are stored. Instead, this information is distributed between the two cerebral hemispheres.

Key memory zones

The memory of a dinner with friends, for example, may be compared to a mosaic that is made up of familiar faces (processed by the visual cortex), the music that you listened to that evening (traces of which remain in the auditive areas) and the aroma of the dishes you ate (which affected the olfactory cortex). Evoking this pleasant moment involves activating the neurons in these different regions, because our experiences leave traces in the brain by modifying the efficiency of certain synapses and creating new ones. It is this capacity of the brain to rewire its circuits that underpins memory. In the case of a dinner with friends, it is the strength of the connections between the neurons in the different areas involved (visual, auditory, olfactory) that conditions the quality of the memory.

Even though memories are distributed in this way, the fact remains that the functioning of the different types of memory depends on specific brain structures. The study of patients with amnesia and the use of medical imaging techniques have made it possible to identify the key zones that are associated with memory.

Frontal lobes This part of the brain is involved in the acquisition and recovery of information that is stored in the memory. The left lobe is used more for encoding and the right lobe more for recall. The frontal lobes are also activated for working memory, when they cooperate with other areas of the cortex, which supply them with short-term information.

Hippocampus The hippocampus and two neighbouring cerebral areas play a key role in the creation of new memories (episodic memory) as well as in spatial memory. The hippocampus is linked by nerve paths to the whole of the cortex. This means it receives information from the different areas of the brain and sends other information back to them in return. It is this retroaction loop that allows the various elements of memories to be linked and consolidated. The hippocampus also participates in the retrieval of information and makes it possible for events to be relived – even if, in the long term, some memories can become independent of it and be evoked without its participation.

Amygdalae The two amygdalae are essential to emotive memory. In particular, they are activated during moments of fear and they process the emotional aspect of memories. The hippocampus and the amygdalae all belong to a set of brain structures called the limbic system, which is known for its role in memory and emotions.

Temporal lobes These two regions of the cerebral cortex are especially important for semantic memory, as well as being central to general memory functions.

Striatum and cerebellum The striatum and cerebellum play major roles in procedural memory – the type of memory associated with acquiring skills and know-how. The striatum is part of a set of structures called the basal ganglia, which are associated with the control of movement. The cerebellum is important for balance and in planning movements.

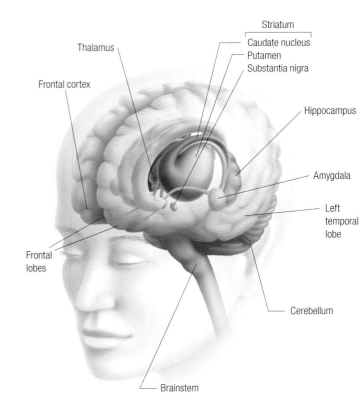

Thalamus

Frontal cortex

Striatum
Caudate nucleus
Putamen
Substantia nigra

Hippocampus

Amygdala

Left temporal lobe

Frontal lobes

Cerebellum

Brainstem

Why forgetting is important for memory

Being forgetful is often thought to be a handicap. Yet forgetting – in other words the temporary or permanent inability to recall a memory or a piece of information – plays an essential role in ensuring that memory functions correctly.

An effective selector

Memory fulfils two functions that may seem contradictory: it records certain information as faithfully as possible and then it organises, compares, extracts common points and makes generalisations. These different operations mean that some details are forgotten. For example, they allow a generic concept to be associated with the word 'dog', rather than a catalogue of animal representations. In practice, with the exception of particularly pleasant or unpleasant events that remain vivid for a whole lifetime, the majority of memories disappear or fade over time.

The true nature of forgetting

The nature of forgetting is still a subject of debate. Is the information permanently erased from the memory or does it remain present but inaccessible? Neurobiological studies carried out on laboratory animals support the first theory – that of the disappearance (or decline) of the trace. In the hours or days following the moment when something is learned, the modifications that take place in the neuronal circuits have a tendency to regress spontaneously if they are not consolidated by a repetition of the task. According to one hypothesis, this phenomenon appears to be linked to the permanent erasing of some circuits, just as paths that are no longer used disappear. On the other hand, we can think of the information that is considered forgotten as not really being lost, only difficult to find. Pieces of knowledge or memories have a tendency to interfere with one another, which sometimes makes it more difficult to retrieve them. In this way, acquiring new information can hinder the recall of data that was previously acquired, or inversely, old memories can hinder the memorisation of new facts. And, according to yet another theory that is close to psychoanalysis, called motivated forgetting, unpleasant or traumatic memories are repressed in the unconscious mind without being permanently forgotten, since therapy can bring them back.

The forgetting curve

After memorising a list of information, we quickly forget almost 70 per cent of it. After that, the loss slows down. The curve shown here is based on the work of the German psychologist Hermann Ebbinghaus (1850–1909). It shows that, contrary to what we may think (the black curve in the diagram), we forget a massive amount a short time after we learn it, and then after that we forget much more slowly (the red curve). The result is that we retain about 20 per cent of the initial memories, and these are likely to be remembered for a very long time. Of course, the richer the initial store of information, the more we retain after a few weeks (the 20 per cent). But above all, this curve is not static: different learning and memorisation techniques (see pages 62–4 and 118–23) in fact allow us to increase the proportion of memories we retain in the long term.

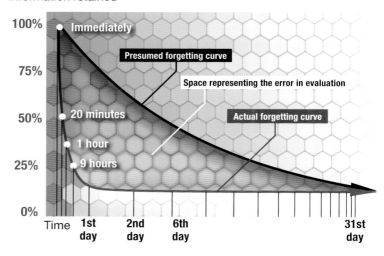

Information retained

100% — Immediately
Presumed forgetting curve
75%
Space representing the error in evaluation
50% — 20 minutes
Actual forgetting curve
1 hour
9 hours
25%

0%
Time | 1st day | 2nd day | 6th day | 31st day

When memory fails

Amnesia is the main disorder associated with memory. The symptom can have many different causes and takes a variety of different forms.

Amnesic syndrome

This is undoubtedly the most serious form of amnesia. In most cases, it is caused by damage (from a car accident, a viral illness or a brain tumour, for instance) that affects both sides of the brain, in the areas associated with episodic memory.

The loss of memory is sometimes limited to the minutes leading up to an accident – for example, after head trauma has caused a brief loss of consciousness. But in the most serious cases it can last for several decades, and these patients lose a substantial portion of their past. Even so, this failure, which involves stored memories, is not the most incapacitating symptom. Patients suffering from amnesic syndrome also have trouble holding on to new memories. They progressively forget what they have done during the day, the content of conversations, the names and faces of the people they have met, what they have seen, and so on. In rare cases, the inability to retain new memories may freeze these patients in time. They don't notice the passing of the years and think that they are the same age as they were at the time of the accident.

Some types of memory, such as working memory, are not affected. People with amnesic syndrome can retain a short list of words or numbers for a few seconds or minutes and repeat it, but they forget it as soon as they stop concentrating on the exercise. The memory associated with skills – procedural memory – is also maintained. And what's more, recent studies have shown that these patients are able to acquire new general knowledge, such as the names of new celebrities or words that have recently entered into the vocabulary. This seems to indicate that their semantic memory has been preserved too.

Korsakoff's syndrome

Among heavy drinkers, alcohol abuse can lead to a deficiency of vitamin B_1, or thiamine, and this causes brain damage. Consequently, these people are incapable of retaining new memories and also experience amnesia in respect of past events. People with Korsakoff's syndome are often unaware of their problem and tend to make up stories, or confabulate, but

At the movies Amnesia has always been a popular theme for movies, although most cinematic versions are not considered to be authentic by experts. Generally they depict amnesia resulting from an accident or a degenerative illness and show how the condition affects the lives of the individual concerned and those close to them. Some more accurate representations include the blue tropical fish Dory (pictured above) who suffers from short-term memory loss in *Finding Nemo* (2003) and Leonard Shelby (Guy Pearce) in *Memento* (2000).

their implicit memory (their ability to remember unconsciously) seems to be unaffected. Sergei Korsakoff (1854–1900), the Russian neuropsychiatrist who identified this syndrome, recounts that in the course of one day a patient of his said hello every time they met because he didn't remember meeting previously, but didn't shake Korsakoff's hand after the first meeting. This seemed to indicate that the patient retained the implicit memory of their first meeting.

Selective amnesia

Other kinds of amnesia concern specific types of information. In semantic dementia, which is linked to the degeneration of certain neurons in the external temporal lobe, patients lose the meaning of words and concepts, leading to progressive language decline – essentially, semantic memory is affected. In frontal amnesia, caused by damage to the frontal lobes, it is above all the ability spontaneously to encode and recall information that is defective. Those affected are incapable of repeating a list of words, although they can recognise some of them. This reveals both a lack of attention and an inability to retrieve information from memory. Other types of amnesia involve being unable to remember faces, objects or gestures.

Temporary amnesia

A strange syndrome known as transient global amnesia can occur in people who are generally over 50 years of age and who are otherwise in good health. During the crisis, which lasts for only a few hours, they lose a section of their past and suddenly forget everything that has only just happened. But they remain perfectly capable of driving a car, and teachers can even conduct a class!

This sudden amnesic event corresponds to an abrupt, selective and temporary loss of episodic memory. Its causes are unclear, but it seems to be due to a temporary malfunction of a vast circuit in the brain that covers the area of the hippocampus and the prefrontal cortex.

Alzheimer's disease

The impairment of memory is usually the first sign of Alzheimer's disease, a condition that is characterised by the atrophy of the hippocampus. Older memories are retained better than more recent facts, but working memory and semantic memory are affected fairly quickly. As the illness evolves, the losses can assume dramatic proportions, and patients can even forget that they have a family.

On the other hand, procedural memory – involving the automatic functions that have been acquired over the years – remains intact for a long time. This is why patients can sing nursery rhymes or execute dance steps even when they are no longer able to speak. Even though in the long term the ability to carry out everyday activities is not spared (writing, getting dressed, washing, and so on), automatic programming of the memory remains efficient longer than the voluntary execution of a movement. Patients who are disoriented when faced with a table that has been set will nevertheless start

eating if handed a fork. This observation has given rise to the idea of devising re-education programs based on this part of the memory that is still functional, with the aim of trying to install new automatic functions that may make daily life easier. The principle is to promote implicit learning through the repetition of gestures, without giving any oral commands, in other words 'to get them to do' rather than 'to tell them to do'. To help patients to situate themselves in their new living environment, it's better to help them make a trip several times in silence while holding them by the arm than to explain the trip to them by giving directions for each stage (such as first right, second left).

Post-traumatic stress syndrome

War, assault or aggression: a violent event can provoke post-traumatic stress syndrome, which can be very incapacitating. The memory of the traumatic event tends to invade the person's daily life – it returns in a loop and the sufferer remains haunted by what has been experienced. For such patients, the normal process of effacing a memory has not been activated.

An event of this kind may sometimes have an opposite effect. In this case, sufferers can forget a whole section of their past, and sometimes even their own name and address. Known as psychogenic amnesia, this condition can last for just a few hours, or can continue for several months.

The impact of such experiences on memory is the result of a stimulation of the amygdalae – two structures in the brain that are involved in processing emotions, particularly fear. The reaction can be stopped in the hours following a traumatic experience by administering propanol (a beta-blocker that is normally prescribed to treat high blood pressure). This is likely to erase not the memory of the traumatic event, but the suffering that is associated with it.

Principal causes of amnesia

● An accident involving head injury
● A stroke, brain tumour, epileptic fit, brain infection, neurodegenerative disorder (Alzheimer's disease, for example) or psychiatric illness
● A deficiency in vitamin B_1 (thiamine), usually linked to chronic alcoholism
● Lack of oxygen to the brain caused by carbon monoxide poisoning, prolonged cardiac arrest or strangulation/hanging
● Other poisoning or the abuse of certain medications
● A psychological shock
● Surgery that has caused damage to the brain

The symptoms vary a great deal, depending on the origin of the disorder. But, in most cases, memories that are associated with episodic memory are particularly fragile.

How attention works

Have you ever had trouble finding your car in a car park? If you didn't take the precaution of noting a few visual landmarks, it was your attention that was at fault, and not your memory.

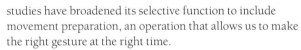

Attention requires effort

Attention is central to the way working memory functions (see page 102). It allows for selective awareness of and response to stimuli, and simultaneously involves the memory and the senses. It selects and temporarily stores pieces of information that have been perceived from the world around us together with other information from the memory and then processes or compares them. This double activity involves making an effort and can't be sustained for very long without being accompanied by a drop in performance and a feeling of fatigue. For this reason, psychologists have defined attention as a mechanism that has only a limited capacity – it focuses on a single idea or a single set of ideas, or selects only one part of the environment that we perceive with our senses, such as a detail in a painting or the sound of a single instrument in a symphony. This is why attention is used mainly for prioritising a few pieces of information, whether from the senses or the memory. Recent studies have broadened its selective function to include movement preparation, an operation that allows us to make the right gesture at the right time.

Attention may be spontaneous (when we are suddenly curious about something, or there is a sudden stimulation arising from our surroundings, such as an unexpected noise) or voluntary (when we have a goal to reach over a shorter or longer time frame). We can alternate between these two forms, as happens when we focus on completing a task and some unusual element in the environment momentarily distracts or alerts us.

Vigilance

Vigilance corresponds to our levels of awareness, receptivity and alertness, which can vary according to the time of day or how tired we are. We need it to maintain our attention, but it is not sufficient in itself: we can be more or less vigilant without being attentive.

When we carry out routine or monotonous activities (driving a car, for example), we often 'tune out': we no longer pay attention to what we are doing and function in a kind of automatic mode. This distraction can have consequences that are unimportant or quite serious, ranging from simple absent-mindedness to an accident (a fall or a car crash). But our brain maintains a minimal level of awareness – vigilance – which for the most part allows us to notice errors in behaviour and to avoid them.

Magical diversions So-called magic tricks are based on visual attention. Using gestures or words, the magician diverts or focuses your attention while using sleight-of-hand to manipulate objects before your very eyes.

Concentration

Concentration is the ability to maintain a good level of efficiency for the duration of a particular activity. One of the first studies on concentration, published in the UK in 1958, was based on observing air traffic controllers on duty. Their work demands that they sustain a high level of attention so that they are ready to receive both visual information from radar control screens and auditory information from colleagues and pilots. The effort that this requires can't be maintained for very long, which explains why people in this profession have limited working hours and need to take frequent breaks.

Problems with concentration

The capacity to concentrate varies from one individual to another, depending on personal and environmental conditions such as level of fatigue, preoccupations, the time of day, the surroundings (whether it is quiet or noisy, for example) and how interesting or important the activity is deemed to be.

Difficulty A difficult task generates an optimal state of concentration. If the level of success targeted can't be attained, or if the influence of the surroundings is too strong, our performance drops. The effort we need to make to focus our attention on an activity that is too complex can't be sustained for long. On the other hand, a task that is too easy or repetitive actually has the same effect: lack of stimulation and interest makes our attention wander and our performance deteriorates.

Sadness When we are sad, all our energy is consumed and we lose interest in other matters. A study published in 2004, for example, showed that the risk of having a car crash was multiplied by four in the period following a divorce. More generally, we know that depressive states or prolonged stress are accompanied by difficulties in concentrating.

Effort How hard we try to do something depends not only on how interesting we find the task, but also on how satisfied we will feel after its completion. The greater the pleasure, the less importance we give to the effort we need to make. In sport, the person who wins a match feels less tired than the one who loses, even though they both put in the same amount of effort.

Is it possible to pay attention to several things at the same time?

We have no difficulty doing several things at the same time if they are associated with the same activity or have the same goal. This means that we can simultaneously be aware of a flower's aroma as well as distinguish it from other flowers by its colour, its form and the arrangement of its petals and its leaves; observe an approaching butterfly; and identify the flower and the butterfly by searching in our memory for other flowers and butterflies whose names we know. We can also make a number of movements while analysing this information – we can turn to look at the butterfly, smile, bend our body, stretch out our hand to the flower or the butterfly and so on.

All this is possible because all these operations are working towards the same goal: that of observing nature. But if we had to answer the phone at the same time, our brain could not take simultaneous account of all the information received, but could only cope with it successively.

Yet two completely different activities can be carried out at the same time if one of them is automatic – following a conversation (controlled activity) and walking or driving (automatic activity), for example. The automatic activities decrease the effort of paying attention and free up our consciousness, which can then focus on other mental or motor activities (see also page 100). In spite of this, it can happen that a controlled activity overwhelms an automatic activity, particularly if the emotional charge is too great. If you are talking on a phone while driving, even though it is hands-free if required by law, and the phone call brings news of a serious event, the analysis of the conversation will take priority over the driving. In this case, there is a high risk of having an accident if you don't stop driving.

How good is your visual attention?

The purpose of the puzzles on this page is to help to stimulate your visual attention and also to increase your capacity for concentration. Try to complete the puzzles as quickly as possible, and don't spend more than five minutes altogether.

Daily life

1. Study this drawing for three minutes, then cover it.

2. Using the letters underneath the items on the right, place each item in its correct position in the drawing.

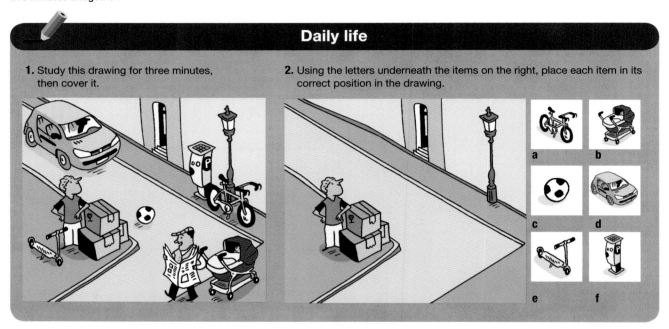

Play on words

By changing one letter in each of the two groups of words below, make two new groups of words in which each group belongs to the same category.

BIKE ....

GLADE ....

Category
....

PARK ....

SUMMER ....

BARE ....

CLUE ....

Category
....

SLUMP ....

WICKER ....

Superimposed shapes

Which three of the shapes below are superimposed in this drawing?

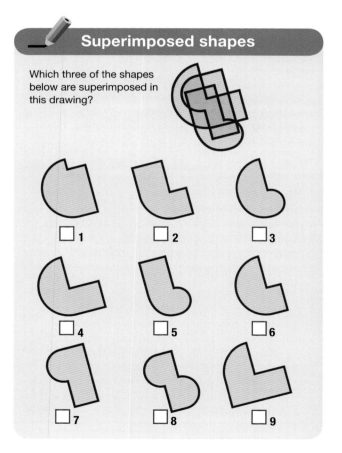

□ 1   □ 2   □ 3

□ 4   □ 5   □ 6

□ 7   □ 8   □ 9

Find the symbol

Find and circle the target symbol.

Target 1 = ☉   **Target 2 = ♄**   **Target 3 = ▨**

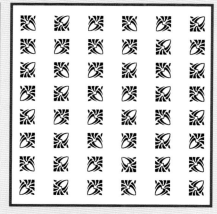

Numbers and letters

1. Sequence of numbers

How many times does the number combination 467 appear in this sequence? Spend no more than one minute on your answer.

27651**467**94634189**467**148672

4390**467**741546290346798290

3646756746294**467**725**467**725

..........7..... 467

2. Letters

How many times does the letter A appear in this opening sentence from Jane Austen's *Pride and Prejudice*? Spend no more than one minute on your answer.

'It is a truth universally acknowledged, that a single man in possession of a good fortune, must be in want of a wife.'

9

.... A

Stroop test

This test shows how difficult it is to process two pieces of contradictory information simultaneously, where one seems controlled (recognising the colours) and the other automatic (reading). The purpose is to name the colour of the letters as quickly as possible when the word is the name of a different colour.
Say the colours of the following words out loud.

Purple   **Orange**   **Green**

Purple   **Red**   **Green**

Blue   **Blue**

You are obliged to make an effort to concentrate because reading the word comes automatically; it imposes itself on you and is an obstacle to verbalising the colour of the letters. This is called the Stroop effect. With practice, the exercise does become easier, as you become familiar with the unusual mental gymnastics, but the Stroop effect nevertheless persists.

Answers: Play on words Bake, glaze, pare, simmer; all are terms used in cooking. Base, club, stump, wicket; all are names of sporting equipment. **Superimposed shapes** 4, 5, 7. **Find the symbol:**

Numbers and letters 1. 467 appears seven times. **2.** A appears nine times.

Is procedural memory automatic?

You only have to learn to ride a bike when you are young to remember how to do it all your life. Simply sitting on the saddle releases a whole series of appropriate actions – holding the handlebars, pedalling and braking – without having to think. Even if you find it difficult to explain how you manage to keep your balance, the reflexes are still there. This type of learning corresponds to a relatively archaic and very robust part of memory that is called procedural memory.

The memory of automatic movements

Automatic movements make up a store of complex motor skills that allow us to ski or play a musical instrument, as well as to eat with a fork, turn a tap on and off, or enter a password or code without being conscious of remembering the right numbers. All these skills have one thing in common: they depend on automatic movements that are so well integrated that we use them without thinking. These automatic movements belong to implicit memory. Most of them are the result of a long learning process that originally required conscious effort, but we have forgotten where, when and how we acquired them. Carrying them out automatically allows us to focus our attention on something else, such as holding a conversation while we are eating.

Automatic or not?

Read the following list carefully and tick everything that doesn't belong to procedural memory.

- ☐ Driving
- ☐ Skiing
- ☐ Your wedding day
- ☐ Writing
- ☐ The perfume of jasmine
- ☐ Your partner's birthday
- ☐ Your shopping list
- ☐ Mental calculation
- ☐ Your bank PIN
- ☐ Sewing

Answers: Your wedding day, the perfume of jasmine, your partner's birthday, your shopping list.

Other kinds of implicit memory

Procedural memory, which we call on automatically, is not the only type of implicit memory. The brain also receives other information that influences our behaviour without us being aware of it.

This is what happens with the conditioned reflexes that produce physiological reactions or certain behaviours when we are faced with a given situation – for example, increased heart rate and sweating when we feel fear or a rush of saliva when we think of a good meal.

Another well-known phenomenon revealed by memory tests is something psychologists call the priming effect. This refers to the effect in which being exposed to a stimulus influences our response to a subsequent stimulus. Again, the priming effect is not governed by our consciousness and is based on perceptive memory. Priming effects can involve the meaning of words. Reading one word, for example, influences our understanding of the words that follow because memory stores associations of meaning. When we read 'Two lines that are par-…', we are more likely to complete the phrase with the word 'parallel' than with 'particular' or 'partnered'.

The fact that memory functions without our knowledge plays a determining role in decision making and judgment. This is a phenomenon that is well known to marketing professionals: even if we don't consciously remember their content, advertisements that activate our perceptive memory or that play on our emotional conditioning strongly influence our purchasing decisions.

Are you sensitive to suggestion?

1. Read the following text, and then do something else for about ten minutes.

Although euro coins and banknotes have been in circulation in France since 2002, many people who grew up with and used francs still assess the value of what they buy in the former currency and not in euros. Even if they no longer systematically convert euros into francs, their reference, which is inscribed in their implicit memory, remains the franc.

The psychologist Romain Guilloux gives the example of small pastries that are sold by weight at 2 euros per 100 grams. 'When we read 2 euros, the social convention inscribed in our implicit memory makes us perceive this amount as if it were 2 francs. Of course we know that 2 euros is a lot more than 2 francs, but we still don't feel the exact difference in value.'

2. Then complete the following words, filling in each space with a letter

a. **B _ _ _ N _ _ E S**

b. **V _ _ U _**

c. **C _ M _ _ T _ R**

d. **H _ _ S _ H _ _ D**

e. **P _ _ C _ O _ O _ I _ _**

f. **L _ _ T _ E _**

Answers: a. banknotes. **b.** value. **c** computer. **d.** household.
e. psychologist. **f.** leather
Normally the words 'banknotes', 'value' and 'psychologist' are found more quickly than the others because they have been read in the text. This is what is called 'perceptual priming': the implicit memory of words that have previously been seen allows you to identify them more quickly, even though this exercise was not related to a memorisation and recovery task.

Working memory: a short-term faculty

Working memory is temporary. Its principal characteristic is its low capacity: it is quickly saturated. Psychological tests show that we can retain on average seven unassociated elements (such as letters, words or numbers) for a few minutes. This is called the span.

Specialised subsystems

There appear to be several distinct stores for working memory. Each specialises in a certain type of information and they operate parallel to one another.

One of them, the phonological loop, deals with the sounds of language. It allows you to retain a list of words or a phone number, for example. It includes a passive storage system with a limited capacity lasting no more than a few seconds, as well as procedures for repeating the information that allow the working memory to be refreshed for the time required. It is this system that is in operation when you mentally repeat a phone number for the time it takes to find a piece of paper to write it down.

Another subsystem of working memory, the visual–spatial notebook, encodes information in a visual form. It permits us to keep spatial arrangements or mental images such as faces briefly in our heads.

These systems seem to be supervised by a kind of central administrator – called the central executive – that coordinates the various processing operations and directs the attention towards a particular type of data.

The final module in working memory – episodic or buffer – is responsible for the link with long-term memory. It allows us temporarily to retain more elaborate memories by linking information across space and time.

Grouping to aid memory

Even if the capacity of working memory is limited, it is still possible to increase it. One of the most efficient ways to do this is by grouping.

Experiments show that we are able to retain an average of seven elements (between five and nine, depending on the individual), regardless of their nature (numbers, words or images) and, above all, their length. Any more than this and the risk of error is significant. In order to increase what experts call the capacity span of working memory, we should group the elements together into longer units. It's difficult to remember ten letters, but if we make them into a word, as in the game of Scrabble, we can remember about seven times as many. So to memorise a list of random numbers, for example, the trick is to associate them in twos and threes, or even create numbers that have a meaning: in 872 319 453 256 781, for example, 87 might be the year you got married, 23 the street number of your house, 19 your daughter's age, 45 is the year World War II ended, and so on. You can also link numbers according to a logical order. To memorise the code 6035, you could remember that 35–5 is half of 60. This process is a way of confirming a number when you are hesitating between several figures.

Devise reminders

To memorise a list of proper names, you can devise a code that will jog your memory – one that uses the first one or two letters of each word, for example.

● Group the initials of all the words in the list together in twos or threes. So to remember the eight planets of the solar system (the ninth, Pluto, has been reclassified as a dwarf planet), starting from the one closest to the Sun and finishing with the one farthest away, we can memorise: MVE MJS UN (Mercury, Venus, Earth, Mars, Jupiter, Saturn, Uranus, Neptune). You can do the same thing with countries and their capitals, anatomical names, a list of presidents, or customers' orders in a restaurant.

● Create a sentence based on the first letter of each word – it's easier to remember than the list of names. You may come up with a sentence that is a little absurd, but this method is often effective. For example, a sentence for the eight planets might be 'My Violet Eiderdown Makes John Sing Until Night'.

The effect of position

When you have to remember a list of words and then recall it immediately, you usually remember the beginning and end of the list far more easily than the middle. The primacy effect (good recall of the words at the beginning) is the result of the transfer of information from working memory to long-term memory. The recency effect (good recall of the words at the end) is associated with maintaining the last words on the list in the working memory. Thirty seconds after reading the list, there is a far greater likelihood that you will remember the elements at the beginning of the list than those at the end: the last elements disappear before the first ones because they are stored in the working memory, where duration is very limited.

MVE MJS UN

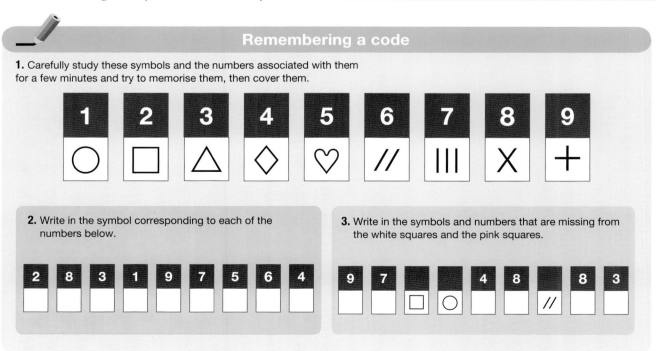

Remembering a code

1. Carefully study these symbols and the numbers associated with them for a few minutes and try to memorise them, then cover them.

1	2	3	4	5	6	7	8	9
○	□	△	◇	♡	//	|||	X	+

2. Write in the symbol corresponding to each of the numbers below.

2	8	3	1	9	7	5	6	4

3. Write in the symbols and numbers that are missing from the white squares and the pink squares.

9	7			4	8		8	3
		□	○			//		

1. Study these 22 words for one to two minutes and try to memorise them. If necessary, you can form associations or groups to make the task easier (see page 120).

polar — apple — chief — director — stitch — toffee — seek — escalator — curve — puree — birthday — general — knitting — size — curtain — mint — almond — attic — double — duplicate — light — growth

2. Cover the words, and then try three different ways of testing your capacity to memorise a list: free recall, suggested recall and recall by recognition (page 105).

a. Free recall Write down the list spontaneously, in any order you wish.

1. ....
2. ....
3. ....
4. ....
5. ....
6. ....
7. ....
8. ....
9. ....
10. ....
11. ....
12. ....
13. ....
14. ....
15. ....
16. ....
17. ....
18. ....
19. ....
20. ....
21. ....
22. ....

b. Suggested recall Use the hints provided to help you to remember the words.

PO _ _ _

Tempting fruit ....

Chewy sweet ....

Second part of a children's game..............

Rearrange FICHE to find a leader ....

Rhymes with 'hint' ....

Anniversary ....

Can be drawn ....

Copy.............................

Carries you up and down.......................

_ L _ _ N _

Of movies or companies.....................

Not heavy or dark.........................

A lofty room...................

From small to big ....

Stature...........................

Can save nine ....

Twice...........................

P _ R _ _

Bend ....

Done with needles..........

High military rank...........

c. Recall by recognition Identify the words on the list by recognising them among other words that are called distractors: some of these have a meaning or a form that is similar to the words on the basic list. Among these 70 words, circle those that appear on the list on page 104.

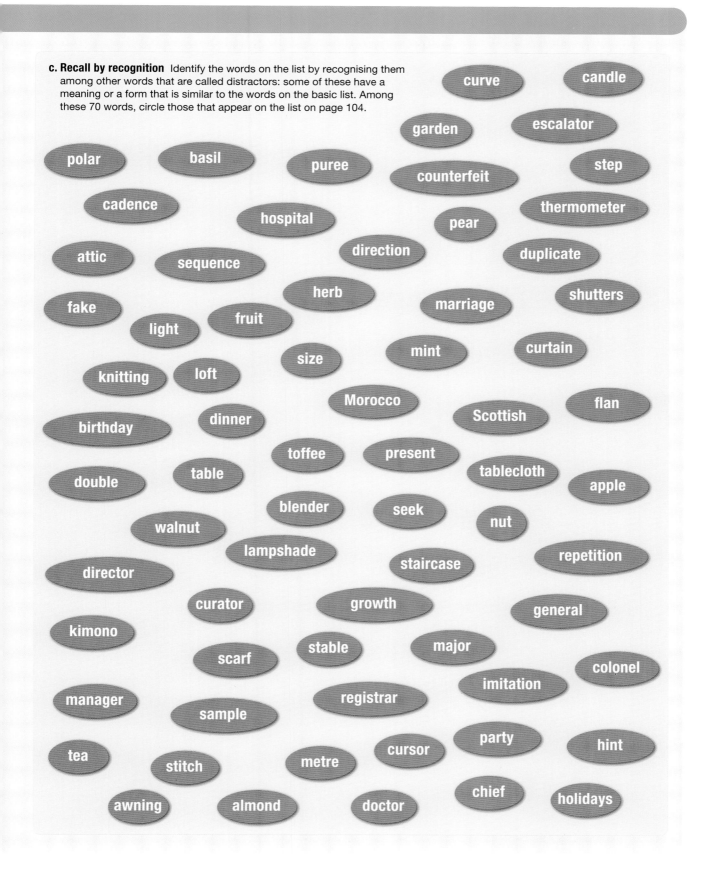

curve · candle · garden · escalator · polar · basil · puree · counterfeit · step · cadence · hospital · pear · thermometer · attic · sequence · direction · duplicate · fake · herb · marriage · shutters · light · fruit · size · mint · curtain · knitting · loft · Morocco · Scottish · flan · birthday · dinner · toffee · present · tablecloth · apple · double · table · blender · seek · nut · walnut · lampshade · staircase · repetition · director · curator · growth · general · kimono · stable · major · scarf · colonel · imitation · manager · registrar · sample · party · hint · tea · cursor · stitch · metre · awning · almond · doctor · chief · holidays

Semantic memory: a cultural heritage

Neil Armstrong, first astronaut to set foot on the Moon; Rome, capital of Italy; an orange, a kind of citrus fruit; 1 kilometre = 1000 metres; Robin Hood, English folklore hero… Our immense store of general knowledge, made up of facts, concepts and vocabulary, corresponds to what is known as semantic memory. We have memorised all this knowledge, but we have generally forgotten where, when and how.

Complementary forms of memory

Semantic memory is different from episodic memory, which involves our personal recollections. We can remember the details of our last trip overseas perfectly well: this comes from our episodic memory. But we can also talk about the tower of Pisa, and even draw it, without ever having seen it: this comes from our semantic memory.

In reality, these two types of memory frequently overlap when we talk about past events. For example, it's thanks to our semantic memory that we know the result of the last national election. But the political importance of the event also allows us to recall the personal memories that we associate with it, which come from our episodic memory. All of us are probably able to remember where we were on 11 September 2001. But, even if we have a precise memory of what we were doing on that day, this doesn't necessarily imply that it is an accurate memory. In an experiment that was carried out in the United States following the explosion of the Challenger space shuttle, students were questioned the day after the tragic event, and then again two and a half years later. On the latter occasion, 40 per cent of the students gave accounts that were different from their first interview, and were even incorrect.

Overlapping memories Anyone who sees an orange knows what it is, but no one knows when they actually memorised it. On the other hand, in response to the question, 'Where were you on 11 September 2001?' or 'What were you doing on that day?', everyone can give an answer, even without having been in the United States either on 11 September 2001 or at any other time. The impact of this event is such that it has been integrated into everyone's memory and very often remains associated with a personal memory.

Processes for acquiring knowledge

How can our brain store such a wide range of general knowledge? Much of what we know is acquired through our education, schooling, experience and reading. At the same time, there's also a form of unconscious absorption that experts call the semantisation of memories. Initially, our memory stores a specific episode in our life (our first plane trip, for example) and then, little by little, as similar experiences are repeated, the memory becomes more general – as we take more plane trips, we draw from them a bank of abstract knowledge about planes.

What's more, it seems to be possible to acquire several kinds of knowledge without ever being aware of it. This has been shown in a recent study involving children with amnesia. When they were born or in the first few weeks of life, they suffered very serious brain damage in the area of the hippocampus, a zone that plays an essential role in episodic memory. As a result, these children don't remember what they have done during the day and have difficulty knowing where and when things occurred (a condition known as tempo-spatial disorientation). Despite this, they manage to acquire a wide store of knowledge: they learn to speak, and their IQ – which is almost in the average range – allows them to have practically normal schooling. These findings suggest that episodic memory and semantic memory are not interdependent.

Collective memory

Each culture is characterised by common beliefs, history, values and abilities. This set of representations, passed from one generation to the next and anchored in our minds as well as in books, tools or customs, forms collective memory. Beyond our individual diversity, then, we all have a common base that is variously composed – according to the type of group, be it a region, a country or the Western world, for example – of things like history, language, cultural references, culinary traditions, emblematic figures and social conventions.

In the past, information was transmitted mainly orally, through words and gestures. This meant that each human being was entrusted with a fragment of collective memory, which could be modified if required and passed on. Today, it is the media, and particularly television, that is the main vehicle for collective memory, and this tends to reinforce our common references, while at the same time making the different collective memories more uniform.

Do you know these places?

Even if you haven't actually visited them, you should recognise most of the following places.

1. ....

2. ....

3. ....

4. ....

5. ....

6. ....

7. ....

8. ....

9. ....

10. ....

Answers: 1. Bridge of Sighs, Venice. **2.** Easter Island. **3.** Statue of Liberty, New York. **4.** St Basil's Cathedral, Moscow. **5.** Temple of Abu Simbel, Egypt. **6.** Taj Mahal, Agra, India. **7.** Eiffel Tower, Paris. **8.** Big Ben, London. **9.** Uluru (Ayers Rock), Australia. **10.** The Parthenon, Athens.

How to develop your semantic memory

Some of us like to learn for the sake of learning: this is what psychologists call a compulsion, which is related to collecting. Collectors focus their attention on objects that they don't yet own. The collecting urge can certainly make us winners when it comes to game shows based on general culture, but that means memorising facts to an almost obsessive level – knowing, for example, the capital of every country in the world, all the kings and queens of England and their reigns, the 12 gods and goddesses of ancient Greece, the dates and locations of all the Olympic Games, or the 53 movies directed by Alfred Hitchcock, their stars and when they were made.

Students are capable of storing away a lot of knowledge very quickly in preparation for an examination or a competitive selection test, but they will progressively forget a large amount of this material and will eventually retain only what is useful for pursuing a career. With maturity, interest and pleasure are major drivers of our learning. When we want to acquire skills and know-how, we spontaneously turn to subjects and activities that are associated with a passion or a particular interest. The development of botanical skills, for example, is a natural progression from a love of gardening. And the quality of paintings produced by an amateur will benefit from having a sound knowledge of fine arts. Being familiar with masterpieces and having the keys to understand them sharpens the eye, a skill that can be put into practice in the amateur's own work.

Internet, the Aladdin's cave of knowledge

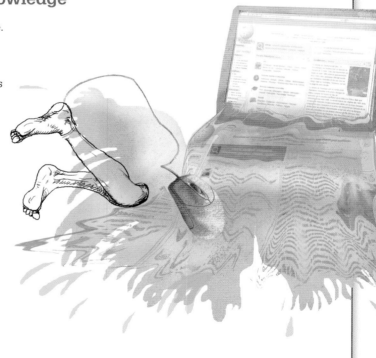

The internet is a marvellous tool for sharing knowledge. Any subject you choose can be covered in its various aspects and contexts, in either a few words or 300 pages, making it suitable for novice and expert alike. Take the word 'hand', for instance. It gives access to websites on anatomy, prehistory (walking on two legs and manual dexterity), art (drawing, sculpting), lateralisation (left-handedness and right-handedness), fortune telling (lines on the hand), beauty (manicure), medical topics (disorders, injuries, exercises, surgery, hygiene), not to mention second-hand goods and many commercial brands using this word.

But this avalanche of instantly available data is a double-edged sword. It certainly does offer a monumental store of information, with links that allow us to move from one subject to another, wherever our curiosity leads, and it gives us access to enriching interactive opportunities (such as discussion forums and being able to ask questions or express an opinion). On the other hand, the information is not sorted, organised or arranged in any order of importance, and its accuracy can't be established. This can leave us totally confused and make it impossible to extract the information we need and to get a general idea of the subject we are researching.

And there's another important question: what place should the internet have in education? Do we really need to make an effort to memorise information when it is constantly available on the web? More generally, the more we use these tools (the internet, GPS, electronic indexes and the like) to assist our memory, are we actually running the risk of weakening it?

In any case, our brains have adapted to these aids by developing new skills to manage them and use them better. According to the results of a study conducted at the University of California and published in 2008, using search engines on the internet may even be of benefit to brain function!

How many words beginning with 'fi' are you able to name? The challenge appears simple, and yet we run out of words fairly quickly. This type of question calls on the lexical memory and has to do with the morphology, or form and derivation, of words, unlike semantic memory tests, which are more concerned with word meanings. The following questions will test both your lexical memory and the richness of your vocabulary.

Try to fill in the table below without using a dictionary. Spend no longer than ten minutes on it.

1. Find ten words (adjectives, nouns or verbs, without repeating two words in the same family) that begin with the letters 'fi'.

fi.................................... fi....................................

fi.................................... fi....................................

fi.................................... fi....................................

fi.................................... fi....................................

fi.................................... fi....................................

2. Find ten names of objects from everyday life that begin with the letter 'm'.

m.................................... m....................................

m.................................... m....................................

m.................................... m....................................

m.................................... m....................................

m.................................... m....................................

3. Find five words beginning with 'ortho-' (from the ancient Greek *orthos*, 'straight, upright, correct').

ortho.................................... ortho....................................

ortho.................................... ortho....................................

ortho....................................

4. Find ten specialisations or professions ending in '-ologist' (from the ancient Greek *logos*, 'speech, study').

....................................ologist ....ologist

....................................ologist ....ologist

....................................ologist ....ologist

....................................ologist ....ologist

....................................ologist ....ologist

5. Find five words ending in '-grapher' (from the ancient Greek *graphos*, 'drawn, written').

....................................grapher ....grapher

....................................grapher ....grapher

....................................grapher

6. Find ten words beginning with 'bio-' (from the ancient Greek *bios*, 'life').

bio.................................... bio....................................

bio.................................... bio....................................

bio.................................... bio....................................

bio.................................... bio....................................

bio.................................... bio....................................

Answers (possible words)
1. fickle, fiction, fiddle, fidelity, fidget, field, fierce, fig, fight, figment, figure, file, fill, fillet, filly, film, filter, filth, fin, final, finance, finch, find, fine, finger, finish, fir, fire, firm, first, fish, fist, fit, five, fix, fizz. **2.** machine, magazine, magnet, mailbox, map, mask, mat, match, medal, medicine, menu, mesh, metal, meter, microphone, microscope, mirror, mitten, mixer, mobile (phone), money, monitor, mop, mortar, mothball, motor, motorbike, motor car, motorcycle, mould, mower, muff, muffler, mug, mural. **3.** orthochromatic, orthodontist, orthodox, orthogonal, orthographic, orthography, orthopaedic, orthoptics. **4.** anthropologist, archaeologist, biologist, cardiologist, climatologist, criminologist, dermatologist, ecologist, gerontologist, gynaecologist, musicologist, ophthalmologist, ornithologist, palaeontologist, pathologist, pharmacologist, psychologist, rheumatologist, seismologist, sociologist, toxicologist, vulcanologist, zoologist. **5.** biographer, bibliographer, cardiographer, cinematographer, choreographer, demographer, geographer, hagiographer, hydrographer, iconographer, lexicographer, lithographer, oceanographer, photographer, radiographer, stenographer, telegrapher, topographer, typographer. **6.** biochemistry, biodegradable, biodiversity, biodynamic, bioethics, biofuel, biogas, biography, biology, biomass, biophysics, biorhythm, biosphere, biopsy, biosynthesis, biotechnology.

How good is your semantic memory?

Have fun testing your semantic memory with this series of questions that dip into the store of cultural knowledge you've been accumulating since childhood.

History

1. What is the common link between Aristotle and Alexander the Great, Abélard and Heloïse, Seneca and Nero, Frédérique de la Harpe and Tsar Alexander I?

....

2. Where is the site of Waterloo?

- ☐ **a.** England
- ☐ **b.** Belgium
- ☐ **c.** Sweden
- ☐ **d.** Germany

3. Who was president of the United States when Japan surrendered on 2 September 1945?

....

4. Put these people in chronological order by numbering them from 1 to 6.

- ☐ **Nebuchadnezzar II**
- ☐ **Constantine I**
- ☐ **Tutankhamen**
- ☐ **Julius Caesar**
- ☐ **Plato**
- ☐ **Mohammed**

5. The dates 1961 and 9 November 1989 mark the rise and fall of which historic structure?

....

Geography

1. The distance between the North Pole and the South Pole is 40,075.017 km.

☐ **True**   ☐ **False**

2. What are the capitals of Turkey, Canada and Honduras?

....

3. The Aleutian Islands are located:

- ☐ **a.** Between Australia and New Zealand
- ☐ **b.** Between Japan and South Korea
- ☐ **c.** Between Siberia and Alaska
- ☐ **d.** Between Madagascar and Tanzania

4. Northern Ireland is not part of Great Britain.

☐ **True**   ☐ **False**

5. Put these cities in order from north to south, numbering them 1 to 9.

- ☐ **Bangkok**
- ☐ **Colombo**
- ☐ **Hong Kong**
- ☐ **Jakarta**
- ☐ **Kuala Lumpur**
- ☐ **Mumbai**
- ☐ **Singapore**
- ☐ **Suva**
- ☐ **Tokyo**

Vocabulary

1. Phobias

a. If you are thalassophobic, you have a fear of
....

b. If you are acrophobic, you have a fear of
....

c. If you are nyctophobic, you have a fear of
....

d. If you are ochlophobic, you have a fear of
....

2. What is an ampersand?
....

3. What is the meaning of *annus mirabilis*?
....

4. What is the name of the linguistic phenomenon that appears in the sentence 'Do you mean he's been mean to you?'
....

5. What is the origin of the phrase 'as old as Methuselah'?

- ☐ **a.** From a character in the Old Testament who is said to have lived 969 years.
- ☐ **b.** From the name given to a type of prehistoric human discovered in the nineteenth century in the region of Methuselah, in modern day Portugal.
- ☐ **c.** From the name of a sorcerer, Charles Methus, who is said to have discovered the secret of eternal youth (a potion of which one had to drink exactly 6 litres, which is the origin of the name 'methuselahs' given to 6-litre champagne bottles).

Science and technology

1. What does the acronym DNA stand for?

....

2. What is electrolysis?

☐ **a.** A technique of molecular separation designed to purify solutions

☐ **b.** A chemical reaction producing electrical activity

☐ **c.** The transformation of electrical energy into chemical energy

3. Who said, 'Sit next to a pretty girl for an hour, it seems like a minute. Sit on a red-hot stove for a minute, it seems like an hour. That's relativity.'

☐ **a.** Stephen Hawking

☐ **b.** Niels Bohr

☐ **c.** Albert Einstein

4. The relationship of three parallel straight lines is transitive.　　☐ True　☐ False

5. Who was responsible for the following discoveries or scientific advances?

a. The Earth rotates around the Sun

b. The telephone

c. The period classification of chemical elements

d. The basis of modern genetics

e. The electric light bulb

f. Penicillin

1. Alexander Fleming

2. Alexander Graham Bell

3. Gregor Mendel

4. Dmitri Ivanovitch Mendeleïev

5. Nicolaus Copernicus

6. Thomas Edison

Arts and literature

1. Who wrapped the Pont Neuf in Paris, the Reichstag in Berlin and the coast at Little Bay in Sydney?

....

2. In painting, what is vanitas?

....

3. Who was the librettist of these three operas by Mozart: *The Marriage of Figaro, Cosi fan tutte* and *Don Giovanni*?

....

4. What is the name given to the author of a private journal?

....

6. Picasso's *Guernica* is painted in black, grey and white.

☐ True　☐ False

7. The first prize at the Venice Film Festival is called the Golden Gondola.

☐ True　☐ False

8. In the novels by Conan Doyle, Sherlock Holmes never said 'Elementary, my dear Watson'.

☐ True　☐ False

5. Who wrote what? Match the pairs correctly.

a. *White Fang*

b. *Lord Jim*

c. *Treasure Island*

d. *Moby Dick*

e. *The War of the Worlds*

1. Robert Louis Stevenson

2. Herman Melville

3. Jack London

4. HG Wells

5. Joseph Conrad

Answers
History 1. The former were the private tutors of the latter. **2.** b. **3.** Harry Truman (following the death of Roosevelt on 2 April 1945). **4.** 1 – Tutankhamen (c. 1345–27 BC); 2 – Nebuchadnezzar II (c. 630–562 BC); 3 – Plato (427–348 BC); 4 – Julius Caesar (100–44 BC); 5 – Constantine I (274–337 AD); 6 – Mohammed (570–632 AD). **5.** The construction and the fall of the Berlin Wall. **Geography 1.** False. 40,075.017 km is the circumference of the Earth at the Equator. As the Earth is slightly flatter at the poles, its circumference through the poles is slightly less: 40,007.864 km. The distance between the North and South Poles is about 20,004 km. **2.** Ankara, Ottawa, Tegucigalpa. **3.** c. **4.** True. Great Britain is comprised of England, Wales and Scotland. The United Kingdom combines these three countries, plus Northern Ireland. **5.** 1 – Tokyo; 2 – Hong Kong; 3 – Mumbai; 4 – Bangkok; 5 – Colombo; 6 – Kuala Lumpur; 7 – Singapore; 8 – Jakarta; 9 – Suva. **Vocabulary 1. a.** the sea. **b.** high places. **c.** the night or darkness. **d.** crowds. **2.** It is the sign '&' which means 'and'. **3.** 'Year of wonders'. This expression is notably used by the scientific community to characterise a year that is particularly fertile in discoveries, for example, 1666 for the work of Isaac Newton, or 1905 because of Albert Einstein. The opposite is an *annus horribilis*. Queen Elizabeth II used this term in relation to the year 1992 (two divorces and one separation among her children and a fire at Windsor Castle). **4.** Homonym; words with the same spelling, but different pronunciations, such as 'contract' (an agreement) and 'contract' (to shrink) are called homographs, and words with the same pronunciation, but different spellings, such as 'cite', 'sight' and 'site', are called homophones. **5.** a. **Science and technology 1.** Deoxyribonucleic acid. **2.** c. **3.** c. **4.** True. If straight line A is parallel to straight line B and if straight line B is parallel to straight line C, then A and C are parallel. **5.** a, 5. b, 2. c, 4. d, 3. e, 6. f, 1. **Arts and literature 1.** Christo Vladimirov Javacheff, known as Christo, a contemporary American artist born in Bulgaria. **2.** Vanitas is a type of still-life painting that uses motifs such as skulls, rotting fruit and hourglasses to symbolise the brevity of human life, the flight of time and the vanity of human desires (riches, pleasures, power, knowledge) in the face of the unavoidable nature of death. **3.** Lorenzo da Ponte. **4.** A diarist. **5.** a, 3. b, 5. c, 1. d, 2. e, 4. **6.** True. **7.** False. It is called the Golden Lion. **8.** True.

Episodic memory: a time machine

If you look at last year's diary, you'll discover that you have forgotten many of the events that you noted there. Over time, memories fade. We can talk in detail about a movie we saw yesterday, but after a few weeks our memory retains only the story and the most powerful scenes.

How memories are made

At first, when you experience an event, it is stored in your brain in a temporary way. The memory of the event can then either fade or become established over a longer period of time. This consolidation phase can last for months or years. It is not a passive process: you remember an event better if you think about it often, talk about it or experience other similar situations. For example, going back to a familiar place makes the events that you have experienced there come back into your mind. Memories can also flood over you when you see a well-known face, hear a certain phrase or smell a particular aroma.

Memory is subjective

By being evoked or repeated, the memory of an event can be reinforced, but it can also be distorted. Some details can assume greater importance, new elements can be added, and we can also change its meaning by reinterpreting the past.

What this means is that memory is not a carbon copy of the past. Our memories change, but this doesn't stop us from thinking that they are accurate, or even from having the impression of reliving them as they happened. It's even easy to give someone false memories. Experiments have shown that after listening to words like sugary, eating, sharp or candy, most subjects are sure that they have heard the word 'sweet', even though it has never been uttered (see also page 101). We can even be convinced that we have seen photos or TV footage of an accident, even though we have only read an account of it.

We shouldn't think of memory's ability to adapt as a handicap. One thing that it allows us to do is to make generalisations based on past experiences and to learn lessons from them. But in some circumstances it can be a problem: for example, in the context of a legal case, techniques of suggestion used by psychiatrists or police officers can lead to the creation of false memories, particularly among children. In this way, some people can be led to make false statements in good faith.

I told you so!

'I was certain it wasn't a good idea to vote for him', 'I thought it was going to be a boy', 'I was sure you were going to say that', 'I knew it'. These little comments that are often irritating are not so much proof of dishonesty or psychic powers as they are illustrations of a kind of prejudice that experts call 'hindsight bias'. This was defined by Scott A Hawkins and Reid Hastie in 1990 as 'a projection of new knowledge into the past accompanied by a denial that the outcome information has influenced judgment'. People sometimes use this device for reasons of self-importance, to show that they are particularly well informed and very knowledgeable, but most of the time it is an involuntary prejudice resulting from the fact that, in retrospect, an event seems obvious. An example drawn from a series of experiments provides a good illustration of this attitude: if people are aware of the correct answers before taking a test, they then overestimate what they would have scored without this prior knowledge.

The weight of emotions

There are some moments you'll remember your whole life through – the death of a much-loved pet, the moment you said 'I do' on your wedding day, the birth of your first child. Whether positive or negative, emotions encourage us to retain memories, with the exception of extreme cases where the event is so intense that it has the opposite effect, resulting in amnesia.

A process of sorting goes on in the memory: we forget most of the repetitive experiences from our daily lives (but not what they have taught us, such as concepts or skills), and only a small number of significant events leave a trace in the episodic memory. These are the memories associated with a context, a date or a place. This could involve meetings, a party, a time of intense happiness, a moment of transition or a time of significant change in our lives.

Memories are made of this While memories of day-to-day experiences quickly fade, a small number of significant events that are associated with a context, a date or a place and positive emotions are retained in the episodic memory.

Generally speaking, we retain pleasant events more easily than unpleasant ones. Emotions, particularly positive ones, reinforce the accuracy of the memory, which as a result includes more details relating to sight, hearing and odour than a negative memory and so appears more real. The role that the emotions play in the preservation of memories has been confirmed by tests that involve remembering lists of words. If these lists include terms that are emotionally neutral (like table or door) while others relate to feelings (like joy or pain), the latter are more easily remembered. Other experiments involving facial recognition have shown that it's easier to remember happy faces than those expressing anger. This suggests that it's easier for us to remember facial expressions that reflect a good image of ourselves.

What impact do emotions have on memory? As well as intervening in the stage in which the memory is encoded, they seem also to be involved in the consolidation phase – in other words, in the long-term storage of the memory. Our frame of mind also influences how we recall memories. So when we're sad, we tend to remember sad events, but when we're happy, positive experiences come back into our minds more easily. And some studies also indicate that people who exert greater control over their emotions remember past events in less detail.

Our first memories

If you ask 50-year-olds to recall the past, they'll probably remember many events that they've experienced over the past few years, but their memories will become fewer as they go back to their thirties. Yet the number of memories will increase again as they think back to their adolescence and their early adulthood, which is a period that is rich in new experiences (first kiss, first love and so on). This is what is called the peak of reminiscence. If we go back even farther, to childhood, we'll notice that our memories before 6 or 7 years of age are very rare, and those before 3 years of age are exceptional. This is called infantile amnesia, and it seems to be due to the immaturity of episodic memory, which is the memory that retains autobiographical episodes. This doesn't mean that young children have no memory. Quite the opposite.

They are able to store an exceptional quantity of knowledge and know-how, and they achieve the feat of learning to speak and write in record time. But they find it difficult to memorise their lived experiences in an episodic manner (by associating them with a place, a date and a specific context). This explains why we have so few memories of our early years. Also, most of the short glimpses of the past dating back to this time don't seem to correspond to real memories, but rather to later reconstructions made with the help of family stories or photos. This doesn't mean that some events experienced by very young children don't leave lasting psychological marks. An early trauma can have disastrous consequences for the formation of personality, although the child won't have any conscious memory of the episode itself.

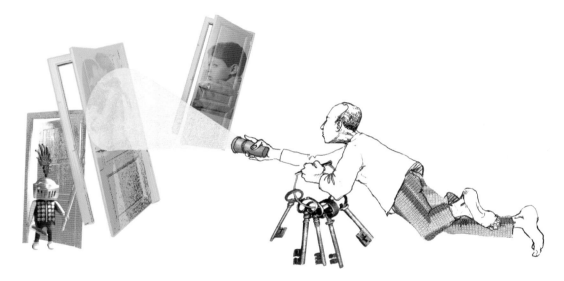

Memories of *Titanic*

James Cameron's epic film *Titanic* (1997) provides a good illustration of the different components of long-term memory. The sinking of the huge liner on its maiden voyage is an event that is recorded in our semantic memory – the memory of knowledge. The tragedy also belongs to collective memory because of its symbolic value as an emblem of human progress destroyed by natural elements. For the elderly woman, Rose, who tells the story 84 years later, the few days of happiness spent with Jack remain clearly engraved in her episodic memory because of their emotional intensity and because they have largely determined her life and her subsequent choices.

For those who saw the movie, the love story between Rose and Jack has perhaps become an ideal, the incarnation of romantic love: this means that it will have been recorded in their autobiographical memory. Implicit memory, that of conditioned behaviour (see page 101), is certainly not absent either – just a few notes of the song 'My heart will go on' are all that is needed for those familiar with the film to see the two main characters standing with their arms outstretched at the front of the ship.

8 TIPS FOR REMEMBERING YOUR LIFE

To store the greatest number of memories possible, you need to keep track of them progressively, so that there are reference points for future reminiscences. Much later, feelings, anecdotes and atmospheres will resurface, even though you may think you have forgotten them. This doesn't mean that you should constantly be obsessed with storing memories or overindulge in nostalgia. It simply provides a way of consolidating your personal story, of enriching the vision of your life and of passing it on to future generations.

1 Take photos or make videos and label them before you forget the context of the moment.

2 Keep a diary, a travel notebook or a blog. Writing every day is, by definition, an excellent way of keeping a record of events. It is also a creative and enriching exercise. A blog also allows you to work with computers and to communicate with others.

3 Note the titles of books that you like and passages that you would like to read again. Keep a record of exhibitions you have seen, and museums and monuments you have visited. All these contribute to the development of your personal culture.

4 Keep recipes associated with your childhood or with people you have met. You could also keep audio or video recordings of meals so that one day you can reactivate the unconscious part of your memory through flavours, aromas or music.

6 Write the first name and family name of your children's friends on their school photos.

7 Keep track of relatives, colleagues and neighbours whom you like and with whom you may one day lose touch.

5 Transfer your films and photos onto CDs to avoid the risk of losing them, and don't forget to label them so as to limit any autobiographical loss.

8 Before you move house, don't forget to take photos of it. Looking at pictures of the bedroom you had as a child or an adolescent, where you lived as a student and places you have lived since then helps you to relive the memories of those times.

Prospective memory: the life ahead of you

Tying a knot in a handkerchief was once a popular memory aid. Nowadays, people are more likely to set the alarm on their mobile phone. Remembering something that has to be done – whether it's an occasional visit to the dentist, or a routine task like taking medication before going to bed – uses prospective memory. For this kind of memory to be effective, we must first carry out the planned action at the right time, and then avoid redoing it or checking several times that it has been done properly.

The role of context

If prospective memory is functioning correctly, it means that we are mentally associating a given action with a context: a place, an event or an individual we may meet. So, remembering to pick up some shopping after work requires a process of monitoring and checking to detect the appropriate signal (catching a glimpse of a supermarket in our visual field, for example). This then obliges us to interrupt the activity we are engaged in at that moment – which might be driving, or thinking of something else – in order to carry out that task. We can then retrieve the list of things we have to buy that is stored in our memory: bread, milk, eggs, fruit…

Prospective memory appears to rely on the interaction between two major structures in the brain: the prefrontal cortex, which is involved in planning actions and temporarily holding information in the working memory; and the hippocampus and neighbouring areas in the temporal lobe, which are responsible for storing information about the task that has to be accomplished.

Jogging the memory

At every age, we call on external aids or crutches to help our prospective memory. We note an appointment in our diary, we draw up an urgent 'To do' list, we leave an object in an obvious place so that we don't forget to return it to a friend, we program a timer and so on. Memory aids like this help us to organise our daily lives and prevent us overburdening our brains with technical information (such as timetables and addresses) that we don't need to know by heart. This is even more important for people who suffer from problems with memory: for them, these aids are indispensable tools, precious reference points that allow them to have better control over their lives and help them not to feel lost or embarrassed, or even belittled, because they are constantly forgetting.

And if you are not in the habit of using a diary, you need to learn how to use it properly, and above all you mustn't forget to consult it! The most commonly used format is the personal organiser with special sections for things like personal details, names and addresses, trips, notes, and year or monthly planner.

People with any sort of brain injury affecting memory are routinely taught to make use of external memory aids. This allows them to be more independent and improves their ability to organise their daily lives without requiring them to spend a lot of time trying to memorise dates and times of appointments, visits from various people, or deadlines of any kind. Internal strategies are also taught, such as the use of mnemonics and making associations with the information to be remembered (see pages 102–3, 118).

The advantages of planning

Planning consists of listing the actions that must be taken in order to reach a goal. A date may be specified for the goal, which gives the constraint of a deadline (party preparations must be completed by the date of the celebration, for example). A budget may also be set, which implies a cost constraint that must be apportioned.

Planning can be more or less complex, depending on what is to be organised: it might be having friends to dinner, losing weight, undergoing various examinations before surgery, launching a new product before summer, assembling kit furniture, organising holidays or a wedding, planning school excursions or having a house built. Not all of these goals require the same intellectual investment. Planning can also be complicated by the time frame (whether it's booking a venue months in advance or making an appointment at the hairdresser's for the same day) or the diversity of what is to be done (from buying tiles to notifying people of your new address). On top of this, unexpected events that are likely to change the implementation of the initial plan can add to the complexity (the plumber is late so you have to delay the painter, which means you have to put back the date you move in; bad weather prevents photography for a catalogue, so all those participating have to be notified and the date has to be rescheduled).

So if you need to plan a task that is rather complex, it's essential to start by determining the stages, then to allocate a time frame for each stage and place them in the order in

which they need to happen. Using a calendar, you start by marking these stages in chronological order, building in some safety margins but also allowing an overlap where several actions can be undertaken at the same time. If proceeding in this way takes you past the target date, some stages will have to be tightened, the safety margins omitted and the allocation of tasks reorganised. For this reason, it is sometimes helpful to plan backwards – in other words, start from the final date that can't be changed and work towards the starting date.

Then, once the action begins, it is very reassuring to cross off each stage on the calendar or the planning board as it has been achieved, in this way giving a concrete form to the progress of the project.

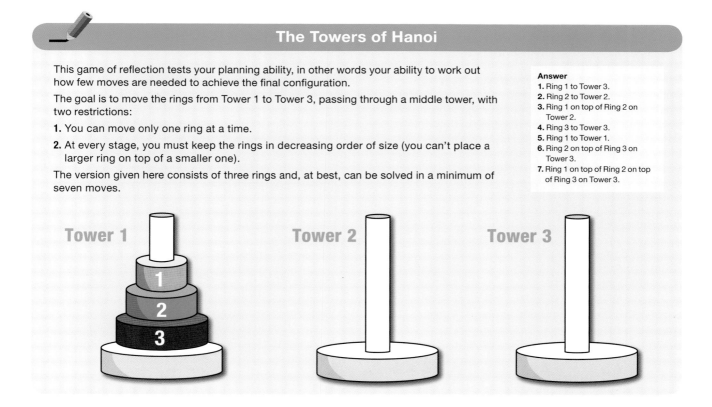

The Towers of Hanoi

This game of reflection tests your planning ability, in other words your ability to work out how few moves are needed to achieve the final configuration.

The goal is to move the rings from Tower 1 to Tower 3, passing through a middle tower, with two restrictions:

1. You can move only one ring at a time.

2. At every stage, you must keep the rings in decreasing order of size (you can't place a larger ring on top of a smaller one).

The version given here consists of three rings and, at best, can be solved in a minimum of seven moves.

Answer
1. Ring 1 to Tower 3.
2. Ring 2 to Tower 2.
3. Ring 1 on top of Ring 2 on Tower 2.
4. Ring 3 to Tower 3.
5. Ring 1 to Tower 1.
6. Ring 2 on top of Ring 3 on Tower 3.
7. Ring 1 on top of Ring 2 on top of Ring 3 on Tower 3.

Tower 1

Tower 2

Tower 3

The mental image

When we perceive something in our environment, we process it in two ways: by means of language – by using words to describe what we see, hear or smell; and by means of an image – by mentally visualising an interpretation of the information given by the brain. It is this internal reformulation of basic sensations in the associative areas of the brain that makes up the mental image.

An indispensable stage

What we perceive is transcribed and recorded by either a visual or a verbal code. Concrete data, such as scenery or an object in our line of vision, produce images, whereas abstract concepts, like democracy or overwork, tend to generate verbal representations.

The ability to construct mental images is the first stage in the memorisation process: we can retain something only by appropriating what our senses capture. This presupposes that we are paying attention to what is around us. In fact, if we neither notice our impressions or what we have learned, nor have the desire to retain and to subsequently recreate them, we create only fleeting perceptions that can't be recorded on a long-term basis in our memory.

How mental images are formed

The following examples of common situations or scenes will help to clarify the idea of a mental image.

1. How many windows are there in your house? How many pharmacies are there in your suburb?

To answer these questions, you don't call on your knowledge. You visually go through the rooms in your house or the streets in your suburb, and you mentally count the number of windows or pharmacies. You carry out the same search for mental images when a person asks you for directions and you go over the route in your head so that you can describe it to them. Similarly, you relive your recent actions and movements in your home in order to find out where you put your keys.

2. Don't think about a pink elephant.

This is a classic game and is generally associated with the promise of a gain if you succeed. Inevitably you do your best not to think about a pink elephant – but that is the only thing you can see. This game is often used in psychotherapy as an example of avoiding thinking about an event.

3. Look at the following names for a few minutes

- Winston Churchill
- Mickey Mouse
- Marilyn Monroe
- Superman

Undoubtedly you've visualised these people or characters – their images are fixed in everyone's memory. The mental image gives a physical presence to something that is visually absent.

Seeing through rose-coloured glasses

Our capacity to develop mental images can help us to prepare for a situation and can influence our mood by chasing away negative emotions. Through the power of the imagination, we are capable of creating scenarios that allow us to be better prepared to face a challenge (such as a sports competition, fear of flying or quitting smoking) and to reinforce our willpower.

When directed by a therapist, visualisation is a technique for relaxation and wellbeing based on the power of the mind over the body and on the biological effects of the emotions and mood. It is used in conjunction with other treatments to counteract stress, insomnia, anxiety and addictions.

Mental images and memory aids

The localisation method consists of imagining places that are very familiar, such as the rooms in a house, or the facades of buildings in a street. You then associate each of these places with something that you would like to commit to memory. To remember milk, bread or soap on a shopping list, for example, you could imagine milk boiling over in the kitchen, the bread popping up in the toaster, the soap in the bathroom, and so on. Then all you need to do to remember the items is mentally to go through the rooms of the house.

Images and words

Studies show that we retain information more easily if it is coded both visually and verbally. Test this yourself with the following exercise in memorising a list.

Test 1

1. Try to memorise this list of words. Study it for one to two minutes, then cover it.

light

suitcase

bowl

chair

fir tree

radio

glasses

no entry

cat

pullover

hairbrush

2. Now write down all the words you remember.

1. ....
2. ....
3. ....
4. ....
5. ....
6. ....
7. ....
8. ....
9. ....
10. ....
11. ....

Test 2

1. Try to memorise this list by looking at the words and their photographs. Study the words and images for one to two minutes, then cover them.

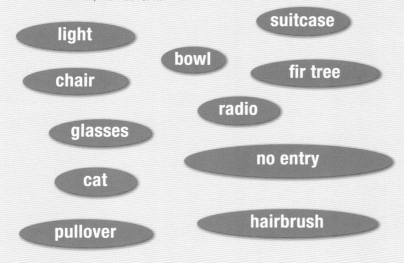

fountain pen

trousers

leeks

toothbrush

alarm clock

plates

cake

keys

doll

2. Now write down all the words you remember.

1. ....
2. ....
3. ....
4. ....
5. ....
6. ....
7. ....
8. ....
9. ....

Compare your results. You should have retained more words in Test 2 because you coded them in two forms: the image and the word. Generally speaking, we record information better if we perceive it and process it in several ways. For example, a text that we have to learn can be read silently or read out loud, it can be heard, copied, summarised or interpreted as a diagram.

Linking information

It's very difficult to memorise unrelated items of information, without any link or hierarchy between them. Just as you need to tidy your desk or put your files in order to be able to function efficiently, your memory needs order and coherent groups. This structuring can be governed by different criteria, and one of the most important of these is logic.

A sense of order

Reasoning allows us to create sequences that facilitate understanding and, consequently, memorisation. Finding an order in a series of words, numbers or sentences or following a train of thought, the plot of a story or the stages in a mathematical proof: these coherent links that we establish through reflection or learning constitute the essential conditions for good memorisation. This is why, even though intelligence and memory can be separated, they also sustain each other. The former helps to organise the data, while the latter provides subject matter and references such as culture, experience and methods of reasoning, which in turn nourish reflection.

Using reference data The memory can function more easily if it can refer to data that it considers significant. You can remember the structure of the drawing on the right, and even the number of lines it contains, because it looks like a familiar structure that we call a house. This is much easier to retain than another structure composed of the same number of lines, but positioned randomly (above), for which we can find no reference.

Association and memory

The words in our mental lexicon are organised like a network of associations that obey a number of different rules. These can be spontaneous (cabinet and medicine) or deliberate (Sydney and Melbourne), common (tomato and sauce) or personal (England and sadness, if you have experienced hard times there). Unlike dictionaries, the criterion of association is not alphabetical, which undoubtedly explains why the questions in the vocabulary quiz on page 109 are relatively difficult.

Word associations In our brain's vast mental lexicon, words are organised in a network of associations to help us call them to mind. While words are grouped by associations such as household furniture, illness, shops or administration, these groups can also be interconnected (cabinet with pharmacy, pharmacy with baker, hospital with administration, and so on).

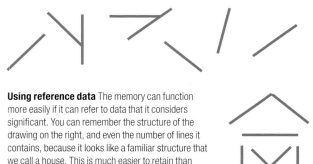

delicatessen

supermarket

baker

butcher

pharmacy

cabinet

illness · doctor

sideboard

chair

medication

house

health · hospital

bed · table

education

administration

researc

desk

parliament

post office

Logical sequences

You probably won't remember these sequences of numbers or shapes unless you can find some kind of logical connection between them. You can then copy them and show them to your friends, or use the logical principle you have memorised to devise new puzzles.

1. Which of the four possible answers given below (a, b, c or d?) is next in this sequence?

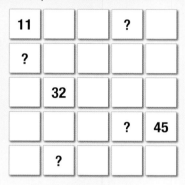

The four possible answers:

a   b   c   d

2. Replace the question marks with numbers.

11			?	
?				
		32		
			?	45
	?			

3. Complete these two series of numbers.

a

b

4. Study the two examples below carefully, then find the number that replaces the question mark.

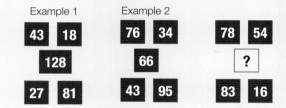

Answers

1. d; each new colour appears in the top right-hand corner and the other dots move clockwise. **2.** First line, 14; second line, 21; fourth line, 44; fifth line, 52. The first figure is the number of the row and the second is the number of the column. **3. a.** 212; the sequence is a list of all the uneven numbers from 1 to 23, arranged in groups of three. **b.** 16; the sequence runs as follows: subtract 9 (36 − 9 = 27), then add 1 (27 + 1 = 28), then subtract 8 (28 − 8 = 20), then add 2 (20 + 2 = 22), and so on, adding one unit to each addition and subtracting one unit from each subtraction. **4.** 148; the first part of the central number is the sum of the even figures from the numbers in the top left box and the bottom right box; complete the central number by adding together the uneven figures on the other diagonal (8 + 6 = 14) and (5 + 3 = 8), which makes 148.

Find the odd one out

The game of finding the odd one out consists of looking for associations between sequences of words in order to remove one that doesn't fit into your logical groupings. Memory functions in this way, like a network of associations that we call on to record new dates or to find a solution for a problem that we have never encountered before. The richer and more diverse the associations, the easier it is to recall or retrieve the information that you have stored in your memory.

Put a line through the odd one out in each the following lists.

1. density, birthrate, inflation, immigration, literacy

2. brain, pancreas, heart, lungs, liver

3. Dwight D Eisenhower
Charles de Gaulle
John Monash
Louis Mountbatten

4. Miami, Cape Town, Madrid, Rio de Janeiro, Mumbai

5. Mexico City, Atlanta, Sydney, Vancouver, Seoul

6. *ET: the Extra-Terrestrial*
The War of the Worlds
Star Wars: the Attack of the Clones
Jurassic Park
Close Encounters of the Third Kind

7. EM Forster
George Orwell
WH Auden
Ernest Hemingway
F Scott Fitzgerald

8. Jessica Watson
Michael Phelps
Cadel Evans
Mark Spitz
Layne Beachley

Answers (note that other answers may be possible): 1. Inflation is an economic term, while the others are used in demography. **2.** The brain is not an abdominal organ. **3.** Louis Mountbatten was a naval commander; the other three were military commanders. **4.** Madrid is not a coastal town. **5.** Vancouver hosted a winter Olympics, while all the other cities hosted summer Olympics. **6.** The film *Star Wars: the Attack of the Clones* was directed by George Lucas, the other four were directed by Steven Spielberg. **7.** WH Auden was a poet, the others were novelists. **8.** Cadel Evans is a cyclist. The other sportspeople are all associated with water: sailing for Jessica Watson, surfing for Layne Beachley, and swimming for Michael Phelps and Mark Spitz.

The benefits of learning by heart

After you have finished school, it can still be useful to continue learning things by heart so you have quick access to the factual information that you use regularly – for example, passwords and PINs, your health card number, phone numbers, addresses, car registration number and bus routes.

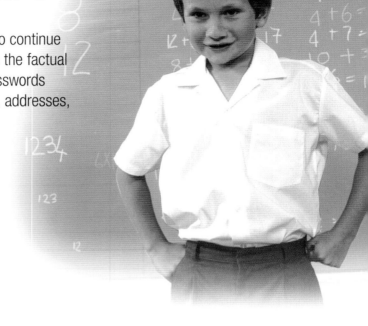

Repetition is important

The only way to retain something long-term is to practise regularly. A sustained but limited effort in time is the equivalent of cramming: once the pressure has passed, the data that has been learned is erased from the memory. The best way to fix information permanently in your mind is to divide the task of learning into stages to give you the time to assimilate the knowledge and then to reactivate it. Try this exercise with a poem of about 20 lines that you particularly like.

● Learn three or four lines a day. Read them, recite them, write them down if that helps you and, if necessary, listen to them. You can record yourself or, with a bit of luck, you may find a recorded version of the poem on the internet. Immerse yourself in the text, and think about its meaning, the choice of the words and the emotions it provokes. Each day repeat what you have learnt on the previous days.

● At the end of a week, recite the complete poem. Continue to do this every day for about a month to consolidate what you have learnt, gain confidence and anchor the text in your procedural memory.

The influence of sleep on memory

There is nothing better than a good night's sleep to keep something in your memory. Nowadays, this has been proved scientifically. Sleeping helps to consolidate memories. On the other hand, depriving someone of sleep alters their ability to learn. But this doesn't mean that we learn while we are asleep: experiments involving hypnopaedia – a method that advocates listening to recorded information while falling asleep – have so far all shown that this method is not effective.

Write it down

Whether you write a summary, take notes during a lecture and revise them later, relate the story of a film, book or trip, or keep a diary – each time you reformulate details or memories, you anchor them a little more firmly in your memory. Rewriting or summarising a text obliges you to analyse its content precisely and understand it perfectly to be able to reconstruct it faithfully in your own words.

Now, start singing!

An artistic activity like singing in a choir brings together use of memory, recall and sharing in a public performance. Added to that is the pleasure of participating in a collective activity and in a project that has to be conceived and carried out to the best of your ability. Singing in a choir requires you to learn a new language (reading music and reproducing the notes vocally) and to work at memorising both the music (the melody line of your own part as opposed to the other voices that are singing other parts) and the lyrics (the words of the songs).

Being a good storyteller has similar benefits. The art of relating anecdotes presupposes that you have a whole store of stories, a 'living memory', as well as the ability to improvise so as to keep the listeners spellbound. The raconteur relies on images that correspond to significant moments in the story and embroiders around these with virtuosity.

6 STEPS TO A BETTER MEMORY

1 Interest and motivation

You can retain things better when you want to remember them, but also when you are obliged to do so. This advice is valid for everyone: setting a goal or having a project, even a frivolous one (remembering funny stories to amuse your friends, or quotations to impress people at social gatherings) is the best way to stimulate your memory.

2 Paying attention

This is necessary for all kinds of memorisation. If you don't pay attention, you don't take in the information correctly. Rest, a favourable environment (calm, sufficient light), good sensory receptivity (good vision and hearing) and the absence of stress are essential to make sure that you correctly receive the information that is to be retained.

3 Developing mental images

We become aware of what our senses are transmitting to us by creating mental images. The information is visualised and converted into words. This mental appropriation of perceptions is the first stage in the memorisation process (see page 118).

4 Organising the information

Putting information in order, giving it meaning and creating a hierarchy helps to anchor the information and integrate it correctly in the long-term memory (see pages 102 and 120).

5 Repetition

To memorise something well, you need to make the effort to repeat it, and sometimes to learn it by heart. It is by reactivating the information regularly – by revisiting it, for example – that you have the best chance of anchoring it in your long-term memory (see page 122).

6 Transmitting the information

Transforming and reformulating facts or knowledge by putting them into your own words in order to recount them, write them, explain them or summarise them is a very efficient and active way of anchoring memories (see page 122).

Observing the stars John O'Neill makes preparations for photographing the night sky at the 24th Winter Star Party held in Florida in February 2008.

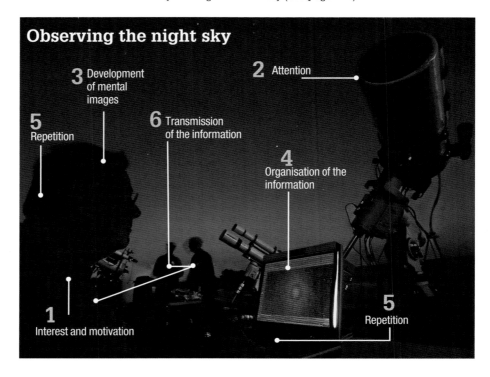

Observing the night sky

3 Development of mental images

2 Attention

5 Repetition

6 Transmission of the information

4 Organisation of the information

1 Interest and motivation

5 Repetition

Language

6

A set of closely linked systems

We all know the word 'picture'. But what does it mean to know a word? When we hear a word we can recognise it, whether it is spoken by a man, woman or child, whether it is said quickly or slowly, or with or without an accent.

The complexity of language

This ability to recognise a spoken word relies on the brain's auditory system and in particular on an area that specialises in analysing speech, which is located at the top of the left temporal lobe. Similarly, when we see a written word, we can also recognise it instantly. Recognition of letters resides in a completely different area belonging to the brain's visual system, which is located under the left occipital and temporal lobes. And we are also familiar with the spelling of words we see – for example, we know that the sound 'r' is written 'are', and this allows us to either read or write it. Experts don't know for sure which part of the brain houses spelling knowledge, but the front part of the temporal lobe and the lower part of the parietal lobe are good candidates.

We know how to articulate the word 'picture' and how to write the letters that comprise it, and this know-how, this motor skill, is based on the practice that our motor cortex has had during childhood. And lastly, we know some more abstract things about this word, things that don't depend on its spoken or written form – for example, its meaning, that it is a common noun, and that it evokes a certain type of memories. The meanings and the memories are themselves dispersed in various areas of the brain.

This analysis is a good illustration of the fact that language resides not in one single area of the brain, but in a number of closely linked systems, some of which specialise in the spoken, heard, read or written language.

Finding that elusive word

The difficulty of bringing a word to mind has been the subject of scientific studies that have examined the organisation of both memory and language. Just as brain damage can help us to understand a process that is lacking, these mental blocks show that language is not a homogenous and direct process, and that it calls on competencies that are distinct, even independent of one another. We want to say a word, we know exactly what it means, we could pick it out from other words, but we can't manage to retrieve its auditory form from our mental lexicon. Generally we know if it's short or long, and we often know the first syllable and can quote words that sound like it. With names of people, we can clearly visualise the person (such as a singer or an actor), we can talk about them (she was in such and such a film, she's the sister of so and so), but we are stumped when it comes to the name itself. When researchers want to study this state without waiting for it to occur spontaneously, they try to provoke it by subjecting people to the 'reverse dictionary game'. How many of the following definitions give you a sense of frustration when you can't find the word?

1. Describes a transgression that is not seriously wrong and can be pardoned.
....

2. The support for an artist's canvas while it is being worked on.
....

3. A group of birds.
....

4. The state of a person who is no longer hungry.
....

5. A beam that spans the opening over a door or window.
....

6. To place one person far above others.
....

7. Describes an area with dwellings.
....

8. A person employed to write what another dictates.
....

9. Behaviour or speech that is very instructive and/or promotes piety and virtue.
....

10. A tendency to form groups, or to model one's behaviour on others.
....

Possible answers: 1. venial. **2.** easel. **3.** flock. **4.** satiated. **5.** lintel. **6.** exalt. **7.** residential. **8.** amanuensis. **9.** edifying. **10.** gregariousness.

The study of language

Ancient Egyptian papyruses mention people with language difficulties linked to brain damage. But the scientific study of such problems began only in the middle of the nineteenth century, based on the relationships between brain damage and well-defined cognitive problems.

The great discoveries

Around 1860, French neurologist Paul Broca described the now-famous case of a patient who had lost the capacity to produce words, even though he understood perfectly well what was being said to him and his intelligence seemed intact. When this patient died, Broca carried out an autopsy and established a link between speech loss and damage affecting a specific area of the left frontal lobe, which has since become known as Broca's area (see also page 13).

Through the following decades, the picture became far more complex. Observation of many other patients indicated that on one hand language problems, known as aphasias, could be extremely varied, and on the other hand the brain damage causing them could affect a number of different areas generally situated in the left hemisphere, well beyond Broca's area. For example, in Wernicke's aphasia (originally described by Polish neurologist Karl Wernicke), unlike the kind of aphasia identified by Broca, enormous problems with understanding language are the result of damage in the left temporal lobe.

Paul Broca (1824–80)
This French neurologist was also the founder of modern brain surgery and anthropology.

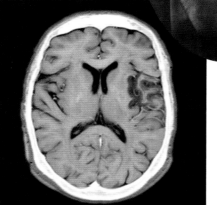

Brain damage
This MRI shows brain damage (blue) resulting from a stroke affecting Broca's area.

Functional imaging

One and a half centuries later, it is still largely unknown how the different regions of the brain involved in language operate and what roles they play. Over the last 20 years, the study of aphasic patients has been partially replaced by the development of functional brain imaging, which allows different cerebral areas to be seen as they become activated when a patient speaks.

Nevertheless, studying patients themselves is still an irreplaceable source of information. Very selective breakdowns in language reveal the finer points of its operation, as the following two cases demonstrate. When one patient speaks, he replaces vowels with other vowels, saying, for example,

'CORIMEL' instead of 'CARAMEL'.

Another patient makes mistakes only with consonants,

saying 'DARAFEL' instead of 'CARAMEL'.
These examples indicate that as speech is programmed the neural mechanisms that select vowels and consonants are quite separate. More generally, these cases illustrate how complex the machinery of language is and how varied aphasic problems can be.

Areas of the brain involved in language

Language mobilises a major part of the left hemisphere, which is dominant for language in more than 90 per cent of right-handed people and in about 70 per cent of left-handed people. Between the development of an idea and its verbal or written expression, many areas of the brain are activated in a few hundred milliseconds, forming a complex network that produces a seemingly simple, easy and spontaneous result. The same applies to reading and listening, which also involve a series of specific mental operations.

The diversity of types of aphasia show not only that specialised structures are allocated to particular language functions, but also that these structures are interconnected – so very different kinds of damage can produce similar problems with language.

THE BRAIN AND LANGUAGE

Prefrontal cortex This region is not involved in the elementary mechanics of language, but it is essential for the organisation of ideas and reasoning, and therefore for planning speech.

Broca's area This area supervises the motor aspect of language: that is, the articulation of words, and so the fluency of speech. The instructions for the articulatory movements that need to be made are sent to the motor cortex, which more directly commands the muscles of the organs that produce speech.

Motor cortex The motor area of the muscles producing sound (the tongue, pharynx and larynx) is activated when we speak. The motor area that controls the dominant hand is activated when we write.

Arcuate fasciculus These are the fibres linking Wernicke's area with Broca's area.

Visual cortex Part of the visual cortex specialises in the recognition of letters, regardless of how they are written (such as lower case letters, capital letters, calligraphy or different typefaces).

Wernicke's area This area is essential for understanding language. It also allows us to choose words according to their meaning and to organise our sentences correctly when we are speaking.

Thalamus In the depths of the left hemisphere, the thalamus coordinates the different areas of language in the cortex. There is no doubt that this role is considerable, as shown by the aphasias that can result from damage to the thalamus, but it is not well understood.

Auditory cortex Part of the auditory cortex in the left hemisphere allows us to recognise the sounds of language (human speech).

The role of the right hemisphere

In most individuals, the literal meaning of words is processed by the brain's left hemisphere, while the implicit content – such as irony, a deeper meaning, humour, metaphors and intonation – is managed by the right hemisphere.

Language problems

Depending on which areas are affected, brain damage can cause problems involving oral expression and comprehension, reading or writing that may or may not be specific. Among the extreme examples of specific problems are: pure word deafness, where patients hear speech only as a series of unintelligible sounds, even though they themselves speak normally; pure alexia, which makes reading impossible, while all the other aspects of language are preserved; or agraphia, which affects how letters are written.

Other disorders concern the most abstract aspects of language like grammar or the meaning of words.

These disorders generally affect the spoken, read, written or heard language alike. With semantic dementia (a degenerative affliction of the temporal lobes), patients progressively lose their understanding of what words mean, and this manifests itself when they try to understand or produce words in their spoken or written form. Another example involves so-called ungrammatical patients who remain capable of producing and understanding isolated words, but who can no longer combine them to form sentences. In most cases, this deficit in an abstract aspect of language affects both spoken and written language, and both its comprehension and production.

Learning another language

Comparative studies have shown that age is not a handicap when it comes to learning a foreign language. Children certainly learn faster and master the foreign sounds better, but adults have greater capacities, cultural baggage and a better knowledge of the world, so that their experience and acquired knowledge largely compensate for any shortcomings. Learning or perfecting a language is extremely beneficial for all of the cognitive functions.

● The areas in the left hemisphere that are linked to language are involved, but they are not the only ones. The right hemisphere is activated for the melody of the language, the hippocampus for the task of memorisation and the frontal cortex for concentration.

● Oral expression stimulates the motor areas of language by requiring new movements for articulation.

● Learning exercises several types of memory, especially working and semantic memories (see pages 102 and 106).

● Learning a new language calls for reasoning and intuition, when we have to reconstruct overall meaning based on a few words we have understood and a particular context. We also have to make an effort to adapt because the structure of each language is different.

● Lastly, this kind of learning presupposes the need or the desire to communicate. Both group courses and travel provide opportunities for us to increase our social contacts and to be open to other cultures.

Social benefits Travel overseas provides opportunities for practising another language and learning about a different culture. Here visitors explore part of the Great Wall of China.

A brain adapted for reading

Pure alexia is a reading problem in which the only way a person can read is by spelling out each letter. It is a consequence of brain damage affecting the underside of the left temporal lobe. In severe cases, alexic patients are incapable of recognising written words, and even letters, even though they can speak, understand and write normally.

A masterpiece of evolution

The example of pure alexia proves that there is a system in the adult brain specifically dedicated to reading, since its destruction affects only this aspect of language. It can't be innate, because the first alphabet was invented only 5000 years ago and at birth our brain is the same as that of our ancestors 20,000 years ago. In order to learn to read with a brain that is not designed for that purpose, we use primitive cerebral systems, which we adapt to this relatively recent know-how.

The first system that is called upon is the visual system. We have inherited a sophisticated visual system from our primate ancestors, and this allows us to recognise the objects around us and locate them in space. When we read a newspaper, we must recognise special kinds of objects, letters and words, and know how they are placed in relation to one another. So when children learn to read, they are training their visual system to recognise groups of letters efficiently. A child who is beginning to read must decipher the words letter by letter. But when adults look at words, they recognise all the letters simultaneously: reading a long word like 'caramel' doesn't take any more time than reading a short word like 'cafe'. This is valid for lower case or capital letters, and for different styles and sizes of writing.

The area devoted to reading

This remarkable expertise is housed in a small area of the cortex located in the underside of the temporal lobe of the left hemisphere, and when it is destroyed the result is pure alexia. This well-defined area belongs to the vast region of the cortex that is used for general recognition of the objects we see around us, but its neurons have been somewhat recycled in the course of learning to read. If it has taken charge of recognising letters, it is no doubt because, even before we learned to read, it specialised in the analysis of small shapes in the central visual field. For our ancestors, perhaps this area played an important role – for example, in identifying types of leaves or animal footprints on the ground.

But the visual system is not the only one that has been affected by reading. The way in which the brain manipulates language, including spoken language, is itself modified by learning to read. If, for example, you are asked to listen to some words and identify those containing the sound 'f', you might not react to the word 'phrase'. Because you know it contains the letters 'ph' and not the letter 'f', you might fail to realise that the letters 'ph' are in fact pronounced 'f'. When we read we have to learn that letter combinations such as 'ph', 'kn' and 'ps' are pronounced 'f', 'n' and 's', respectively.

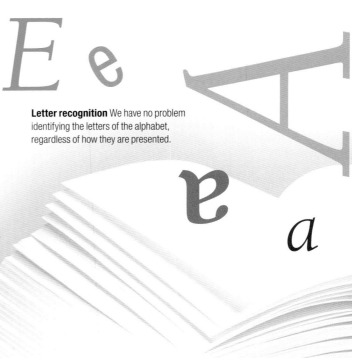

Letter recognition We have no problem identifying the letters of the alphabet, regardless of how they are presented.

How do we read?

We have precise vision only within a small angle of about two degrees from the point where our gaze is focused. Outside this angle, the clarity of our vision declines rapidly. We free ourselves of this constraint by constantly making our eyes jump from one point to another in rapid jerks. As we read, we move our eyes four or five times a second. Each time we focus, we see a 'window' that covers about 4 letters to the left and 14 letters to the right of the point of focus (since we read from left to right). In fact, we see only the 4 or 5 letters at the centre of this window really clearly. This relatively narrow vision obliges us to halt our gaze on almost all of the words in the text we are reading.

In general, our eyes focus on a point between the beginning and middle of the word, which is the optimal position for recognising the word in question. When we focus on a word, we are already gathering some information about the following words, which are imperfectly visible in the right part of our window of perception. In particular, we notice the blank spaces separating the words to come. This allows us to adjust the following jump forward so as to make it fall more or less on the optimal point of the word that follows. Anticipating in this way allows us to avoid focusing on words that are quite predictable and not very informative – like 'and' or 'which' – that we often pass over without stopping.

The system that controls the movement of our eyes during reading is closely associated with the language system that permanently analyses the words we perceive. This means that we spend less time focusing on a word if it's short and familiar, if it has regular spelling, if it's possible to predict its presence from the preceding words, and so on. A minority of our eye movements go backwards rather than forwards in the text we are reading. This happens when we encounter a difficulty or an ambiguity that obliges us to return and check a word we have already read.

Speed reading

The purpose of speed reading methods is to allow us to extract the meaning of a text by skimming it very quickly. The principle is to make ourselves reduce the number of times we focus so that, with practice, we can skim 600 words in one minute, compared with 250 words a minute in the course of normal reading. This means that a large proportion of the words are not read.

Critics of the method say that the time saved is at the expense of a detailed understanding of the text, because part of the information is necessarily ignored. Those who defend the method maintain that the contrary is true, basing their opinion on readers' answers to questions after normal or speed reading of a text: the speed reader understands and memorises just as well, but expends less effort on attention than the person reading normally.

You can make up your own mind by applying this method to different sorts of reading, such as professional documents, articles in encyclopaedias, essays, popular fiction and literature.

The influence of context

Knowing what words mean is not always enough to understand a text you read or hear. Often it's not possible to grasp the meaning of a message without interpreting and analysing the context.

● **Ambiguity** Expressions that have a double meaning throw some light on the importance of context, because the analysis carried out by the brain as we read sometimes prevents us from seeing their ambiguity. For example, the sentence 'John is painting my house' could mean that John is painting the house itself, or that he is painting a picture of the house. Similarly, the following sentences can be understood in two different ways: This minister married my sister; Include your children when baking cakes; Visiting relatives can be boring; Students hate annoying professors; Union demands increased unemployment.

● **Puns** Sometimes ambiguity can be used for humorous effect in a play on words, or a pun. If a word has two meanings and both of them can be read into a sentence in a meaningful way, then this can be entertaining, as shown in the following verse from a poem attributed to Edgar Allan Poe:

I'll tell you a plan for gaining wealth,
Better than banking, trade, or leases;
Take a bank-note and fold it across,
And then you will find your money IN-CREASES!

When we use a pun in speech, we can accompany it with a nudge or a wink to alert the listener to the double meaning. In writing, even if puns are not in capital letters as in this poem, they are at least placed at stressed or significant points in the text. Often a pun is the punch line of a joke.

● **Homographs** Many words, known as homographs, have the same spelling but different meanings. 'Port' can mean a suitcase, a harbour or an alcoholic drink. Each of these has a different etymology – 'port' meaning suitcase is short for portmanteau, while 'port' meaning a harbour is from the Latin *portus*, and 'port' meaning a drink is from the name of the Portuguese city Oporto. Usually context allows us to understand which meaning of 'port' is intended. Some words have many different meanings. The word 'set', for instance, has more than 100 meanings in the dictionary and yet we have no trouble understanding which meaning is required.

● **The context of time** Very occasionally we find a word whose meaning has changed so much over time that its new meaning is the complete opposite of its original meaning. An example of this is 'nice', which once meant 'foolish' (from the Latin *nescius*, 'not knowing', 'out of one's mind'), but which has come to mean 'pleasing'. In the sixteenth and seventeenth centuries, there was a period when it was difficult to know which meaning was intended. In cases like this, the language can't cope with the situation and one meaning becomes obsolete.

● **The priming effect** This effect, which also plays a role in activating the mechanisms of memory (see page 101), helps us to guess some words even before we have read them in their entirety. If the word 'birthday' is followed by 'pres-', for example, we immediately guess it is 'present' and not 'preserve'.

Eye drops off shelf

Red tape holds up new bridge

Milk drinkers are turning to powder

Vaccine may contain rabies

Kids make nutritious snacks

Funny lines Newspaper headlines need to put over a message in as few words as possible, but this makes them prone to ambiguity, which can often have a humorous effect, intended or not.

Your repertoire of words

Who would dare to boast that they know all the words in the English language? Even lexicographers are far from mastering all the words that appear in dictionaries, which range, according to publishers, from about 20,000 in junior dictionaries to 100,000 in general dictionaries and as many as half a million words in the complete *Oxford English Dictionary*.

Vocabulary

According to various investigations, the average person probably has a vocabulary of about 3000 basic words, up to 7000 day-to-day words, and up to 20,000 words when any special jargon, be it stamp collecting or nuclear physics, is included. This is just a rough estimate, but it highlights the gap between the richness of the English language and the number of words we use competently. And a distinction should also be made between active vocabulary and passive vocabulary (the terms whose meaning we know, but which we hardly ever use).

In 1930, a British linguist, Charles Kay Ogden, developed the concept of Basic English. This consisted of a limited vocabulary of 850 words that supposedly couldn't be replaced by other words. The concept was initially popular but the difficulties of working in such a system proved to be too great.

Educationalists have drawn up similar lists of basic vocabulary that children acquire by certain ages, beginning with about 50 words at the age of 18 months. Alongside this common general vocabulary, individuals develop their own lexical palette, influenced by their family context and the environment. Where one person will respond with 'of course', another will say 'certainly' or 'indeed' and yet another person will say 'cool' or 'wicked'. This individual use of language constitutes what linguists call an idiolect. Language is also the reflection of a historical and geographical context, of a particular vision of the world – for example, 'camel' has a dozen synonyms in Arabic, and the Inuits have a whole host of single terms to describe different types and states of snow.

Word associations

In 1998 two French researchers, Ludovic Ferrand and Xavier Alario, submitted a list of 366 words to 89 students. They asked the students to freely associate each word with the first word that came to mind. Below are some of the words that scored more than 60 per cent of identical pairs. Do the test yourself to see if you have the same word association references.

1. **Album** . . . .
2. **Racquet** . . . .
3. **Aquarium** . . . . .
4. **Hive** . . . .
5. **Nest** . . . .
6. **Umbrella** . . . . . .
7. **Scissors** . . . .
8. **Barrel** . . . .
9. **Electric switch** . . . .
10. **Lock** . . . .
11. **Lettuce** . . . .
12. **Cradle** . . . .
13. **Tap** . . . .
14. **Paintbrush** . . . . .
15. **Vase** . . . .
16. **Alligator** . . . .
17. **Giraffe** . . . .

Answers
1. Photograph. 2. Tennis. 3. Fish. 4. Bee. 5. Bird. 6. Rain. 7. Cut. 8. Wine.
9. Light. 10. Key. 11. Salad. 12. Baby. 13. Water. 14. Paint. 15. Flowers.
16. Crocodile. 17. Neck.

When snow is not just snow The Inuits distinguish a snowflake (*qanuk*) from the fine particles of snow and ice combined (*kanewluk*); a light snow fall (*muruaneq*) from a snow storm (*pirta*); or freshly fallen snow on the ground (*nutaryuk*) from snow that has been lying there for a longer period (*qanikcaq*) or snow that is about to melt (*navcaq*).

How rich is your vocabulary?

Banal, capacious, indigent, lucid, vociferous – these words belong to the average vocabulary of anyone who has completed their secondary schooling. Do you use these sorts of words regularly, or do you prefer more general terms?

Five by five

Rearrange each of the two sets of letters below to make five words for each.

Each word must use all five letters.
Proper nouns are not allowed.
Plurals are allowed.

A E M T S   E I N R S

1. ....   1. ....
2. ....   2. ....
3. ....   3. ....
4. ....   4. ....
5. ....   5. ....

Synonyms

For each adjective in the list on the left, find a synonym (a word with a similar meaning) from the less common words in the list on the right.

1. cheery	a. amiable
2. clear	b. banal
3. dull	c. cantankerous
4. enthusiastic	d. capacious
5. foolish	e. ebullient
6. forbidden	f. fallacious
7. friendly	g. fatuous
8. grumpy	h. hapless
9. misleading	i. illicit
10. noisy	j. indigent
11. poor	k. intransigent
12. spacious	l. lucid
13. stubborn	m. nefarious
14. wicked	n. sanguine
15. unlucky	o. vociferous

What's that word?

We often use words like 'thingo', 'whatsit' and 'thingummyjig' when we can't find, or perhaps don't want to use, the right word. In the following sentences, replace each of the nonsense terms with the correct word to make a well-known expression (the meaning is given in brackets).

1. She just doesn't cut the **whatsy**. (She doesn't have the necessary ability.)
....

2. It was like the **what-d'ye-call-its** of Hercules. (Feats that are so difficult they seem impossible.)
....

3. He is a take no **dooverlackies** kind of man. (He has an overly aggressive attitude.)
....

4. She was as cool as a **thingummyjig**. (She was calm and confident.)
....

5. He is one card short of a full **what-d'ye-m'-call-it**. (He is mad or eccentric.)
....

6. Take that with a grain of **thingo**. (Have some reservations about believing that.)
....

7. Don't try to pull the **whatsit** over my eyes. (Don't try to deceive me.)
....

8. He let the **thingummy** out of the bag when he mentioned the surprise party. (He inadvertently revealed a secret.)
....

Bric-a-brac

This apparently simple game tests the richness of your vocabulary. You must think of as many words as you can that start with a given letter – but the exercise is not as easy as it appears.

A person names one of the 26 letters of the alphabet (B for example), and finds a word starting with that letter (such as bric-a-brac). The next person (progressing clockwise) finds another word (such as baseball), the next person finds another word, and so on. Proper names and conjugated verb forms (such as 'is', 'are', 'was' and 'were', which are all forms of 'am') are not allowed. A player who suggests a word that has already been said is eliminated. After a few rounds, you can limit the time taken for each round by using an hourglass or a stopwatch.

Crossword

Crosswords are an excellent way to build up your personal word bank. Test both your vocabulary and your general knowledge with this straightforward puzzle.

Across

1. Impose on another's generosity; scrounge
7. Allay or moderate; make less severe
8. Spirited public debate or knight's combat
10. Go beyond (a limit); infringe
12. Jubilant, triumphant
14. Burden, blame or responsibility
16. Sharp instruments for piercing small holes in leather
17. Symbol or figure used to represent a word
20. Deceptive, misleading
23. Fundamental and distinctive character or spirit
24. Freed from guilt or blame; exonerated
25. Molten material beneath Earth's crust from which igneous rock is formed

Down

1. Coax or persuade by flattery
2. Central or essential part of something
3. Seek favour by servile behaviour
4. Mournful song or poem in memory of the dead
5. Spectacular display; pomp; ostentation
6. Robberies
9. Lacking freshness or effectiveness through constant use or repetition; hackneyed
11. Free from deceit or cunning; artless
13. Term used to indicate the maiden name of a married woman
15. Feeling of irritation or resentment; vexation
16. Noisy public quarrel or disturbance; fracas
18. Dangerous or foreboding atmosphere
19. Section of wall between two sloping roofs
21. Mountain goat with long curved horns
22. In ancient Greek architecture, a long, covered colonnade

Use your imagination

Make up a sentence for each of the following sets of letters. Each word in the sentence must begin with the given letter. Proper names are allowed.

1. S.......... r.......... l.......... t.......... w..........

2. E.......... l.......... f.......... t.......... s..........

3. C.......... b.......... s.......... m..........

4. T.......... m.......... s.......... b..........

Answers

Five by five 1. mates, meats, steam, tames, teams. **2.** reins, resin, rinse, risen, siren.
Synonyms 1. cheery/sanguine. **2.** clear/lucid. **3.** dull/banal. **4.** enthusiastic/ebullient. **5.** foolish/fatuous. **6.** forbidden/illicit. **7.** friendly/amiable. **8.** grumpy/cantankerous. **9.** misleading/fallacious. **10.** noisy/vociferous. **11.** poor/indigent. **12.** spacious/capacious. **13.** stubborn/intransigent. **14.** wicked/nefarious. **15.** unlucky/hapless.
What's that word? 1. mustard. **2.** labours. **3.** prisoners. **4.** cucumber. **5.** deck. **6.** salt. **7.** wool. **8.** cat.
Crossword Across: 1. cadge. **7.** palliate. **8.** joust. **10.** transgress. **12.** exultant. **14.** onus. **16.** awls. **17.** lexigram. **20.** fallacious. **23.** ethos. **24.** absolved. **25.** magma. **Down: 1.** cajole. **2.** gist. **3.** fawn. **4.** elegy. **5.** pageantry. **6.** heists. **9.** rite. **11.** guileless. **13.** nee. **15.** pique. **16.** affray. **18.** miasma. **19.** gable. **21.** ibex. **22.** stoa.
Use your imagination Many sentences are possible; here are some examples:
1. She runs like the wind; Secret rivers loop through woodlands; Some rabbits left the warren. **2.** Everyone looks forward to spring; Ellie listened for the signal; Each lighthouse faces the sea. **3.** Chasing birds seems mean; Cooks brought steaming minestrone; Can Ben see me? **4.** The moon shines brightly; Time marches swiftly by; Tom munched sweet biscuits.

Enriching your vocabulary

A language is learned by immersion and imitation. As young children are plunged into a sea of words and lulled by the speech of those who nourish and protect them, they acquire a linguistic stock, which is then developed when they go to school.

From passive to active

In adulthood, our linguistic environment varies according to the path that each of us chooses. But it's always possible, particularly through reading, to enrich and refine our capacity for self-expression and to resist the lowest common denominator, which consists of favouring the words that everyone uses and immediately understands. If reading enriches our vocabulary, this is not so much the result of learning new words as of being steeped in a stock of words that we already know, but which is broader than the vocabulary we normally use. We rarely interrupt our reading to look up a word in the dictionary because the context is often sufficient to grasp the general meaning. On the other hand, by regularly reading well-written texts, we mobilise our passive vocabulary, which becomes more familiar: we move it from the status of a dormant stock to that of an active vocabulary.

The benefits of writing

When one writer was asked about his style and choice of words, he explained that he systematically rejected the first word that came into his head and picked another that was not necessarily a rare word, but was a little more carefully chosen or precise – for example, 'roadway' instead of 'road', 'fabric' instead of 'material', 'throng' instead of 'crowd', 'fleeting' instead of 'passing', 'festive' instead of 'colourful', 'courtesy' instead of 'politeness', 'conceal' instead of 'hide', 'request' instead of 'ask' and 'alarm' instead of 'fear'. This method may produce writing that is a little pretentious, but it is also a concrete way to mobilise passive vocabulary.

Writing obliges us to call on all our lexical resources: rereading what we have written with a critical eye, correcting it, thinking about words to find the right one, or looking for synonyms to avoid repetition. And as far as writing is concerned, the effects of practice are very noticeable: the more we write, the better we write, and the faster we write too.

Learning new words

Educational practice seems to go through cycles in which children's acquisition of vocabulary by learning lists of words comes in and out of fashion. To fix words in a child's memory, they must be activated outside school, otherwise they will be progressively forgotten like a lot of useless trinkets. Motivation is crucial in learning. When the enthusiasm for dinosaurs in children's literature was at its peak, young children could list a surprising number of long and complicated dinosaur names that their teachers wouldn't have attempted to teach them.

Why shouldn't we do the same? Every day, choose a word or expression from the dictionary. Avoid terms that are very rare or highly specialised and that would be impossible to put into use in everyday life. Instead, choose words whose meaning you already vaguely know, at least in the context of a sentence, but that you don't use spontaneously. Then force yourself, even if it seems a little artificial at first, to integrate them into your everyday vocabulary so as to fix them in your mind. Don't hope to retain them all: some of them will resist your efforts, but others will gradually become part of your personal lexicon and you'll be surprised to hear yourself using them with ease and spontaneity.

Using a dictionary

When we stumble over an unknown word, the most common and efficient reflex is to consult a dictionary. Whether the dictionary is general or specialised, it makes it possible to understand a word in all its accepted meanings. Examples illustrate the various common usages and put the different meanings into a context. Knowing the word's etymology is especially useful. Deconstructing a word to understand its origin and sometimes also knowing the context in which it first appeared make the word easier to remember.

Write without making mistakes

We learn certain rules in spelling, such as 'i after e, but not after c' and dropping a final 'e' before adding '-ing'. Equally important in spelling is our visual memory, which allows us to recognise the appearance of words or to know the correct way to write unknown words by analogy with known words. So we're more likely to write 'analgesic' than 'analgesick', because we are familiar with other words ending in '-ic'.

Spelling lesson

Look carefully at the following words. Eleven of them are spelt incorrectly. Can you find and correct them?

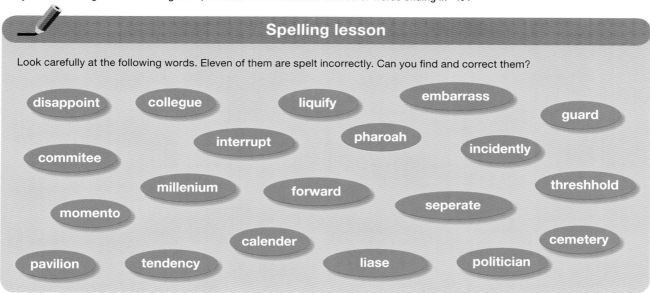

disappoint   collegue   liquify   embarrass   guard

interrupt   pharoah   incidently

commitee

millenium   forward   threshhold

momento   seperate

calender   cemetery

pavilion   tendency   liase   politician

Do they agree?

In English, certain words in each sentence have to agree in number with each other. This means that the ending of the word, or sometimes its whole form, must match.

Look at the following sentences and choose the correct word.

1. One of the teaspoons seem/seems to be missing.

2. The committee reached its/their decision.

3. A number of its members is/are not happy with the outcome.

4. Most of the audience is/are female.

5. The crowd shouted its/their approval.

6. Ten years is/are a long time.

7. Where is/are my hat?

8. Where is/are my gloves?

9. Both Nina and her sister Ann play/plays for our team.

10. The result of the election was/were not known for three days.

11. Everyone in the choir was/were present.

12. All the singers was/were in the room.

Reverse dictation

Find the 15 mistakes in this text.

The epitarths on Roman tombstones were addresed to passer-bys. One from the 2nd century BC describes the qualitys of a Roman dutyful wife: 'This is the tomb of a lovley women. Her parent's named her Claudia. She loved her husband with all her heart. She beared two sons; one she leaves hear on earth, the other she have already placed under it. She was charming in speach, yet pleasent and proper in manor. She managed the house well and span wool.'

Word power

1. probity is:
- [ ] **a.** procedure
- [ ] **b.** honesty
- [ ] **c.** self-righteousness

2. credo is:
- [ ] **a.** obsession
- [ ] **b.** system of principles or beliefs
- [ ] **c.** trustworthiness

3. ethic is:
- [ ] **a.** standard of behaviour
- [ ] **b.** precision
- [ ] **c.** reliability

4. prevarication is:
- [ ] **a.** scarring or marking
- [ ] **b.** building method
- [ ] **c.** being evasive or deliberately unclear

5. procrastination is:
- [ ] **a.** deferring to a later time
- [ ] **b.** desire to have children
- [ ] **c.** prediction

6. inference is:
- [ ] **a.** accusation
- [ ] **b.** reasoned conclusion
- [ ] **c.** representation

7. impasse is:
- [ ] **a.** stalemate
- [ ] **b.** impractical condition
- [ ] **c.** confrontation

8. anomaly is:
- [ ] **a.** unnamed quality
- [ ] **b.** likeness
- [ ] **c.** abnormality

The right word

In each of the following sentences, a word is used incorrectly. Replace it with the appropriate term, which is often very close in sound to the term given.

1. The soft music had a very soothing affect. ....

2. He brought some bread at the corner shop. ....

3. We rowed our dingy all the way across the river. ....

4. Crowds gathered to watch the stars arrive at the movie premier. ....

5. Go fourth and conquer the world. ....

6. A weather vein shows the direction of the wind. ....

7. Your invited to our party. ....

8. I don't know wether to stay or go. ....

9. It was hard to except that our dream had failed. ....

10. The kite was born away by a strong gust of wind. ....

11. The company perpetuated a fraud against the bank. ....

12. The security light is activated by a censor. ....

A more elegant word

Replace the common verbs 'to do', 'to put' and 'to have' with another verb that is more precise or more elegant.

1. On our last holidays we **did** the south of Italy. ....

2. He **put** on five kilos in three months. ....

3. Who **did** that picture? ....

4. I **had** a lot of trouble with that yesterday. ....

5. This restaurant **has** an excellent reputation. ....

6. Have you **done** the invoices yet? ....

7. Please **put** used towels in the basket. ....

8. I won't **have** it, I tell you! ....

9. **Put** the milk in now. ....

10. Each of these boxes **has** something inside. ....

Answers
Word power 1. b. **2.** b. **3.** a. **4.** c. **5.** a. **6.** b. **7.** a. **8.** c.
The right word 1. effect. **2.** bought. **3.** dinghy. **4.** premiere. **5.** forth. **6.** vane. **7.** you're. **8.** whether. **9.** accept. **10.** borne. **11.** perpetrated. **12.** sensor.
A more elegant word (other choices are possible) **1.** visited, toured, explored. **2.** gained. **3.** created, painted, drew. **4.** encountered, experienced, faced. **5.** enjoys, boasts. **6.** prepared, generated, finished. **7.** place, throw, leave. **8.** tolerate, condone. **9.** add, mix, pour. **10.** contains, holds.

Language is a living thing

We don't all express ourselves in the same way. What is a footpath in Australia, New Zealand and India is a pavement in Britain and South Africa, a sidewalk in North America and a footway in engineering jargon. Geography, social group, generation and professional environment all influence the language we use. Jargon in different occupations, sports or hobbies allows us to appreciate through language the richness and complexity of our world, and the subtlety of expertise of which we have only superficial knowledge.

Are changes in language of concern?

'Nowadays, people don't speak as well as they used to.' We often hear statements like this, but they are purely intuitive and are often based on the mistaken belief that language is something stable, and that there is a perfect point of balance, a golden age, which people generally situate in their own youth. But language is a living thing that is spoken and written by a multitude of individuals. The way we use words is influenced by changes in modern life and leads to permanent changes in language: some words disappear while others are established through frequent use, whether they are invented words (neologisms) or words borrowed from other languages.

To avoid either falling victim to the 'it was much better before' syndrome, or blindly and systematically praising the ability of vocabulary to adapt, it is realistic to accept that language is subject to processes that both enrich and diminish it. Words, expressions and some verb tenses will disappear from common usage, but other, new terms will be adopted, which in their turn will make it possible for us to make subtle distinctions or to express feelings and opinions more specifically.

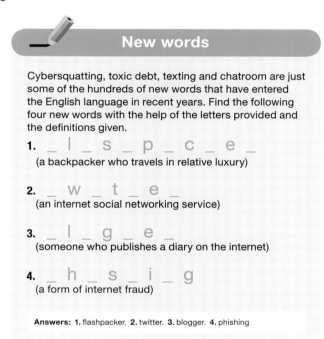

New words

Cybersquatting, toxic debt, texting and chatroom are just some of the hundreds of new words that have entered the English language in recent years. Find the following four new words with the help of the letters provided and the definitions given.

1. _ l _ s _ p _ c _ e _
(a backpacker who travels in relative luxury)

2. _ w _ t _ e _
(an internet social networking service)

3. _ l _ g _ e _
(someone who publishes a diary on the internet)

4. _ h _ s _ i _ g
(a form of internet fraud)

Answers: 1. flashpacker. **2.** twitter. **3.** blogger. **4.** phishing

---

Nautical language

The vocabulary of sailors is very different from the words we use on land, even for common items such as bed (berth), bedroom (cabin), sleeping area (quarters), floor (deck), ceiling (overhead), left side (port), right side (starboard), front of the ship (bow) and rear (stern). Sailors swab the decks (mop the floors), stow (put away) equipment, and let go (drop) or weigh (bring up) the anchor, while a line is any length of rope, but a halyard is the rope or wire used to hoist and lower a sail. It's a ship, not a boat, but sailors in the navy call submarines boats and refer to submariners as boat people. And each nautical tradition, be it the navy, merchant navy or yachting, has its own specialist terms as well. Some of our everyday expressions have come directly from the language of sailors, many dating back to life on board ship in Nelson's day – for example, 'hand over fist' (the correct way of pulling on a rope), 'to know the ropes' (to understand all the different ropes and their uses), 'to toe the line' (when sailors gathered for food or pay each had to step forward to a line on the deck), 'to sail close to the wind' (to proceed with the sails in a position where a single gust of wind might blow the vessel over), and 'under the weather' (originally alluding to seasickness).

Do you understand your doctor?

Some doctors don't appreciate patients using their professional jargon. And yet, if there is one area where it's important to understand each other and to be able to communicate without being intimidated or feeling excluded, it is in the area of health. It's impossible to learn all the medical terms, but we can easily memorise the most common ones.

True or false?

1. Aetiology
is the study of diseases that can be transmitted from animals to humans.

True ☐ False ☐

2. An idiopathic illness
is an illness whose cause is unknown.

☐ ☐

3. Physiology
is the study of how the human body functions.

☐ ☐

4. A syndrome
is an illness that appears suddenly.

☐ ☐

5. A somatic illness
is an illness that is linked to the mind.

True ☐ False ☐

6. A clinical examination
is an examination carried out in a laboratory, a medical imaging centre, a clinic or a hospital.

☐ ☐

7. A conservative treatment
is a treatment that is continued from one consultation to the next.

☐ ☐

8. A prophylactic treatment
is a preventive treatment.

☐ ☐

Specialists and specialisations

Match each specialisation with its corresponding definition.

a. **Oncology**

b. **Stomatology**

c. **Orthoptics**

d. **Endocrinology**

e. **Urology**

f. **Angiology**

g. **Nephrology**

1. Study and treatment of diseases of the kidneys
2. Study of the blood vessels
3. Treatment of diseases of the mouth and teeth
4. Study of tumours
5. Treatment of abnormalities in the function of the eye muscles
6. Study and treatment of diseases of the urinary tract
7. Study of the glands that secrete hormones, such as the thyroid gland

Multiple choice

Choose the correct answer.

1. Fever, cough and diarrhoea are:

☐ a. symptoms
☐ b. illnesses

2. Difficulty swallowing is:

☐ a. dysuria
☐ b. dysphagia

3. A loss of smell is:

☐ a. anosmia
☐ b. anoxia

4. The substance in the cavities of bones is:

☐ a. bone marrow
☐ b. spinal cord

5. Red cells are:

☐ a. erythrocytes
☐ b. leucocytes

Answers: True or false 1. False. Aetiology is the study of causes of diseases. **2.** True. **3.** True. **4.** False. A syndrome is a pattern or set of symptoms that occur together. **5.** False. Somatic means 'relating to the body'; a psychosomatic illness is one in which a physical disorder is caused or strongly influenced by the emotional state of the patient. **6.** False. A clinical examination is the physical examination conducted by a doctor during the consultation after enquiring about medical history and symptoms. The doctor may advise additional tests; these may be carried out in a laboratory. **7.** False. A conservative treatment is a treatment that does not require surgical intervention, such as the removal of all or part of an organ. **8.** True. **Specialists and specialisations** a. 4. b. 3. c. 5. d. 7. e. 6. f. 2. g. 1. **Multiple choice 1.** a. A symptomatic treatment treats the symptoms of a disease and not its cause. **2.** b. Dysuria is difficulty urinating. **3.** a. Anoxia is a decrease in the quantity of oxygen in the blood. **4.** a. The spinal cord is located within the spinal canal. **5.** a. Leucocytes are a type of white blood cell.

The power of words

Like gestures, words can be the bearers of many different emotions, ranging from the violent to the gentle and bringing laughter, fear or comfort. They can also be used to manipulate people in the form of advertisements, speeches or political slogans that are capable of influencing desires, thoughts and actions.

Magical words

The work of Sigmund Freud has highlighted the very strong healing capacity of words – a quality with which confessors or shamans were already familiar from experience. In the practice of psychotherapy and psychoanalysis, words are decisive. A patient can bring personal troubles out into the open by talking about them, and the therapist evaluates the impact of the problem. In this way, the therapist legitimises the patient's experience and – as a result of this re-evaluation mediated by words – the individual becomes fully aware of her or his situation and can accept and deal with it successfully.

Words can also seduce, intoxicate and exalt. The practice of writing love letters has had a long history, but in its current metamorphosis onto the internet it has taken a cyber-twist. Words have shown themselves to be very powerful indeed. There are many stories of people who have 'met' online and fallen in love through emails, only to find that when they meet in real life things are not quite the same.

Where words reach their full potential is in poetry. Caught up in the music of the poem, ordinary words reveal all their beauty and power of expression. Poets who bring the words together draw them from deep within their memory,

sensitivity and creativity. And it is striking that it is to these words of poetry that people in extreme situations have turned when they instinctively felt the need to hang on to a vestige of humanity. Primo Levi and Eugenia Ginzburg, who were deported to Nazi and Soviet camps respectively, have each related how calling on their memory and reciting poems to themselves or their fellow prisoners helped them to resist the dehumanising treatment that they received from their persecutors and under the concentration camp system.

Political speeches

When we listen to a politician speaking without paying strict attention to the words, our opinion tends to be influenced not by the quality of the arguments presented but rather by the following observations:

● The longer the speech, the more credible it is.
● She is an expert, so she must be right.
● The more arguments there are, the truer the message.
● If everyone applauds, it's because it's good.
● Attractive people are more credible than others.
● If she talks without pausing to catch her breath, she knows what she is talking about and she is a master of her subject.
● Her expression shows that she is convinced by what she says, so she must be right.

Reading, an art of living

If you've got out of the habit of reading and you want to take it up again, you initially need to have a little willpower – you need to read regularly to gain benefits and enjoy it.

Reading is something that you choose to do, a time that you decide to give yourself. Once you can successfully set aside the time, you are completely free to decide how to proceed. You can start a book but not finish it because you don't like it; you can read two or three books at the same time, switching between them as the mood takes you; you can read a book slowly or keep turning page after page until you reach the end; you can share your enthusiasm and your disappointment with others in reading groups and book clubs; you can jump from one book to another and explore different works by the same author, or work your way through the bibliography of a subject that you want to know more about; you can scan the shelves in libraries or bookshops to discover new horizons, and so on. Reading is an art of living, a time to stand back and give yourself space. And some books can stay with you all through your life because they transform you, shed light on who you are and bring you renewed pleasure and riches each time you read them.

Once upon a time...

Can you work out the title of each well-known work from these first sentences? (Hint: if your intuition fails you or it's taking you a while to remember, the list of works at the bottom of the page may be of help.)

1. Somewhere in La Mancha, in a place whose name I do not care to remember, a gentleman lived not long ago, one of those who has a lance and ancient shield on a shelf and keeps a skinny nag and a greyhound for racing.

   ....

2. Call me Ishmael.

   ....

3. It was the best of times, it was the worst of times, it was the age of wisdom, it was the age of foolishness, it was the epoch of belief, it was the epoch of incredulity, it was the season of Light, it was the season of Darkness, it was the spring of hope, it was the winter of despair, we had everything before us, we had nothing before us, we were all going direct to Heaven, we were all going direct the other way – in short, the period was so far like the present period, that some of its noisiest authorities insisted on its being received, for good or for evil, in the superlative degree of comparison only.

   ....

4. Far out in the uncharted backwaters of the unfashionable end of the Western Spiral arm of the Galaxy lies a small unregarded yellow sun.

   ....

Moby Dick

The Wonderful Wizard of Oz

Anna Karenina

Peter Pan

The Bible

Alice's Adventures in Wonderland

The Stranger

5. Alice was beginning to get very tired of sitting by her sister on the bank, and of having nothing to do: once or twice she had peeped into the book her sister was reading, but it had no pictures or conversations in it, 'and what is the use of a book,' thought Alice, 'without pictures or conversation?'

....

6. It was a bright cold day in April, and the clocks were striking thirteen.

....

7. Two households, both alike in dignity,/In fair Verona, where we lay our scene,/From ancient grudge break to new mutiny,/Where civil blood makes civil hands unclean.

....

8. Once there were four children whose names were Peter, Susan, Edmund and Lucy.

....

9. In the beginning God created the heaven and the earth.

....

10. Mr and Mrs Dursley, of number four, Privet Drive, were proud to say that they were perfectly normal, thank you very much.

....

11. Happy families are all alike; every unhappy family is unhappy in its own way.

....

12. There is a lovely road that runs from Ixopo into the hills. These hills are grass-covered and rolling, and they are lovely beyond any singing of it.

....

13. All children, except one, grow up.

....

14. Mother died today.

....

15. Dorothy lived in the midst of the great Kansas prairies, with Uncle Henry, who was a farmer, and Aunt Em, who was the farmer's wife.

....

Don Quixote

The Lion, the Witch and the Wardrobe

Romeo and Juliet

Nineteen Eighty-Four

The Hitchhiker's Guide to the Galaxy

A Tale of Two Cities

Cry, the Beloved Country

Harry Potter and the Philosopher's Stone

Answers: 1. *Don Quixote*, Miguel de Cervantes. **2.** *Moby Dick*, Herman Melville. **3.** *A Tale of Two Cities*, Charles Dickens. **4.** *The Hitchhiker's Guide to the Galaxy*, Douglas Adams. **5.** *Alice's Adventures in Wonderland*, Lewis Carroll. **6.** *Nineteen Eighty-Four*, George Orwell. **7.** *Romeo and Juliet*, William Shakespeare. **8.** *The Lion, the Witch and the Wardrobe*, CS Lewis. **9.** The Bible. **10.** *Harry Potter and the Philosopher's Stone*, JK Rowling. **11.** *Anna Karenina*, Leo Tolstoy. **12.** *Cry, the Beloved Country*, Alan Paton. **13.** *Peter Pan*, JM Barrie. **14.** *The Stranger*, Albert Camus. **15.** *The Wonderful Wizard of Oz*, L Frank Baum.

Spatial skills

7

Don't lose your bearings!

Having a sense of direction means quickly finding your way in an unfamiliar environment. It means being able to return to a starting point after changing direction a number of times and without using a map. This ability is based on a geometric perception of space and an ability to remember where places are when they are no longer in the field of vision.

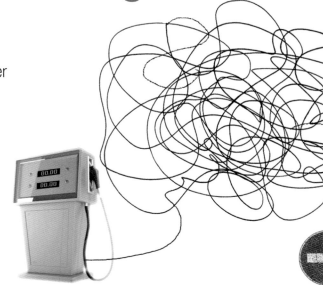

Spatial memory

We don't think about the route to take when we go out to do the shopping because the brain can remember spatial relationships between a number of reference points. A detailed image of the streets we go along every day is stored in our mind. On a larger scale, we know the locations of major buildings in our home town or how to get to the place where we usually spend our holidays. Basically, spatial memory saves us a considerable amount of time and shows that we have adapted to our environment.

How do we find the place where we parked the car? Two strategies can be used, separately or together, with varying degrees of success, depending on the individual. We can work out the way back to the car by remembering the different streets we took (such as, 'I turned left here, then went straight ahead'). But usually we combine recall of the route travelled with events or encounters ('That was where I saw a cat') and reference points along the way. This route memory, then, is mainly kinaesthetic memory, or memory related to movements (see page 20). It is reinforced by visual memory as well as episodic memory, which stores the sequence of experiences.

A mental map

Some people have developed a strategy known as mapping memory and can grasp the overall layout of places, producing a kind of map which they then review in their mind to choose a route, which could be different from the original one. Mapping memory is based on the relative positions of reference points, regardless of the position of the observer – a strategy that is called allocentric. In contrast, route memory is based on the area around the observer and is said to be egocentric.

Research in the field of neurophysiology has shown that many parts of the brain, mainly on the right side, are involved in these two types of memory. Some are used for the two types, while others function with one or the other. Brain imaging has shown that route memory activates networks of neurons in the parietal and frontal lobes, whereas mapping memory triggers networks in the right hippocampus. It has also been reported that damage to this area of the brain causes substantial loss of spatial memory, and that damage to the parietal cortex can be responsible for the curious syndrome of unilateral spatial neglect, a disorder in which the patient is unaware of articles to the left of the body. People affected by this condition may, for example, shave only the right side of the face or eat only half of what is on their plate.

Mental GPS To find your way in an environment that has no reference points – for example, in a forest or a maze – you need to be able to devise a mental map of the area. The map is then adjusted in real time to correspond with the movements you make. It's a bit like having a GPS inside your head!

Taxi drivers

Finding their way around a large city can turn into a nightmare for people with no sense of direction. This doesn't appear to be a problem for taxi drivers, who seem to have a mental mapping system as efficient as a GPS.

A paper published in 2000 by a team of neurologists at the University College of London presented the findings of a study of London taxi drivers using magnetic resonance imaging. It reported that the longer their taxi-driving experience, the larger the posterior part of the hippocampus had become. This discovery seems to indicate that these professional drivers stored their knowledge of the city's 250,000 streets in that part of the brain. But how do they tap into this store? To find the answer to that question, the researchers gave each driver a game console with virtual images of the City of London. They discovered that the hippocampus reached peak levels of activity when the drivers were planning their route, while other areas of the brain took over at intersections near key sites, as well as when the drivers were looking around or trying to second-guess the behaviour of other drivers.

A sense of direction

You may think that these questions and exercises are very easy, which means you have a good sense of direction. If not, it means that you are not using your sense of direction in your everyday life, or even that direction is just not your strong point.

1. Which direction does the front of your house or apartment building face? ....

2. How far is it (approximately) from your home to the nearest shop? ....

3. Sketch the outline of your country and mark your town or city. (Don't copy a map, and take no longer than a couple of minutes.) ....

4. Draw a plan of your home, showing the shapes and relative sizes of the rooms as accurately as you can.
....

5. Draw a map of your local area, marking a route that is familiar to you so that someone who doesn't know the area at all can follow it. ....

The great escape

In the American TV series *Prison Break*, supernatural figures such as angels and devils are tattooed on the body of the main character, but hidden behind them is a map of the prison where he is being held. This extraordinary stratagem has been devised to help him to escape.

Is this strategy plausible? The scriptwriters insist that the tattoos designed by Tom Berg really do conceal the plans of a prison. To find the plans, the protagonist has to remember the meaning of various clues marked on him. The infirmary, for example, is a certain part of the anatomy of one of the figures. While these patterns superimposed on the prison plans might make it impossible for the untrained eye to decipher the relevant information, the protagonist, a talented engineer, finds them extremely helpful for working out the prison layout. They could be compared to the outlines of figures or animals that help us to find and remember the positions of stars on constellation maps.

Improve your spatial memory

The following exercises are designed to help to improve your memory for maps and routes. They will help you to learn how to visualise an object from various angles and to sharpen your skills when working with different scales.

Aerial views

Which one of the aerial views matches the ground-level picture?

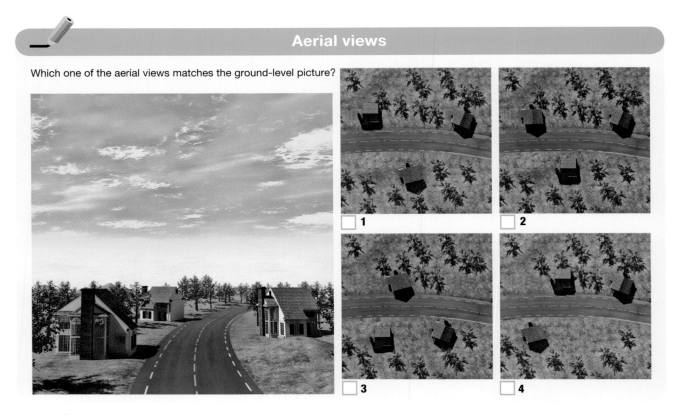

Different viewpoints

The main picture (left) shows a series of crop circles – those mysterious formations that sometimes appear in fields of grain. The four smaller pictures (right) also show crop circles. Three of the four pictures show the same circular patterns that appear in the large picture, but from different angles. The fourth picture shows a completely different series of circles. Which is the odd one out?

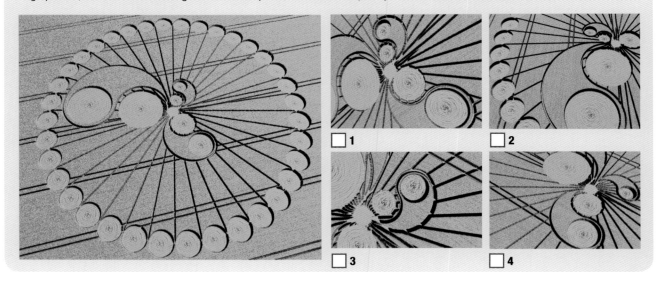

The right route

1. Study the route marked on this map, then cover the picture.

2. Mark the route taken and number the different stops.

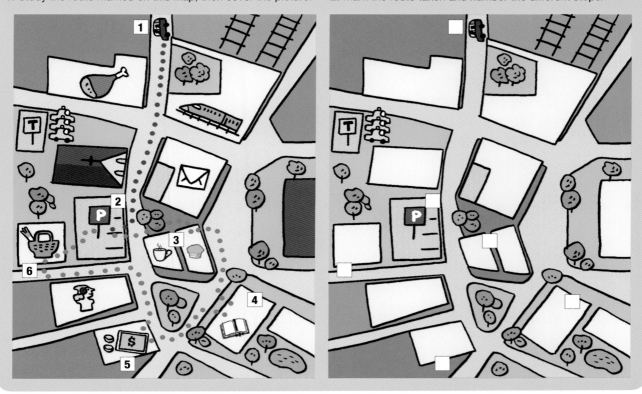

Matters of scale

Maps and plans are drawn to scale, with the length marked in proportion to the distance measured. The relationship between the two is given as the scale.

$$\text{Scale} = \frac{\text{distance on the map}}{\text{distance on the ground}}$$

This means that if the scale is given as 1:200,000, 1 centimetre on the map represents 200,000 centimetres, or 2 kilometres, on the ground.

1. Find the best route

Alice is preparing to cycle from Atown (A) to Beetown (B). When she studies her map (scale: 1:200,000), she sees two options:

• via Ceetown (C), taking two straight stretches of road that she can easily measure on the map: AC=15 centimetres and CB=10 centimetres.

• via Deetown (D), making a total distance of 60 kilometres according to the map.

The road from A to C is very steep and Alice will be able to cycle at only 25 km/h. The road between C and B is downhill and she can average 40 km/h. The road via D is flat and she will be able to pedal at 30 km/h. She plans to leave at 2 pm and would like to arrive before 3.45 pm. Which route must she take?

2. Real scale

On the public transport map (scale: 1:1000) the length of the plaza in the city centre measures 15 centimetres. On the map from the tourist office (scale 1:600), the width of the plaza measures 15 centimetres. What is the actual size of the plaza?

3. Small scale

Lily is buying an apartment. The real estate agent has given her a plan showing the bathroom as a square with the side marked as 4 metres and measuring 12 centimetres on the plan. What measurements does the plan show for the living room, which is 6 metres x 4.5 metres?

Dimension and proportion

What do a landscape gardener, a dental prosthesis maker and a window dresser have in common? They all have an excellent appreciation of shape and volume. This means they can picture three-dimensional objects when presented with two-dimensional drawings, interpret building plans and estimate distances and proportions.

The world in 3D

The ability to see a three-dimensional image is the result of binocular vision, which makes it possible to assess depth and distance. In humans, the two eyes simultaneously take in information from two slightly different angles. The brain is constantly amalgamating the images on each retina to produce a perceived image. The same skill is used to gauge movement: the path and speed of an object are perceived by comparing images registered at different moments. This is how children gradually learn to anticipate the position of a moving object so that they can catch a ball and, with practice, can even learn to juggle with two or three balls.

Add volume

How the brain processes visual information is a vast area of study. Does the brain reconstruct three-dimensional objects from a series of cross-section images? Or, as argued by US researchers in the 1990s, does it recognise some objects immediately? Whatever the method, the cognitive process of recognising objects is extremely swift. For a long time it was thought that a shape had to be isolated in a larger visual context before it could be categorised, but a study conducted in 2005 showed that the two stages occur simultaneously.

In 2007, Belgian neurobiologists tried to identify the areas of the brain stimulated during three-dimensional perception by observing MRI scans of primates. Their findings showed that the centre that processes visual data on spatial position, speed and direction appears to be located in part of the anterior intraparietal cortex, an area also involved in the visual control of hand movements.

The golden ratio

Does the brain respond to certain proportions in particular? Many artists and architects are convinced that there is an ideal proportion that is the most pleasing to the eye. This so-called divine proportion is said to have inspired the builders of the pyramids in Egypt and the architects of ancient Greek temples, as well as Renaissance artists and, more recently, the architect Le Corbusier and the artist Salvador Dali.

The divine proportion is defined as the ideal ratio between the length and width of a rectangle and was called the 'golden ratio' by the ancient Greeks. The two rectangles shown below are golden rectangles: they have the same proportions – that is, the same coefficient of proportionality known as the golden ratio, 1.618.

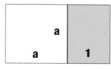

The golden ratio is the result of the equation
$a^2 = 1 + a$.
Solving the quadratic equation, we get:

$$a = \frac{1 + \sqrt{5}}{2} \approx 1.618$$

Divine proportion Many of the proportions of the Parthenon in Athens are golden ratios. This golden number can also be found in ratios between the height and width of the Mona Lisa's face.

Can you put things in perspective?

Drawings with cubes are often used to test three-dimensional (3D) perception. The intention is to distinguish a 3D drawing from other slightly different arrangements or its mirror image. When the brain compares the drawings, it has to rotate, reposition and twist the images mentally as though these were actual physical movements of the objects. Construction games with building bricks and blocks are said to develop children's spatial intelligence. If you didn't spend much time playing such games as a child, you may find that you don't perform very well in this type of test.

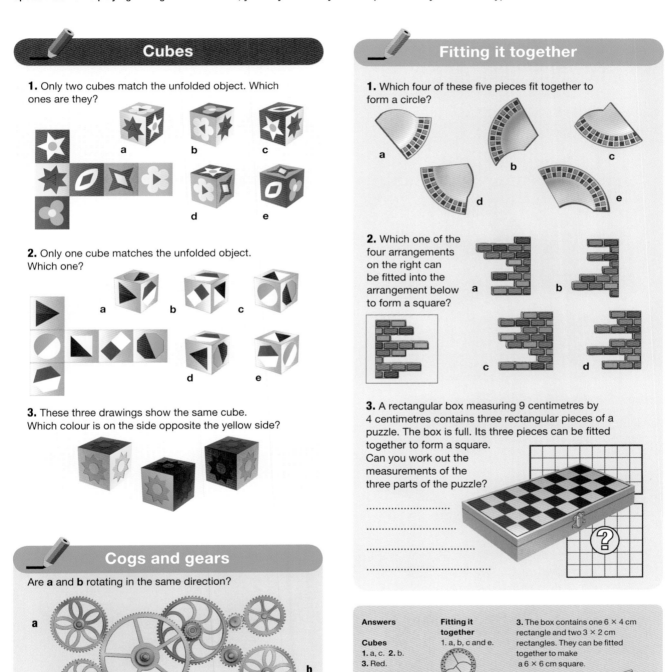

Cubes

1. Only two cubes match the unfolded object. Which ones are they?

a   b   c

d   e

2. Only one cube matches the unfolded object. Which one?

a   b   c

d   e

3. These three drawings show the same cube. Which colour is on the side opposite the yellow side?

Cogs and gears

Are **a** and **b** rotating in the same direction?

a

b

☐ Yes   ☐ No

Fitting it together

1. Which four of these five pieces fit together to form a circle?

a   b   c

d   e

2. Which one of the four arrangements on the right can be fitted into the arrangement below to form a square?

a   b

c   d

3. A rectangular box measuring 9 centimetres by 4 centimetres contains three rectangular pieces of a puzzle. The box is full. Its three pieces can be fitted together to form a square. Can you work out the measurements of the three parts of the puzzle?

....
....
....
....

Answers

Cubes
1. a, c. 2. b.
3. Red.

Cogs and gears Yes.

Fitting it together
1. a, b, c and e.

2. d.

3. The box contains one 6 × 4 cm rectangle and two 3 × 2 cm rectangles. They can be fitted together to make a 6 × 6 cm square.

Odd one out

Which is the odd one out in the following groups?

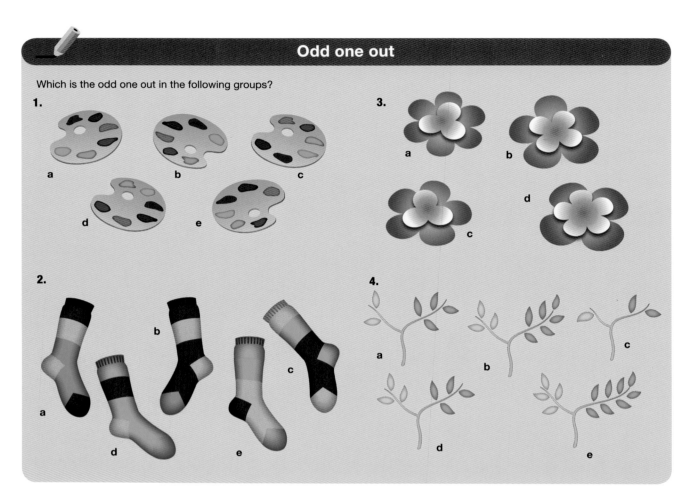

1.

3.

2.

4.

The perfect cut

This cake is in the shape of three squares placed together, with a cherry in the middle of one of them. Can you divide the cake into two equal parts with a single cut that also slices the cherry in half?

The tilted glass

Draw a line to indicate where the top of the liquid is when the glass is tilted.

Answers

Odd one out 1. b. It is the only palette with colours that don't change in a clockwise direction. **2.** b. The top and toe of the sock are not the same colour. **3.** c. Unlike the others, the flower doesn't have nine petals. **4.** d. There should be six leaves on the right branch (twice the number on the left) to fit the series.

The tilted glass

Tiling

The perfect cut

Tangrams

The tangram is an ancient Chinese puzzle consisting of seven shapes cut from a square – five triangles, a square and a parallelogram. These seven pieces can then be arranged to form the outline of a variety of other figures. All seven pieces must be used for each new combination and there can be no overlapping. The game exercises the ability to perceive shapes (arranging geometric figures in various positions), the sense of proportion and also the imagination when players devise their own tangrams.

1. Make your tangram shapes by cutting seven pieces from a sheet of paper or cardboard as shown on the right, then arrange them to produce the figures below.

2. These two figures have been made using the seven pieces of the tangram. Can you explain why they are different?

Answers

Conveying information visually

To gain a better understanding of a text and to remember it, the simplest method is to focus on the key ideas by highlighting them or writing them down. Another way to single out the essential facts is through graphic representation, which gives information an additional visual form that is immediately understood by the brain. A clear, smart diagram can be more effective than a long explanation.

A knowledge tree

Pie charts, graphs and diagrams are the standard tools used to present quantitative data in visual form. Less common are mind maps, which can present a range of information in a tree format: the main subject is placed at the centre of the page and branches are drawn radiating out from it, each one with a key word and subdivided into further branches. The whole picture shows all aspects of the subject at a glance, with all their logical links and hierarchy. Mind maps use language (key words) and visual symbols with colour codes, pictograms and large and small arrows, depending on the link.

The idea dates back to Aristotle, but was formally set down by British popular psychology author Tony Buzan, who coined the term mind mapping. Mind maps provide both a summary and a panoramic view of an issue or a plan and have a range of applications, from taking notes to presenting a complex organisational chart or planning a project (for example, a wedding, as shown here).

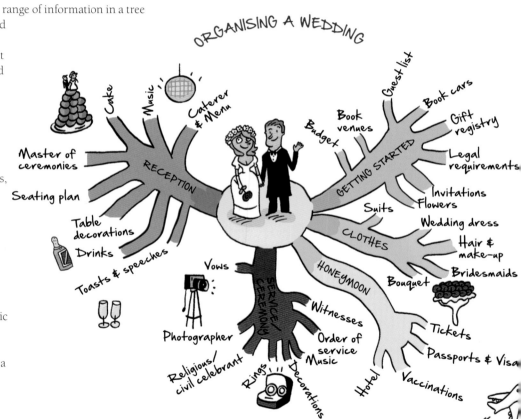

A whole-brain exercise

According to Tony Buzan, this visual arrangement of ideas and thoughts is very efficient because it uses all parts of the brain: the left hemisphere for logic, language and sequential analysis, and the right hemisphere, which is often overlooked in learning processes but is involved in global processing, creativity, and visual and spatial skills. While there is no unanimous endorsement of the theory that the brain is divided into two functionally distinct hemispheres, these maps are still interesting for a number of reasons. They require prior reflection to isolate the essentials, as well as a structural effort to organise ideas and actions; these procedures help to clarify thought and make information easier to remember. Mind maps also involve creative and spatial organisation. And their visual format probably gives a fairly accurate idea of the way the brain collects information – that is, through association and visualisation.

Test your spatial skills

Geometric perception of space and the expression of quantities are both processed in the same part of the brain, the parietal cortex. All humans have these abilities, regardless of our formal training: we are all able to find reference points and to assess distances and compare quantities approximately, without doing any calculations. Geometry and arithmetic first came from these intuitive spatial and numerical observations and later developed into subjects of scientific study to forecast results through reasoning instead of experimentation. Just as we can exercise language or reasoning skills by playing games involving vocabulary or logic, so we can also test our spatial skills with challenges that involve geometric shapes, proportions and volume.

Geometric shapes

1. How do you calculate the perimeter of a triangle?

....
....
....

2. What do you get when you multiply the diameter of a circle by *pi*?

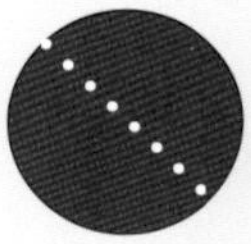

x Pi = ...

3. How do you calculate the area of a rectangle?

....
....
....
....

?

4. The bisecting line, from the apex (a) to the mid-point on the opposite side (b), divides the triangle into two triangles of equal area.

☐ **True** ☐ **False**

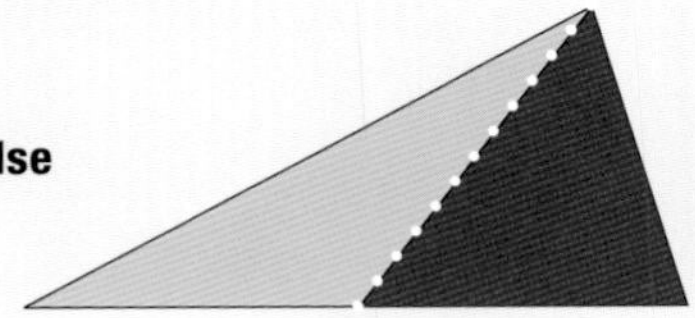

A

B

5. How is the area of a triangle calculated?

....
....
....
....

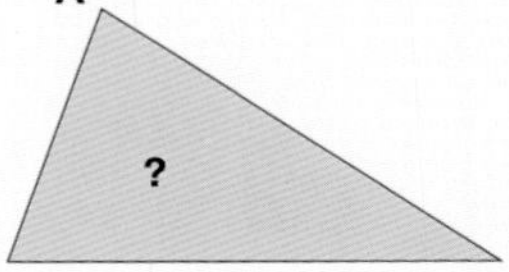

A

?

B   C

6. The diagram below is made up of six triangles formed by straight lines, all intersecting at the same point and running from the apex of the large triangle to the mid-points on the opposite sides.

Do all the triangles have the same area? If so, why?

....
....
....

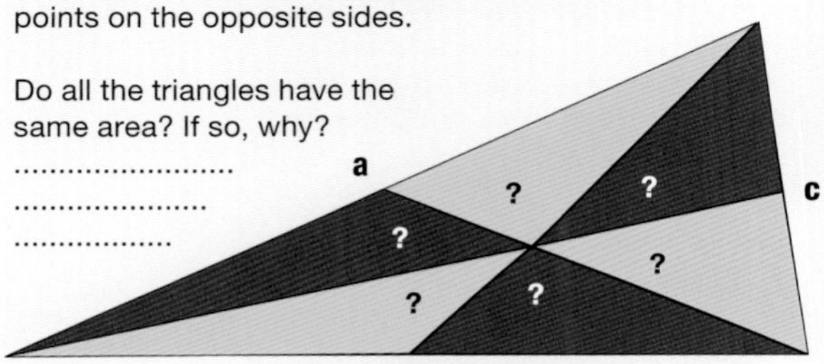

a   ?   ?   c
        ?
    ?   ?
b

7. The area of each of these five equilateral triangles is 1 m². By looking at the diagram without writing down any calculations, what is the area inside the dotted lines?

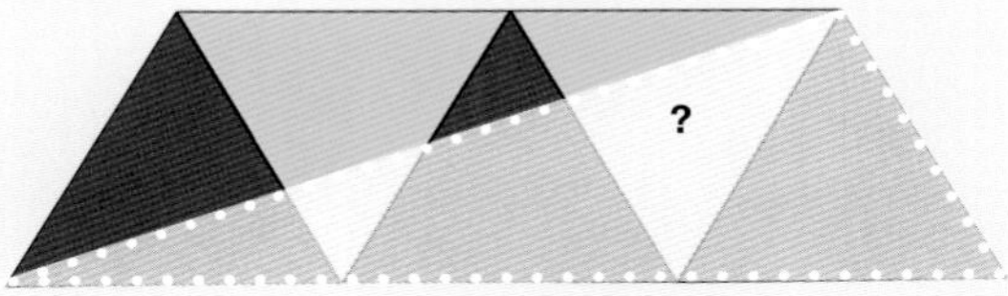

?

....
....

8. If the two sides of a rectangle are multiplied by 10, the area is multiplied by a factor of

☐ **a.** 10
☐ **b.** 20
☐ **c.** 100

?

9. If the radius of a circle is divided by 2, then the area is divided by 4.

☐ **True** ☐ **False**

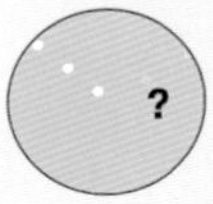

?

Answers: see page 156

1. How tall is the tree?

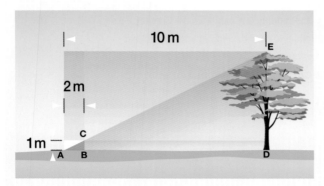

10 m

2 m

C

1 m

A B   D

E

....

2. Grandpa planted these two flower beds, one red and one blue, in the middle of his lawn. He says that the area of the red flower bed is the same as the area of the remaining lawn. Is he right?

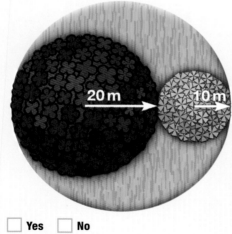

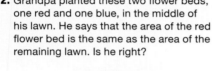

20 m   10 m

☐ Yes ☐ No

3. Three children want to divide their square block of chocolate into three equal pieces. The dividing line has to go through A. Where do they have to position point M (where a straight line from A intersects with BC) and point N (where a straight line from A intersects with CD)?

D   C

A   B

4. A is the fire-fighting centre where a water-bombing plane is based. A fire has broken out at point F. At which point on the river does the plane have to fill up with water to put out the fire as quickly as possible?

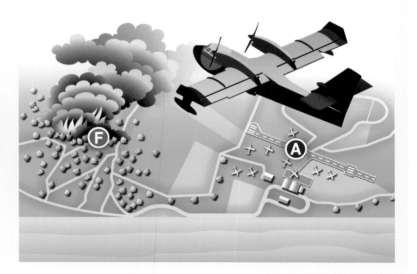

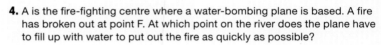

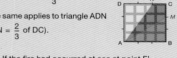
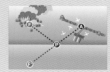
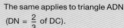

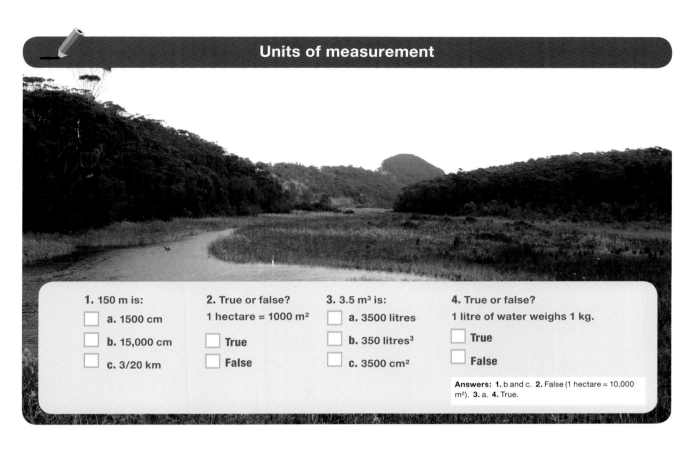

Units of measurement

1. 150 m is:

☐ **a.** 1500 cm

☐ **b.** 15,000 cm

☐ **c.** 3/20 km

2. True or false?

1 hectare = 1000 m²

☐ **True**

☐ **False**

3. 3.5 m³ is:

☐ **a.** 3500 litres

☐ **b.** 350 litres³

☐ **c.** 3500 cm²

4. True or false?

1 litre of water weighs 1 kg.

☐ **True**

☐ **False**

Answers: **1.** b and c. **2.** False (1 hectare = 10,000 m²). **3. a. 4.** True.

Proportion and the Rule of Three

1. What mathematical operation can be used to go from the top line to the bottom line (or conversely, from the bottom to the top)?

20	40	60	80	100
3	**6**	**9**	**12**	**15**

2. A recipe has the following ingredients and quantities to serve 7 people. What quantities are needed to serve 4?

For 7 people	For 4 people
245 g flour	...... g flour
91 g butter	...... g butter
350 g sugar	...... g sugar
10.5 g baking powder	...... g baking powder

3. Every evening the manager of a menswear shop lists the number of garments sold that day, entering them by category. Here is one of the daily records:

Jeans	Shirts	Pullovers	Jackets	Total
36	12	8	24	80

For statistical purposes, the manager prefers figures expressing the proportion of sales of each category of garment to be calculated as a percentage. Can you complete the table?

Jeans	Shirts	Pullovers	Jackets	Total
36	12	8	24	80
......%	......%	......%	......%	100 %

Answers: **1.** To go from the top to the bottom, multiply by 0.15 (15%). From the bottom to the top, multiply by 20 and divide by 3. **2.** Take each quantity and divide by 7 then multiply by 4, which gives 140 g flour, 52 g butter, 200 g sugar and 6 g baking powder. **3.** Each number has to be multiplied by 1.25 (100 = 80 × 1.25); alternatively, you can divide by 4 and multiply by 5 to reach the answer: jeans 45%, shirts 15%, pullovers 10% and jackets 30%.

Logic

8

A widespread ability

Logic and reasoning are difficult to define because they cover a wide range of mental skills. In simple terms, reasoning is the ability to acquire new knowledge solely on the basis of what has already been acquired.

The principles of reasoning

Reasoning means drawing conclusions from known data – a kind of mental gymnastics that is often called inference. There are two types of reasoning, deductive and non-deductive, and there are also two main kinds of non-deductive reasoning – inductive and abductive.

Deductive reasoning aims to draw a conclusion that must be true if the starting points (the premises) are true. It often involves the mechanical application of rules of logic. The best-known examples are syllogisms, arguments of a special kind that are based on two statements or premises. The most famous of these (called a singular syllogism) is:

● All men are mortal. *Major premise*
● Socrates is a man. *Minor premise*
● Therefore Socrates is mortal. *Conclusion*

Successful deductive reasoning like this is said to be valid: if the premises are true, the conclusion has to be true as well.

Non-deductive reasoning is more difficult to grasp. It aims to provide good reasons, knowing that it is not giving any guarantees or watertight proofs. Two main kinds, induction and abduction, are usually distinguished, but we will see others later.

Inductive reasoning typically involves extrapolating or generalising from what has been experienced to what hasn't. You may, for example, generalise from the fact that all the crows you have seen are black to the conclusion that all crows are black, or just extrapolate to the conclusion that the next crow you see will be black. Conclusions may thus be drawn, but there is no logical certainty. If, for example, you are told that a cat, a panther and a cheetah each has 30 teeth, you may infer that all felines have 30 teeth, even if this conclusion is not dictated by logic. Induction is the basis of experimentation. It mostly uses the same concepts in the conclusion as in the premises.

Abductive reasoning, by comparison, is not as restricted and typically involves finding explanations for information you may have. It is sometimes called reasoning or inference to the best explanation. It may be as mundane as concluding that it rained last night if the path is wet this morning, or as remarkable as Gregor Mendel's conclusion that certain unobserved factors (now called genes) were responsible for the frequencies of inherited traits in plants.

Cats have whiskers

Socrates has whiskers

Therefore Socrates is a cat

The seat of reason

According to neurologists, the area of the brain involved in reasoning is indisputedly the prefrontal cortex – the very front part of the brain – which is more highly developed in humans than in any other animal species.

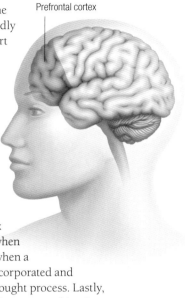

Prefrontal cortex

But the two hemispheres do not play equal roles in reasoning. Studies comparing the abilities of patients with brain damage to the left and right prefrontal cortexes have shown that damage to the left has a far greater impact on reasoning skills, both deductive and non-deductive. Nevertheless, the right prefrontal cortex may still have significant involvement when reasoning relies on incomplete data or when a certain degree of ambiguity has to be incorporated and tolerated in the different stages of the thought process. Lastly, reasoning is not a basic function, but relies on a combination of other skills, such as memory retention, calculation or the ability to develop hypotheses.

Problems with reasoning

Patients with brain damage to the prefrontal area have difficulties that affect the most sophisticated aspects of their intellect, including reasoning.

Clinical tests conducted to diagnose frontal brain damage include questions such as 'You have bought 2 kilos of tomatoes at $3 a kilo and paid with a $20 note. What will the greengrocer do?' Patients with frontal brain damage will struggle to find the answer. They can do the basic arithmetic (3 × 2 and 20 – 6), but are unable to develop the strategy needed to solve the problem.

Another challenging question for such patients is 'What do a banana and an orange have in common?' Most patients describe each item individually, noting the shape and flavour, but cannot give the answer expected, which is that they are both pieces of fruit. This is because they find it difficult to infer a single underlying idea from specific cases.

Logical deduction

On the planet Logica, two large, rival cities are always diametrically opposed: Vera City, capital of the land of the Franks, and False Port, capital of the land of the Rogues. The citizens of Vera City, the Franks, always tell the truth, while the citizens of False Port, the Rogues, always lie. Any statements made must therefore be either true or false.

Can you work out the following conundrums?

1. Rick: 'Malina is from False Port.'
Malina: 'Rick is from....'
A sudden noise blocks out the rest of the conversation.

How did Malina end her sentence?

....

2. Zara: It's my birthday today.
Joe: If it's Zara's birthday, then I'm a Rogue.

What are the nationalities of Zara and Joe?

....

3. Daniel: 'I am Nina's brother and we have the same nationality.'
Nina: 'Daniel and I are not brother and sister.'

What are the nationalities of Daniel and Nina?

....

4. Sharon: 'Wally likes everyone from his own country, but doesn't like the people from the other city.'
Wally: 'To tell the truth, I don't like Sharon.'

Only the nationality of one of the two can be established. Which one?

....

Answers: 1. False Port. If Rick is from Vera City, he is telling the truth and Malina is lying, so she will say that he is from False Port. If Rick is from False Port, he is lying and Malina is telling the truth and she will say that he is from False Port. **2.** Zara is a Rogue and Joe is a Frank. If Zara is telling the truth, then what Joe says makes no sense, as it cannot be a true statement that tallies with Zara's statement, or a lie if Zara is lying: it is not her birthday and what Joe suggests is true. **3.** Daniel is a Rogue and Nina is a Frank. If Daniel were telling the truth, Nina would be his sister and would be a Frank, which is the opposite of what she has said, so Daniel is a Rogue. As he is lying and maintains that he has the same nationality as Nina, then she must be a Frank. **4.** Sharon is a Rogue. If Sharon were a Frank, Wally would say, regardless of his nationality, that he likes Sharon. If he were a Frank, this would be because he would have the same nationality; if he were a Rogue, it would be because she was not the same nationality and he would be lying. Therefore Sharon is a Rogue, but we can't decide about Wally.

Brain training and Sudoku

Sudoku requires a number of different brain functions: logic, because deduction is the basis of the game, but also attention and memory. Concentration is of fundamental importance because distraction will be an obstacle, ultimately making it impossible to solve the puzzle, since the point where the mistake was made often can't be found. Memory is put to the test: trying to note all clues on the grid would make it unreadable. Different pieces of information need to be managed at the same time, so a well-organised memory is an essential tool.

Rules of the game

A Sudoku puzzle is a nine-by-nine grid of squares, subdivided into nine sections of three squares by three. The goal is to complete the grid using the numbers 1 to 9, so that each horizontal line, each vertical line and each section contains the numbers 1 to 9 in any order.

Different methods

Here are three methods to help solve easy or medium-difficulty Sudoku puzzles. Other techniques can be used for more difficult ones, but require a certain amount of practice.

● The section method

This is the simplest, most effective method. Choose a number and one of the nine sections, then ask: 'Where can the number fit into this section?' If there is only one possible option, then the number can be written in the one square where it fits.

In the example shown on the left, for the number 4 there is only one choice possible in the top left section.

● The line method

The same principle applies, but using a horizontal or vertical line, asking 'Where can this number go?' If there is only one possible solution, the number can be written in the square on the line.

● The duo or trio method

This method, which can produce spectacular results, is based on a simple rational argument. If one line has two squares that can contain only two numbers, then the same numbers cannot appear anywhere else on the same line. The same process can be used for vertical and horizontal lines and for sections; the same argument can also be applied to three numbers in three squares.

In the example given, the squares in the last vertical line on the right have three options noted; the three squares must contain 2, 7 and 9, which means that these figures cannot appear anywhere else in the same line, such as the square in the second line, which means that this square has to be a 5.

Grid 1

Find the solution using the methods described above.

	8		1				7	
1					5		6	3
						9		8
3					2			7
					9			
	4		6	1			5	
		3						9
4	2				7			
	7	9	3			6		1

Grid 2

Find the solution using the methods described above.

4				6				1	
	1			4		8			
		6		5				7	
2		8	5						
	5			1			6		
				6	9			2	
7				4		1			
		7		5			3		
	2			9				5	

Logical sequences

So-called logical sequences or series depend more on induction than on deduction. The rest of a sequence has to be worked out by finding a rule that applies to the first elements. This shows whether the person has good powers of observation, analysis or even intuition.

Complete the following logical sequences

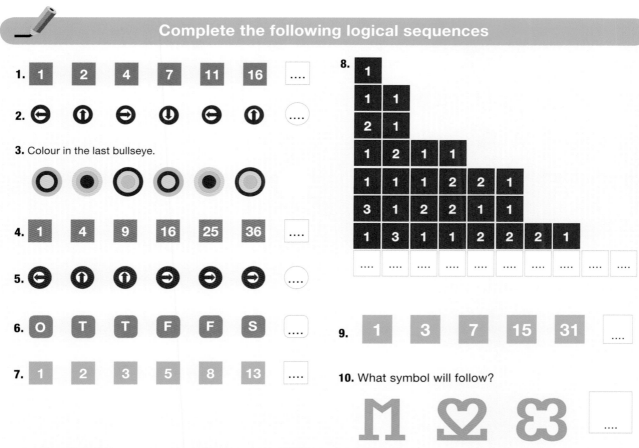

1. 1 2 4 7 11 16 ....

2. (arrows) ....

3. Colour in the last bullseye.

4. 1 4 9 16 25 36 ....

5. (arrows) ....

6. O T T F F S ....

7. 1 2 3 5 8 13 ....

8.
1
1 1
2 1
1 2 1 1
1 1 1 2 2 1
3 1 2 2 1 1
1 3 1 1 2 2 2 1
....

9. 1 3 7 15 31 ....

10. What symbol will follow? ....

11. Researchers often start by using a method in which they interpret a series of observations based on what they intuitively feel is the law that governs them. In this table, the first three lines (mauve squares) list the values of three parameters, A, B and C, while the last line, D, gives the result (blue squares). What is the principle used to complete the table?

A	0	1	2	0	1	2	2	1	2	2	4	1	1	2	0
B	0	1	2	1	2	3	2	2	1	4	4	2	3	1	2
C	0	1	2	2	3	4	1	2	2	6	2	4	1	1	4
D	0	0	0	−4	−4	−4	3	−1	−2	−8	6	....	....	....	....

Answers, page 163
1. 22. The differences occur with increasing numbers 1 (+1, +2, +3...) **2.** ↻ The move from one arrow to the next is by simple clockwise rotation. **3.** ○ The shift from one bullseye to the next is done by exchanging the colours (yellow becomes red, red becomes green and green becomes yellow), making it possible to work out the next three bullseyes. **4.** 49. The figures are the square of consecutive whole numbers (1^2, 2^2, 3^2...). **5.** ↺ The arrows change in a clockwise direction, repeating once, then twice, then three times, and so on, before moving on to the next position. **6.** S (the first letter of 'seven'). Each letter is the first letter of the words for the numbers. **7.** 21. Each number is the sum of the two previous numbers. **8.** 1113213211. The sequence is written down as it is read out: one one (11) for the 1 on the top line; two one (21) for the 11 on the second line; one two, one one (1211) for 21, and so on. **9.** 63. Multiply by 2 than add 1. **10.** The sequence is comprised of the figures 1, 2, 3, 4, each facing its own mirror image. **11.** The principle used to complete line D is: A + 2B − 3C. The answers are therefore: −7, 4, 1 and −8.

Intuition and logic

Scientists are often viewed as experts in logic who are capable of formulating extremely rigorous rational arguments. And yet many discoveries that have revolutionised the world of knowledge have called for intuition rather than rational deduction.

Complementary abilities

Intuition is often defined as an immediate kind of knowledge that doesn't require any conscious mental effort. But, of course, it doesn't come from nothing: it's the result of processing and synthesising information gained from past experience and external indicators. Some of the information we receive from the senses may be processed unconsciously and compared to impressions and knowledge already stored in our memory bank. This could help us to analyse complex situations and may explain why a fleeting impression is sometimes all that is needed for us to make a decision.

Is it better to be intuitive or logical? This question is not particularly meaningful, as these two different ways of thinking are not mutually exclusive, but complement and support each other. Intuition may play a key role in the reasoning process of experts, but unless an initial analysis is undertaken there are no paths to explore. Some brilliant ideas seem to have come about automatically – for example, it's difficult to imagine a world where the wheel was not invented. Nevertheless, great inventors are probably those who base intuitive judgment on sound reasoning and a thorough knowledge of their subject – people like Louis Pasteur, Isaac Newton and Marie Curie.

Abductive reasoning and the supersleuth

Sir Arthur Conan Doyle's fictional detective, Sherlock Holmes, is admired by readers for his powers of reasoning based on careful observation, but what Holmes calls 'deduction' is not strictly speaking deductive reasoning. His more spectacular reasoning is mostly non-deductive, and specifically abductive, leaving scope for creativity. He relies on clues, often acutely observed, to reach a conclusion. If, for example, he finds a basket containing medical instruments, the best explanation is that the owner is probably a doctor. But some of his hypotheses are far-fetched – when he assumes that a dog didn't bark because it knew the thief, he is overlooking or judging as implausible other possible causes (such as that the dog may have been asleep or deaf). Sherlock Holmes relies on his intuition to think of the most plausible explanations or reasons – this is typically abduction.

Inspector Maigret, the hero of Georges Simenon's novels, relies on his intuition when investigating criminal cases. He solves them by immersing himself in the lifestyle and environment of the criminals he pursues, trying to discover the real person hiding behind the suspect being questioned. Although he appears to be daydreaming, he is simply going where his intuition leads him. Like Holmes, he bases his investigations on abductive reasoning, but while Holmes relies on tangible clues, Maigret trusts his impressions and his understanding of human nature.

Master of 'deduction' Sherlock Holmes has been portrayed by many actors, among them British actor Basil Rathbone, who brought the famous fictional detective to the screen in 14 movies.

Find the context

The American philosopher, Charles Peirce, coined the term *abduction* to recognise the role that is played by the imagination in reasoning when also based on knowledge. This is what we do when we use clues to help us to explain a phenomenon or an observation: if we notice a car stranded in the middle of the road, we will probably assume that it has broken down, but the link is not always that straightforward, as can be seen in the following examples.

The two sentences below don't appear to be part of the same story. Give them meaning by devising a context in which they could logically be included.

At that time he had only $1000 in his account. That meant he lost only $5000.

Answer: This exercise is based on a true story, but you can devise others. Members of an investors' club were offered the opportunity to buy futures – that is, contracts setting the purchase price of listed securities in advance. David thought it was a good deal, as the share price for BDB clearly seemed to be undervalued, so he took the maximum amount, for $10,000. He had only $1000 at his disposal, but club members enjoyed special conditions that required only a 10 per cent payment at the time of purchase. Unfortunately, three months later the financial crisis hit and BDB shares dropped to half the price they were when David bought the futures. At that time he had only $1000 in his bank account. That meant he lost only $5000.

Reasoning by analogy

Analogical reasoning, another non-deductive kind, operates through the association of ideas, in which a rational argument that applies in one context is transposed to another. In this way, the framework of a problem is ignored so that similarities with another problem can be found. This type of thinking, also called lateral thinking, makes it possible to see a problem in a new light and gives free rein to creativity.

A comparative method

Analogy is the relationship that exists between a number of things. In mathematics it is related to proportions, that is, to the quality of ratios – 'A is to B as C is to D' means that four numbers, A, B, C and D, are in a proportional relationship, the ratio between A and B being equal to the ratio between C and D (A:B = C:D). This principle can be applied to other areas to explain a complex idea, to solve a problem or to express feelings, which are by definition subjective; it is the principle upon which the visual analogue scale is based (a scale on which people indicate visually where they fall between two opposing categories).

Metaphor is a figure of speech that uses a type of analogy. An abstract, subjective or new situation is compared with one that is more concrete and so more meaningful for the reader or audience, but this is done without fully stating the comparison. When someone is called a shark, the analogy is that the person behaves in a social setting in the same way as a shark does in its environment, that is, as a great predator. Poetry is the ultimate domain of metaphors and analogy, but computer language also uses analogy. A computer virus spreads in the same way as a biological virus: it can lie dormant for a period and then suddenly revive.

Can you reason by analogy?

Mathematical and verbal analogies
Complete the following by adding the required figure or word.

1. **12** is to **8** as .... is to **5**

2. **Pre** is to **amble** as .... is to **script**.

3. **Moon** is to **Earth** as **Earth** is to ....

Visual analogy

is to   as   is to

Analogical conundrums

1. If Jaqueline appreciates enigmas, Nina adores animals, Oscar likes racing and Janis loves singing, then Edward enjoys:

   Crosswords ☐ Football ☐ Dancing ☐ Drawing ☐ Canoeing ☐

2. Mr Jason is a celebrity disc jockey with a leading radio station broadcasting in both amplitude modulation and frequency modulation. Printed on his business card is Jason DJ FM-AM.

   What is the initial of his first name? ....

Answers: Mathematical and verbal analogies 1. 7.5, as 12 = 8 + (8/2). **2.** Post. The term is a prefix forming a compound word (preamble, postscript). **3.** Sun. (The Moon is a satellite of Earth and Earth is a satellite of the Sun.) **Visual analogy** The colours are reversed and the pattern rotates 45 degrees. **Analogical conundrums 1.** Drawing. There is a link between the last three letters of each name and the first three letters of the interest or hobby, so EdwARD enjoys DRAwing. **2.** J. The letters J a s o n D J F M A M are the initials of the months of the year, starting from July. The initial of his first name is therefore J, as in June.

We are not completely cerebral beings

In life, we don't generally make decisions based on cool, calculated rational thought, weighing up arguments for and against an action without any emotional considerations. The link between rational thought and emotions in decision making has now become an area of study in cognitive neuroscience.

Cerebral skills

The neurologist Antonio Damasio and his team at the University of California have studied patients suffering from damage to the lower side of the frontal lobes, just above the eye sockets, called the orbitofrontal cortex. These individuals were incapable of making appropriate decisions in everyday life. This problem left them open to disappointment and even disaster in every sphere – social, professional and personal – and was in dramatic contrast to the excellent results they scored in all the standard mental function tests, especially reasoning.

The first such case reported in the medical literature was that of Phineas Gage, a US railway construction foreman. In 1848 an explosion drove a large iron rod right through his left frontal lobe. He survived, was not paralysed and showed no apparent loss of mental function. But he began making erratic decisions and as a result he lost his job and all contact with his family, friends and society.

These cases shed light on what we all experience sooner or later. Our decisions are based on rational assessment of a situation as well as our emotional response. When confronted with a complex problem, it may be difficult to make a rational choice in favour of one solution rather than another. Some decisions may even trigger a sense of physical distress, to the point where it is impossible to reach a decision and impossible to explain why.

Impossible dilemmas

The relationship between reason and emotion is clear for some decisions. Imagine that you are beside a railway line and you see a train speeding along it. Then farther down the line you spot five people who can't see the train coming and will be run down if you don't act. You are beside the switch at the points and can divert the train onto another track. Unfortunately, there is a man on the other track and he can't see the train coming either. You are confronted with the following dilemma: either you do nothing and five people will be killed, or you divert the train and the five people will be saved, but you will be responsible for the death of the man. Most people consider it is acceptable to divert the train onto a track where it will hit only one person instead of five.

Now here's another story. You are on a bridge above a railway track. A train is coming and will run down five people if you don't act. There's no railway switch point, but you can still do something. There's a man beside you on the bridge and you can push him onto the track. If you do, the train will hit him then stop, saving the other five people. Unlike the previous example, most people find this act to be abhorrent and morally wrong.

The moral of the story

We have two very different views of the 'right' moral attitude, even though in both stories it is a question of saving the lives of five people by killing one. On the one hand, there is abstract, utilitarian reasoning, which makes us think that the right decision is to save five people, even if one has to be killed. On the other hand, there are intuitive moral considerations that are expressed as emotions. From this point of view, the two stories are different. In the first situation, you are not directly confronted with the man who is to be sacrificed, whereas in the second you have to touch your victim: the personal and emotional implications conflict with the arithmetical argument.

Researchers have used functional imaging to test subjects who are given similar problems to solve. According to whether they are confronted with a decision that can be made on the basis of rational arithmetical calculations or a dilemma involving personal and emotional commitment, the systems activated in the brain are not the same. When the dilemma becomes intolerable, other areas of the brain are triggered in order to manage the conflict and to attempt to control emotions.

Are we rational beings?

We often make the wrong judgments or decisions. And sometimes people criticise us for not being objective, or even worse, for being hypocritical. This is because, besides errors due to faulty logic, we often make mistakes that can be attributed to psychological mechanisms – in other words, to the way we process information.

Taking the easy way out

'If they said it on TV, then it must be true.' This maxim doesn't require any in-depth reasoning; it simply needs to be applied to get a result, which might even prove to be correct. This way, there's no need to check the level of expertise or the sources of the person giving the information. But when a decision or a judgment we need to make is an important one, we assess the information available thoroughly and examine the arguments for and against. When we want to reach a reliable conclusion, then, we use complex procedures. We need to devote a great deal of energy to this reasoning process, but the result is very likely to be the right one.

Most of the time we follow the first model, applying the principle of cognitive economy. In situations where there is little or nothing at stake, we use simplified procedures to reach a conclusion, without assessing all the possible options. And as simple explanations work effectively in many cases, we feel justified in taking this approach.

Hasty judgments

Researchers use the term *heuristic* to describe the kind of rules, not always reliable, that are economical in terms of time and energy and allow us to make quick decisions. Here are a few examples of this kind of biased or fallacious reasoning.

Majority heuristic This refers to conforming – believing that the opinion of the majority is right, that consensus in support of a theory or behaviour pattern must prove it to be right.

Recognition heuristic We naturally give greater importance to things we know. Which city has the larger population, Berlin, Germany, or Belo Horizonte, Brazil? If you said Berlin, you made the wrong choice. The best-known cities do not necessarily have the largest population.

Time heuristic In this case, the belief is that anything requiring a great deal of time must be good.

Availability heuristic News stories that are given the greatest media coverage are more present in our minds because they are more accessible in our memory banks, but this doesn't necessarily show how important or true they are.

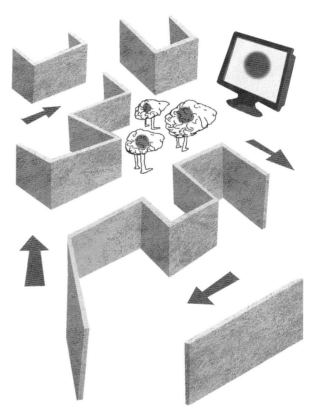

Alien invasion On October 30, 1938, American actor Orson Welles narrated a radio adaptation of *The War of the Worlds*, by HG Wells. The announcement of an invasion by Martians, complete with news flashes, was so realistic that it sparked panic among listeners, with some even fleeing their homes.

When we confuse cause and effect

Cart-before-the-horse arguments, where the effect is said to be the cause, are often presented humorously, for example: 'Nature has provided for all our needs. It has made sure that apples grow in Tasmania where they drink so much cider.' Yet we often come across this kind of reverse reasoning in everyday life, as the following examples illustrate.

● 'Of course you feel tired; you're taking antibiotics.' The widespread idea that antibiotics cause fatigue comes from the observation that the two events often coincide and from concluding that there is therefore a causal relationship. The truth is that the fatigue is caused by the illness requiring antibiotics, not by the treatment.

● 'Whenever police are at that intersection, there's a huge traffic jam!' The reverse argument is more likely: because there is a traffic problem, the police have come along to deal with it.

Fate or coincidence?

We sometimes think we see connections between events that are totally unrelated because we underestimate the likelihood that they are just coincidences. Depending on the circumstances, chance can be called good luck, bad luck, destiny, providence or the fickle finger of fate. It's as though people have a need to find meaning in random events that have no connection at all. When reading one day we may notice an unusual or technical term, and then the very next day we are surprised to discover it in another context. This makes us think that it couldn't possibly be a simple coincidence, that it must be some sort of sign. But unusual words or odd facts attract our attention for the simple reason that they are uncommon; when we see them again in a different context, we remember the first time we came across them precisely because it seemed so strange. When we say something like 'I was wandering around, and as though by chance such and such a thing happened', it shows that we don't believe in chance and that our brain is always trying to find meaning in the information it is processing.

Coincidence or lucky number?
Laëtitia Le Corguillé, France's BMX champion, won the silver medal at the 2008 Olympics in Beijing on 22 August, at the age of 22. She comes from Côtes d'Armor, which is administrative region number 22 in France, and her racing number was 22.

The impact of stance and expression

Sit up straight and smile. No doubt you are feeling better already. Even if you are sceptical, it's a fact that physical bearing, posture and facial expressions influence how we process information. Researchers asked two groups of students to watch a cartoon film; one group had to hold a pen between the teeth (imitating a smile), while the other group held a pen in the mouth, puckering the lips. They discovered that the first group found the film funnier than the second group did. We are not consciously aware of it, but the simple fact of imitating an emotion may influence the emotions we experience.

Called a sensorimotor effect, this phenomenon highlights the strange relationship between the body and the brain. To a certain extent, it's possible to change our emotional state simply by simulating expressions and posture. And that's why we should sit up and try to smile as much as possible.

Other psychological influences

Our perceptions are also influenced by a number of other factors that are explained in other parts of this book:
● Stereotypes and preconceptions that relate to gender (page 80) or influence memory performance (page 85)
● Memory bias: factors that influence or alter our ability to remember lists (page 103) or events (episodic memory, page 112)
● Language perception: factors that influence our opinion, as in political speeches (page 141)
● Facial expressions used to control emotion (page 195)
● The emotions of others: empathy, sympathy and compassion (page 207).

When time drags or flies

A common effect produced by the senses is the impression that time is going very slowly when we are bored (watching an uninteresting TV program or being present at a dull dinner party) or when we are experiencing something unpleasant or stressful. The last minute of a football match always seems too long if your team is leading by only a slim margin. In contrast, the last week of your holiday always seems to pass very quickly.

The amount of pleasure an event gives us, then, influences the length of time it appears to last. In one study, researchers asked participants to watch, for a fraction of a second, an unknown person who was either smiling or looking angry. When questioned afterwards, they all thought they had spent longer looking at the angry person. In another research project, psychologists simulated an attack on a professor in front of students. The altercation lasted 34 seconds, but witnesses estimated that it had gone on for almost 70 seconds.

Good luck or bad luck?

1. In China, which number is regarded as lucky?
- [ ] **a.** 3
- [ ] **b.** 8
- [ ] **c.** 13

2. In many Western cultures, the number 13 is regarded as unlucky. Where does this idea come from?
- [ ] **a.** The number of apostles at the Last Supper
- [ ] **b.** The number of steps leading to the gallows
- [ ] **c.** The thirteenth card in the Tarot deck (death)

3. What word means 'fear of the number 13'?
- [ ] **a.** Triskaidekaphobia
- [ ] **b.** Thirteenaphobia
- [ ] **c.** Triodekaphobia

4. In Japan and nearby countries, which number is regarded as so unlucky that people try to get telephone numbers that do not include it?
- [ ] **a.** 4
- [ ] **b.** 6
- [ ] **c.** 9

5. In Italy, which number is regarded as unlucky?
- [ ] **a.** 12
- [ ] **b.** 17
- [ ] **c.** 21

6. In the Chinese calendar, which month is called the 'ghost month'?
- [ ] **a.** The third
- [ ] **b.** The fifth
- [ ] **c.** The seventh

7. In Spanish-speaking countries, which day is regarded as unlucky?
- [ ] **a.** Friday the 13th
- [ ] **b.** Tuesday the 13th
- [ ] **c.** Friday the 17th

Answers: 1. b. In China, the number 8 is always associated with good luck. That's why it's lucky to have a dinner party with 8 guests and why the opening ceremony of the Beijing Olympics began at 8 o'clock, 8 minutes and 8 seconds on 8 August 2008. **2.** a. Judas, the thirteenth apostle, was the traitor. **3.** a. **4.** a. The number 4 has the same pronunciation as the word for death. **5.** b. In Roman numerals, the number 17 is written as XVII, and its anagram in Latin, 'VIXI', translates as 'I have lived', meaning 'my life is over'. **6.** c. It is said that in the seventh month of the year spirits and the ghosts of deceased ancestors visit the world of the living. **7.** b

Mental arithmetic

Systems for manipulating numbers have been developed by all cultures, with varying degrees of sophistication, but they all use the same basic skills. When doing mental arithmetic, the first skill that is needed is the ability to understand and work with quantities, a skill that we share with many animals.

The law of numbers

Pigeons can be taught to tap a button with their beak 12 times to get seeds. They learn to do so very quickly, although they often make mistakes – it's as though they have an approximate idea of the number 12. Similar experiments can be conducted with rats, monkeys and even dolphins. The ability to count is a very useful skill for animals in the wild. It can help them to choose the tree with the most fruit, for example, or to make decisions in a social context. When chimpanzees meet other chimpanzees, they start by assessing the relative strength of the other group before deciding how to behave. If they are outnumbered by more than 50 per cent, they will head off in another direction. The same ability to assess quantities has been observed in babies only a few months old, well before they can speak.

Tasks that call for manipulating quantities mainly involve a part of the cortex located in a fold of the parietal lobe.

Expressing quantities

The second basic skill that is needed for mental arithmetic is language, the ability to match symbols to units. Humans use symbols – figures – to represent quantities. A pigeon can't tell the difference between 29 and 30, but we have words and distinctive numerals, and we know that 29 and 30 are different, even though the quantities denoted are close. Symbols have also made it possible to develop complicated methods of calculation. It is almost impossible to multiply five hundred and twenty-nine by six hundred and thirteen without using Arabic numerals.

The representation of numbers as words and digits is centred in the language areas of the left half of the brain. Mental calculation demands more than the ability to represent numbers and to use symbols. It also requires the ability to reason and to combine concepts, which involves the cortex at the front of the frontal lobes.

Wrong numbers

Difficulties with doing mathematics, called dyscalculia, may be caused by brain damage, but some developmental disorders seen in children can also affect their ability to calculate, producing a condition comparable to dyslexia, the reading disorder. As mental calculation depends on the concerted efforts of different brain systems (working with quantities, using symbols, and reasoning), brain damage can cause several types of disorders. Aphasic patients (those with a language impairment) may be unable to work accurately with words and figures because they can't read numbers out loud, recite multiplication tables or find the right answer to a very simple sum such as 4 + 5. At the same time, because they may be able to assess quantities in an approximate way, they will recognise that the sum 4 + 5 = 2 is wrong. On the other hand, some patients may be perfectly able to read multiplication tables and recite them by heart, but may never be able to manipulate quantities correctly, will find the simplest subtractions impossible to do and may even argue that five is greater than six.

Degrees of magnitude

The concept of degrees of magnitude is part of mathematical intelligence. It's not so much a question of remembering figures as an ability to reason on the basis of knowledge acquired. To find blatant errors in quantitative data, it's often more useful to have a critical and curious mind than to have mathematical skills.

Can you estimate degrees of magnitude?

To answer most of these questions, there's no need to write down the equations, as the purpose is not to do accurate calculations, but rather to quickly gauge the degree of magnitude, rejecting wrong answers by roughly working out the mental arithmetic and using both your reasoning skills and your knowledge.

1. Are these equations right or wrong? Allow only a few seconds for your decision

True False

a. 25.364 + 24.278 = 51.642 ☐ ☐

b. 12/15 = 8/10 ☐ ☐

2. The bottle shop is selling a case of 12 bottles of Chateau Grand for $239 a case. Chateau Showy is being sold by the half-case of six bottles, with a seventh one thrown in for free, for $145. Quickly compare the prices per bottle. Is the more expensive one Chateau Grand or Chateau Showy?

☐ **Chateau Grand**

☐ **Chateau Showy**

3. In the novel *State of Fear* by Michael Crichton, a forecast made in 1988 was that the temperature of the world would increase by 0.35°C within ten years. The increase as measured was only 0.11°C. According to one of the characters, the error of 300% could be compared to the difference between a three-hour flight and a one-hour flight. Why is this comparison invalid?

4. What is the distance between Cairo and Cape Town?

☐ **a.** Approximately 6000 km

☐ **b.** Approximately 12,000 km

☐ **c.** Approximately 15,000 km

5. True or false?

True False

a. The Eiffel Tower is 320 metres high. ☐ ☐

b. A barrel of oil contains 1600 litres. ☐ ☐

c. A bathtub contains approximately 150 litres of water. ☐ ☐

6. Which speed is the fastest?

☐ **a.** 1 m/s ☐ **b.** 1 km/min ☐ **c.** 30 km/h

7. You sleep an average of 468 minutes a night. After 85 years you will have slept for:

☐ **a.** 10–15 years ☐ **b.** 15–20 years

☐ **c.** 20–25 years ☐ **d.** More than 25 years

Think small

We find it easier to think in small numbers, as our working memory is quickly overtaxed when handling large numbers. To simplify work with high numbers, we just need to move to powers. The number 3,621,895 can be written as 3.621895×10^6, making it easy to see the number of figures involved. The rule for multiplying powers is very simple: $10^a \times 10^b = 10^{a+b}$. If you are asked to multiply 3,621,895 by 309,554,186, you should write it out as follows:

$$3{,}621{,}895 \times 309{,}554{,}186 = 3.621895 \times 10^6 \times 3.09554186 \times 10^8$$
$$= 3.621895 \times 3.09554186 \times 10^6 \times 10^8$$
$$= 3.621895 \times 3.09554186 \times 10^{14}$$

We can see that $3.621895 \times 3.09554186$ is between 10 and 11. And $10 \times 10^{14} = 10^{15}$. The answer is therefore just above 10^{15}, which is 1,000,000,000,000,000: a million billion!

The same type of calculation can be done on a microscopic scale. For example, 0.00000000349 is written as 3.49×10^{-9}.

The rules are the same and can be used to multiply small numbers, or to multiply very large and very small numbers together.

Answers: 1. a. False. You can tell immediately that the equation is wrong. 25.364 is less than 25.5 and 24.278 is less than 24.5. Together they do not add up to 50. **b.** True. This can easily be checked, either by the equation 12 x 10 = 8 x 15, or by observing the change from 8/10 to 12/15 by multiplying the numerator and denominator by the same number, 1.5, and not changing the fraction. **2.** You are trying to find a degree of magnitude, not the exact price per bottle. For Chateau Grand, you round off the price of the crate to $240, so one bottle costs slightly less than 240/12, i.e. $20. You do the same for the second wine: 145 is more than 140, but not by much, so one bottle costs slightly more than $140/7, which is also equal to $20. The degrees of magnitude are equivalent, but a bottle of Chateau Grand is slightly less expensive than a bottle of Chateau Showy. **3.** The percentage is correct, but it compares flight times, which are absolute values, with differences. For the comparison to be valid, the reference should have been the temperature forecast and the actual temperature. **4. b. 5. a.** True. **b.** False, it is only 10% of that quantity (159 litres). **c.** True. **6. b. 7. d** (more than 25 years).

Beat your own record in mental arithmetic

According to the Japanese neuroscientist, Ryuta Kawashima, who created a training program using a game console, simple and speedy mental arithmetic could be more effective for maintaining efficient cognitive function than solving complicated problems. There is no consensus on this among scientists, but mental arithmetic does stimulate mental alertness. On the question of speed, we can all feel that time pressure is a good stimulant. These equations are to be done as mental arithmetic, as quickly as possible, without writing anything down or using a calculator.

Quick sums

Try to do the sums one after the other, as quickly as possible, using as many tricks as you can to make it easier.

Look for tens to simplify the calculations. For example:
$464 - 198 = (464 - 200) + 2$

For sums with more than two numbers, be smart and group together certain numbers and break them down to get as many figures as you can ending with a 0.

For example: $400 + 708 - 9 = 400 + (708 - 9)$
or: $706 + 525 - 6 + 175 = (706 - 6) + (500 + 100) + (25 + 75)$

a. $28 + 32 =$ ....
b. $477 + 223 =$ ....
c. $75 - 35 =$ ....
d. $354 - 298 =$ ....
e. $18 + 23 + 22 + 47 =$.....................
f. $56 - 12 + 44 - 8 =$ ....
g. $25 + 25 + 25 + 25 + 25 =$ ....
h. $250 \times 10,000 =$ ....
i. $253 \times 247 =$ ....
j. $10 \times 58 + 10 \times 42 =$ ....
k. $12 \times 59 - 11 \times 57 =$ ....
l. $568 - 49 =$ ....
m. $568 + 49 =$.....................
n. $1300 - 370 =$ ....
o. $1300 + 401 - 11 =$.....................
p. $456 + 69 =$ ....
q. $456 - 57 =$ ....
r. $235 + 95 =$ ....
s. $235 - 39 =$ ....
t. $8.5 + 0.75 + 2.5 + 0.25 =$ ....
u. $25 \times 109 \times 4 =$ ....
v. $202 + 1625 - 2 + 175 =$ ....
w. $2 + 4 + 6 + 8 + 8 + 4 + 6 + 2 =$.....................
x. $(2009 \times 15) + (2009 \times 32) + (2009 \times 53) =$ ....
y. $32.8 \times 37.25 - 37.25 \times 12.8 =$ ....
z. $1018 + (9 \times 1018) =$.....................

The unknown quantity

Find the missing number.

a. $11 \times$ .... $= 121$ b. $13 \times$ .... $= 377$

c. .... $\times 28 = 2856$

d. $630 \times$ .... $= 2520$ e. .... $\times 56 = 252$

Multiples of 3

For any number that can be divided by 3, the sum of its digits can also be divided by 3. Which numbers below cannot be divided by 3?

1   3   82   2007   9927
14   26   97   117
128   1789   252   1515   222

Find the missing symbol

Complete these equations by entering the symbol $(+, -, \times, \div)$ for the appropriate operation. Parentheses may be added if needed.

a. 25 ..... $13 = 12$
b. 19 ..... $13 = 247$
c. 473 ..... $43 = 11$
d. 575 ..... $238 = 337$
e. 5 ..... 5 ..... 5 ..... $5 = 0$
f. 5 ..... 5 ..... 5 ..... $5 = 10$
g. 5 ..... 5 ..... 5 ..... $5 = 20$
h. 5 ..... 5 ..... 5 ..... $5 = 26$
i. 5 ..... 5 ..... 5 ..... $5 = 50$

Multiplication by 5 or 25

It's easy to multiply by 5 or 25. Find the answers to the multiplications here, without writing anything down.

a. 9 × 5 = ...

b. 13 × 5 = ...

c. 28 × 5 = ...

d. 32 × 5 = ...

e. (24 − 10) × 5 = ...

f. (34 + 8 − 4) × 5 = ...

g. 15 + (24 × 5) = ...

h. (789 × 5) − 45 = ...

i. 11 × 25 = ...

j. 29 × 25 = ...

k. 78 × 25 = ...

l. (42 − 22) × 25 = ...

m. (33 − 10 + 2) × 25 = ..

n. 625 + (5 × 25) = ...

o. (12 × 25) − 50 = ...

What about by 11?

Multiplying by 11 in your head is even easier! Find the answers to the sums below.

a. 25 × 11 = ...

b. 34 × 11 = ...

c. 28 × 11 = ...

d. 39 × 11 = ...

e. 37 × 11 = ...

f. (48 × 11) + (52 × 11) = ..

g. (48 × 11) + 52 = ...

h. (88 + 77) − 5 × 11 = ...

The correct change

You have paid the following amounts with a $100 note. As quickly as possible, write down the change given.

75	24	36	18	73	89	91	4	17	29	11	65	71	37	49	8	41	55	67
......	......	......	......	......	......	......	......	......	......	......	......	......	......	......	......	......	......	......

Series of calculations

To go from the starting line to the result, a series of calculations are carried out:
- Multiply the number by 2.
- Take away 2.
- Add triple the starting number.
- Add 7 to the result.

Complete the table by finding a trick to save time.

Start	1	3	5	9	10	13	19	24	29	109	1009	1999	2009
Result	......	......	......	......	......	......	......	......	......	......	......	......	......

Coded numbers

Find the following numbers.

a. A third of twice 18 ....

b. Half of three times 222 ....

c. 3 plus twice 25 ....

d. Twice the sum of 30 plus 18 ....

e. Half the difference between 36 and 24 ....

Balance

The left tray of the scales has three oranges and the right tray has two apples and a 50 g weight. If each orange weighs 60 g, how much does an apple weigh? Both trays have the same weight and the scales are balanced.

Each apple weighs ....

Answers
Quick sums a. 60. **b.** 700. **c.** 40.
d. 56. **e.** 110. **f.** 80. **g.** 125.
h. 2,500,000. **i.** 62, 491. **j.** 1000.
k. 81. **l.** 519. **m.** 617. **n.** 930. **o.** 1690.
p. 525. **q.** 399. **r.** 330. **s.** 196. **t.** 12.
u. 10, 900. **v.** 2000. **w.** 40. **x.** 200,
900. **y.** 745. **z.** 10,180.
The unknown quantity a. 11. **b.** 29.
c. 102. **d.** 4. **e.** 4.5.
Multiples of 3 1, 14, 26, 82, 97, 128
and 1789 are not divisible by 3.
Find the missing symbol a. 25 − 13.
b. 19 × 13. **c.** 473 ÷ 43. **d.** 575 − 238.
e. 5 + 5 − 5 − 5. **f.** 5 + 5 + 5 − 5.
g. 5 + 5 + 5 + 5. **h.** (5 × 5) + (5 ÷ 5).
i. (5 × 5) + (5 × 5). **Multiplication
by 5 or 25 a.** 45. **b.** 65. **c.** 140. **d.** 160.
e. 70. **f.** 190. **g.** 135. **h.** 3900. **i.** 275.
j. 725. **k.** 1950. **l.** 500. **m.** 625.
n. 750. **o.** 250. **What about
by 11? a.** 275. **b.** 374. **c.** 308.
d. 429. **e.** 407. **f.** 1100. **g.** 580.
h. 110. **The correct change** 25, 76,
64, 82, 27, 11, 9, 96, 83, 71, 89, 35, 29,
63, 51, 92, 59, 45, 33. **Series of
calculations** In this series of
calculations, the starting number is,
in effect, multiplied by 5 and then
has 5 added to it to reach the result.
The trick is to add 1 to the starting
number and then multiply this by 5 to
get the same result. Answers: 10, 20,
30, 50, 55, 70, 100, 125, 150, 550,
5050, 10,000, 10,050.
Coded numbers a. 12. **b.** 333.
c. 53. **d.** 96. **e.** 6.
Balance 180 g = 2 apples + 50 g,
so the weight of an apple is
(180 − 50) ÷ 2 = 65 g.

Mathematical problems

These problems exercise the memory, making use of rules learned at school, plus logic and common sense. Maths is needed in everyday life to manage a budget, check bills and make financial choices. The fact that we feel uncomfortable or embarrassed if we find it difficult to work out a division without assistance is a clear sign that maths can be considered a basic cultural acquisition, just as language is.

Simple sums

Addition and subtraction can be done directly as mental arithmetic. For multiplication we need to retrieve tables learned by heart and stored in the memory, but the operation is simple compared to division, which is a complex exercise both to understand and carry out.

Sudoku calculations

To get to the answer at the bottom, you must complete this grid just as you would a Sudoku square, by using all the numbers from 1 to 9. Each number can be used only once. Each vertical line has the highest numbers at the top and the lowest at the bottom.

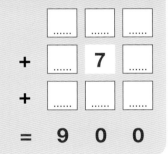

Repeated numbers

Which sets of repeated numbers are hidden behind the symbols in the following equation?

.... = 4321

The missing link

Complete the letter 'N' using the numbers 1 to 7 (1 and 7 are already marked) so that the three numbers on each arm of the figure add up to the same total.

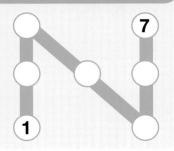

Squared

In the diagram on the left, the equation starts with the number 9 and goes through four consecutive operations (× 2, ÷ 3, + 4 and − 1), to get back to the original number, 9.

Fill in the squares in the diagram on the right so that the four sums are correct. What number needs to be entered in the top left-hand square?

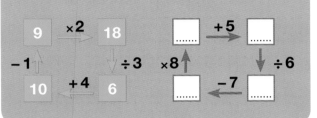

Pyramid

Find the seven numbers missing from this pyramid. Use each number from 1 to 10 once only. The number marked on a brick placed above two other bricks must equal the difference between the numbers on the two lower bricks.

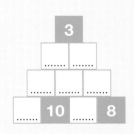

Answers

Sudoku calculations Two pairs of numbers can be put in the two columns on the right: 3 and 8, or 5 and 6 (they have to add up to 11). The option of 3 and 8 is eliminated, as it cuts off all options in the middle column.

```
    135
  + 276
  + 489
  = 900
```

Repeated numbers There is only one solution: 4444 − 222 + 99 − 0 = 4321.

The missing link Two solutions are possible. *Solution 1:* left vertical line, top to bottom: 5, 6, 1; diagonal line, top to bottom: 5, 4, 3; right vertical line, top to bottom: 7, 2, 3. *Solution 2:* left vertical line, top to bottom: 6, 5, 1; diagonal line, top to bottom: 6, 4, 2; right vertical line, top to bottom: 7, 3, 2.

Squared To find the answer, you must solve the following equation:

$(x + 5) \div (6 - 7) \times 8 = x$
$(8x \div 6) + (40 \div 6) - (336 \div 6) = x$
$8x \div 6 - 296 \div 6 = x$
$8x - 296 = 6x$
$2x = 296$
so $x = 148$.

Pyramid

Division

We have all learnt how to do division but, unlike many things we have learnt that become automatic reflexes, division can be forgotten.

The first reason for this is probably because division can be used in two ways. Division is an operation for sharing. In everyday life we may, for example, have to divide $400 between 5 people. But we also may need to know a number of parts: for example, a grocer might want to put 40 eggs into boxes of 12 and needs to know how many boxes are required.

The second reason is technical. Division is a complicated operation combining multiplication and subtraction, and producing a result that often has two numbers, a quotient and a remainder: in the eggs example the number of boxes (quotient) is 3, and there are 4 eggs left over (remainder).

$$
\begin{array}{r}
3 \quad \leftarrow \text{Quotient} \\
\text{Divisor} \rightarrow 12\overline{)40} \quad \leftarrow \text{Dividend} \\
36 \\
\hline
4 \quad \leftarrow \text{Remainder}
\end{array}
$$

Simple division

Do the following division.

$$45\overline{)746}$$

Fill in the gaps

In the following divisions, the intermediate subtractions are missing. Find the figures to replace the asterisks.

a.
$$
\begin{array}{r}
*7 \\
3\overline{)5*} \\
30 \\
\hline
** \\
\end{array}
$$

c.
$$
\begin{array}{r}
1* \\
9\overline{)**4} \\
90 \\
\hline
** \\
\end{array}
$$

b.
$$
\begin{array}{r}
13 \\
*\overline{)1*4} \\
80 \\
\hline
** \\
\end{array}
$$

d.
$$
\begin{array}{r}
14 \\
\overline{)12} \\
90 \\
\hline
** \\
\end{array}
$$

Riddle

When Tony was asked his age, his mother answered with a riddle.

– Divide my son's age by 2, and the remainder is 1.
– Divide my son's age by 3, and the remainder is 2.
– Divide my son's age by 4 and the remainder is 3.

How old is Tony? (He is not an adult.) ....

Giant omelette

For a special celebration, a restaurant manager is preparing a huge omelette made with 2009 eggs and has ordered 14 gross of eggs (one gross = 12 dozen).

How many eggs will be left over?

....

Rubbish reduction

In a waste management plant, everything is processed.

• Each group of **5 garbage bags** is compressed to form **1 cube**.
• Each group of **5 cubes** is compressed to form **1 cylinder**.
• Each group of **5 cylinders** is turned into **1 cone**.
• Each group of **5 cones** is turned into **1 huge sphere**.

2009 garbage bags were brought in today. What will be left over?

....

Magic numbers

• Think of a three-figure number.
• Write it down twice and you will have a six-figure number.
• Divide it by 7.
• Divide the result by 11.
• Divide the result by 13.

Do you know why you have ended up with the original number? ....

Answers

Simple division

$$
\begin{array}{r}
16r26 \\
45\overline{)746} \\
-450 \quad | \; 10 \\
\hline
296 \\
-270 \quad | \; 6 \\
\hline
26 \\
\end{array}
$$

Fill in the gaps

a.
$$
\begin{array}{r}
17 \\
3\overline{)51} \\
30 \\
\hline
21 \\
\end{array}
$$

c.
$$
\begin{array}{r}
16 \\
9\overline{)144} \\
90 \\
\hline
54 \\
\end{array}
$$

b.
$$
\begin{array}{r}
13 \\
8\overline{)104} \\
80 \\
\hline
24 \\
\end{array}
$$

d.
$$
\begin{array}{r}
14 \\
9\overline{)126} \\
90 \\
\hline
36 \\
\end{array}
$$

Riddle We know that:
– (age) – 1 is a multiple of 2, and so therefore is (age) + 1.
– (age) – 2 is a multiple of 3, and so therefore is (age) + 1.
– (age) – 3 is a multiple of 4, and so therfore is (age) + 1.

Therefore (age) +1 is a multiple of 2, 3 and 4. The number 12 fits (the next one is 24), so Tony is 11 years old.

Giant omelette 14 gross of eggs is the same as 14 × 144 eggs, i.e. 2016 eggs. There will be 7 eggs left over.

Rubbish reduction Each successive stage is divided by 5:
2009 = 5 × 401 + 4 (bags)
401 = 5 × 80 + 1 (cube)
80 = 5 × 16 + 0 (cylinder)
16 = 5 × 3 (spheres) + 1 (cone)
The remainder is 4 bags, 1 cube and 1 cone, plus the 3 spheres produced by the series of processes.

Magic numbers If the number at the start is abc, the six-digit number is abcabc, which is equivalent to abc × 1001. But 1001 = 7 × 11 × 13, so 1001abc ÷ abc = abc.

Fractions and proportions: revision of basics

Proportion is the statement of equality of two or more fractions. For example, 4/8, 12/24 and 350/700 all express the same proportion, which can be simplified and written as 1/2.

To determine if two fractions express the same proportion, there is one very simple rule: multiply the numerator of one by the denominator of the other. If the two multiplications produce the same result, then the fractions are equal.

For example, with the two fractions: $\frac{24}{28}$ and $\frac{18}{21}$

$28 \times 18 = 504$
$24 \times 21 = 504$

The size of a fraction is not changed when the numerator and denominator are multiplied by the same number.

The size of a fraction is not changed when the numerator and denominator are divided by the same number. This is the principle of simplification. When a fraction cannot be simplified any further, it is said to be irreducible.

Greater than or less than?

Compare the fractions and numbers below and circle the correct answer.

– less than: $<$
– greater than: $>$
– equal to: $=$

a. 5/4 in relation to 1	$<$	$>$	$=$
b. 5/2 in relation to 2	$<$	$>$	$=$
c. 8/5 – 1 in relation to 1/2	$<$	$>$	$=$
d. 1/4 in relation to 3/12	$<$	$>$	$=$
e. 3/4 – 1/2 in relation to 1/8	$<$	$>$	$=$
f. 4/3 – 11/33 in relation to 2 – 15/(3 × 5)	$<$	$>$	$=$
g. 2 × 3 × 5/16 in relation to 2	$<$	$>$	$=$

The unknown quantity

Complete the following fractions.

a. 0.2 = ... /5

b. 1.25 = ... /50

c. 0.625 = ... /10,000

d. 3.2 = ... /20

e. 0.045 = ... /10,000

f. 15/4 = ... /8

g. 0 = ... /8

h. 3/4 = ... /100

i. 3/..... = 75/175

j. 25/3 = 75/.....

k. 2 = ... /17

l. 68/50 = 34/.....

Decimal conversion

Express all the values on the top line as tenths and write them below.

1	$\frac{1}{5}$	$\frac{4}{5}$	$\frac{1}{2}$	$\frac{6}{5}$	$1+\frac{6}{5}$	$4-\frac{1}{5}$	$\frac{7}{2}$	$\frac{6}{3}$	$\frac{5}{2}$	100	$\frac{10}{25}$	$4-\frac{3}{2}$
$\overline{10}$	$\overline{10}$	$\overline{10}$	$\overline{10}$	$\overline{10}$	$\overline{10}$	$\overline{10}$	$\overline{10}$	$\overline{10}$	$\overline{10}$	$\overline{10}$	$\overline{10}$	$\overline{10}$

Addition and multiplication

Complete the additions in the table below.

+	$\frac{1}{7}$	$\frac{2}{7}$	$\frac{3}{7}$	$\frac{4}{7}$	$\frac{5}{7}$	$\frac{6}{7}$	1
$\frac{3}{14}$							
		$\frac{13}{21}$					

Complete the multiplications in the table below.

×	$\frac{1}{7}$	$\frac{2}{7}$	$\frac{3}{7}$	$\frac{4}{7}$	$\frac{5}{7}$	$\frac{6}{7}$	1
$\frac{14}{5}$							
				$\frac{2}{3}$			

Make things simple

Reduce the following fractions to their simplest form.

a. $\dfrac{2 \times 3 \times 5}{10 \times 11}$ = ...

b. $\dfrac{2007 \times 2008 + 2008 \times 2009}{2007 + 2009}$ = ...

c. $\dfrac{3 \times 12 \times 25 \times 26}{5 \times 6 \times 13}$ = ...

d. $\dfrac{(27 + 3) \times (27 - 3)}{3 \times 5 \times 6 \times 16}$ = ...

Answers
Greater than or less than? a. 1. **b.** > **c.** > **d.** = **e.** > **f.** = **g.** <
The unknown quantity a. 1. **b.** 62.5. **c.** 6250. **d.** 64. **e.** 450. **f.** 30. **g.** 0. **h.** 75. **i.** 7. **j.** 9. **k.** 34. **l.** 25.
Decimal conversion 10, 2, 8, 5, 12, 22, 38, 35, 20, 25, 1000, 4, 25.
Addition and multiplication
First table First line: 5/14; 7/14; 9/14; 11/14; 13/14; 15/14; 17/14.
Second line: 7/21 (or 1/3); 10/21; 13/21; 16/21; 19/21; 22/21; 25/21; 28/21.
Second table First line: 2/5; 4/5; 6/5; 8/5; 2; 12/5; 14/5.
Second line: 7/6; 1/6; 1/3; 1/2; 2/3; 5/6; 1; 7/6.
Make things simple a. 3/11. **b.** 2008. **c.** 60. **d.** 1/2.

Percentages

Remember that one of the classic traps is to add or subtract percentages that do not apply to the same entity (e.g. two consecutive increases in a price, or an increase and then a reduction). The basic rule for calculating a percentage is: a 30% increase is the equivalent of multiplying by 1.3 and a 25% decrease is the equivalent of multiplying by 0.75.

Selected maths problems

These questions will no doubt bring back memories. With a bit of practice and logic, you'll see that you'll soon remember how to solve equations.

 Percentages

1. A shopkeeper cut a price by 20% and then the next month increased the new price by 20%.
   How much will the customer pay in relation to the initial price?
   - ☐ **a.** The same
   - ☐ **b.** More
   - ☐ **c.** Less
   - ☐ **d.** It depends on the initial price

2. A shopkeeper increased a price by 20% and then granted a 20% discount to a customer.
   How much will the customer pay in relation to the initial price?
   - ☐ **a.** The same
   - ☐ **b.** More
   - ☐ **c.** Less
   - ☐ **d.** It depends on the initial price

3. The price of a watch will be going up by 10%, but you know that the jeweller will then discount it by 10%. Should you buy it before the increase or after the discount?
   ....

4. The manager of company A, Ms A, gave her staff a 2% salary increase at the beginning of the year and when they protested she immediately gave them a further increase of 1%. The manager of company B, Mr B, gave his staff a single salary increase of 3%. Which company gave the higher increase?
   ....

5. Real estate prices went up by 15% in 2009 compared to the previous year (2008), then went down by 14% in 2010 (compared to 2009).
   What is the difference between 2008 and 2010?
   - ☐ **a.** 1% increase
   - ☐ **b.** An increase of just under 1%
   - ☐ **c.** No difference
   - ☐ **d.** A drop of just over 1%

6. To calculate taxable income, Nation A has asked taxpayers to deduct 20% from gross income and then a further 10% from the reduced amount. Nation B has the opposite approach: first a 10% deduction, then 20% from the reduced amount. Which nation has the lower income tax?
   - ☐ **a.** Nation A
   - ☐ **b.** Nation B
   - ☐ **c.** No difference
   - ☐ **d.** It depends on the initial amount.

7. Banks A and B have approved overdrafts. At the end of each month, Bank A adds up the total daily sums overdrawn by its customers and takes 0.05% of the total. At the end of each year, Bank B adds up the total daily sums overdrawn by its customers and takes 0.05% of the total. Which bank gains the greater benefit?
   - ☐ **a.** Bank A
   - ☐ **b.** Bank B
   - ☐ **c.** Neither. It's the same.

 Hello!

Your telephone bill lists phone calls charged at a rate of 30 cents per local call plus a monthly line rental fee of $21. If x is the number of local phone calls over the billing period, which formula will be used to calculate the amount of the bill for 1 month of local calls?

- ☐ **a.** $21 \times (x + 0.30)$
- ☐ **b.** $(0.30 \times 21) + x$
- ☐ **c.** $(0.30 \times x) + 21$
- ☐ **d.** $(0.30 \times x) + (21 \times x)$

 Train trip

A travel agent has a special offer: if you buy a return ticket by express train, the return will be half the price of the outbound journey. The return ticket costs $27. How much would a one-way ticket cost?

 A stroke of luck

You have tossed a coin ten times. The first nine times it has landed tails. What is the probability of it being tails a tenth time?

- ☐ **a.** Less than 1 chance in 2 (less than 50%)
- ☐ **b.** 1 chance in 2 (50%)
- ☐ **c.** More than 1 chance in 2 (more than 50%)

Answers to percentages
1. c. **2.** c. **3.** After the discount, the watch will be 1% below the original price. If it cost $100, it would be $110 after the increase and $99 after the discount. **4.** Company A. **5.** d. 100 in 2008 becomes 115 in 2009 and 98.9 in 2010. **6.** c. Starting with 100, the taxable income in both cases becomes 72. **7.** a. Bank A increases the overdraft every month by charging overdraft fees on a monthly basis.

Answers to selected maths problems: Hello! c.
Train trip The price of the one-way ticket is $18.
A stroke of luck b. The chances are always one in two and, as each toss is independent, the previous tosses are irrelevant.

Creativity and action

9

Change and continuity

Human beings generally dislike change and are careful to organise their lives around routines. These life habits make us feel secure and comfortable because they enable us to avoid being confronted by the stress of uncertainty. They allow us to rely on what we already know and things we can already do: familiar itineraries, skills we have mastered, well-known environments, rituals, and so on. On the flip side of this nicely polished coin, the absence of novelty can lead to boredom over time.

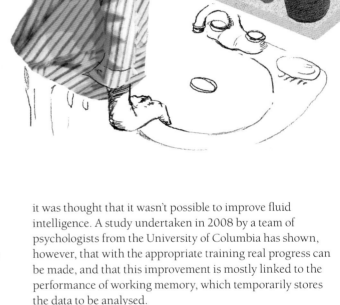

Faced with the unexpected

A certain amount of exposure to things that are new or unexpected allows the brain to be stimulated and curiosity to be aroused. This is why being adaptable to change and able to bring change about ourselves are factors that engender success and wellbeing. But this doesn't mean we should change all our habits: the stimulation we get from innovation works better when our personal environment retains well-known and reassuring traits.

The term of 'executive functions' became widely accepted in cognitive psychology in the 1990s and refers to all the cognitive processes that are activated by new situations. These mechanisms of adaptation are mainly located in the frontal lobes and include several faculties or functions:
● sustained and focused attention, which allows us to perceive the change, select the relevant information and prevent automatic or routine responses
● the capacity to develop a strategy for solving a problem or reaching a goal
● the capacity to plan, which allows us to implement a strategy
● mental flexibility, which is the capacity to modify our way of thinking and our behaviour so as to adapt to change. This is what allows us to change a plan of action while it is being executed, depending on the responses from the environment.

A skill to be cultivated

Mental flexibility more or less corresponds to the notion of fluid intelligence, which is used for resolving new problems, rather than crystallised intelligence, which is based on experience and knowledge (see also page 68). For a long time it was thought that it wasn't possible to improve fluid intelligence. A study undertaken in 2008 by a team of psychologists from the University of Columbia has shown, however, that with the appropriate training real progress can be made, and that this improvement is mostly linked to the performance of working memory, which temporarily stores the data to be analysed.

All through our lives, we can also improve our capacity to face change. While tests and exercises allow us to evaluate and train our purely intellectual flexibility, adaptability also depends on personal factors such as motivation, emotions and feelings. Having both an open mind that is free of dogmatism as well as the capacity to be self-reflective are valuable assets that make it possible to prepare ourselves for change, to think about new opportunities, to avoid focusing on failures or things we have abandoned, and to see the positive aspects of any new situation.

Test your mental flexibility

Everything that we do each day, even the most trivial of actions, calls on our mental flexibility. If you've kept coffee in the same cupboard for years and then you decide to move it, for the next few days you'll need to resist your first impulse to look in the old place and update your memory in order to find it. A waitress taking an order in a restaurant must update the list of dishes she has memorised if a customer changes his mind halfway through the order. Tests of mental flexibility are based on the same principle, that is, resisting automatic responses and applying changes in the instructions.

Colours

Read the written word aloud when it is underlined and say only the colour of the text when the word is not underlined.
Example: <u>blue</u> , you say 'blue'; red, you say 'green'.

green   grey   brown   <u>green</u>   purple

pink   <u>blue</u>   orange   black   orange

black   <u>red</u>   <u>purple</u>   red

More or less

Add 3 to each number and then subtract 3 from each number as quickly as possible.

	+ 3	– 3		+ 3	– 3		+ 3	– 3
7	10	4	14			13		
8			15			33		
20			5			18		
31			40			25		

Answers: **7,** 10, 4. **8,** 11, 5. **20,** 23, 17. **31,** 34, 28. **14,** 17, 11. **15,** 18, 12. **5,** 8, 2. **40,** 43, 37. **13,** 16, 10. **33,** 36, 30. **18,** 21, 15. **25,** 28, 22.

Crossing the bridge

Four people want to cross the bridge to Shelly Island at night. They have just one lamp between them and can only arrive on the island two by two. In addition, they're not travelling at the same speed. They take 10, 5, 2 and 1 minutes respectively to cross the bridge.

How can all of them manage to cross in exactly 17 minutes?

....
....

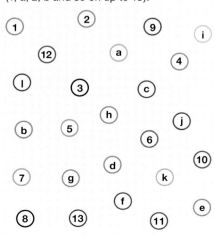

Answer: 1. The person who takes 1 minute and the person who takes 2 minutes should cross the bridge first (+2 minutes). **2.** Then the person who takes 1 minute should go back across the bridge (+1 minute). **3.** The person who takes 10 minutes should cross next with the person who takes 5 minutes (+10 minutes). **4.** The person who takes 2 minutes should go back across the bridge (+2 minutes). **5.** The person who takes 1 minute and the one who takes 2 minutes should then cross the bridge (+2 minutes). Total: 17 minutes.

Numbers and letters

This exercise is called a 'route test' and takes place in two stages. Each stage is timed, and the difference in time between the two corresponds to the 'alternating cost', in other words, the mental effort required to alternate between following two instructions such as classifying numbers and classifying letters (stage 2), instead of following a single instruction as in stage 1.

Stage 1: Link the numbers together in increasing order as quickly as possible without lifting your pencil.

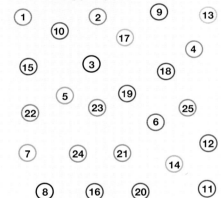

Stage 2: Do the same thing as before, but this time alternate a number and a letter (1, a, 2, b and so on up to 13).

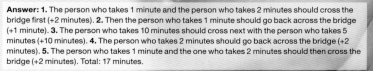

Are you set in your ways?

Are you someone who mainly enjoys what you know already or do you genuinely take pleasure in something new?

	Yes	No
1. You have radically changed your job at least once in your life.	☐	☐
2. You have moved house at least once in the course of your adult life (more than 100 kilometres away).	☐	☐
3. You often order the same thing in a restaurant.	☐	☐
4. You often go to the same place on holiday.	☐	☐
5. The following words make you feel ill at ease: improvisation, impromptu, unpredictable.	☐	☐
6. You make new friends easily.	☐	☐
7. You have a limited circle of friends.	☐	☐
8. You generally have your meals at the same time each day.	☐	☐
9. You watch the same television programs each week.	☐	☐
10. You have changed some of your habits to contribute to the protection of the planet (for example, you make fewer car trips, buy local products, turn off pilot lights).	☐	☐
11. You immediately call the repairman if your TV breaks down.	☐	☐
12. Your friends and acquaintances are generally people of your generation.	☐	☐
13. You like organised trips (package tours or holiday clubs).	☐	☐
14. You have learnt one or more new sports as an adult.	☐	☐
15. You only sleep well in your own bed.	☐	☐
16. You have already spent more than six months overseas in the course of your adult life.	☐	☐
17. After a failure or a disappointment, you take some time to forget or forgive.	☐	☐
18. You are interested in new trends in music.	☐	☐
19. When you are on holiday, comfort is a secondary consideration. What's important to you is discovering new worlds (landscapes, cultures and activities).	☐	☐
20. You closely follow and adopt technical innovations (computers, telephone systems, digital photography).	☐	☐

Results

Depending on your answer, tick either box A or box B.

	A	B		A	B
1.	No ☐	Yes ☐	12.	Yes ☐	No ☐
2.	No ☐	Yes ☐	13.	Yes ☐	No ☐
3.	Yes ☐	No ☐	14.	No ☐	Yes ☐
4.	Yes ☐	No ☐	15.	Yes ☐	No ☐
5.	Yes ☐	No ☐	16.	No ☐	Yes ☐
6.	No ☐	Yes ☐	17.	Yes ☐	No ☐
7.	Yes ☐	No ☐	18.	No ☐	Yes ☐
8.	Yes ☐	No ☐	19.	No ☐	Yes ☐
9.	Yes ☐	No ☐	20.	No ☐	Yes ☐
10.	No ☐	Yes ☐		A	B
11.	Yes ☐	No ☐	Total	☐	☐

Interpreting the results

● **More than 15 As.** You are a creature of habit. That's not necessarily a failing: appreciating your daily life is also a strength that enables you not to feel frustrated or dissatisfied with your situation. What's more, having a routine and set points of reference provides you with a reassuring stability that allows you to cope with difficult times. But being attached to habits is limiting if it prevents you from acting. It can then lead to passivity or even rigidity in the face of events that require flexibility, an open mind or a re-examination of certain principles.

● **More than 15 Bs.** Your life is not governed by routine. Change and innovation don't frighten you. Your curiosity and your open mind give you access to alternative models. Your taste for new experiences also allows you to face changes with greater serenity. The flip side? The boredom and weariness that you may feel in everyday life.

● **An intermediate score.** Both of the tendencies described above apply to you, because depending on the area (work, friendships, relationships) and the circumstances, you are either more likely to prefer routine or you can be inclined towards innovation. If you are constantly torn between these two inclinations, you may well have to manage this contradictory situation. As the US novelist Thornton Wilder put it: 'It's when you're safe at home you wish that you were having an adventure. When you're having an adventure you wish you were safe at home.'

7 TIPS FOR MOVING WITH THE TIMES

1 Don't think of modernity as a threat

To make sure you don't feel excluded, you must remain inquisitive, keep informed, and not automatically reject everything new. Trends in fashion and art are not threatening. Handling modern communication tools, such as the internet, is something that anyone can do with a bit of practice.

Dare to change The Zimmers is a British rock band that challenges misconceptions about the elderly. It has some 50 members with a cumulative age of about 3700!

6 Don't say, 'It used to be better'

Education, courtesy, language… We often have the tendency to idealise the past, or even to see it differently from what it really was, because it is tempting to take refuge in the good old days. Nostalgia is an ambiguous feeling that associates the sweetness of memories with the bitterness of loss. Frequent recourse to nostalgia is a defensive reaction to change and shows a certain inability to adapt to the present.

2 Renew yourself

It's never too late to acquire new knowledge or new talents. To keep your finger on the pulse of the modern world, take a general approach. Follow current affairs, read contemporary novels to immerse yourself in the current atmosphere, or essays to understand the times we live in. Attend lectures, join guided tours, go to university, start new hobbies or sports…

7 Try a change of scenery

When we are completely wrapped up in our daily lives, we forget that there is another place, other worlds and other people we might meet. We repeat the same actions and the same rituals in a framework that is always identical. You only have to travel, even without going very far, to discover new or forgotten sensations and to step out of the person you normally are and find the new 'you'.

3 Widen your circle

Don't mix only with people of your generation. Being confronted with other ways of thinking is enriching for both parties and allows you to move away from conversations you're used to having.

4 Dare to start something

Instead of being filled with regrets, why not say to yourself, 'If I don't do it now, when am I going to do it?' The important thing is to live your dreams right now, without setting yourself unrealistic goals. Take the plunge and start an activity or join an association: you'll discover new interests, challenge yourself, start questioning yourself again and feel more fulfilled. Above all, you'll gain a sense of the future.

5 Change your points of view

The world is moving on, so move with it! If you have fixed ideas and ready-made opinions, this may be because you feel out of step with the times. Jazz, rock and miniskirts were all criticised by our elders, just as rap or texting are criticised today. Show tolerance and flexibility!

SMS language

SMS language was designed to send messages that are short enough to appear on phone screens, but today it's also used on other devices. Here are a few common words, phrases and expressions.

Do you know what they mean?

1. **lol** ....
2. **ur** ....
3. **?4u** ....
4. **gr8** ....
5. **c-u-l8ter** ....
6. **i-h8-it** ....
7. **4eva** ....

Answers: 1. laugh out loud. **2.** your/you're. **3.** I have a question for you. **4.** great. **5.** see you later. **6.** I hate it. **7.** forever.

Find fulfilment through action

Whether it's giving up smoking, following a diet or learning a foreign language, nothing would be possible without motivation. It's motivation that determines our involvement in action and that allows us to mobilise the necessary energy to reach our goals.

A range of motivations

The first target for motivation is the satisfaction of basic biological needs like hunger or thirst. When these are met, we can devote ourselves to other aspirations. Based on this model, in 1954 the US psychologist Abraham Maslow proposed a hierarchy that prioritises human needs. First come our physiological needs, and then, in order of importance, the following needs: security and protection, belonging, the esteem of others, self-esteem and, finally, personal accomplishment.

Today Maslow's theory is considered to be too simplistic. For some, the need for personal accomplishment is predominant. Others seek power or are at their best in their social relations and as members of a group. Motivation is also largely the result of conditioning: compliments from parents reinforce a child's desire to be successful at school. More generally, our behaviour is determined to a large extent by rewards and the pursuit of pleasure.

The reward circuit

What are the biological bases of motivation? In the course of evolution a circuit of special neurons has developed to promote the behaviour linked to our survival and to the survival of the species. This network is called 'the reward circuit' (see page 218) and mainly links two areas that are among the most primitive in the brain. The first is an area of the midbrain called the ventral tegmental area, which receives information about the body's needs – for example, when the blood sugar level drops and we have to eat – and which anticipates the feeling of pleasure that corresponds to the satisfaction of the need. The second of these areas is called the nucleus accumbens; this belongs to the limbic system and delivers the reward in the form of a feeling of pleasure. This network is stimulated by the neurotransmitter dopamine, which has been nicknamed the 'pleasure molecule'. This substance also plays a key role in drug dependency.

The reward circuit is not exclusively linked to the satisfaction of our vital needs, however. It is also a learning circuit that encourages us to renew the pleasant experiences we have had in the course of our existence. It is associated with memory and is the basis of our motivations, and so also the basis of most of our behaviour. The results that reward our efforts – the pleasant sensations, the compliments or gratifications – encourage us to continue.

Volunteering Is participation as a volunteer really unselfish? Providing practical aid and support are partly a response to personal motivations, such as building self-esteem and attracting the esteem of others, or feeling the need to act in accordance with our convictions. The satisfaction we feel in helping others doesn't devalue the humanitarian action in any way: on the contrary, it is evidence of a heightened level of personal discipline.

Taking risks Our approach to risk taking is also regulated by the reward circuit. Researchers have determined two opposing profiles: those who don't need strong stimulation to be satisfied (low-sensation seekers), and those who seek new extreme experiences (high-sensation seekers) to feel pleasure. In the latter group is Liya Brumer who, at 80 years of age, made a tandem skydive with an instructor.

Project yourself into the future

'When we don't like life, we go to the cinema.' You may not agree with this statement made by French film director François Truffaut, but if 'we go to the cinema' is replaced with 'we watch television', this sentence highlights the importance of action as opposed to contemplation. Steering the course that your life takes brings a unique feeling of accomplishment and mastery over your destiny. It presupposes the ability to tolerate a certain amount of uncertainty and to have the capacity to see yourself in plausible scenarios, something that the brain knows how to do in the short term. In fact, whether we mentally simulate a situation or we actually put it into practice, we engage the same neurons. In a way, then, perception is a simulated action that already constitutes a decision. What's more, the premotor cortex – in the frontal lobe of the brain – becomes active even before we undertake any effort: it is this 'cognitive warming up' that allows a skier mentally to recognise a slope and its curves. Similarly, it is what allows film actors to put themselves in the right frame of mind before the director calls 'Action!'

This doesn't mean that you should systematically put off decisions and actions to another day when it's possible to make or do them in the present. Make a list of small tasks as well as larger projects that you are constantly putting off and assign deadlines for their completion.

Similarly, make the most of your retirement. Plan for this period by trying to imagine a new rhythm of life and a different relationship with time – one that doesn't depend on the demands of a job. Then take the opportunity to review your deeper aspirations and your dreams and define your priorities, because at last you will have the time to clearly distinguish between what is urgent and what is important.

How to start something new

● Trust your intuition in areas where you are already quite experienced. In other areas, compare your choices with more rational arguments.
● In order to help you overcome indecision, you can list the advantages and disadvantages of each option (for and against).
● The technique of mind mapping (see page 154) is also a good way to visualise all the aspects of a project or a decision, and this seems to limit any uncertainties.
● Make sure you can tolerate a certain amount of ambiguity and risk. To embark on something new, you often need to have an optimistic vision of the future and to be able to move forward without stable reference points.

New opportunities Retirement provides the opportunity to undertake new projects, even for someone who has occupied the highest role in government. After leaving office, former US president Bill Clinton set up the William J Clinton Foundation, which has established a number of worldwide initiatives to identify and implement solutions to the world's most pressing challenges.

Unlock your creativity

In the corporate world, creativity is defined as the capacity to come up with a product, a service or an idea that is both new and relevant. This skill is not reserved solely for the professional world: we use it every time we find a way to adapt to a new situation or when we think outside the box to come up with new ideas and new ways of doing things.

Creative techniques

These techniques help to free us from our habitual reflexes and ways of thinking. They encourage us not to simply follow our natural inclinations and to see beyond our intuition. They also rely on the collaboration of people with different backgrounds and expertise, which in turn enriches the points of view and brings a variety of perspectives to the same problem.

Brainstorming This is the best known of these methods, but it is often deemed not to be very efficient. It involves giving free rein to the production of ideas, even the most incongruous ones, and avoiding any censorship, so as not to inhibit the imagination of the participants.

Analogy This involves looking for similarities between different fields in order to transpose the methods of reasoning or solutions from one to another. Bionics, for example, establishes analogies between the living world and technical inventions: between birds and planes, for example, or between burdock, a herb whose flowers attach to clothes, and Velcro®.

Crunching This involves re-analysing an object or a service to bring out new ideas by asking questions in which the object can be reconsidered from an unconventional perspective. We can ask, for example, what it would be like if it were expanded or reduced, if it were combined with another object or had another function, or if its use were to be changed or adapted. In this way, a TV series, a film or a video game whose essential elements are extracted to create a derivative work are objects that have been expanded and modified.

The six hats method Edward de Bono, a psychologist and specialist in creative thought, originated this approach, which involves exploring a question from six different angles. The protagonists who are responsible for solving a problem will take turns wearing the six hats: the white hat describes the facts and the data in a neutral way; the red hat gives the emotional point of view; the black hat underlines the risks and weaknesses of an idea; the yellow hat gives the creative point of view; and the blue hat directs the debate, as its role is to take a step back and try to identify a global vision.

Give free rein to your imagination

The puzzles given below are both visual and text-based. Their purpose is to help you go beyond what you see and also to imagine scenarios that make apparently unsolvable puzzles possible.

Change your point of view

What do you see in this drawing?

....

Transformation

How can you change 'IX' into 'six' by adding one single element?

....

Accident

A man and his son are the victims of a traffic accident. The father is unhurt, but the son, who is injured, is taken to hospital. The doctor who examines him suddenly cries out 'My God! It's my son!'

How is this possible? ....

Geometrical mystery

Why are manhole covers round?

....

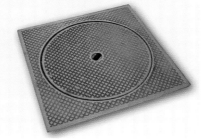

Mystery object

'A frame without a picture,
a bridge without a river,
two glasses that cannot be filled.'

What am I? ....

The right choice

What would you do in the following situation? (This scenario is taken from a recruitment test.)

Returning home in the middle of a terrible storm, you drive past a bus stop where three people are waiting.

The first is a sick elderly woman who must get to hospital as quickly as possible.

The second person is a friend who is a doctor who saved your life a few years ago.

As soon as you catch sight of the third person, you immediately fall in love: this is the person that you want to spend the rest of your life with.

In your sports car you have room for only one passenger. What do you do? ....

Horse race

In this two-horse race, the competitors have agreed that the winning horse will be the one that crosses the finishing line last.

Yet when the race starts, both riders try to go as fast as possible. Why? ....

Answers: Change your point of view Depending on whether you concentrate on the white areas or on the black parts of the figure, you will see either two faces looking at each other (in white) or a vase (in black). **Transformation** You must add 'S' in front of 'IX' to make the word 'six'. **Accident** The doctor is a woman and she is the boy's mother. **Geometrical mystery** For safety reasons, because this is the only shape that ensures that the cover doesn't fall into the hole by accident (a square cover can fall because the diagonal of a square is longer than its side). **Mystery object** A pair of glasses. **The right choice** You give the car keys to the doctor who can drive the elderly woman to hospital. You stay and wait for the bus, which allows you to get to know the person of your dreams. **Horse race** The two riders have swapped horses.

Exercise your imagination

Children invent scenarios: they create a character, imagine threats, adventures and heroic deeds ('If I were a pirate, I would have hidden a treasure, and you would have found my hideout…'). The whole game continues in this way, like a story they tell themselves in the conditional tense.

Try to rediscover this pleasure by trying your hand at writing. Apart from stimulating your imagination, working with language exercises your memory, thought processes and concentration.

1. Try out some writing games, for example. The fact that they have rules and a starting point (such as a photo, the beginning of a sentence, set words or a theme) will help you to take the plunge and stimulate your imagination, because they force you to call on all your resources. Invent a story using as many of the following groups of words as you can:

total sincerity

the ultimate choice

from the very first second

the hotel manager

This time I've got it!

a young academic

the plates in the dishwasher

2. How do you begin? Start with one of the following questions and continue the thread. Make a rough draft and don't hesitate to change the text as you go because writing is above all something you learn by re-reading what you have written.

'**Where will you go without me?**' ....

'**What am I doing here?**' ....

'**What is the point in telling the truth?**' ....

'**Are you sensitive to the cold?**' ....

'**What is the rule of three again?**' ....

'**Who wants to come for a walk?**' ....

'**How much more proof do you need?**' ....

3. Starting each sentence with 'I remember', try briefly to write down some memories that are both concrete and evocative for others. To help you get started, here are some examples from a collection of such memories:

- I remember the advertisements painted on the walls.
- I remember the buses with platforms: if you wanted to get off at the next stop, you had to press a buzzer, but not too close to the previous stop, or to the next one.
- I remember Lee Harvey Oswald.

I remember ....

What do you see?

Try to make sense of these unusual images.

Answer: This is a boy somersaulting on a trampoline.

Answer: These are pilgrims in front of the Kyaikhtiyo Pagoda, Myanmar, which is built on top of a boulder overhanging a rock ledge.

The soul of an artist

Modern societies tend to neglect artistic education. At school and in most of the professions, it's easier for your knowledge to be recognised than your sensitivity or your artistic creations. Yet research has shown that practising an art is extremely beneficial, both for your brain function and for providing some balance in your life.

Growing up with Mozart

Drawing, making pottery or sculpture, singing or dancing are all different ways of developing your sensitivity, your imagination and your creativity. These pursuits also promote self-confidence, concentration, control of your body (dance) or motor coordination (as in music and sculpture).

According to some theories, the positive effects that artistic activities have on the brain could even be far more important than their other benefits. In 1993, researchers at the University of California confirmed that children can reinforce their spatial skills simply by listening to a few bars of Mozart every day. Following on from that, the hypothesis was put forward that music encouraged the learning of mathematics and sciences. While the 'Mozart effect' has not really been confirmed, researchers continue actively to explore the impact of different creative activities on the brain.

Creative genius and eccentricity

Is creative genius linked to madness? This question has intrigued psychiatrists for a long time. While not all artistic people have been committed to a mental asylum as was Camille Claudel, many have displayed eccentricity or unbalanced behaviour – for example, Michelangelo, Vincent van Gogh and William Blake. Studies have established a link between creativity and manic-depressive psychosis. The neurobiological bases of this creativity have yet to be explained, because even though many hypotheses have been proposed, the nature of genius still escapes researchers.

The study of pathologies that cause brain damage has shed some light on which parts of the brain are linked to creative skills. The case of Tommy McHugh, an English mason, came to light in the early 2000s. Although Tommy had never previously shown any interest in the arts, after suffering a brain haemorrhage he became an obsessive painter and also started writing compulsively. A Harvard neurologist, Dr Alice Flaherty, attributed Tommy's sudden urge to create to modifications in the temporal lobe resulting from the haemorrhage. An expert in the neural basis of creativity, she also thought that van Gogh's genius might have been linked

to epilepsy located in this same lobe. In a similar vein, the French neuropsychologist and organist Bernard Lechevalier took an interest in the brains of musicians. According to him, musical intelligence involves structures found throughout the brain, and studies using medical imagery have indeed shown that melody, rhythm and tone are processed by different areas of the brain.

Other research seems to show that musicians are more likely to use divergent thinking (a method of finding new solutions to problems in a spontaneous and free-flowing manner), as distinct from the more common convergent thinking, which is measured by IQ and follows logical steps to arrive at the 'correct' solution. Experts have also noted that musicians have a particular aptitude to integrate how they call on the two cerebral hemispheres. This is probably linked to the fact that, in order to play an instrument, the two hands function separately but must also work together in a similarly integrated manner.

The arts as therapy

Practising an artistic discipline can help people to express their emotions. Guided by a therapist, it becomes a means of releasing anguish and overcoming emotional and relationship blocks. When people can't express their suffering verbally, therapies using music or the visual and performing arts can help to remove defence mechanisms and to overcome difficulties. Arts therapies are recommended for many different patients: for example, after an emotional shock or depression, to treat alcoholism and food-related problems, as well as to help autistic children and adults.

These therapies can take very different forms. The plastic arts (such as ceramics or sculpture) and puppetry are used to resolve internal conflicts and to allow the unconscious to be expressed. Performing arts such as dance can improve certain psychomotor skills. Body work (such as manipulative therapy or working with the breath) allows patients to reconstruct their image and encourages self-esteem, and may be suggested to treat stress or addictions. Music therapy helps to manage emotions and facilitates relationships with others. Listening to music has a soothing effect, singing releases tension and stimulates memory, and practising an instrument encourages motor coordination.

Therapy for body and mind Dance therapy aims to make a person more self-aware and to release blockages. Physically, it improves circulation, coordination and muscle tone. Mentally and emotionally, it reinforces self-affirmation and allows the expression of emotions that are sometimes difficult to put into words, such as anger, frustration or the feeling of isolation.

Artistic education

The French neuropsychiatrist Roger Vigouroux has explained how the brain 'makes something beautiful' out of a perception, and how it integrates emotional and rational elements in order to appreciate the aesthetic value of a work. The frontal lobe, which is the seat of complex processes such as memory, reasoning or conceptualisation, plays a key role in our critical sense. A certain kind of aesthetic emotion seems to be intuitive and immediate, but our sensitivity stems above all from our lived experience. It involves our memory, our culture (colour symbolism, for example, is not the same in Western and Eastern cultures) and of course, our ability to decode a work, whether it be visual or auditory. While artistic sense seems to be relatively universal, art forms vary enormously in different eras and societies – not everyone spontaneously appreciates modern jazz or abstract art, for example.

The earlier in life we have been exposed to the arts, the easier it is to learn to practise them. But it's never too late: perhaps when you have more free time you'll find that you have a hitherto unsuspected leaning towards pottery making or contemporary dance.

Discovering art Children learn about art not only by looking at paintings – through visual discovery – but by creating their own paintings, which allows them to represent and interpret the world around them.

7 TIPS ON DISCOVERING THE ARTS

1 Overcome your prejudices

'A child of 5 could do that!' 'Opera is not for me.' 'I wouldn't like one of those in my garden!' These are some of the clichés or prejudices we hear about the arts and artists. Remember that in every era pioneers of new art forms have been criticised, as were the great impressionist painters, for example, whose works are so admired today. So be careful about making hasty judgments, and retain your curiosity.

2 Train your senses

When you view or listen to a work, take the time to become familiar with it. What does it evoke for you? What feelings, either positive or negative, does it inspire in you? How is it constructed? Use your senses, your memory, your intelligence and your humour. Let an association of ideas emerge. Little by little, you'll accumulate points of comparison that will enrich your perception.

3 Educate yourself

Take an interest in artists, in their approach to art, in their lives. If you have questions when you are standing in front of an abstract painting, take the trouble to read the information about the painter's style in the exhibition catalogue. Study the explanatory notes provided in museums, read about the opera in the program, attend lectures, and so on. There are many ways of learning how to view and listen to works of art.

4 Let yourself be surprised

Sometimes it's a chance encounter that will move you the most. You might be visiting an artist's studio on an open day, or pausing in front of a performer during a festival, or listening to some street musicians.

5 Introduce beauty into your daily life

'A first-class soup contains more creative treasures than a second-rate painting', said the psychologist Abraham Maslow. There are the mainstream arts – and then there are all the others! Paying attention to aesthetics in your everyday life is a way of developing your artistic sensitivity.

6 Don't censor yourself

Choose whatever activity attracts you. Inhibitions are often acquired with age. If you feel like taking up an artistic activity but don't know which one to choose, try something related to a discipline that gave you pleasure when you were a child. Put your complexes back in the cupboard. Of course, you're no Renoir or Mozart, but the essential thing is that you enjoy it.

7 Develop your skills by copying

If you want to be a writer, first try copying out by hand the pages of the texts that make an impression on you. This will help you to understand what was happening in the minds of their authors. Do this exercise not only with literary works but with drawings, paintings or sculptures. Try to create in the style of others and use many sources of inspiration, for as US playwright Walter Mizner said, 'Copy from one, it's plagiarism; copy from two, it's research.' You can then move away from your models and find your own style.

The emotions

10

The whirlwind of feelings

Anger, fear, joy, surprise, disgust, sadness: we are continually affected by emotions, but do we really know what happens when we are moved and why we read the expression of an emotion so easily on another person's face?

Body and soul

The word emotion comes from the Latin *emovere*, which means 'to put into motion'. We know that the first manifestations of emotion are physical. Our heartbeat accelerates, our breathing becomes faster and we perspire. But emotion is affective and subjective too; when we feel sad, we not only feel as though we have a lump in the throat, but we are also plunged into a very particular frame of mind – a subtle mix of unpleasant thoughts, moral suffering and negative feelings. This transition from the physical to the psychological constitutes the very basis of emotion.

The physiological changes in response to an emotion are transmitted to the brain by means of nerve sensors located throughout the whole body. We feel the emotion in the very depths of our being, and the brain transforms this physical feeling into a subjective experience. Emotion is defined as an exchange between the body and the mind, like a dialogue orchestrated by the brain.

A universal language

All around the world, irrespective of culture, the basic emotions are externalised in the same way. So fear is always expressed on the face by a wide-eyed stare, raised eyebrows and clenched lips. It is thought that contracting the upper part of the face increases the field of peripheral vision so that it is easier to detect possible threats in the environment. In this way, the facial expression of fear is an ideal response, allowing humans to react faster when confronted by danger.

Each of the other emotions, such as joy, sadness or disgust, is also accompanied by a very particular expression that is the result of contracting certain facial muscles. The American psychologist Dr Paul Ekman has catalogued some 46 basic movements of the facial muscles by analysing precisely which ones are moved more and which less in the expression of each emotion.

A system of emotional resonance

We recognise other people's emotions, we can understand them and, to a certain extent, we also feel them. This faculty of empathy is said to be linked to the activation of a particular class of neurons called mirror neurons. They have the special ability to become activated both when we carry out an action and also when we see someone else carrying out an identical action. So when the specific muscles on the face of the person to whom we are speaking contract to express joy, our mirror neurons become activated as if we were going to contract the same muscles. We know what the other person's face is expressing and we feel the same emotion through mimicry.

Empathy Seeing someone yawn often provokes an irrepressible urge to yawn as well. One study appears to show that the contagious nature of yawning is an unconscious manifestation of empathy: we too feel the same emotion that the other person's face is expressing.

Smile!

To a certain extent, we can control our facial expressions to hide an emotion or lessen its effects. But controlling our expression can also regulate the emotional feeling itself – so the simple mechanical act of smiling, for example, actually improves mood. In one experiment, researchers asked participants to draw geometric figures while holding a pen between their teeth – either in the most comfortable position (with the pen between their lips), or taking care not to touch the pen with their lips. In the latter case, they had to contract the zygomatic muscle, which is normally activated when we smile. At the end of the test, the researchers noted that those who had not touched the pen with their lips were in a much more positive and happy mood.

This example shows that when we are happy and we smile, our brain registers both the feeling of happiness and the corresponding facial contractions. Connections are formed between the motor aspects of the feeling and the areas in the brain that promote subjective feeling. When the motor aspect is revived, these connections automatically reawaken the corresponding emotion.

There are many applications of this connection between the physical and the subjective: for example, forcing ourselves to keep a calm face when anger wells up inside helps to diminish the emotional impact of what we find annoying.

Nevertheless, we shouldn't abuse this method of controlling emotion, because if we resist our emotions too often (something that psychologists refer to as 'emotional suppression'), it can have harmful effects on mood and self-esteem in the long term.

Make believe Actors and especially mime artists – like Marcel Marceau, pictured here in his famous persona Bip the Clown – can simulate emotions and make us believe in their authenticity. But there are many facial signs that allow us to detect hypocrisy and lies or, conversely, sincerity. In fact, American researchers have listed some 10,000 micro-expressions of this kind that are likely to betray us.

Primary emotions

All human beings can feel six primary emotions: fear, disgust, joy, sadness, anger and surprise. In addition to these, there are a large number of nuances or secondary emotions that also belong to the realm of sentiments: examples of these are shame, disdain, guilt, pride, indignation and empathy.

● **Fear** A sudden fright or a threatening situation activates the brain's amygdala, and this provokes a reflex reaction of flight or avoidance, or perhaps muscle tension preparing the body for confrontation, or even complete immobilisation. In the latter case, the person seems to be paralysed. Other areas of the brain register these jolts in the body and allow us to become aware of the emotion we feel. To detect fear on someone else's face, you have only to look at their eyes.

● **Disgust** This powerful emotion is automatically unleashed at the sight of rotten food and involves the front part of the insula, a part of the cortex that belongs to the limbic system (see page 21). A feeling of disgust triggers a characteristic contraction of some of the muscles of the face, which in turn causes the eyebrows to be lowered, the eyes to narrow and the muscles surrounding the nose to pucker.

● **Joy** In a spontaneous smile, the zygomatic major muscle raises the corners of the mouth, and the contraction of the orbicularis muscle causes the eyes to narrow, forming crow's feet. To tell whether the expression is natural or simulated, look at the person's eyes: it's possible to force a smile with the mouth, but it's more difficult to mimic a narrowing of the eyes.

● **Sadness** Lines at the corners of the mouth can betray a sad temperament, because they are caused by repeated contractions of the muscles that are activated when a person is sad.

● **Anger** This is both a negative emotion and a defensive reaction when confronted with a real or symbolic threat. It is expressed by facial contraction (frowning and wrinkling the brow, grimace).

● **Surprise** This is a fleeting expression: raised eyebrows furrow the forehead, the eyes become enlarged and round, and the open mouth forms an oval shape. Although it is neither a positive nor a negative emotion, surprise does have a favourable connotation: when people are asked about surprises they remember, they will generally mention happy or pleasant times.

The emotional brain

Emotion is the result of a dialogue between the body and the brain. The first stage of this exchange is the perception of a stimulus, which sets the body in motion. This internal modification is then mapped by the brain and transferred to an area of emotional awareness, which provides the subjective feeling and allows us to put a name to this emotion, to think about it and to remember it.

Perceiving a stimulus

In response to a frightening emotional stimulus, image or noise, the first areas of the brain to be activated are the sensory areas, particularly the visual areas. They transmit the information to a sensory relay station, the thalamus, and then to the amygdala, which gives instructions to different areas of the brain, including a core of nervous tissue in the midbrain (called periaqueductal grey matter) and the hypothalamus.

The behavioural response The periaqueductal grey matter coordinates the muscles and, in the case of fear, produces a fight-or-flight reaction or, if the emotion is positive, causes the facial muscles to contract to produce a joyful expression.

The visceral response The amygdala also activates the hypothalamus, which modifies the body's nervous and hormonal equilibrium. The lateral hypothalamus activates the sympathetic nervous system, which causes increases in heart rate, breathing rate, blood pressure and perspiration. The paraventricular hypothalamus initiates the release of cortisol, a stress hormone that allows us to better utilise the glucose in muscles to fight or flee.

Becoming aware of emotion

The coordinated actions of the amygdala, the periaqueductal grey matter and the hypothalamus place the body in a state of intense readiness to react: the energy of cells is mobilised and the muscles are contracted. Messages about these physiological changes go back to the brain, where they are perceived by two structures: the insular cortex, or insula, and the cingulate cortex.

The conscious, subjective response It is the cingulate cortex that makes us aware of our emotions and allows us to interpret them as feelings. This part of the cortex interacts with the areas of the brain that are associated with language, making it possible for us to name the feeling, to become aware of it and to talk to others about it.

THE EMOTIONAL PARTS OF THE BRAIN

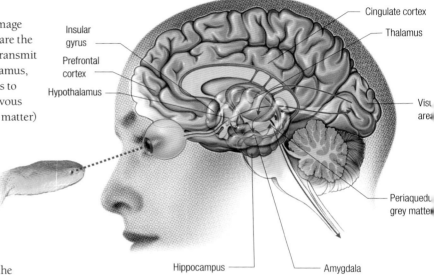

Cingulate cortex
Thalamus
Insular gyrus
Prefrontal cortex
Hypothalamus
Visual area
Periaqueductal grey matter
Hippocampus
Amygdala

Detecting emotion The insula detects the internal state of the body. It allows us to feel the muscular and visceral changes caused by the source of the emotion, and to create a sort of neuronal file that corresponds with this internal configuration of the body. If the body is placed in a similar state on another occasion, the insula will be able to identify the sensation, so allowing us to become more familiar with our emotions.

Other reactions to emotion

There are some other reactions that involve specific parts of the brain.

Anticipation The prefrontal cortex, the seat of reasoning, allows us to anticipate emotions and to react to danger by planning an appropriate action.

The memory of emotions The hippocampus stores memories and associates emotions with contexts: this is why your heart beats faster when you return to the places where you have been happy, or why the memory of a past event can suddenly unleash an emotion.

When we can't feel emotion

When certain emotional centres of the brain are damaged, either by a stroke or an invasive surgical operation, a person's emotional life can be changed considerably, or even completely destroyed.

Failure of the amygdala

The amygdalae are essential for decoding emotions, particularly threatening signals. Damage to these structures leads to a number of problems, especially an incapacity to discern fear or anguish on the face of another person and in the intonation of their voice. There is an amygdala in each of the brain's hemispheres, and the effects differ according to which one is damaged. If the left amygdala is affected, the patient is incapable of recognising joy on faces. If the right amygdala is damaged, the patient can no longer identify signs of sadness.

A connection breakdown

In other cases, it's not the amygdala itself that is damaged, but the nerves linking it to an area of the brain whose function is to identify a person by their face. Since this area is operational, patients who have suffered damage to these nerves are perfectly capable of recognising the face of someone they know well, but the image can't be transmitted to the amygdala because the connection has been broken. For this reason, such patients don't experience the emotion that would normally be associated with this face. An adolescent with this kind of damage can see a woman and notice that she resembles his mother, but he doesn't recognise her, because he doesn't feel the emotions that he has always associated with his mother. He concludes that this woman is not really his mother, but rather someone who looks like her.

This disorder is called the double, or Capgras, syndrome, because patients usually believe they are dealing with doubles of the people close to them, or even impostors who are trying to usurp their loved one's identity. As a result, they experience paranoia, accompanied by frequent outbursts of persecutory delusions. One of the most famous cases of Capgras syndrome is that of a woman who believed that a different double of her husband came home each night and that she had slept with more than 80 husbands.

No words to express it

In other cases, the emotion is present, but it can't be expressed in words. Called alexithymia, this is a frequent problem, with varying degrees of severity, and affects men in particular. Patients can't find the words to express their emotions: as soon as the conversation turns to an emotional subject, they stammer, perspire and feel embarrassed.

This disorder is the result of abnormal activity in the cingulate cortex, an area in the brain that is responsible for the transition between the raw emotion and awareness of it, notably by means of language. Alexithymic patients feel all the internal changes in their body caused by emotion, such as stronger heartbeats, a lump in the throat and sweating, but they don't understand what these changes mean. It's as if emotion remains at a distance and is something foreign. Often an examination of their past reveals that at key moments in their childhood they weren't able to associate words with their feelings. Their vocabulary for doing this remained deficient, and they are now faced with a handicap that can be very harmful to their social life. In addition, the physical manifestations of their emotions often make these patients think that they are ill – that they are suffering from tachycardia, for example. This probably explains the frequency of cases of hypochondria among alexithymic individuals.

Falling in love

There is only a fine line between emotion and feeling. For some neurologists, a feeling is an emotion that has become conscious. Seen in this light, there is an emotion that precedes the feeling of love, a sort of mechanical attraction that brings two people together before they are aware of what is happening to them or can talk about it.

The paths of love

How is this attraction produced? Mainly through three channels: sight, hearing and odour. When a man meets a woman he likes, the automatic attraction mechanisms are engaged.

Research has investigated these olfactory effects and found that volatile molecules contained in sweat or genital secretions, called pheromones, disperse into the air until they settle in the nasal cavity and activate one of the centres of sexual desire, the hypothalamus. The body is then placed in a state of excitement that is favourable to the development of the feeling of love.

Two mechanisms then intervene: a selection, which makes one person more attracted to another specific person, and an amplification, or idealisation, which will actually lead to the feeling of love.

Finding a soul mate

Can we explain the mechanism of selection, in other words, the moment when we focus attention on one person rather than another? Why do we fall in love with this person and not with that person? Personality and environment are naturally involved, as is chance, but, according to certain studies, surprisingly there are also chemical factors. We are more sensitive to the pheromones of a partner whose immune system is compatible with our own. From the point of view of the evolution of the species, this selection mechanism allows unions whose offspring are more likely to be resistant to diseases.

Apart from this criterion linked to our survival, facial characteristics obviously play a role in the attraction process: some are universally appreciated, such as symmetry, the fineness of the skin texture, the size of the eyes, the shape of the chin and the distance between the eyes and the eyebrows. But often, attraction also reflects conditioning in our childhood years. According to studies carried out by Polish and British psychologists, if a woman had a good relationship with her father when she was a young girl, as an adult she will be attracted to a man whose face reminds her of her father.

The development of feeling

After attraction has occurred, the emotion reaches the areas in the brain that make us aware of the attraction. Specifically this involves the front areas of the cingulate cortex, which links the physical effects of the emotion with the subjective and conscious feeling. Before this structure intervenes, we feel vaguely unsettled, agitated and uneasy. Afterwards, we can recognise what we have experienced, describe it with words and link it to memories. It's then that we realise that this is love, and can delight in it, be overwhelmed by it and constantly turn our thoughts towards the loved one.

'Intrusive thoughts' In the movie *West Side Story*, the obsessive nature of the feeling of love is epitomised in the song 'Maria', in which Tony can't stop saying Maria's name, 'the most beautiful sound' he has ever heard.

A deceived lover The Othello syndrome takes its name from Shakespeare's tragedy *Othello* – seen here in the 2007 production at London's Globe Theatre – in which manipulation and deceit triumph over love and convince Othello that his beloved wife, Desdemona, has been unfaithful.

An obsessive passion

At this stage in the love relationship, psychologists refer to 'intrusive thoughts'. The face or voice of the loved one fills every moment of the day, wherever the person happens to be, disrupting concentration and destroying appetite. The feeling of love is completely tied up with this obsession. Research conducted at Italy's University of Pisa has noted that people in love even exhibit changes in their blood that can be compared to those observed in obsessive compulsive disorder – an illness in which the same thought keeps on returning, despite efforts to get rid of it.

The loved one is the source of a strong emotional charge: at the sight of the beloved, the brain releases large amounts of the pleasure hormone dopamine into the areas that are essential for recognising pleasant feelings, which are linked to the reward circuit (see page 218). This biochemical reaction ensures that there is attraction, at least for a time. According to the psychiatrist Donatella Marazzitti from the University of Pisa, this attraction is of limited duration and doesn't last longer than 18 months! An enduring attachment may follow, even if the passionate desire gradually wanes as the dopamine diminishes. Other hormones, called enkephalins, are then instrumental in making the bond into a long-term relationship by creating a feeling of wellbeing and a positive kind of dependence.

Through rose-coloured glasses

Studies carried out by Semir Zeki at the University of London have shown that the brains of people who are in love seem particularly peaceful and serene. The area responsible for fear, the amygdala, appears to be switched off. Another area of the brain that is often active in case of depression is also dormant, as is critical judgment: the person in love sees life through rose-coloured glasses. This disposition can be explained by the fact that during the sexual act the brain releases a hormone, oxytocin, which promotes feelings of intimacy and confidence in the other person.

The Othello syndrome

This syndrome is attributed to a brain injury. Medical archives tell the story of a 61-year-old woman who, after having a brain tumour removed, began to suspect her husband of being unfaithful to her with a 70-year-old woman who was a member of her golf club. She kept him under surveillance day and night, and was persuaded that her imaginary rival secretly entered their house while she was asleep. No one was able to convince her that her suspicions were simply delusions. Her obsession was attributed to the fact that her right orbitofrontal cortex had been removed at the same time as the tumour. This area of the brain, located above the eyes, allows us to take new data into account and to revise or update our judgments. For example, if you think that your friends refused your invitation because they didn't want to see you, and you later find out that their child was ill on that day, your orbitofrontal cortex will become active and revise your initial hypothesis.

What is emotional intelligence?

Emotions are often automatic and involuntary reactions to situations that represent a threat or pleasure. They are essential for survival: fear makes us flee from danger, while pleasure motivates the sexual act, which propagates the species. But can emotions be reduced to reactions for survival alone? Obviously not, for they also constitute feelings over which individuals can exert their intelligence.

Reason and emotion

The French philosopher René Descartes (1596–1650) established a clear boundary between reason and emotion, and maintained that the former should free itself from the influence of the latter to find the path towards truth. But Descartes also reflected on the way in which human beings can introduce reason and intelligence into their emotional experience. Unlike animals, humans can feel their emotion internally, be conscious of it, name it and decide, in the name of free will, whether it is appropriate in a precise context. In a situation where it is realistic to confront danger, humans are therefore capable of deciding to fight, despite the initial feeling of fear that urges them to flee. Here Descartes laid the foundations for what, four centuries later, we call emotional intelligence.

A special intelligence

Emotions are not just biochemical upheavals that enslave us: they are messages sent to us by the body and the brain that we must know how to interpret. This means we have to call on our intelligence, but it is a very special kind of intelligence – emotional intelligence. This term designates the capacity to feel emotions, to identify them in ourselves and in others, to elucidate their causes and to use them to make decisions, but also to take a step back and control ourselves so that we don't passively suffer the effects of raw emotion. According to studies, the most emotionally intelligent people have greater professional success and more stable relationships and gain more pleasure from social contacts.

Aspects of emotional intelligence

1 Self-knowledge helps us to make choices based on our deeper convictions rather than on external pressures or social conventions. It allows us to lead a life that is more in tune with our true nature.

2 Mastering emotions is the capacity to avoid being dominated or swamped by emotional outpourings, to keep our cool and show restraint.

3 Self-motivation allows us to resist impulses and to bear a certain amount of frustration in order to reach an objective that is more fulfilling, but farther away in time. This attribute is essential for finishing tasks and persevering in a course of action or training.

4 Empathy (see page 207) is the ability to recognise and understand the emotions of others: it's knowing how to put yourself in someone else's shoes.

5 Interpersonal relationship skills (see page 209) allow us to maintain good relationships with others, create a convivial atmosphere and inspire empathy.

How to control your emotions

Emotions are both allies and enemies. They can either help us to make good decisions or lead us to act too quickly and contrary to commonsense. Choosing the path that allows us to live life well is difficult, however, because we have to be open to our emotions without letting ourselves be controlled by them.

Controlling impulsiveness

Impulsive behaviour is a classic example of allowing emotions to control what we do. Being impulsive means finding it difficult to put off an immediate pleasure, even though waiting until later might give greater pleasure. With impulsive people, an area in the brain, the striatum, becomes activated too strongly when they are faced with a desire that they find irresistible. It's possible that this impulsive tendency may be partly inherited through the genes.

In childhood and adolescence, impulsiveness is a natural tendency. Maturity is characterised by being able to take a long-term view and resist immediate feelings. And that is precisely one of the roles of education – to set limits and rules so that impulsiveness is replaced by restraint, the capacity to put off pleasure and contain emotional outbursts. Mobile phones probably play a negative role in relation to restraining impulsiveness, because they encourage the immediate and uncontrolled expression of emotions.

Sweet deal Suggest the following to a young child: either she can have one sweet now, or she will get two if she waits until you've finished your shopping. This sweet test offers a choice between immediate pleasure and a pleasure that is deferred, but greater.

Tyrannical emotions

Addictions to tobacco, drugs, alcohol or video games are typical examples of problems where emotions are in control. When a substance or an activity gives us pleasure, we want to renew the experience. The dependent individual wants to feel the same emotions by repeating the same behaviour, but is obliged to keep on increasing the stimulation because repetition generally diminishes the feeling (the addiction phenomenon). In such cases, harmony between life and emotions can be restored by ceasing to seek emotion for its own sake and instead allowing it to resume its natural role, which is that of a messenger that helps us to make decisions.

The reasons for anger

Irritation and anger are feelings that relentlessly build up inside us. We can contain them for a certain time at the cost of a great effort of willpower, but ultimately this censoring does little to calm us down and can even lead to resentment and stress. Curiously, an angry outburst doesn't bring relief either: at the time, expressing anger gives us the impression that we feel better, but in the long run it makes us feel bitter and ill at ease.

Psychologists recommend a strategy that everyone can use to deal with overwhelming surges of emotion: it's called automatic control. It is based on how we interpret the world around us – the view we take of a situation, rather than the situation itself. It uses an essential law of emotion: the fact that emotion is not produced by a situation, but by the interpretation that we give it. So, in each emotional situation, we should question or reflect on the real origin of our reaction, whether it's due to jealousy, stress, a feeling of guilt or memories of the past. Undertaking this introspective analysis is useful for two reasons: it's often all we need to do to calm down, and it helps us to know ourselves better, which is an essential skill for emotional intelligence.

Taking time out

There are obviously other ways of living with our emotions in a healthy way. The first is to understand that most of our emotions will diminish over time. In a heated debate or an argument with a spouse or partner, it is sometimes sufficient to go outside and take a breath of fresh air for a few minutes in order to return in a calmer frame of mind. Studies have also shown that at the time of experiencing a disappointment we always overestimate its intensity and duration. Becoming aware of the volatile nature of our emotions helps us to get through the present, because we are able to see that everything will return to normal one day.

Turning our minds to something completely different can also be effective. Soft music reduces the level of the stress hormone cortisol in the blood, and most of us can attest to the diversionary power of movies, sport or music. Pride and self-image can also constitute strong motivations; the main thing is to avoid hiding emotions on a permanent basis.

Learning from our emotions

The prefrontal cortex, which is located at the front of the brain, stores emotional experiences linked to past situations and reactivates them in response to present situations. For example, if the emotional process is working well, a young man whose girlfriend has left him because of behavioural problems will begin to feel negative emotions if he starts to behave in the same way with his new girlfriend. If he becomes aware of these emotions, he will correct his behaviour so as not to experience another break-up.

This capacity to avoid repeating mistakes allows us to make progress in our lives. To make the most of this, it's not necessary to try to develop our emotional sensitivity. Instead, we should think about what is preventing us from following the path suggested to us by our intuition, preconceived ideas about success, education or intimate relationships. Temporarily abandoning these habitual mental patterns allows us to take our emotions into account more effectively.

Time factor A psychological experiment revealed that football fans who are devastated by the defeat of their favourite team are convinced that their disappointment will last several weeks, but the reality is that it is often forgotten the very next day.

The vocabulary of feelings

Match each word in the column on the left with the corresponding primary emotion in the column on the right.

1. Remorse
2. Apprehension
3. Bliss
4. Contrition
5. Wrath
6. Revulsion
7. Fright
8. Horror
9. Loathing
10. Delight
11. Spite
12. Amazement
13. Hilarity
14. Irascibility
15. Repugnance
16. Stupefaction

a. **Anger**
b. **Disgust**
c. **Joy**
d. **Fear**
e. **Sadness**
f. **Surprise**

Answers: 1. e. **2.** d. **3.** c. **4.** e. **5.** a. **6.** b. **7.** d. **8.** d. **9.** b. **10.** c. **11.** a. **12.** f. **13.** c. **14.** a. **15.** b. **16.** f.

Look for the animal

Find the name of an animal that allows you to complete each of these expressions associated with emotions.

1. **Have**.................. **in your pants.**
2. **Be an eager** ....
3. **Like a red rag to a** ....
4. **Have**.........................**in your stomach.**
5. **Feel like a**.........................**out of water.**
6. **Caught like a**......... **in the headlights.**
7. **Be like a** .... **on hot bricks.**
8. **Be like a** .... **with two tails.**
9. **Get someone's**............................... .
10. **Act like a**................**with a sore head.**

Answers: 1. Have ants in your pants (restless). **2.** Be an eager beaver (keen, full of enthusiasm). **3.** Like a red rag to a bull (cause anger, rage, fury). **4.** Have butterflies in your stomach (nervous). **5.** Feel like a fish out of water (uneasy, uncomfortable). **6.** Be caught like a rabbit/deer in the headlights (surprised and frightened). **7.** Be like a cat on hot bricks (tense, nervous, agitated). **8.** Be like a dog with two tails (excited and happy). **9.** Get someone's goat (make irritated or annoyed). **10.** Act like a bear with a sore head (grumpy, irritable).

Are you an angry person?

The situations described here often provoke disproportionate reactions that indicate an inability to contain emotions and calmly evaluate the importance of certain facts. Answer these questions to find out whether you can control yourself or whether you let your feelings get the better of you.

Often Rarely

1. You get very irritated and are in a terrible mood when you're stuck in traffic jams, waiting in a long queue in a shop or are cut off after spending a long time on hold on the phone.

2. After a trying day at work, when you get home you find your children making an awful noise while they are playing. You can't help shouting at them, even though you know that your irritation has more to do with your own tiredness than with the children's noisy play.

3. You curse when everyday objects are not in perfect working order.

4. You're exasperated by delays – such as your train being slightly late or a detour that makes your drive home take longer than usual – even if they don't have any significant consequences.

5. You are enraged if you can't find something when you need it because the object isn't in its usual place.

Total ☐ ☐

Interpreting the results

● **More than four responses of 'Often'**
You find it hard to take a step back, even though you are probably aware that your reactions are excessive. You know that being irritated and angry is not helping the situation. The easiest course of action is to remove yourself from the context: listen to the radio in the car, go for a walk and breathe calmly, or use the excuse that there is something urgent you must do in order to break off a conversation that is turning nasty.

● **Five responses of 'Rarely'**
If you are always able to remain calm, either this is a sign of maturity and serenity, or it indicates that you are constantly suppressing your emotions, which can be harmful over a long period of time.

● **Other combinations of responses**
You contain your anger in certain circumstances, but you explode in others. Just be careful not to go to extremes. If you suppress your feelings, it could generate resentment. On the other hand, if you give in to your emotions, it could create conflicts that are often unjustified.

Uncontrolled fears

Fear is a natural, healthy emotion that allows us to be alert and to react to danger by fleeing or fighting. Nevertheless, it can assume a greater or lesser importance, depending on each person's life experiences and personality.

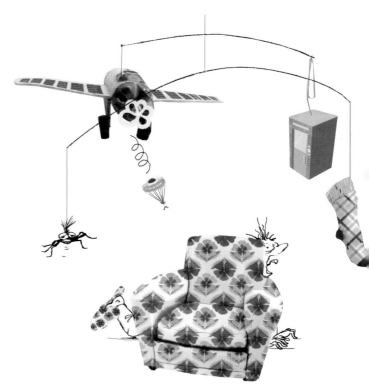

Phobias

Phobias affect about one person in ten. An individual's particular phobia – be it spiders, planes or lifts – can instantly bring on characteristic symptoms of fear: increased heart rate, muscle contraction, perspiration, hyperventilation, the sensation of suffocating and others. The emotion, visible on the person's face, seems to swamp all their thoughts and emotional reference points without them being able to control it.

A spider on the ceiling

According to researchers, a phobia activates a brain circuit called the lower fear circuit, as opposed to the upper circuit. These two circuits are routes that fear is likely to follow in order to enter the psyche. The upper circuit starts at the eye when the phobic individual sees a spider, for example. It then reaches a nerve relay station, the thalamus, before moving on to the brain's visual areas, where the image is consciously perceived and analysed. The information is then transferred to the amygdala, which orchestrates all of the physical reactions associated with fear – the muscle contraction and the release of hormones like cortisol. In this upper circuit, fear is accompanied by a conscious analysis of the danger, but in the lower circuit the path taken by the information is faster and simpler. The image is captured by the eye and then sent to the thalamus. From here it is sent directly to the amygdala, without passing through the brain's visual areas, which consciously analyse the nature of the danger. In other words, the reaction is fast, automatic and uncontrollable.

A phobia generally takes root in childhood. When a child is frightened of a spider, the brain's lower circuit is automatically activated, but the parents' assurances and the child's ability to verbalise feelings call on the upper circuit. This allows the child to adapt to different situations and to use reason so he doesn't feel in danger when faced with a spider. A phobia can develop if this learning doesn't take place, or if a traumatic experience reinforces the nerve connections of the lower path.

Obsessive compulsive disorder

A fear that lasts for a long time becomes anxiety. In certain people, this takes the form of obsessive fears – for example, of dirt or of illness. Such people try to overcome these fears through ritualised behaviour, such as washing their hands dozens of times a day to avoid contamination.

In obsessive compulsive disorders (OCDs), nerve connections work in a loop, constantly reactivating the same fixed ideas. The obsessions move around within a closed circuit that includes three nerve relay stations: the orbitofrontal cortex (at the front of the brain), the thalamus (in the centre) and the striatum (around the thalamus). OCD can have at least two causes: either a defect in the first of these stations, one of the functions of which is to adapt behaviour to changes in the environment, or an excessive amount of glutamate in the brain. This arousing molecule, which stimulates neurons, provokes hyperactivity in the loop circuits that support the obsessive ideas. In some cases, the excessive glutamate could be the result of a genetic predisposition.

Behavioural psychotherapy

Phobias and OCDs are treated using a combination of medication and a form of psychotherapy known as behavioural psychotherapy. A technique involving brain surgery is also being evaluated in the treatment of some OCDs that are resistant and severe.

The different therapeutic techniques used in behavioural psychotherapy are based on the principle of regularly and progressively exposing patients to their phobias and obsessions. Sufferers describe their troubles and thoughts and eventually also undertake special exercises until the condition abates.

Sadness, a fleeting visitor

Sadness is a painful feeling: something that anyone can feel after an unhappy event. It is a normal reaction that is generally overcome with time: as with every emotion, it often doesn't last long.

Sadness is a normal feeling

Brain imagery shows that the emotional system of a person who feels sad is very active, as is the prefrontal cortex, the front part of the brain that thinks things through, analyses emotions and creates mental images. Nerve fibres originating in the prefrontal cortex can activate a pleasure centre, called the nucleus accumbens, which in some way makes the sadness 'consolable'. Although you are sad, when friends invite you out for a drink, you enjoy talking to them and even laughing with them, thanks to this cerebral reward circuit (see page 218).

Bereavement, longer-lasting sadness

The death of a loved one is a particularly painful experience: the response to bereavement evolves slowly and goes through a number of relatively well-defined stages. A study conducted at Yale University involving 233 people who had experienced the loss of a loved one identified five key stages in their response: incomprehension, then grief and nostalgia, followed by anger and revolt, apathy and, finally, acceptance. This last stage generally starts seven to eight months after the loss, but it is progressive and is not completed until two years, on average, have elapsed.

It may seem surprising that a situation that appeared to be unacceptable and intolerable does come to an end after two years for most people. When they are overwhelmed by sorrow, people who have lost a loved one can't imagine that two years later they will have returned to a normal existence and that they will suffer far less. Emotions have a beginning and an end, and most psychological studies show that their duration is generally overestimated.

The survival instinct

The examples of people who have survived in situations of extreme distress show to what extent a human being has unsuspected resources of motivation and perseverance. For example, in 1912–13 Australian Antarctic explorer Sir Douglas Mawson survived frostbite, hunger, the toxic effects of vitamin A in the dog's livers he had eaten and a fall into a crevasse to drag himself over more than 160 kilometres of blizzard-swept ice and snow and finally reach safety. What kept him going was not only his stubborn refusal to give up but also his love for his young bride-to-be Paquita Delprat, according to his great-granddaughter Emma McEwin in her book *An Antarctic Affair*. The Austrian psychoanalyst Viktor Frankl has attributed his survival in the hell of the Nazi concentration camps to similar factors. In the depths of despair, he clung to life by thinking of his family and by imagining himself in 30 or 40 years time – old, grey-haired and thinking back over a long and fulfilling life.

The fact of existing for others or for a specific objective seems to have helped these two men to overcome seemingly insurmountable obstacles. They did this by projecting their thoughts beyond the blizzards or the barbed wire and visualising a future that would vindicate their triumph over adversity.

Against all odds After losing his dogs, supplies and the other members of his exploration team, Sir Douglas Mawson (1882–1958) was motivated by his will to survive and his love for his future wife to struggle on alone in the face of hunger, physical weakness and extremely harsh Antarctic conditions until he finally reached the expedition's base camp.

Depression, a pathological sadness

Depression, which is different from sadness or gloominess, is an illness characterised by ongoing mental suffering that has an impact on all the physical and mental functions.

A subdued state

Depression, a state of low mood and loss of interest or pleasure, is a condition in which it is impossible to enjoy anything, as if the positive emotions were numbed. This pleasureless state manifests itself through a general slowing down, feelings of lethargy and an inability to look forward to anything. People with depression have trouble getting up in the morning, because tackling the day ahead seems like an impossible task. Aversion to activity and lack of motivation, often accompanied by strong anxiety, cause such people to withdraw and become unsociable, which in turn leads to low self-esteem.

The precise cause of depression has not been identified. Three factors might be involved to varying degrees, depending on the form of the illness: hereditary aspects, particularly in bipolar disorder, a chemical anomaly in the brain and adverse or negative life events.

A bad chemical formula

In depression the neuronal circuits that allow the emotions to be regulated no longer work correctly. The prefrontal cortex, which is indispensable for developing and carrying out projects, is no longer sufficiently active. This anomaly results in a loss of energy and interest as well as the inability to envision the future. On the other hand, the amygdala is hyperactive, which causes a rush of negative emotions. Normally, the prefrontal cortex limits the emotional activity of the amygdala, but this brake is missing in people with depression, who are then consumed by dark thoughts. This downward spiral can be attributed to a lack of serotonin, which is a neurotransmitter that allows the prefrontal cortex to limit the emotional charge of the amygdala. A large number of antidepressants target serotonin by seeking to normalise its level of concentration in the nerve cells.

A distorted self-image

Very often, people with depression have a tendency to have low self-esteem. Psychiatrists have recently established that this is the result of overactivity in a specific area of the brain – the dorso-medial prefrontal cortex – whose role is to provide us with the sense of self, with our faults as well as our qualities. In the case of depression, changes occur in the way this area operates, characterised by a focus on negative aspects. Patients see only their less favourable personality traits and can find nothing positive about themselves. This negative self-image can be corrected through behavioural and cognitive therapy.

Social factors

Social context is a powerful generator of stress, and it has long been known that repeated stress leads to despondency and even despair. When the body is in a permanent state of stress, it produces cortisol, a hormone that destroys the neurons in the areas involved in memorising, learning and motivation. This process weakens the brain's defence mechanisms against harmful thoughts.

Depression worsens with isolation and daily stress, and so unemployment makes people particularly vulnerable. Individuals who put all their energy into reaching socially desirable objectives can be profoundly affected by a sense of failure when they suddenly find themselves isolated, exhausted and seemingly worthless.

The sympathetic brain

Without the support of a friend, spouse, partner or a sympathetic listener, how would we face the difficulties of life? Empathy is the eminently human capacity to understand what the other person is feeling, whether they are crying, laughing or admiring a sunset.

Sharing emotions

Empathy is the ability to understand from the inside what the other person is thinking and feeling. Sympathising is defined as the fact of aligning our thoughts and feelings with those of the other person. 'I sympathise with him' means 'I partially identify with what he is thinking and feeling; I don't just understand what is happening, I associate myself with it'. Sympathy retains a certain distance, but this disappears in the case of compassion, when the confidant feels real suffering in the face of the other person's suffering.

What determines the progression from empathy to sympathy, and then from sympathy to compassion, is the degree of distance from the other person's emotions. The brain is equipped with structures that allow us to identify emotions and reproduce them in ourselves. It can fully accept them, or take a step back to protect itself from them.

This means there are three degrees of emotional closeness. When it is controlled, as is the case with empathy, it allows us to understand what the other person is feeling, but without being overwhelmed by it. A psychotherapist can be empathetic towards a patient, but not necessarily in sympathy nor in a relationship of compassion. Sometimes we can even seek to understand the emotions of others for destructive reasons: cruelty and hatred presuppose that we know the pain our enemy feels and that we know how to amplify it.

Interest that is not always disinterested

Altruism, paradoxically, does not necessarily imply emotion. The humanistic altruism of Kant, for example, is a philosophical posture of principle, which demands that we should not do to others what we would not want them to do to us.

Biologists and psychologists generally distinguish four types of altruism. Parental altruism leads us to devote ourselves to those who share a part of our genetic heritage (such as a mother for her child). Reciprocal altruism is altruistic behaviour that brings some expected return favour (I am helping you so you will help me later). Wartime altruism leads some individuals to risk their lives for their group, their country or their ideas. Finally, altruism for the sake of publicity is behaviour that increases a person's

Feeling for others The brain reacts to another person's suffering. If you ask people to imagine what a footballer feels after sustaining an injury, they activate their own pain networks, even though they don't feel pain themselves.

prestige and makes others view them favourably (such as celebrities who establish charity organisations and then inform their public about them). In this last case, such people gain direct benefits from their altruistic behaviour.

None of these forms of altruism is in fact totally lacking in self-interest. Most often, altruistic behaviours vary according to the circumstances and what incentives are offered. If you make someone feel guilty, that person may become more generous for a certain period of time. Similarly, a man can be altruistic – by helping someone in the street, for example – if he sees a pretty woman smiling at him because, through her approval, he will have a better image of himself and his ego will be flattered. To understand the nature of pure altruism, we need to turn to philosophy or to spontaneous emotional compassion, such as is advocated by Buddhism.

Altruism, then, is a complex concept that is subject to many different influences. Empathy certainly plays a role, but what is also involved is the desire to make ourselves feel more important or to temper our own emotions, particularly our sense of guilt.

A question of distance

Considerable progress has been made in understanding empathy since the discovery of mirror neurons. These neurons are located in the premotor frontal area and have the special ability to become activated in the same way, whether we see someone carrying out an action or whether we do it ourselves.

When we watch someone cry, we also prepare ourselves to cry, but without necessarily doing so. The desire to imitate is strong, but whether we actually carry out the action depends on the barriers that we put up against the feeling of sadness. Mirror neurons are responsible for imitating an action, but not a feeling. We see the facial movements of the person we are speaking to and the mirror neurons reproduce them in the same way as a mime artist would. And we know that miming an emotion can lead us to feel the stirring of the same emotion in ourselves. It is then up to each of us either to let this emotion develop or to hold it in check and retain a more distant relationship with the person we are speaking to.

Two parts of the brain have been identified that allow us to share other people's emotions without being entirely caught up in their feelings – the median frontopolar lobe and the right lower parietal cortex. These allow us to avoid immersing ourselves in a feeling that is identical to that of the person to whom we are speaking and to keep our emotional distance.

A nation in mourning When Britain's Princess Diana died tragically after a high-speed car crash in France in 1997, there was an unprecedented outpouring of public grief. Carpets of flowers were laid outside Kensington and Buckingham palaces, people lined up for ten hours or more to sign books of condolence and wept openly in the street on the day of her funeral. Clearly, the depth of emotion felt by many people went beyond that of empathy to feeling the loss quite personally and, of course, feeling deeply for the two boys who had lost their mother.

Learning by imitation
Mirror neurons form the biological basis of imitation, which is an essential mechanism for learning, particularly in the very young.

The power of the imagination

According to some neurobiologists, mirror neurons and imitation are not the only foundations of empathy. We also access the feelings and emotions of others in a relatively abstract way. This is what allows us to imagine the suffering felt by another person in a situation that we have never experienced. We can't share this suffering through the imitated reaction of an identical experience, because we have never felt it, so we need to use our imagination. This doesn't call directly on the mirror neurons; instead, it activates a particular area located at the front of the brain, the ventromedial prefrontal cortex.

Human beings are sociable animals

Sociability is one of the main aspects of human personality. According to contemporary psychological theory, it is one of five broad categories, or dimensions, of human personality traits, the other four being emotional stability, level of conscientiousness, degree of extroversion and openness.

Who is sociable?

According to the psychological classification of personality, each person's temperament is considered to be a combination of varying degrees of the five basic factors. In one individual, emotional stability will be more noticeable, whereas in another it will be extroversion that will be dominant, and so on.

Sociable people demonstrate a strong pleasantness component, which is defined as the desire for cooperation and social harmony. This capacity is often determined or acquired quite early in life.

How can a pleasant or sociable individual be recognised? There are a number of characteristics or behaviours that are often present in such people.

- They are very considerate, friendly and helpful.
- They are ready to put their personal interests aside or to moderate them to reach compromises with others.
- When in a group, they are rarely directly confrontational and spend time consulting others.
- They rarely express a negative opinion about individuals or about human nature in general.
- They know how to put a given situation, the stakes or a conflict into perspective – that is, they can imagine what it is like to be in another person's shoes.
- They are sensitive to the difficulties experienced by others and don't like to see others suffer.

The opposite of sociability is a lack of interest in other people's problems and, in contact with others, a tendency to be introverted and less inclined to compromise.

Are you sociable?

		A	B
1. You are interested in people, in their lives, in their troubles and their joys.	**a.** True **b.** False		
2. You are quite sensitive to other people's feelings.	**a.** Often **b.** Rarely		
3. You are soft-hearted and easily moved to tears and often feel sorry for others.	**a.** True **b.** False		
4. You always make sure that people feel at ease in your home or elsewhere.	**a.** Often **b.** Rarely		
5. Your friends find it easy to confide in you.	**a.** True **b.** False		
6. You set aside time for others (family, friends, contacts).	**a.** Often **b.** Rarely		
7. Other people's problems don't concern you.	**a.** Often **b.** Rarely		
8. Other people don't really interest you, and you are often criticised for not knowing how to listen.	**a.** Often **b.** Rarely		
9. You're not very concerned about what happens to your acquaintances.	**a.** Often **b.** Rarely		
10. You can be aggressive or even nasty.	**a.** Often **b.** Rarely		

	A	B
Total		

Interpreting the results

For each 'A' response to the first six questions, score 1 point. For each 'B' response to the last four questions, score 1 point. Add up the total to get a sociability score out of 10. If you have a low score, note that it's possible to live perfectly well without being particularly sociable. But if this makes you unhappy and you don't like having few social contacts, try to change things by examining each of your answers to this questionnaire.

Beware of egocentric tendencies!

You will undoubtedly recognise yourself in some of these failings, the objective of which is to make us seem important and preserve our self-image.

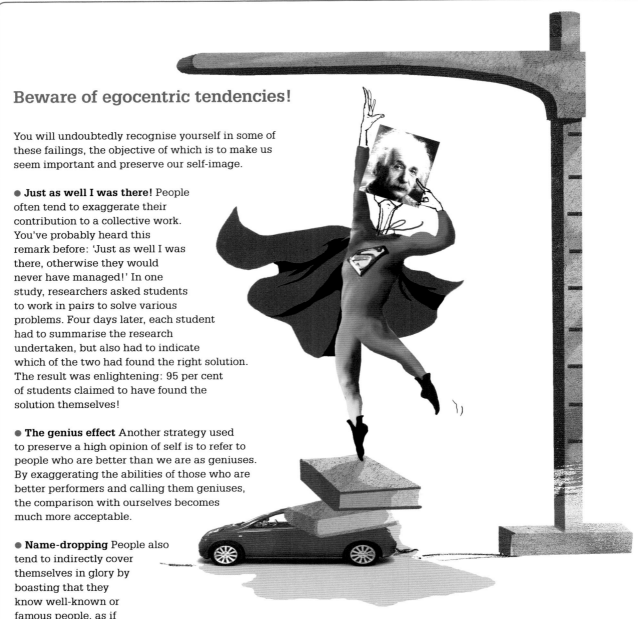

● **Just as well I was there!** People often tend to exaggerate their contribution to a collective work. You've probably heard this remark before: 'Just as well I was there, otherwise they would never have managed!' In one study, researchers asked students to work in pairs to solve various problems. Four days later, each student had to summarise the research undertaken, but also had to indicate which of the two had found the right solution. The result was enlightening: 95 per cent of students claimed to have found the solution themselves!

● **The genius effect** Another strategy used to preserve a high opinion of self is to refer to people who are better than we are as geniuses. By exaggerating the abilities of those who are better performers and calling them geniuses, the comparison with ourselves becomes much more acceptable.

● **Name-dropping** People also tend to indirectly cover themselves in glory by boasting that they know well-known or famous people, as if some of their prestige is transferred in some way. Someone is likely to say something like 'I spent an excellent evening at my friend's house – you know, the surgeon…', but you rarely hear 'I spent an excellent evening with my friend, the garbage collector'.

● **Our friends are better than we are!** If we are sometimes stricter or less generous with our friends than with strangers, psychologists consider this to be another strategy for safeguarding our self-esteem. In one study a group of men were asked to participate in an experiment with their best friends. Each had to answer questions in an intelligence test while sitting beside their friend. The researchers noticed that the participants tried to influence their friend's work negatively by supplying him with worthless or even incorrect information. In contrast they didn't behave like this with a stranger. How can this attitude be explained? Perhaps it's because we don't want to admit that a friend – that is, someone with whom we can compare ourselves – might be better than us in areas that we consider important. This social comparison threatens our self-esteem. Paradoxically, sabotaging the success of a friend or damaging his reputation is not rare behaviour.

7 TIPS FOR IMPROVING YOUR SOCIAL NETWORK

1 Share your emotions

Bringing people together to experience shared emotions is one of the basic forms of human social behaviour. Psychological studies show that when human beings experience an intense emotion, such as on the birth of a child or the death of a loved one, they react by wanting to share their feelings with friends or those who are close to them. The function of this reaction is to strengthen connections with others: it is a social cement that we should not deny ourselves.

2 Be polite

Courteous behaviour makes a good impression and gives us a better image in social settings. Studies show that not only do people retain a positive memory of someone who addresses them politely, but they also pay more attention to what that person says and respond more favourably. Courtesy and good manners are essential for making a good first impression.

3 Smile

A friendly smile is a good way to make sure people remember you. Studies carried out at Brazil's University of São Paulo have shown that you will be perceived as more intelligent, extroverted, pleasant and sociable if you approach others with a smile. What's more, people will remember your face and your name for much longer.

4 Offer hot drinks

Serving coffee or tea at the right moment can encourage good communication. Studies at the University of Brisbane have demonstrated that people are more attentive to the person they are talking to after they have had a coffee and they react more favourably to what the person says. Another study carried out at the University of London found that people are regarded as more friendly if they offer a warm drink to the person they are talking to, because the brain associates the warmth from the contact with the cup with emotional warmth!

5 Make eye contact

Looking directly at the person you are talking to makes you appear more convincing and gives the impression that you are trustworthy. A psychological experiment found that when a request to sign a petition or to make a donation is accompanied by direct eye contact it is ten times more likely to be granted.

6 Put others at ease

Establishing a feeling of trust is essential and can be achieved quite simply. For example, by nodding your head you encourage the other person to continue talking and this leads to a greater degree of satisfaction with the outcome of the conversation.

7 Get a dog!

Taking a dog for a walk helps you to make friends, according to an experiment carried out at the UK's University of Warwick. The participants went for walks in the town, some accompanied by dogs and others alone. The researchers noticed that other people were more likely to start a conversation or have a joke with those who were walking with dogs. It seems that pets are social catalysts.

A subtle alchemy

Happiness is made up of all the good and positive things that happen to us, whether they are actual events or our experience of happy moments that have some special significance.

A question of nature?

Happiness is something that human beings possess to a greater or lesser degree. This predisposition or capacity to be happy can be seen in people who keep smiling no matter what happens. Others, on the other hand, always look gloomy or are constantly irritated and complain about what are often minor problems. A happy disposition seems to be based on certain aspects of character that may have some genetic basis.

Studies have shown that twins generally experience happiness to a similar degree, even if they are raised separately. Just as they have the same genetic heritage, they also seem to enjoy the same capacity for happiness. To what extent can the differences in the subjective wellbeing of individuals be attributed to their genes? What psychologists have found is that the happiest people have a particular psychological profile: they tend to be extroverted, emotionally stable, pleasant socially and conscientious. These character traits, with the exception of the last one, are partly associated with biological factors, and particularly with the action of two neurotransmitters, dopamine and serotonin.

That some people can be predisposed towards happiness seems plausible when we consider the two extremes represented by inconsolably depressed people and those who are deliriously happy. Between these two extremes, individuals can think about the meaning of their own existence and decide, if not to be happy, then at least not to attach too much importance to things that don't matter.

The conditions for a successful life

The first lesson we can learn from the psychological studies investigating happiness is that it is rarely encountered if it is seen as the accomplishment of predefined goals. Based on statistics, a psychologist at the University of South Carolina concluded that neither dreaming of a great love nor hoping for professional success led to the feeling or a state of happiness. It seems that pursuing such objectives arouses a strong expectation that is bound to be disappointed by reality or can even lead us to set goals that are higher than the previous ones. While achieving goals brings an intense feeling of wellbeing that can be compared to pleasure, this feeling quickly fades until it returns to the level of wellbeing that we felt previously. This has been shown by a study of lottery winners: after a moment of exaltation, most of them return to the same level of internal happiness that they had experienced before their win.

Happiness is contagious

Happiness obeys a particular logic of contagion, as demonstrated by an extensive study involving 4739 people carried out at the University of California. Using answers to questionnaires, psychologists noted that as the years went by those people who were surrounded by happy people in turn became happier themselves, and that the opposite was true for people surrounded by morose individuals.

Live life in the present

How can we find happiness on our doorstep? The key word seems to be concentration. According to American psychologists, the happiest people are those who manage to become totally absorbed in particular pursuits, whether this involves do-it-yourself projects, embroidery, writing fiction or fishing. Focusing the mind on a thought or an action leads people to forget about themselves and, above all, to be oblivious to the temporal dimension of existence. They no longer think about the future or the past, but only about the here and now.

Happiness, however, is still a difficult concept to grasp. There's always the risk of making it a condition, an imperative, a goal to be reached, whereas all the psychological research on the topic shows that happiness is not found if it becomes the objective of a systematic search.

Positive thinking

At the end of the twentieth century, the American psychologist Martin Seligman developed a structural and rational theory around what he called positive thinking. According to him, historically most psychological research had concentrated on mental illness and on dysfunctional emotions and ways of thinking. He felt it was therefore important to return psychology to a more noble purpose, that of giving people the capacity to be happier, more creative and more talented. This was the beginning of cognitive psychology, which is based mainly on an approach that assumes individuals will take themselves in hand. Each of us is responsible for our own life: this is the first message of positive psychology.

Laughter and a sense of humour

What is more liberating, more contagious and more soothing than laughter? For laughter brings about reconciliation: it releases tensions, makes people happy, spreads to others and puts them at ease. But why is it so heartening and rousing? And what happens in our brain when we laugh?

Laughter yoga Clubs practising this new kind of exercise routine are springing up around the world. This complete wellbeing work-out is the brainchild of Dr Madan Kataria, an Indian physician who started the first laughter club in Mumbai in 1995. It begins with simulated laughter as a group exercise, but soon turns into real, contagious laughter. Here members of a club in France demonstrate the tiger laugh.

What causes laughter?

In 1998 during surgery, a Californian neurobiologist was surprised to see his patient start laughing for no reason when electrodes were implanted in a cerebral area called the supplementary motor area. This is the area that regulates the movements we make when we laugh – in other words the contraction of the muscles of the mouth, larynx and chest. But the deeper origin of laughter is the brainstem, inside a small structure that acts as a coordination centre by stimulating the nerve impulses that lead to the rhythmical expulsion of air and the action of the vocal chords. A third element takes care of the cognitive dimension of laughter, whether it is caused by an incongruous situation or by a joke. This is the frontal lobe of the right hemisphere, which decides whether an action or a story is amusing and then sends a message to the coordinating centre to begin the process that will release laughter.

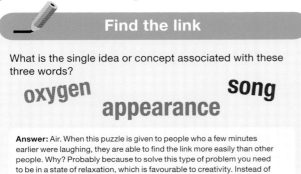

Find the link

What is the single idea or concept associated with these three words?

oxygen   **song**
        appearance

Answer: Air. When this puzzle is given to people who a few minutes earlier were laughing, they are able to find the link more easily than other people. Why? Probably because to solve this type of problem you need to be in a state of relaxation, which is favourable to creativity. Instead of concentrating on one particular word, you need to take a step back and consider a number of different approaches. Laughter encourages this type of reasoning, whereas stress or negative emotions focus our attention on a single aspect of our environment.

When life is funny

The brain's right frontal lobe is the seat of a sense of humour and it operates in a special way. It anticipates what is likely to happen. For example, a man is walking along a footpath, and he will probably continue along this path. But if he slips on a banana skin, this change in the scenario provokes a sudden inversion of electrical activity, which awakens the centre that releases laughter. This means that humour is motivated by an unexpected event or double meaning of a word, as in a play on words.

Laughter is good for you

A study carried out in 2007 in the USA showed that when we laugh the brain releases the main neurotransmitter of pleasure, dopamine, which is involved in all types of enjoyable experiences. And what's more, the release of dopamine seems to be good for our health. A psychologist from the University of Kentucky studied 179 accounts of the life led by a group of nuns in a convent and noted that the most cheerful among them lived an average of ten years longer than the others. This can be explained by the fact that joy inhibits the release of cortisol, a stress hormone that eventually causes hypertension and cardiac problems.

Laughter also helps us to think. A team of psychologists at the University of Washington found that a group of people who completed some tests after watching comic films took a broader approach to problems, demonstrated greater creativity and obtained better results in memory exercises. They also observed that the group showed evidence of greater activity in the prefrontal cortex, an area of the brain involved in attention and working memory.

A healthy mind in a healthy body

11

Feeling blue

Keeping your brain healthy is closely dependent on taking care of your body, adopting an appropriate healthy lifestyle and having good social relationships. The interdependency of mental and physical states is particularly highlighted by the fact that some illnesses affect both the mind and the body.

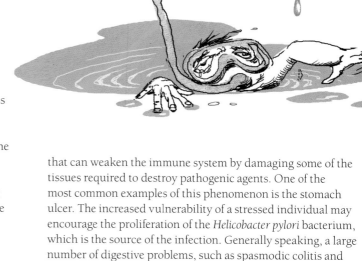

When the mind affects the body

More than half of the illnesses encountered by doctors are psychosomatic – 'psycho' means relating to the mind, and 'somatic' means relating to the body. These illnesses are characterised by quantifiable organic or functional problems that are caused, promoted or amplified by emotional phenomena. The part of the body affected depends on each person's biological predispositions, and the seriousness of the condition depends on how strongly psychological aspects affect physiological aspects, and vice versa. Psychosomatic illnesses mainly affect those who have trouble externalising their emotions, tend to be sensitive and anxious, find it quite difficult to adapt or show strong aggressive impulses and express their suffering in this way.

The effects of stress

When we are affected by an intense emotion such as stress, the sympathetic nervous system stimulates the secretion of adrenaline and noradrenaline, which in turn provokes an increase in blood pressure and blood sugar. This means that the brain, heart and muscles will be supplied with blood more quickly. This reaction is intended to help us either cope with a fight more effectively or flee as quickly as possible. If episodes of stress are too frequent or last too long, they can contribute to the development of diabetes or cardiovascular disease. They can also cause an excessive production of cortisol, a hormone that can weaken the immune system by damaging some of the tissues required to destroy pathogenic agents. One of the most common examples of this phenomenon is the stomach ulcer. The increased vulnerability of a stressed individual may encourage the proliferation of the *Helicobacter pylori* bacterium, which is the source of the infection. Generally speaking, a large number of digestive problems, such as spasmodic colitis and gastric reflux, have a strong psychosomatic component.

When it's all too much

Migraines are common psychosomatic complaints. They often affect perfectionists, who demand a lot of themselves and who also tend to take refuge within themselves. When such people make a prolonged effort, the sympathetic nervous system is overstimulated. This is followed by a sudden change in the level of serotonin – a neurotransmitter that is especially involved in the mechanisms that control suffering – as well as painful vasodilation, the expansion of cranial blood vessels.

A number of skin diseases also have a strong psychosomatic component: eczema, urticaria, pruritus and especially psoriasis and lichen planus. And even back problems can be psychosomatic. In an American study, people who had suffered from back problems were so concerned about recurrence that when they carried out everyday tasks they overcontracted some muscles and made many unnecessary movements, to the extent that they used some muscles 27 per cent more than is normally required, which then caused a recurrence of their back problems. Other study participants who had no apprehensions about previous back problems carried out the same tasks by adopting postures that were more appropriate and therefore less likely to cause distress.

Autoimmune diseases

Hormonal and chemical disturbances in the body that are caused by stress can also lead to increased production of some kinds of lymphocytes (the cells that are responsible for immune responses) and, consequently, to stronger defence reactions, some of which are directed against the body itself. These reactions can then set off what is known as an autoimmune condition, such as multiple sclerosis or rheumatoid arthritis.

How stressed are you?

Complete the following questionnaire with reference to the recent past and trying to be as truthful as possible.

	True	False
1. I am often tense.	☐	☐
2. I feel like I have a weight on my shoulders.	☐	☐
3. I often feel pain (in my back, in my head, in my stomach).	☐	☐
4. I constantly feel overwhelmed.	☐	☐
5. Most of the time I am preoccupied.	☐	☐
6. I can't always manage to control my reactions.	☐	☐
7. Generally speaking, I have a tendency to worry.	☐	☐
8. I am easily irritated.	☐	☐
9. I have trouble staying still.	☐	☐
10. I am more fearful than most people.	☐	☐
11. My ideas are not clear.	☐	☐
12. I rarely feel sure of myself.	☐	☐
13. I am afraid of new situations.	☐	☐
14. I check what I'm doing several times.	☐	☐
15. I have palpitations or a lump in my throat when I do something that I regard as important.	☐	☐

Calculate your score: count 1 point for every 'True' answer.

Total points ☐

Interpreting the results

● **Under 5 points.** You are not particularly affected by stress and you get through most situations quite well. You manage to take a step back from events and remain calm and assured. A minimum of anxiety is a good thing, because it is a way of adapting to external aggressions. What's more, a small amount of stress can be stimulating.

● **Between 5 and 10 points.** You are subject to stress and quickly thrown off balance. You are easily overcome by your emotions, and this could have an impact on your morale and your health. To avoid letting yourself be overwhelmed, you need to put a few simple rules into practice.

– Reduce the sources of stress by working on your environment. Choose what news you want to hear by reading it in newspapers. Give yourself a real treat each day. Put things into perspective: what seems so important today will be of little concern tomorrow.

– In addition, control your reactions to stress by working on yourself. Practise relaxation by breathing using your stomach and exhaling fully. Adopt a balanced diet. Begin some gentle exercise such as walking, swimming or a light work-out in the gym.

● **More than 10 points.** Your daily life is totally taken over by stress and simple advice is not enough. You can get help through therapy:

– either through discussion, by talking to a counsellor about your anxieties and learning techniques to overcome them

– or by using physical methods, such as relaxation and exercise.

Is stress our best friend?

When we are faced with an event that demands a fast and appropriate response, the brain will raise the alarm and set off a chain of physiological reactions. If this sequence happens too frequently and intensely, it can lead to an inner disturbance that results in extreme fatigue and problems with memory, mood and behaviour, or even a psychosomatic illness. On the other hand, when it happens rarely, it acts as a stimulant and allows us to adapt to a new situation, face a danger or a challenge, improve our performance or even excel in something. And it can even get rid of some health problems. People who are subjected to a situation of intense stress can suddenly find that they no longer suffer recurrent allergy attacks, because in such cases the noradrenaline and cortisol that are released have anti-inflammatory and antihistamine effects.

The brain held hostage

People who are stressed, worried and immature, have narcissistic tendencies, feel different and vulnerable and have poor self-esteem are more likely to develop an addiction to substances that act on the central nervous system.

A downward spiral

Psychoactive substances – such as tobacco, alcohol and drugs, as well as medications such as benzodiazepines or barbiturates – modify the chemistry of the central nervous system. By removing inhibitions and lowering anxiety, they create in their users a temporary sensation of relaxation, wellbeing, control over the surrounding environment and even euphoria. Used regularly, they can lead to states of dependency – both psychological, in which users believe they can no longer function without their help, and physical, in which attempts to reduce or stop using produce withdrawal syndromes such as behavioural problems, sweating, shaking or convulsions.

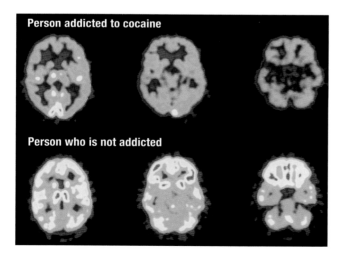

Person addicted to cocaine

Person who is not addicted

Brain activity and addiction These PET scans show that the activity in the brain of a cocaine addict after 4 months of abstinence is still slower than the activity in the brain of someone who is not addicted. Different degrees of cerebral activity are indicated by colours ranging from blue to red, with red indicating the most significant activity and blue the least activity.

When the body drinks, the brain drinks too

All psychoactive products that can lead to addiction, with the exception of benzodiazepines, artificially increase the release of dopamine, a neurotransmitter known as the pleasure molecule. This acts as a transmitting agent to neurons located in the areas of the brain that form what is called the reward circuit. Its release is responsible for all the sensations of pleasure that we can feel, whether we are savouring a tasty meal, enjoying a show, becoming passionate about a match or engaging in sexual intercourse. So the release of this molecule can easily lead individuals who have experienced the wellbeing induced by a psychoactive substance to seek a state that they consider pleasant as often as possible, even if that means they can no longer control their impulses. In the long term, this state of mind can disrupt the cerebral circuits involved and reduce blood flow to the brain, which means that the supply of glucose and oxygen is also reduced. Conversely, the weaning process will restore balance in the production of neurotransmitters, which entails a chemical readaptation of the brain.

The enigmatic placebo effect

The placebo effect is defined as the beneficial action exerted by a substance that has no properties capable of curing a patient's symptoms. Comparative clinical tests carried out to evaluate the effectiveness of new medication show that about 35 per cent of people tested experience this effect. Until recently, the phenomenon was considered to be purely psychological, but several studies carried out by neurologists at the University of Michigan have shown that it is the result of modifications that take place inside the brain. Medical imaging has shown that the expectation and hope aroused by the administration of a placebo product or by a medical appointment are sufficient in some people to stimulate the release in the reward circuit of two categories of neurotransmitters: dopamine and endorphins. These are anti-pain molecules that are produced naturally by the body.

Why it is difficult to stop smoking

One of the neurotransmitters that is naturally present in the reward circuit is acetylcholine. In order to transmit the nerve impulse, acetylcholine attaches itself to the neurons that release dopamine. Curiously, acetylcholine has a biochemical structure that is close to that of one of the 4000 components of tobacco, nicotine. Once it is introduced into the body, nicotine imitates the action of acetylcholine and artificially stimulates the neurons that produce dopamine. As it penetrates the brain, a smoker will be tempted to smoke more and more in order to feel pleasurable sensations – that is, to satisfy the demands of the nicotine receptors, whose number has increased. This is why the use of substitute products for nicotine is recommended to help those who wish to give up smoking.

Sombre figures

According to official figures for Australia in 2004–05, almost 900 deaths per year (out of a total number of some 130,000 deaths) are caused by drugs, with the vast majority of them being attributable to the consumption of opiates such as heroin. In addition, about 3500 Australians die every year as a result of the harmful consumption of alcohol, while about 15,000 deaths are caused by tobacco.

Jumbled words

Rearrange these letters to make words that are related to the mind or the body.

1. **SUALAMHOPYTH** ....
2. **CANIDRICA** ....
3. **OINTMENAL** ....
4. **LITOROCS** ....
5. **BOYLONOGIROCH** ....
6. **THYMHOBIR** ....
7. **MONACHSATILCEE** ....
8. **RALINDEANE** ....
9. **DRAINROLEANEN** ....
10. **THIMARPOYHE** ....
11. **COGLYNGE** ....
12. **NOTOIRENS** ....
13. **PORHIDNNE** ....
14. **MOTSANRERTUNETRI** ....
15. **RBNIA** ....
16. **BALPOCE** ....
17. **CHACELYLITONE** ....

Answers: 1. hypothalamus. **2.** circadian. **3.** melatonin. **4.** cortisol. **5.** chronobiology. **6.** biorhythm. **7.** catecholamines. **8.** adrenaline. **9.** noradrenaline. **10.** hypothermia. **11.** glycogen. **12.** serotonin. **13.** endorphin. **14.** neurotransmitter. **15.** brain. **16.** placebo. **17.** acetylcholine.

Our internal clock

The rhythms of life are governed by a tiny brain structure found in the hypothalamus, the central biological clock. Respecting the patterns of activity it imposes on us can help us to make the best use of our time and improve the quality of what we do.

When the brain beats the rhythm

Our central biological clock is synchronised to a 24-hour cycle, or circadian rhythm, that corresponds to Earth's rotation. This internal clock regulates functions such as sleep, alertness and the frequency of eating, as well as the production of some

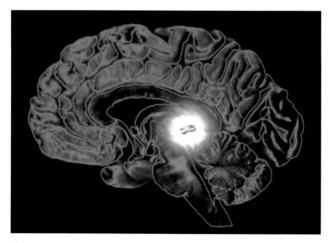

Pineal gland Also called the epiphysis, this tiny structure in the brain – about the size of a grain of rice – produces the sleep hormone melatonin, which regulates our central biological clock.

hormones. Among these are melatonin, which is known as the sleep hormone and is generally secreted between 9 pm and 7 am, and cortisol, which prepares the body to resume activity in the morning by raising its temperature. The biological clock can be influenced by external parameters such as light, which reaches it through the retina and the optic nerve, and by the constraints of each person's individual timetable. It also obeys internal genetic parameters that determine, for example, whether an individual is spontaneously a morning or an evening person.

Chronobiology and biological rhythms

By identifying the times of the day when we are in better shape, chronobiology allows us to adopt a timetable that is the best fit with our biological rhythm, whether we want to think, work, relax, sleep, make love, play sport or eat. The obligations of daily life don't always allow us to follow these biorhythms, however. If the difference between our biorhythms and the rhythms our schedule imposes on us is too great, it can lead in the long term to problems with mood, persistent tiredness and even depression. Working at night, if it is not accompanied by periods of regenerative sleep, and shift work can often cause major health problems such as insomnia, cardiovascular and gastric illnesses, hormonal disturbances, premature ageing and some kinds of cancer.

The right time to take medication

To optimise the effectiveness of certain medications and limit their side effects, it is better to take them at specific times of the day. If aspirin is prescribed to prevent cardiovascular problems, it would be more effective to take it in the evening than in the morning. Similarly, nonsteroidal anti-inflammatory drugs are tolerated better by the stomach if they are ingested at the end of the afternoon or in the evening. Influenza vaccine is more effective when it is administered in the afternoon, and an anaesthetic that is given for a dental procedure lasts longer if it is administered around 3 pm.

Against the clock Working at night or in shifts (early morning or late in the evening) can disrupt biological rhythms and lead to health problems.

Biological rhythms round the clock

● Between 7 and 8 am The body experiences a period of transition between wakefulness and sleep, called the period of post-sleep inertia. If body temperature is lower than 36.8°C, we are not yet quite ready to start the day. The production of cortisol peaks, and body temperature and blood pressure rise. We secrete catecholamines (adrenaline and noradrenaline), which break down sugars and fats. It's time for a good, wholesome breakfast and some exercise.

● From 9 to 11 am Blood sugar and temperature are at optimum levels, and this is when we are most alert and have maximum intellectual capacity and effectiveness.

● Between 12 and 1 pm This is the ideal time to eat the main meal of the day, between four and five hours after breakfast.

● From 1 to 3 pm Levels of cortisol and adrenaline fall, which means that we are less alert and our capacity to concentrate also drops. A break or a nap is a good idea.

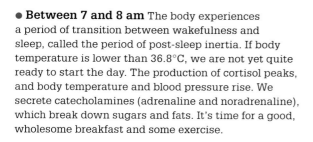

● From 3 to 7 pm Blood sugar, body temperature and adrenaline rise again. We are in good shape intellectually and physically (most sporting records are established between 5 and 7 pm). This is the time to make the most of every minute, but don't forget to have a short break and to rehydrate the body every 90 minutes.

● From 7 to 8 pm Body temperature drops and the secretion of melatonin resumes and increases as darkness falls. It's dinner time. It's best to avoid sweet dishes, otherwise the drop in insulin level will lead to a night-time sugar clearance, which, if we are not active, will turn into fat.

● From 9 to 11 pm Body temperature, blood pressure and cortisol are at their lowest levels. Our degree of alertness gradually decreases. It's time to go to bed.

● Between 2 and 5 am This is the least active phase. It's also the time when accidents are most likely to happen, particularly car accidents. Around 4 am, sleep becomes lighter. We may tend to wake up spontaneously and then have trouble getting back to sleep.

● From 5 am We gradually move back into an active phase. Our cortisol level rises.

A good night's sleep

Our internal clock determines the period in the circadian cycle when we sleep, which is generally at night. During this time, which is made up of several cycles, the body appears to be totally passive, but the same cannot be said of the brain, whose activity never stops.

A vital need

Influenced by our internal clock, neuronal circuits in the brainstem that stimulate sleep via certain neurotransmitters block other neuronal circuits that condition waking up. According to specialists, our average sleep needs are between seven and eight hours in a 24-hour period. The amount of time we allocate to sleep can vary: it can depend on cultural criteria, such as the custom of having a siesta in hot countries, or on age, because the waking–sleeping biological rhythms of older people are usually less well synchronised. The consequences of lack of sleep show how indispensable it is to our ability to function well. People who don't sleep long enough have mood problems and difficulty concentrating, lack energy and suffer from reduced alertness and performance (31 per cent of bad sleepers have accidents at work, as opposed to 19 per cent of good sleepers) as well as relative hypothermia (feeling cold).

The brain never sleeps

A person who is in a deep sleep gives the impression of absolute passivity. This is in appearance only, however, because it masks the activity of an organism that is fully engaged in physical and intellectual regeneration. During periods of deep sleep, the pituitary gland secretes most of its daily production of growth hormone. This substance, which is indispensable to the physiological development of children and adolescents, stimulates the synthesis of glycogen and proteins in adults. This allows the body to recover energy and promotes the regeneration of bones, muscles and tissues. Deep sleep also improves the elimination of some toxins, allows muscles that have been working all through the day to rest and enables the immune system to work better. Studies of people with insomnia have actually demonstrated that their levels of lymphocytes (cells that help to fight infection) were lower than those of good sleepers. Other studies of individuals

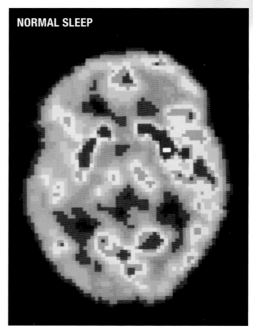

NORMAL SLEEP

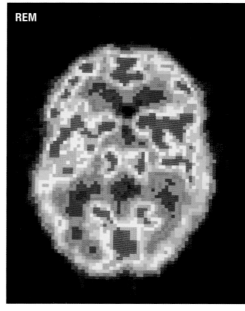

REM

PET scans of sleeping subjects More colour at the red end of the spectrum, as seen in the REM scan (bottom), indicates that there is greater brain activity during this period of sleep than during normal sleep (top).

who sleep less than six hours a night showed that a reduction in deep sleep encouraged excessive weight gain and development of type 2 diabetes, because tissues normally affected by insulin became more resistant to this hormone.

Sleep on it

During a recurrent kind of sleep known as rapid eye movement sleep, or REM sleep, the brain consumes as much, if not more, oxygen than it does during waking hours and just as much glucose – which is proof of its energy requirements at this time and, consequently, of the intensity of its activity. This observation can be confirmed both by electroencephalogram (EEG), which reveals that the cortex is just as active during this period of sleep as during the day, as well as by medical imaging techniques such as PET scans, which show the cerebral regions that are the most activated.

In particular, the limbic system, which is linked to the emotions and to some of the brain's visual areas, is very dynamic during the periods of dreaming that occur during REM sleep. It is clear from this that REM sleep is a natural emotional and psychological outlet. PET scans of sleeping subjects have also proved that the areas involved in a learning activity during the day – for example, the hippocampus – are also reactivated at night during episodes of REM sleep. These experiments demonstrate the fundamental role of sleep in consolidating memory. During REM sleep, the hippocampus is also thought to be involved in regenerating neurons that are linked to our innate behaviour and the way it adapts to external demands.

How sleep requirements change with age

● **Newborn** 16 hours, half of which is REM sleep.

● **At 6 months of age** Between 14 and 16 hours.

● **At 3 years of age** Between 12 and 14 hours, around 60 per cent of which is deep slow sleep.

● **From 6 to 12 years of age** Between 9 and 11 hours. Sleep is nocturnal. Children generally sleep for half an hour longer at the weekend than during the week. Slow sleep represents about 75 per cent of the total sleep time. The organisation of sleep cycles moves closer to that of adult cycles.

● **Adolescent** Between 9 and 11 hours. There is a reduction in deep slow sleep and REM sleep, which are replaced by light sleep.

● **Adult** Between 6 and 10 hours, 20 per cent of which is REM sleep.

● **Over 60 years of age** An average of 7 hours and 30 minutes.

● **Advanced age** The phases of nocturnal sleep are shorter and naps during the day compensate for this. The time spent in REM sleep and deep slow sleep decreases more and more.

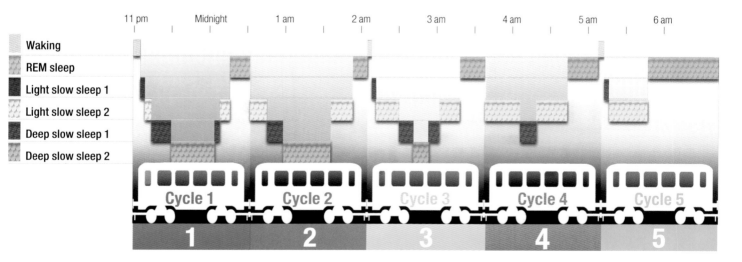

Sleep cycles Our sleep is generally composed of a series of four to five cycles, each lasting about 90 minutes. Each cycle has a phase of slow sleep, which is divided into four stages (two stages of light sleep, representing 40 to 50 per cent of a cycle, and two stages of deep sleep, representing 10 to 20 per cent of a cycle). Each cycle also has a phase of REM sleep, the length of which increases as the night progresses. The order of these different sequences is regulated by special neurons in the hypothalamus.

How well do you sleep?

Complete the following questionnaire and try to be as truthful as possible.

True False

1. I have trouble getting to sleep. ☐ ☐

2. I often have sleepless nights. ☐ ☐

3. I wake up early. ☐ ☐

4. I have nightmares. ☐ ☐

5. I am often the last person to go to bed. ☐ ☐

6. I don't need an alarm clock. ☐ ☐

7. I find it difficult to change my sleep pattern (when travelling, for example). ☐ ☐

8. I wake up tired in the morning. ☐ ☐

9. I sometimes have moments during the day when I feel drained. ☐ ☐

10. I often need to have a sleep during the day. ☐ ☐

11. I wake up several times during the night. ☐ ☐

12. I feel apprehensive about going to bed. ☐ ☐

13. I can't bear to sleep away from my own bed. ☐ ☐

14. After being out all night (at a party or on New Year's Eve, for example), I find it difficult to get to sleep. ☐ ☐

15. I doze after meals or on public transport. ☐ ☐

Calculate your score: count 1 point for every 'True' answer.

Total points ☐

Interpreting the results

● **Fewer than 5 points**

You have no or few problems sleeping. For the moment you have a sleep pattern that suits you, and you manage to keep your sleep separate from the tensions and cares of the day. You rarely have difficulty sleeping.

● **Between 5 and 10 points**

Your sleep is fragile and the slightest irritation will disturb it. Try preparing during the day for the night ahead in the following ways:

– Do some kind of physical exercise, except in the three hours before you go to bed.

– An hour before you go to bed, start unwinding: no violent films or intellectual activity that is too intense. Do things that relax you.

– Create the right atmosphere in your bedroom: calm, temperature of 19°C, soft colours, pleasant decor.

– Avoid stimulants, especially at the end of the day: no coffee or tea or caffeine-based drink after 2 pm.

● **More than 10 points**

Sleep is playing tricks on you and this can have repercussions for your health. If the advice here is not sufficient, you should consult a specialist.

– Follow the advice given in the point above; avoid heavy evening meals (with fats and alcohol) and don't eat too late.

– Adopt a regular rhythm of sleeping and waking.

– If you can't sleep, don't stay in bed tring to sleep at all costs.

– Hot baths and showers just before going to bed are not a good idea, because they raise the body temperature and delay the moment when you actually fall asleep.

Should you take tablets to help you sleep?

Although sleeping tablets may be prescribed when insomnia has clear circumstantial causes (jet lag, a temporary stressful period), they should be used sparingly, not continuously, and not for longer than three weeks. Because of their side effects – drowsiness, problems with memory, concentration and balance, a return of anxiety during the day, as well as the risk of dependency and addiction – it is preferable to choose other treatments instead, such as adopting a more appropriate lifestyle, changing daily rhythms, using relaxation techniques or seeking psychological help. Another disadvantage of sleeping tablets is that they reduce the duration of REM sleep.

The benefits of physical exercise

Regularly engaging in physical exercise at any age has beneficial effects not only for the body but also for brain function, especially through stimulating the production of neurotransmitters that contribute to wellbeing.

Move and eliminate!

In a 1995 study, a group of elderly people who were in good health, but normally sedentary, experienced a significant increase in the amount of time spent in deep sleep after six months of regular physical exercise. Apart from the effect it has on sleep, physical exercise has other benefits. It helps to reduce and manage weight, levels of cholesterol and triglyceride, as well as the risk of developing osteoporosis, rheumatic conditions and diabetes. It also allows us to retain a good degree of mobility and endurance and to improve our intellectual ability. Overall, according to a 2008 British study, regular exercise gives us extra years of healthy life.

What kind of exercise is best?

It's better to choose activities involving gentle endurance, such as walking, developing muscle strength and stretching exercises. To stay in good physical and mental condition, you need to do 30 minutes of physical exercise, if possible every day or on a minimum of three to five days a week. Endurance activities (hiking, cycling, dancing, swimming) involve a sustained effort of low to moderate intensity, with the objective of giving the heart a work-out. You'll gradually feel less and less out of breath and your daily performance will improve. Activities that develop muscle strength improve joint stability and will help you to maintain or adopt a good posture. They include everyday activities such as climbing stairs, carrying your shopping, standing up and sitting down several times in a row, as well as doing sit-ups or lifting weights. Stretching exercises, such as yoga, tai chi and even simply using the vacuum cleaner, help you to retain flexibility in your joints. If you do a variety of these sorts of activities, you'll feel the benefits after a few weeks – and not only will you be fitter, your involvement in group activities will allow you to expand your social circle.

Stretch and relax When practised regularly, yoga helps to keep your body flexible and also assists in strengthening resistance to fatigue and stress.

Meditation and the brain

Those who practise yoga and other meditation techniques often find that their blood pressure, pulse rate and level of anxiety drop and that their immune response improves. Studies have tried to discover whether brain mechanisms are involved in these changes. Electroencephalograms (EEGs) taken of subjects in a meditative state have revealed hyperactivity in the left prefrontal cortex, an area associated with positive feelings such as joy and liveliness, and reduced activity in the right prefrontal cortex, which is linked to negative feelings such as sadness and depression. When EEGs of Buddhist monks were compared with those of people who occasionally practise meditation, the monks showed an increase in neuronal activity two or three times greater than that of the occasional practitioners, and there was evidence that their parietal areas were also involved. These observations suggest that intense mental activity during meditation involves several different parts of the brain at the same time, and after thousands of hours of practice it produces permanent changes in physiology and cerebral connections. Magnetic resonance imaging has also shown that the cortex of elderly people who practise several hours of meditation each week is thicker than the cortex of individuals who don't meditate. These conclusions could be of interest in fighting mental ageing, because the thickness of the cortex – that is of the layers of neurons – tends to decrease with age. According to some hypotheses, meditation might also increase the level of serotonin in the brain, just as some antidepressants do.

The feel-good factor

Exercising or playing a sport induces a state of wellbeing linked to the release of endorphins, which are neurotransmitters produced by the pituitary gland with a molecular structure close to that of opiates. They have the effect of removing stress and momentarily calming anxiety. Physical activity also leads to an increase in the secretion of serotonin, a neurotransmitter that is considered to be a kind of natural antidepressant. Studies of people with depressive tendencies have shown that those who take medication that increases serotonin production are more likely to suffer a relapse than those who regularly exercise or play a sport.

Give your brain a boost!

Physical exercise also helps to keep the cardiovascular system functioning well by improving cardiac performance and the condition of blood vessels responsible for carrying blood, and therefore oxygen, to neurons in the brain. By improving the supply of blood and oxygen to the brain, exercise stimulates neurons and helps to keep them active. When doctors from the University of Boston monitored 18,000 women over 70 years of age, they discovered that the most sedentary of these women had a 20 per cent higher risk of experiencing a degeneration of their mental faculties than those who regularly played a sport. What's more, engaging in an appropriate physical activity encourages the renewal of neurons and their connections, mainly in the hippocampus, which is an area that is essential for memory function. From this point of view, exercise also provides good protection against neurodegenerative diseases. According to recent studies, exercise might reduce the risk of developing Alzheimer's disease, which begins in the hippocampus, and might also slow the progress of the disease once symptoms appear.

How fit are you?

You've made some good resolutions: you've decided to increase the time you spend doing physical exercise or to resume a sporting activity that you gave up a long time ago. This means you need to take stock of the situation and find out which are your strong points and what you need to improve. The following tests will help you, but before doing any of these check with your doctor.

1 Flexibility

This is carried out without a preliminary warm-up so that you can evaluate your true level of flexibility. Test your shoulders one after the other, starting with the right one. First put your right hand behind your neck, with the palm turned towards your back. Then put your left hand up behind your back, with the palm turned away from your body. Estimate the distance between the two hands. Test the other shoulder in the same way, reversing the position of the hands.

Results

The two palms are flat against each other.	☐ Very good
The fingers are flat against one another.	☐ Good
The middle fingers of each hand are barely touching.	☐ Average
The hands are not touching.	☐ Poor
The hands are very far away from each other.	☐ Very poor

2 Muscular strength

This is very simple. Try to do as many push-ups as you can without any time limit. For men, this test is done with the tips of the toes touching the ground, the arms straight and the back straight. For women, the position is identical, but the knees touch the ground. You should stop this test when you can no longer do the movements correctly.

Results

Age 50 to 59 years	Age 60 years and over		
21 or more	18 or more	☐	Very good
13 to 20	11 to 17	☐	Good
10 to 12	8 to 10	☐	Average
7 to 9	5 to 7	☐	Poor
Less than 7	Less than 5	☐	Very poor

3 Cardiovascular endurance

See how long it takes you to cover a distance of 2 kilometres, walking as quickly as you can, but without pushing yourself.

Results

Age 50 to 59 years	Age 60 years and over		
Less than 16 min	Less than 16 min	☐	Very good
From 16 min to 18 min 45 s	From 16 min to 19 min 30 s	☐	Good
From 18 min 45 s to 19 min 30 s	From 19 min 30 s to 21 min	☐	Average
From 19 min 30 s to 21 min	From 21 min to 23 min	☐	Poor
Longer than 21 min	Longer than 23 min	☐	Very poor

4 Balance

Place a watch or a clock in front of you. Standing with bare feet, place the sole of one foot against the inside knee of the other leg. Keep your arms beside your body and start timing yourself as soon as you have reached a balanced position. Stop timing as soon as your heel becomes less firm on your supporting leg. This test should be carried out for a maximum of 60 seconds.

Results

Age 50 to 59 years	Age 60 years and over		
16 s or more	14 s or more	☐	Very good
12–15 s	10–13 s	☐	Good
8–11 s	6–9 s	☐	Average
4–7 s	3–5 s	☐	Poor
Less than 4 s	Less than 3 s	☐	Very poor

A brain running at full capacity

Appropriate and varied food can improve the brain's performance and help to delay cognitive decline. In fact, the brain has very specific nutritional needs that must be satisfied in order to maintain its special composition and ensure that it is in tip-top working order.

An indispensable source of energy

The brain needs fuel to function. But unlike other organs that can utilise lipids, such as muscles, it must be supplied with glucose 24 hours a day. The brain actually consumes 120 grams of glucose per day, which is supplied by what we eat and by our liver stores.

This is why we need to eat carbohydrate foods such as cereal grain products, legumes and fruit. It is advisable to eat some of these foods at every meal so that the slow-acting carbohydrates they provide are spread throughout the day and the blood sugar level is kept stable.

Natural shields

It is imperative to protect nerve cells from ageing too quickly. By choosing foods that are rich in protective micronutrients, you will significantly increase your chances of retaining good brain function for a long time. This means that your diet should include oily fish, nuts and canola oil, which are sources of omega-3 fatty acids. These unsaturated fats, which are present in the structure of neuronal membranes, are in fact essential for transmitting information between neurons.

You should also eat lots of fruit and vegetables, which provide important vitamins, such as vitamins C and E, as well as polyphenols. These substances are antioxidants, which slow down the ageing of cells by neutralising the action of free radicals, the molecules that attack neurons. And don't forget to drink plenty of water. Water actually makes up 70 per cent of brain tissue and promotes the elimination of undesirable or potentially toxic substances. Some trace elements – such as zinc or selenium – also protect brain tissue from wear and tear. These are found in meat, fish, nuts and wholegrain cereal foods like brown rice.

Is fish good for the memory?

We have long been told that eating fish will improve brain function, including memory. Fish is a good source of protein and fat-soluble vitamins, but most of all it is the omega-3 content of fish oil that plays a key role in brain function. Fatty fish such as salmon and sardines contain the most omega-3. So don't hold back – eat fish two or three times a week and choose oily fish regularly!

Is your brain well fed?

Do you have good or bad food habits? It's time to take stock. Complete this questionnaire to find out whether you are feeding your brain correctly or whether you need to make some changes.

True False

1. I have a substantial breakfast each morning. ☐ ☐

2. I eat bread, pasta or other starchy foods at every meal. ☐ ☐

3. I make sure I eat at least five portions of fruit and vegetables each day. ☐ ☐

4. I like dairy products and I have them at every meal. ☐ ☐

5. At dinner time I have a light meal and I never snack after dinner. ☐ ☐

6. I eat seafood at least twice a month. ☐ ☐

7. I regularly use canola oil in my cooking. ☐ ☐

8. I eat red meat or offal at least twice a week. ☐ ☐

9. I don't put sugar in my tea or coffee and I don't eat sweets or desserts very often. ☐ ☐

10. I make sure I drink regularly throughout the day, drinking a total of about 1.5 litres of water daily. ☐ ☐

11. I don't add very much salt to my cooking and I don't add salt at the table. ☐ ☐

True False

12. I regularly use spices, fresh herbs, garlic and onion in cooking. ☐ ☐

13. I eat dark chocolate from time to time, in small quantities. ☐ ☐

14. I sprinkle food with brewer's yeast or wheat germ. ☐ ☐

15. I regularly eat nuts (such as walnuts, hazelnuts and pine nuts) as snacks or use them in cooking. ☐ ☐

16. I drink one or two cups of tea or coffee a day, never more. ☐ ☐

17. I like pulses (lentils, chickpeas, beans) and include them in meals once or twice a week. ☐ ☐

18. I eat oily fish such as salmon or sardines twice a week. ☐ ☐

19. I don't eat snacks and I never miss meals. ☐ ☐

20. I rarely eat fatty foods (preserved meats, fried food) or dishes with a sauce. ☐ ☐

Calculate your score: add up all the 'True' answers.

Total points ☐

Interpreting the results

● **Up to 5 points**
You need to improve the quality of your diet urgently! By eating in a more balanced and varied way, you'll notice a rapid improvement in wellbeing, with better sleep, digestion and concentration. But above all, in the long term, you'll be promoting optimal brain function!

● **From 6 to 10 points**
If you make some better food choices, your daily menus will be more balanced and you'll improve your brain performance into the bargain! Choose one or two simple goals (such as eat less sugar, eat more fruit or more fish) that will allow you to make progress as the months go by.

● **From 11 to 15 points**
Your diet is relatively varied and balanced. This is an advantage that will enable your brain to stay in perfect health! Check the eating plan starting on page 232 to find out what else you can do to improve your menu and boost your cerebral functions even more!

● **From 16 to 20 points**
A balanced diet is clearly one of your main preoccupations. You make the right choices and what you eat helps to protect your brain from premature ageing. Continue in this way, but make sure you also enjoy your food, which is essential for your psychological wellbeing!

Take care with food supplements

It's tempting to think that certain substances could improve brain performance or fight the ageing of cells. But the effectiveness of vitamins, trace elements or amino acids in capsule form still remains to be proved. Instead it's better to use commonsense and opt for dietary habits that are healthy and long-lasting. If you want to enrich your diet with useful micronutrients, try natural methods, which are more efficient. Here are some examples:

● Brewer's yeast, sold as dehydrated flakes, is an excellent source of vitamin B_1, which is essential for transmitting nerve impulses. Brewer's yeast also contains a large number of trace elements – including selenium and zinc – that have anti-ageing properties. All you need is one tablespoonful a day. Try adding it to yogurt or salads.

● Wheat germ is a source of vitamin E and zinc and helps to protect tissues, particularly brain cells. Sprinkle a tablespoonful of wheat germ flakes each day onto your breakfast cereal or add some when you are making soups or desserts. The effectiveness of wheat germ depends on consuming it regularly, so taking infrequent large doses is of no use.

● Powdered algae and seaweed flakes are natural condiments that are great with fish and rice. The minerals, trace elements and protective antioxidants in seaweed and algae foods

---

What you should avoid

Too much alcohol and an excessive intake of saturated fats (butter, cream, cheese), sugar and salt are all harmful to brain function and accelerate the ageing of the brain. Even some essential micronutrients such as selenium can become dangerous if you consume too much of them. Rather than looking for a miracle pill that is capable of stopping the degenerative processes, use your commonsense. Eat balanced meals by selecting foods that are rich in protective micronutrients and avoid dishes that are too fatty and too salty – and, of course, limit your intake of alcohol.

---

might be one reason for the longevity observed in Asian populations. Add a pinch two or three times a week to one of your dishes.

Lastly, your doctor or your dietitian can advise you about taking a particular supplement if you have an obvious deficiency or require a temporary boost. But do avoid using supplements without seeking advice – they may not be appropriate and may even cause an imbalance in your body.

The brain and food

How good is your knowledge about the effect of food on the brain and its operation?

	True	False
1. Selenium can be dangerous for your health if you have too much.	✓	
2. Algae and seaweeds are generally a rich source of proteins.		✓
3. Because the brain works during the night, you should eat a substantial meal in the evening.		✓
4. The brain consumes mainly fibres and fats.		✓
5. White and red meat are the principal animal sources of omega-3.		✓
6. Brewer's yeast is a rich source of vitamin C.		✓
7. Melatonin is often called 'the good-mood hormone'.		✓
8. Skipping breakfast keeps you hungry, making you more alert.		✓

	True	False
9. Vitamin B_1 helps the transmission of nerve impulses.	✓	
10. Antioxidants help to protect the body against cellular ageing.	✓	
11. Rich, fatty foods have a low glycaemic index (GI).	✓	
12. The trace elements zinc, copper and iron are essential for the body to function normally.	✓	
13. Tryptophan is an essential amino acid, but the body is unable to produce it.	✓	
14. Chocolate contains caffeine, which contributes to wakefulness and to increased heart rate.	✓	
15. White rice is a rich source of vitamin B_1.		✓

Answers: 1. True. **2.** False. **3.** False. **4.** False. **5.** False. **6.** False. **7.** False. **8.** False. **9.** True. **10.** True. **11.** True. **12.** True. **13.** True. **14.** True. **15.** False.

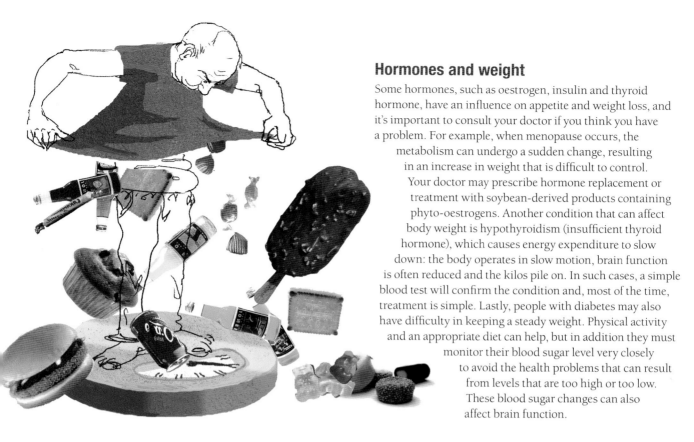

Hormones and weight

Some hormones, such as oestrogen, insulin and thyroid hormone, have an influence on appetite and weight loss, and it's important to consult your doctor if you think you have a problem. For example, when menopause occurs, the metabolism can undergo a sudden change, resulting in an increase in weight that is difficult to control. Your doctor may prescribe hormone replacement or treatment with soybean-derived products containing phyto-oestrogens. Another condition that can affect body weight is hypothyroidism (insufficient thyroid hormone), which causes energy expenditure to slow down: the body operates in slow motion, brain function is often reduced and the kilos pile on. In such cases, a simple blood test will confirm the condition and, most of the time, treatment is simple. Lastly, people with diabetes may also have difficulty in keeping a steady weight. Physical activity and an appropriate diet can help, but in addition they must monitor their blood sugar level very closely to avoid the health problems that can result from levels that are too high or too low. These blood sugar changes can also affect brain function.

Managing weight

The brain plays an essential role in regulating weight. It continuously receives information about the body's energy needs and this allows it to decide whether we need food. This means that an individual's weight should remain stable, because in theory food intake is intended simply to cover energy needs. But the way many people eat today produces a confusion of messages, which leads to inappropriate responses from the brain.

A diet that is too strict or monotonous can lead to frustration and result in sudden bouts of overeating. Such diets inevitably lead us to regain weight: this is the yo-yo effect, which is just as bad for the figure as it is for the morale! On the other hand, many processed foods, such as confectionery, soft drinks and fast foods, are designed to override our natural sense of appetite satisfaction. Their heightened flavours tempt us and conceal large amounts of added sugars and fats. Eating too many of these foods or alternating between periods of overeating and strict dieting only serves to destabilise the natural regulation performed by the brain. How can we escape from this cycle? By adopting a varied and enjoyable diet, focused on fresh, unprocessed foods, that allows us to rediscover our normal feelings of hunger and satisfaction and still have the pleasure of occasional treats.

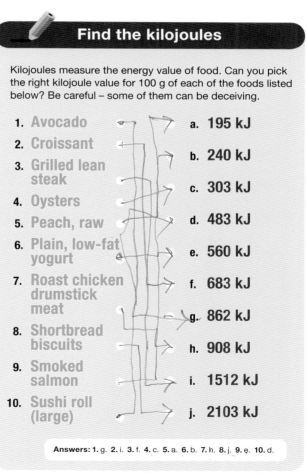

Find the kilojoules

Kilojoules measure the energy value of food. Can you pick the right kilojoule value for 100 g of each of the foods listed below? Be careful – some of them can be deceiving.

1. Avocado
2. Croissant
3. Grilled lean steak
4. Oysters
5. Peach, raw
6. Plain, low-fat yogurt
7. Roast chicken drumstick meat
8. Shortbread biscuits
9. Smoked salmon
10. Sushi roll (large)

a. 195 kJ
b. 240 kJ
c. 303 kJ
d. 483 kJ
e. 560 kJ
f. 683 kJ
g. 862 kJ
h. 908 kJ
i. 1512 kJ
j. 2103 kJ

Answers: 1. g. **2.** i. **3.** f. **4.** c. **5.** a. **6.** b. **7.** h. **8.** j. **9.** e. **10.** d.

20 days to nourish your brain

The brain is a very special organ and we are only just beginning to understand its nutritional requirements. It consumes energy (in the form of glucose), and to function efficiently it also needs a lifelong supply of specific vitamins and minerals. Over the years, diet may also help to delay the premature ageing of brain cells. If you adopt a better diet, you can improve your cognitive skills, protect your brain from the effects of ageing and even improve its ability to recover from damage.

In this section you'll find an easy-to-follow eating plan: in 20 days and with 20 new approaches to your diet, you'll learn how to change your eating habits and give yourself the best possible chance of keeping your brain in tip-top condition.

Each day focuses on a particular nutrient or eating habit, with detailed explanations and practical suggestions. You'll find out, for example, how you can boost omega-3 fatty acids in your diet, how a light evening meal will ensure a good night's sleep or how you can increase your magnesium intake. And, as you go along, you can enjoy putting these new principles into practice by trying out the accompanying recipes, which are as easy to make as they are delicious – because, of course, eating better should also be a pleasure!

Browse through the pages of this dietary guide in any way that you like, selecting what appeals to you and varying the menus with the seasons. You'll find that the examples we've given can easily be adapted to your own tastes and needs. For many of the dishes, alternative ingredients are suggested so that you can make substitutions according to what is available (turn to page 4 for alternative food names). And with the daily menus you can choose whether to serve the main meal at midday or in the evening. This allows you to change the recipes and menus to suit your own lifestyle, while still following the general guidelines for better eating habits. In the menus, recipes that are featured on the same page are indicated by a coloured dot.

Enjoy!

Stimulating taste buds and neurons: bitter and sour tastes

The external stimuli that your senses perceive are constantly being detected, analysed and decoded by your brain. Stimuli for taste and smell play an important role: any new flavours, unusual aromas or unknown textures force your brain to decode previously unknown data and record it in the memory. This keeps your brain on permanent stand-by, so that it stays alert and efficient, improving its overall function. So don't hold back: introduce some variety into your daily diet.

Today's resolution!
To use a variety of spices in my cooking to keep meals interesting, stimulate the taste buds and arouse the senses. Some spices also help digestion and contain important nutrients for health.

Food preferences

With time, we tend to become set in our dietary habits and stick to what we like best, what we think is healthy or simply whatever is easiest to prepare. This cosy monotony can send our senses to sleep. The information transmitted by sensors becomes so familiar that it no longer triggers any surprise or need to adapt. We stop being consciously aware of the taste and aroma of food because we are so used to it.

Try this little experiment: wander around your usual supermarket or shopping centre. You'll soon realise that you rarely notice any of the smells around you, and yet there are many. Then go into an ethnic food store you don't usually visit: the smells may seem quite strong, sometimes even overwhelming, as you encounter new fruits, unusual spices, or unfamiliar dried meats or seafood. This is a good exercise for the brain, as it is forced to deal with new information. The same applies to the food you eat: unfamiliar dishes or unusual combinations will force your brain to wake up and to revive previously underused neuronal circuits.

Stimulate your senses!

Modern Western food is blander and milder than it used to be, particularly fruit and vegetables. Eggplant, cabbage, carrots, brussels sprouts and witlof are all examples of produce with a characteristic bitterness that has now largely been bred out. New types of grapefruit have been developed to be sweeter, and many of the most popular varieties of apples these days are less tart than traditional types. Here are a few tips to take you off the beaten track and awaken your senses.

● Seek out older varieties of fruit and vegetables, like old-fashioned apples (Bramley and Granny Smith), yellow grapefruit, parsnips, swedes and kohlrabi.

● Choose organic vegetables, which have a stronger flavour because they take longer to grow.

● Bring a touch of bitterness back to your dishes. Today's menus rarely have a bitter flavour, yet there are plenty of health-giving plants that are pungent and bitter, such as rocket, watercress or dandelion leaves, which add bite to your salads.

● Use plenty of spices, fresh herbs, garlic and onion, which are also rich in protective antioxidants. Try some cumin, chives or red onion for a change.

● Taste new, exotic or traditional dishes as often as possible. What's important is to stimulate the brain by getting away from routine.

Flavour	Food
Bitter	Yellow grapefruit, citrus rind, witlof, rocket, artichoke, bitter melon, beetroot leaves, coffee
Acidic	Citrus fruits, older apple varieties such as Bramley and Granny Smith, redcurrants, cranberries, slightly unripe fruit, green papaya or mango, vinegar, pickled cucumbers
Hot and spicy	Chillies, pepper, Indian curries, green and red Thai curries, ginger, watercress, radish, mustard, wasabi
Sulphur-like	Cabbage, broccoli, brussels sprouts, kohlrabi, radish, garlic, onion, leeks
Tannin	Well-steeped tea, rhubarb, celery, persimmon, plantain, dry red wine

Quinoa, tomato and radish salad

Preparation time: 20 minutes   **Cooking time:** 10 minutes   **Serves 4**

100 g quinoa
2 tomatoes
10 red radishes
1 spring onion
1 tablespoon wine vinegar

2 teaspoons sesame seeds
2 tablespoons canola oil
2 tablespoons flat-leaf parsley, finely chopped

1 Place the quinoa in a fine colander and rinse with cold water. Cook for 10 minutes in boiling water, and then drain carefully.

2 Wash the tomatoes, wipe dry and dice. Wash and trim the radishes and slice finely. Peel the spring onion and chop finely, including the green stem.

3 Combine the quinoa and salad vegetables in a salad bowl. In a separate bowl mix the vinegar, sesame seeds and pepper; add oil and whisk. Pour the dressing onto the salad, add parsley, season to taste and toss.

4 Refrigerate and serve chilled.

Bracing fruit cocktail

Preparation time:
10 minutes
Refrigeration time:
2 hours
Serves 4

1 carrot
1 Granny Smith apple
1 mango
1 pomelo (or grapefruit)
2 cm fresh ginger
Juice of 1 lime
Black pepper

1 Refrigerate the carrot and fruit for at least 2 hours before starting.

2 Wash and dry the carrot and apple; trim the carrot and cut the apple into 4 pieces. Peel the mango, remove the flesh from the stone and roughly cut into pieces. Peel the pomelo and ginger.

3 Juice the carrot, apple, mango, pomelo and ginger in a juice extractor.

4 Add the lime juice and a pinch of black pepper and mix well. Serve immediately.

Tip If you don't have a juice extractor, you can use 100 per cent pure fruit juice bought from the supermarket. Just mix in some finely grated ginger, freshly squeezed lime juice and black pepper immediately before serving.

Summer menu

Breakfast
Half a grapefruit
Toast with orange or lime marmalade
Yogurt
Tea or coffee

Lunch, or light meal
• Quinoa, tomato and radish salad
Goat's cheese
Walnut bread
Cherries

Afternoon snack
• Bracing fruit cocktail
Grainy crackers with cheese and pickles

Dinner, or main meal
Chicken curry
Basmati rice
Spicy chutney
Indian salad of cucumber, herbs and plain low-fat yogurt
Sliced melon of your choice

Winter menu

Breakfast
Porridge sprinkled with ginger, cinnamon and honey
Mandarin
Coffee, or smoked tea such as lapsang souchong or Russian caravan

Lunch or light meal
Watercress or spinach soup
Pumpkinseed bread
Rocket salad
Kiwi fruit

Afternoon snack
Gingerbread
Lemon or ginger tea

Dinner or main meal
Lamb casserole with garlic and parsley
Steamed carrots, parsnip and celeriac
Baked apple with citrus zest and spices

Wake up your brain: breakfast

Breakfast is the most important meal of the day. When you wake up after 8 to 12 hours without food, your brain works sluggishly, drawing on the depleted sugar reserves left in the body. Eating a full, well-balanced breakfast is the only way to get your brain up and running again, so that you don't suffer from moments of fatigue or a lack of efficiency and concentration until you eat at lunchtime.

Today's resolution!
To start each day with at least three different foods – a dairy product, some fruit and bread – for a breakfast that provides plenty of energy. I'll also include a drink for fluid replacement.

Why have breakfast?

A number of studies have proved the nutritional value of breakfast. People who eat an adequate breakfast demonstrate greater mental efficiency all through the morning: they are more alert, have fewer accidents at work and perform better in tests involving logic and thinking. It has also been shown that people who have breakfast are less likely to put on weight – yet another argument in favour of this often neglected meal.

Having breakfast is far from being a universal practice. Either because we don't have time or because we don't feel hungry, most of us settle for a hot drink, sometimes with a bit of toast. According to current dietary guidelines, breakfast should account for 25 per cent of our total daily energy intake – that is 2000 to 2500 kilojoules.

Like the other meals of the day, breakfast should supply a variety of nutrients: this is essential for the body to function properly. During sleep, the brain continues to consume glucose, virtually its only source of energy. Early in the morning, your energy reserves are almost exhausted and it's imperative to replenish the body's fuel supply. A cup of black coffee is just not enough.

Ideally breakfast should include at least three different food groups: a cereal grain food providing complex carbohydrates, vitamin-rich fruit and a dairy product for calcium. A drink will round off the meal, providing the liquid needed to rehydrate the body.

How to have an appetite in the morning

Lack of appetite at breakfast is often related to poor eating patterns the previous day – for example, eating too late or too much in the evening, or snacking all through the day. This means that your digestive system doesn't get the breaks between meals that it needs.

Start by eating less in the evening and gradually vary your breakfast. Have tea or coffee with some toast and jam; after a few days add a fruit juice, and later a dairy product such as yogurt, or milk with cereal. Then increase the quantities and vary the food you eat for breakfast on a daily basis. Within a few weeks you won't be able to do without this special moment in the day.

Food groups*	Nutritional content	Food
Beverage	Water, minerals	Coffee, tea, herb tea, juice
Cereal grain product	Complex carbohydrates, B vitamins, minerals, fibre	Bread (preferably wholemeal), crispbread, porridge or breakfast cereal with low sugar content, muesli
Dairy and soy products	Protein, calcium, vitamins A and D	Milk, yogurt, soy milk, soy yogurt, yogurt smoothie, cottage cheese, cheese
Fruit and vegetables	Carbohydrates, fibre, antioxidants	Fresh or dried fruit, stewed fruit, fruit juice, tomato, mushroom, spinach, vegetable juice
Additional source of protein (optional)	Protein, iron	Egg, bacon or ham, sausage, cold meat, smoked or canned fish, nuts and seeds

*For a balanced breakfast choose one food from each group.

Parmesan scrambled eggs

Preparation time: 15 minutes **Cooking time:** 10 minutes **Serves 4**

6 eggs

100 ml low-fat milk

30 g parmesan cheese, freshly grated

1 slice leg ham (optional)

10 g margarine fortified with omega-3

Pepper

1 Break the eggs into a bowl. Add the milk and pepper to taste, and beat lightly with a fork. Add the parmesan and combine well.

2 Dice the ham finely, if using.

3 Heat the margarine in a non-stick frying pan. Fry the ham over a low heat, stirring frequently, for 3 minutes.

4 Add the egg mixture and cook for 5 to 7 minutes over a low heat, stirring occasionally with a wooden spoon. Remove from heat when the egg mixture starts to look just set. Serve immediately while still hot.

Raisin and honey pancakes

Preparation time: 20 minutes

Refrigeration time: 1 hour

Cooking time: 1 hour

Makes about 10 pancakes

30 g margarine fortified with omega-3

200 g self-raising flour

30 g raw sugar

2 eggs

1 cup (250 ml) low-fat milk

40 g raisins

30 g crushed hazelnuts

1 tablespoon sunflower oil

½ lemon

60 g honey

1 In a small saucepan melt the margarine over a gentle heat, and then allow to cool slightly.

2 Combine the self-raising flour and sugar in a bowl and make a well in the centre. Break the eggs into the well, add the milk and melted margarine, and mix to make a smooth batter.

3 Add the raisins and hazelnuts and mix well. Cover with plastic wrap and let the batter rest (in the refrigerator) for approximately 1 hour.

4 Using a brush, lightly oil a non-stick frying pan and heat. For each pancake, pour a small ladleful of the batter into the pan and cook over a medium heat for 2 to 3 minutes on each side. Cover the pancakes with a tea towel to keep warm.

5 Squeeze the half lemon. Heat the lemon juice and honey in a small saucepan for 2 minutes, stirring continuously. Serve the pancakes hot, drizzled with the lemon-flavoured honey.

Tip The pancakes can be cooked the day before and reheated in a frying pan.

Breakfast menus

1 Savoury breakfast
Tomato juice
● Parmesan scrambled eggs
Mushrooms
Toast
Tea or coffee

2 Sweet breakfast
● Raisin and honey pancakes
Low-fat ricotta
Kiwi fruit
Hot chocolate

3 Light breakfast
Sliced cheese and tomato
Wholegrain crispbread with omega-3-fortified margarine
Pear
Tea or coffee

4 Quick breakfast
Wholegrain toast and peanut butter
Mandarin
Banana and yogurt smoothie

Give your brain a chance to recover: eat a light dinner

At night, the brain sorts and organises the information it has collected during the day; it also rests and dreams. It's essential that these stages occur so that we can be in top mental form the next day. To ensure a good night's sleep – and better brain function – there's nothing better than a light, well-balanced evening meal.

Today's resolution!
To cut down on meat and cheese at dinnertime for a better night's sleep. These foods are high in protein and take too long to digest.

Not too much, not too little

When you sleep, your body rhythms change. Your heart rate and respiration slow down and the body's cells burn fewer kilojoules. Only the brain continues to work in top gear, compiling information and sensory stimuli that have accumulated during the day. For this task to be performed efficiently, the other organs in the body must rest. So take care not to overload your digestive system with a huge meal late in the evening, because digestion uses a great deal of energy – digestive juices are secreted, gastric and intestinal muscles contract, and nutrients are broken down and assimilated. On the other hand, while a very rich dinner can disturb the brain's nocturnal cycle, eating too little can leave you hungry, starving your brain and nervous system, which then slow down. At night, your brain still needs glucose to function. If you experience any of the following symptoms regularly, your evening meal may not be allowing your brain to recover:
• You feel heavy and bloated after dinner.
• You have stomach discomfort, heartburn or acid reflux.

• You fall asleep less than an hour after eating, then wake up later and have difficulty getting back to sleep.
• You have nightmares or dreams about food.
• You feel thirsty or hungry in the middle of the night.
• You have no appetite, or nausea on waking in the morning.
There's just one solution to all these problems: change what you eat for dinner.

How to plan your dinner

First, make sure you are not eating too late. Aim to eat your evening meal at least two to three hours before you go to bed. Second, it must be a complete meal – that is, it must include food from each of the different food groups. To aid digestion, limit how much of each you eat and choose low-fat dishes. Instead of a large serve of meat accompanied by small amounts of vegetables, try reducing the size of your meat serve and presenting it as a salad or stir-fry. Plan your menu around the following ingredients:
• One serve of a starchy food such as bread, potato, rice or pasta, and at least two serves of non-starchy vegetables or salad. You can combine the two if you like: for example, tomato and rice salad, steamed carrots and potatoes, or vegetable soup with noodles.
• One small serve of a protein food such as meat, chicken, fish, egg, a slice of ham or some tuna salad.
• One dairy food such as cheese, yogurt or low-fat ice cream.
• One serve of fruit.
Your dinner should supply the carbohydrates your brain needs to function efficiently. If you don't want to eat meat in the evening, be careful not to miss out on proteins – choose a vegetable source of protein (see the accompanying chart). And don't forget to drink one or two glasses of water during your meal, followed by a herb tea later, because dehydration has a negative effect on the brain.

Food	Protein content
Animal protein	
Beef, lamb, chicken or pork (50 g)	15 g
1 cup (250 ml) of milk	10 g
Cheese (30 g)	8 g
1 egg	6 g
Yogurt, low fat (125 g)	6 g
Milk-based dessert with eggs (125 g)	6 g
Vegetable protein	
Tofu (100 g)	8 g
Legumes, such as lentils (100 g)	7 g
Bread (50 g)	4 g

Beef and beetroot salad

Preparation time: 20 minutes **Serves 4**

120 g mache (lamb's lettuce), rocket or mixed salad greens

2 cooked beetroots

150 g cooked beef or lamb

1 red onion, finely chopped

½ bunch parsley (curly or flat-leaf), finely chopped

1 teaspoon mustard

1 tablespoon balsamic or red wine vinegar

1 tablespoon olive oil

Freshly ground black pepper

1 Wash the salad greens in cold water, then dry and place in a serving dish. Peel the beetroot; dice and arrange on top of the greens.

2 Cut the meat into thin strips and add to dish.

3 To make the dressing, mix the mustard, vinegar and pepper in a bowl, and then slowly whisk in the oil until smooth. Add the onion and parsley.

4 Pour the dressing over the salad and serve immediately.

Tip This recipe is a good way of using up leftover cooked meat.

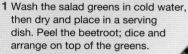

Eggs florentine

Preparation time: 20 minutes
Cooking time: about 30 minutes
Serves 4

2 bunches English spinach, washed thoroughly

1 clove garlic

100 ml low-fat cream

Grated nutmeg

4 large eggs

120 g mozzarella cheese

Freshly ground black pepper

1 Preheat the oven to 210°C. Place the spinach in a heatproof bowl and pour boiling water over it. Let stand for 5 minutes to soften, and then drain. As soon as the spinach is cool enough to handle, squeeze it firmly in your hands to remove the excess water, then chop finely. Return the spinach to the bowl.

2 Finely chop the garlic and add to the spinach. Add the cream, and then pepper and nutmeg to taste. Mix well.

3 Arrange the spinach mixture in a flat ovenproof dish. Using the back of a spoon, make four evenly spaced wells in the spinach. Break one egg into each.

4 Cut the mozzarella into fine slices and cover the spinach. Bake for approximately 20 minutes, or until the cheese is golden brown and the egg whites are cooked.

Tip To save time, you can use 500 g frozen spinach – you don't need to thaw it before cooking.

Light dinner menus

1 Cool and refreshing
• Beef and beetroot salad
Linseed bread
Fromage frais or yogurt
Apricots

2 Comfort food
Noodle soup
• Eggs florentine
Grapes, or melon of your choice

3 Dining with friends
Salmon and leek tart
Mixed salad greens
Baked apples served with Greek-style yogurt

4 Country-style
Tomato soup
Grainy bread
Chive omelette
Green salad
Baked custard

For a healthier brain: say no to toxins!

Many substances in the food we eat have toxic effects on the nervous system: toxins from food bacteria, additives used to preserve food, pesticides, aluminium, heavy metals such as mercury, or even alcohol. These noxious substances, even when ingested in only tiny quantities, can prevent the brain from functioning properly. So it's better to avoid them if you want your brain to remain healthy and active for as long as possible.

Today's resolutions!
– Be aware of food safety.
– To buy organic foods and avoid preservatives if possible.
– To prefer unprocessed food and home-cooked dishes.
– To reduce my alcohol intake.

How to avoid toxic substances

It's all but impossible to avoid toxic substances completely. Food products all contain residual traces of pollutants (pesticides) at varying levels, as well as substances intended to enhance the flavour, colour and texture of food and to conserve it. To limit the impact of pollutants and additives on your health, take care when you are shopping and cooking.

● Be careful with hygiene when cooking and storing your food. Toxins from food poisoning bacteria can be much more harmful than pesticides or other chemical residues and are a far more common cause of food-related health problems. Keep hot food hot (above 60°C) and cold food cold (below 6°C). Refrigerate leftovers promptly – don't leave food to cool at room temperature.

● Preferably choose organic produce, which is now easier to find, even in supermarkets. While it may still contain traces of pollutants from adjacent areas, the water or air, no chemicals are actively used during cultivation and this means that the level of fertilisers and pesticides in organic produce will always be lower than in conventionally grown produce.

● Don't use aluminium foil or cookware when preparing acidic foods such as fruit and vegetables. The acidity can dissolve the aluminium, which combines with the food. Instead cover acidic foods with plastic wrap and use baking paper instead of foil when cooking lemon or tomato in a parcel (en papillote).

● In general, choose unprocessed foods that have no additives (preservatives, or artificial colour or flavouring). The potential long-term effects on the body of such additives are not fully known. Rediscover the pleasure of home-cooked dishes.

● Buy a variety of species of fish and seafood. Pollutants found in fish and crustaceans (such as mercury and toxic micro-organisms) vary with the species and where it was caught. In general, mercury is a concern mainly in the larger or longer-lived fish species such as tuna, marlin, swordfish, shark, orange roughy (sea perch) and catfish. Such fish should be limited to one serve per week (one per fortnight for children and pregnant women).

● Finally, be careful with alcohol. It is indeed a drug and today there is clear evidence of its toxic effects. For example, it can damage neuronal membranes and disrupt the delicate balance of neurotransmitters, the tiny compounds that move information from neuron to neuron. Rather than counting how many glasses or cans you consume, it's more accurate to count standard drinks, as recommended by health authorities, because different beverages can contain varying amounts of alcohol. A standard drink is any alcoholic beverage that contains a specified amount of alcohol, which may vary (it is 10 grams in Australia and New Zealand, for example, but 12 grams in South Africa), and the number of standard drinks contained in the bottle or can is stated on the label. The accompanying chart lists alcoholic beverages and how much of each counts as a standard drink in Australia and New Zealand. In general, recommendations are to limit daily intake to around two or three standard drinks per day, with several alcohol-free days each week.

Type of beverage	1 standard drink (10 g alcohol)
Full-strength beer/cider (4.8% alcohol)	210 ml (60% of a can)
Light beer (2.7% alcohol)	375 ml (1 can)
Wine or champagne (average 10% alcohol)	100 ml (small glass)
Port/sherry (average 18% alcohol)	60 ml
Spirits (average 40% alcohol)	30 ml (1 nip)
Ready-mixed spirits (5% alcohol)	200 ml (half a can)

Fish parcels with diced vegetables

Preparation time: 25 minutes **Cooking time:** 30 minutes **Serves 4**

4 fish fillets (trout, whiting, flathead or yellowtail; about 120 g each)
1 carrot
1 zucchini
½ red capsicum

1 clove garlic
1 tablespoon olive oil
30 g sun-dried tomatoes in oil
1 bunch fresh basil, chopped
Freshly ground black pepper

1 Preheat oven to 200°C. Rinse the trout fillets and pat dry with a paper towel.

2 Wash the carrot, zucchini and capsicum; peel the carrot, trim the zucchini and capsicum, and dice. Peel the garlic and chop finely.

3 Heat the oil in a frying pan and fry the vegetables and garlic for 10 minutes over a high heat until browned. Add pepper to taste. Cut the sun-dried tomatoes into pieces.

4 Cut four large squares of baking paper and place one trout fillet on each. Top each fillet with the vegetables, sun-dried tomatoes and some basil. Wrap up the parcels and cook for 20 minutes. Serve hot.

Non-alcoholic fruit cocktail

Preparation time: 10 minutes **Refrigeration time:** 2 hours **Serves 4**

1 small rockmelon
300 g white seedless grapes
200 g raspberries (fresh, or frozen and thawed)
A few lemon balm or mint leaves
Juice of 1 lemon

1 Refrigerate the fruit for at least 2 hours before preparing. Peel and slice the melon. Wash the grapes.

2 Process the melon, grapes and raspberries in a juice extractor.

3 Pour the juice into 4 glasses. Add lemon balm or mint leaves and a few drops of lemon juice to each glass. Serve immediately.

Summer menu

Breakfast
Wholegrain toast with peanut butter or tahini
Strawberries, blueberries or raspberries
Reduced-fat Greek-style yogurt
Tea or coffee

Lunch or light meal
Prawn and lime salad
Soy yogurt
Sourdough bread

Afternoon snack
Tea or coffee
Apricots

Dinner or main meal
• Non-alcoholic fruit cocktail
Stir-fried turkey with vegetables and cashews
Brown rice
Sliced fresh peach
Low-fat ricotta with honey

Winter menu

Breakfast
Fruit and nut loaf, toasted, with margarine
Orange
Hot chocolate

Lunch or light meal
Vegetable soup
Wholegrain roll
Goat's cheese
Sliced fresh pineapple

Afternoon snack
Hot lemon tea with honey
Fig biscuit

Dinner or main meal
• Fish parcels with diced vegetables
Celeriac salad
Steamed potatoes
Plain yogurt
Kiwi fruit

A brain stimulant and antidepressant: chocolate

Chocolate, or more accurately the cocoa in it, can have both stimulating and calming effects. It is a relaxant and an antidepressant and helps to improve alertness. It contains magnesium and antioxidants and has a high concentration of protective substances. Chocolate is a treat that can safely be used on a regular basis, but because it is very high in kilojoules it is important to keep to small amounts. This is easier with good-quality chocolate, as the flavour is much stronger and more satisfying.

Today's resolutions!
– To choose dark chocolate with a high cocoa content (at least 50 per cent cocoa).
– To eat one or two squares each day, but no more.

Beneficial effects

It's well known that chocolate can improve concentration; it contains caffeine and theobromine, two substances that increase the heart rate and help you to stay focused and alert. It has been calculated that one block of dark chocolate provides as much of these two substances as a cup of strong coffee. But as chocolate is usually eaten in small quantities, its stimulating effect is quite mild.

Chocolate is also well known for its antidepressant effect, which is attributed to its magnesium content and its stimulation of serotonin in the brain. Serotonin is a neurotransmitter that acts as a natural antidepressant, and magnesium is a mineral that is essential for normal neuromuscular function and has relaxing effects. When you eat chocolate, there is a spontaneous release of endorphins, hormones that give you a sense of wellbeing, and this, too, could explain why chocolate relieves anxiety. Even though countering stress and depression may just look like an excuse for eating chocolate, it's nevertheless one of the rare food sources that combine all these soothing substances. Sweets without chocolate don't have such clearly positive effects on mood.

And there are even more good things about chocolate. It has an invaluable antioxidant effect, because it is rich in polyphenols – compounds that protect the cells from premature ageing caused by excess free radicals.

Eating chocolate sensibly

As we have seen, chocolate is much more nutritious than other sweet products such as sugar, honey or sweets, but it's also very high in kilojoules, with an average of 2300 kilojoules per 100 grams. So it should be consumed in moderation – 10 to 15 grams a day is enough to reap the benefits. And choose chocolate that has more than 50 per cent cocoa

(the best-quality chocolate contains 70 to 80 per cent cocoa). This is the only way to be sure that there is only a small amount of added sugar and the right concentration of protective substances.

Avoid high-fat, sugar-rich, chocolate-flavoured sweets that contain very little cocoa, such as sweetened drinking chocolate powder, white chocolate, cream desserts, snack bars and all those other kinds of chocolate munchies that don't provide the same nutritional content as quality dark chocolate. These products have the same kilojoule content as chocolate, but are overloaded with sugar and provide no stimulation for the brain.

Food	Energy content
1 teaspoon (10 g) unsweetened cocoa powder	150 kJ
2 teaspoons (10 g) sweetened drinking chocolate powder	170 kJ
1 square (10 g) dark or milk chocolate	220 kJ
1 chocolate truffle (15 g)	310 kJ
1 tablespoon (20 g) chocolate spread	430 kJ
1 small chocolate snack bar (40 g)	920 kJ
1 standard chocolate snack bar (50–60g)	920 kJ
1 portion chocolate mousse (100 g)	1250 kJ

Chocolate fondue with fresh fruit

Preparation time: 20 minutes **Cooking time:** 1 minute 30 seconds **Serves 4**

1 punnet strawberries
1 tart apple
2 kiwi fruits
1 banana
2 large mandarins or small oranges

Juice of 1 lemon
120 g dark chocolate (50% cocoa)
4 tablespoons low-fat milk
100 ml fresh single cream

1 Hull the strawberries. Peel and slice the apple, kiwi fruits and banana. Peel the mandarins or oranges and separate into segments. Cut each segment in half and remove the seeds.

2 Place the fruit into separate bowls and sprinkle with lemon juice to stop browning.

3 Break the chocolate into squares and place in a microwave-proof dish. Add the milk and cream and melt in a microwave oven for 1 minute 30 seconds (or heat over a saucepan of simmering water until melted). Stir until smooth and pour into a serving dish. Guests use wooden skewers to dip pieces of fruit into the melted chocolate mixture.

Chocolate and raspberry brownies

Preparation time:
25 minutes
Cooking time:
15 minutes

Serves 4

60 g dark chocolate (70% cocoa)
15 g butter or margarine
3 tablespoons caster sugar
1 teaspoon vanilla essence
1 egg
30 g cornflour
100 g raspberries, fresh or frozen
1 tablespoon raw sugar

1 Preheat the oven to 180°C. Break the chocolate into squares and place in a microwave-proof dish. Add the butter, sugar and vanilla and melt in a microwave oven for 1 minute (or heat over a saucepan of simmering water until melted). Stir until smooth and leave to cool slightly.

2 Add the egg and cornflour.

3 Stir the raspberries carefully into the mixture without crushing them.

4 Pour the mixture into a small rectangular cake tin (10 x 18 cm) lined with baking paper. Smooth the surface and sprinkle with raw sugar. Bake for 15 minutes. Cool before removing from the tin. Cut into eight squares and serve.

Summer menu

Breakfast
Wholegrain crispbread and cheese
Sliced melon of your choice
Soy milk shaken with 1 tablespoon cocoa and 1 teaspoon sugar

Lunch or light meal
Tomato and basil soup
Walnut bread
Green salad
Yogurt or fromage frais

Afternoon snack
• One chocolate and raspberry brownie square
Green tea

Dinner or main meal
Roast chicken with sage
Steamed new potatoes
Steamed vegetables
Rocket and parmesan salad
Plums

Winter menu

Breakfast
Banana and orange yogurt smoothie
Porridge with hazelnuts and raisins
Wholemeal toast and fig jam
Hot chocolate

Lunch or light meal
Lentil soup
Witlof salad with ham and walnuts
Pear

Afternoon snack
Fruit tea
Mandarins

Dinner or main meal
Baked fish
Roast sweet potato
Broccoli purée
Grated carrot and celeriac coleslaw
• Chocolate fondue with fresh fruit

Hydrate your brain: drink enough liquid

Brain tissue consists mainly of water, so for optimum brain function a good intake of water is essential. It allows nutrients, including glucose, to circulate and unnecessary substances to be eliminated. So remember to drink enough, so that your brain stays hydrated all day long.

Recognising thirst

Thirst is a vague sensation, and plenty of people, especially young children and the elderly, have difficulty recognising it. The time that you actually need to drink is before you feel thirsty. Adequate fluid intake is important not only for muscles, but also for nerve and brain tissue. Mild dehydration can cause headache, a sense of confusion or loss of balance: the brain needs to be perfectly hydrated for optimal functioning. The daily requirement is about 2.5 litres of water, but you don't need to drink this much, because nearly half of it comes from the water content of the foods you eat. In fact, fruit, vegetables, meat, fish and dairy products contain between 75 and 95 per cent water. The remaining water (some 1.5 litres) comes from the fluids you drink – water, tea, coffee, fruit juice and soup.

Can our needs change?

Air temperature and physical activity also influence our water requirements, which can increase to 3 litres a day when it is very hot. If you don't like drinking water, choose other non-acidic drinks, preferably without sugar, such as herb tea, green tea or coffee (weak or decaffeinated). For the sake of your teeth, avoid relying on juices or soft drinks to quench your thirst – even sugar-free soda water contains acid that can damage tooth enamel. Remember, too, that you can always make water more tempting by adding a squeeze of lemon or orange juice, or a few drops of liquorice extract, then keep it chilled. And mineral water often contains significant amounts of calcium and sometimes magnesium as well, which is another little bonus to keep the body in balance.

Pineapple and lemon granita

Preparation time: 15 minutes
Freezing time: about 2 hours

Serves 4

3 lemons
4 tablespoons pure pineapple juice
3 tablespoons caster sugar (or sweetener)

1 Squeeze the lemons and pour the juice (about 150 ml) into a jug. Add pineapple juice and 250 ml water.

2 Add the sugar (or sweetener, if you are limiting your kilojoule intake). Whisk well to dissolve.

3 Pour the mixture into two ice-cube trays and freeze for 2 hours.

4 Just before serving, take the ice cubes out of the freezer and place in a food processor. Turn on for a few seconds to crush the ice. Pour the granita into 4 glasses and serve immediately.

Tip You can also make this drink in an ice-cream machine.

Hydration regimen
Daily total: about 1.5 litres water

Breakfast
1 warm drink (200 ml of tea, coffee or herb tea)
1 glass water or fruit juice (150 ml)

Mid-morning
1 glass water (150 ml)

Lunch
2 glasses water (300 ml) during the meal

Mid-afternoon
• 1 glass pineapple and lemon granita (250 ml) or 2 glasses water (300 ml)

Dinner
1 soup (250 ml) and 1 glass water (150 ml)

Late evening
1 herb tea (200 ml)

Protect your brain's arteries: reduce your salt intake

Today's resolutions!
– To taste food before adding any salt.
– To use aromatic herbs and spices to give flavour to dishes during cooking, instead of adding salt.

Too much salt can lead to hypertension and damage your arteries, including those that carry blood to the brain. If these arteries become weakened and less flexible, they are less efficient. Even if you think your salt intake is low, be on the lookout, as most food contains hidden salt.

Our excess intake of salt (sodium) is not so much the result of the salt we sprinkle on home-cooked meals. It's more likely to come from cheese, preserved meats, bread, breakfast cereals, biscuits, cakes and other types of manufactured food. For most people, the salt in these foods represents three-quarters of overall sodium intake. This doesn't mean that we should embark on a totally salt-free diet, because sodium is essential for good health. So how can we avoid having too much salt?
• Instead of pretzels and crackers, serve unsalted nuts, seeds and raw vegetables with pre-dinner drinks.
• Limit your intake of cheese to a maximum of one portion (30–40 grams) a day and choose lower-salt varieties such as ricotta or fresh goat's cheese.
• Eat preserved meats only once or twice a week at most.
• Instead of salt, use spices and fresh herbs to flavour food.
• Steaming food retains its original flavours and makes it possible to reduce the amount of salt you add.

Food	Sodium content
50 g raw ham or salami	1000 mg
1 mug of packet soup	1000 mg
30 g blue cheese	600 mg
180 g canned green beans	600 mg
30 g crackers or salted seeds	400 mg
30 g camembert cheese	300 mg
60 g white bread (2 slices)	300 mg
100 g canned tuna in brine	300 mg
180 g fresh or frozen green beans	4 mg

Low-salt menu

Breakfast
Fruit or juice
Muesli with nuts and dried fruit
Yogurt
Tea or coffee with milk

Lunch
Cold roast meat salad
  with fresh goat's cheese,
  cucumber, capsicum,
  onion and lettuce, dressed
  with olive oil and balsamic
  vinegar
Low-salt crispbreads
Peach

Afternoon snack
Vanilla fromage frais or yogurt
Green tea

Dinner
Spiral pasta or penne
• Salt-free tomato sauce
Baked plums with homemade
  custard

Salt-free tomato sauce

Preparation time:
15 minutes
Cooking time:
25 minutes
Serves 4

800 g ripe tomatoes
1 clove garlic
1 onion
2 tablespoons olive oil
1 pinch paprika
Freshly ground black
  pepper
2 sprigs basil

1 Place the tomatoes in boiling water for 2 minutes. Drain, rinse under cold water and peel. Dice over a bowl to catch the juice.

2 Heat the oil in a heavy enamel pot, add the finely chopped onion and garlic, and cook over a medium heat, stirring continuously.

3 When nicely browned, add the diced tomato, paprika and pepper. Simmer uncovered over a low heat for 15 minutes.

4 Chop the basil finely and add to the sauce immediately before serving.

For sustained energy: natural sugars

Glucose is produced in the body by breaking down the carbohydrates in food. It is the main source of energy for brain and nerve tissues, which consume a minimum of 120 grams of glucose a day. This doesn't mean that we have to eat sugary foods for the brain to work properly. Quite the opposite. Sugar and foods containing added sugar should make up only a small proportion of our energy intake. Instead, choose naturally sweet foods that contain fruit or dairy sugars – these provide a more sustained energy boost, as well as important nutrients to help the brain work even better.

Today's resolutions!
– To reduce the amount of sugar I add to my coffee, tea or herb tea to one teaspoonful (or none at all).
– To reduce the sugar in desserts by replacing it with more fruit and spices.

Fuel for the brain

The brain consumes large amounts of glucose and any shortfall will cause fatigue and a drop in alertness. A quick, easy fix might be to eat a sweet or a biscuit, but the effect is deceptive. Eating something very sweet only makes the problem worse, because after an initial apparent improvement the fatigue returns worse than ever. When you eat only sugar, your blood glucose level rises rapidly – and your brain certainly benefits from the additional energy – but your body reacts to this sudden uptake of sugar by secreting insulin, a hormone that lowers the blood glucose level. So then you feel sluggish again, your efficiency drops and often you may feel ravenously hungry. On the other hand, when simple sugars are eaten in small quantities in the course of a balanced meal, they don't have such a dramatic effect on blood glucose, so there is no need to cut them out entirely.

Excessive intake of sweet foods has another undesirable effect on health. Most sweets have virtually no vitamins, minerals or essential nutrients, so when you overindulge they can cause dietary imbalance. If you eat too many high-kilojoule sweets with very little food value, you will gradually lose your muscle tone and energy, and put on weight. The kilojoules in sweets are empty – instead of improving your mental and physical performance levels, they will gradually exhaust you.

How to restrict your sugar intake

Just as with salt intake, don't simply target the spoonful of sugar that you add to your tea or coffee, but look for the sugar that's hidden in various food products. Cut down on biscuits, cakes, sweet drinks and sweets, as well as on commercially produced desserts and sweetened fruit products. Many ready-made savoury dishes also contain sugar, but we rarely notice this. Always read the label carefully to check the ingredients.

Reduce the amount of sugar you add to hot drinks or dairy products, limiting it to 25 g a day – that is, five teaspoons of sugar. If you also like to drink soft drinks (cordials, lemonade or cola), choose low-kilojoule versions and remember to check that the label says 'no added sugar'. Whenever possible, make your own desserts, reducing the sugar in the recipe by 30 per cent. Gradually you'll rediscover the natural flavour of food and reduce your taste for anything that is highly sweetened.

Food	Sugar content
1 teaspoon (5 g) sugar	5 g
1 teaspoon (10 g) jam	8 g
1 bran muffin (70 g)	10 g
35 g breakfast cereal	10 g
1 fruit yogurt (125 g)	15 g
1 ice-cream cone (80 ml)	20 g
1 iced cupcake (50 g)	20 g
1 can (330 ml) soft drink	25 g

Quick spicy pear crumble

Preparation time: 15 minutes **Cooking time:** 15 minutes **Serves 4**

4 pears
Juice of ½ lemon
2 star anise
1 pinch cinnamon

400 g low-fat (20%) cottage cheese, well chilled
1 vanilla bean
6 plain sweet biscuits

1 Peel and dice the pears; sprinkle with the lemon juice to prevent browning.

2 Place the diced pear in a small saucepan with the star anise and cinnamon. Cook over a high heat, stirring frequently, for 15 minutes, until soft and slightly caramelised. Remove the star anise and leave the cooked pear to cool.

3 Place the cottage cheese in a bowl. Split the vanilla bean in half, remove the seeds using the blade of a knife and mix them well into the cheese until smooth. Crush the biscuits on a plate.

4 Divide the vanilla cream between 4 small bowls and top with the warm pear. Sprinkle with biscuit crumbs and serve immediately.

Apple and hazelnut tart

Preparation time:
40 minutes
Refrigeration time:
30 minutes
Cooking time:
50 minutes

Serves 4

150 g flour (plus a little more for flouring the work area)
75 g butter
30 g hazelnuts
800 g apples
Juice of ½ lemon

1 Put the flour in a bowl. Add the salt and butter cut into small pieces. Rub together with your fingertips until the mixture resembles fine breadcrumbs. Add 100 ml warm water, mix quickly and shape into a ball. Cover with plastic wrap and place in the refrigerator to rest for 30 minutes.

2 Preheat the oven to 180°C. Chop the hazelnuts roughly. Peel and dice the apples.

3 Place two-thirds of the apples in a saucepan and stew over a low heat for 15 minutes, stirring frequently. Sprinkle the lemon juice over the remaining diced apple and set aside.

4 Roll out the pastry and place in a 22 cm pie tin. Prick the base with a fork. Spread the stewed apple over the base, and then add the diced raw apple. Sprinkle with crushed hazelnuts. Bake for 35 minutes. Serve warm or cold.

Summer menu

Breakfast
Freshly squeezed orange juice
Country-style bread, toasted, with sliced tomato and cottage cheese with herbs
Plain yogurt with fresh passionfruit pulp
Tea or coffee with milk

Lunch or light meal
Tomato quiche
Radicchio salad
Reduced-fat Greek-style yogurt
Sliced peach

Afternoon snack
Small handful of nuts
Cherries
Tea or coffee

Dinner or main meal
Tuna kebabs with basil
Sautéed zucchini
Tabouleh salad
● Quick spicy pear crumble

Winter menu

Breakfast
Unsweetened porridge sprinkled with chopped walnuts, dates and sultanas
Orange
Lemon or orange tea

Lunch or light meal
Swiss cheese, sun-dried tomato and salad sandwich on wholegrain bread
Sliced pineapple

Afternoon snack
● Apple and hazelnut tart
Weak coffee

Dinner or main meal
Lamb fillets with rosemary
Braised leeks
Mashed potato
Steamed vegetables
Fruit salad of kiwi fruit and mandarin segments

For energy that lasts all day: slow-acting carbohydrates

The brain functions in a very special way – it is continually burning up glucose, but has no glucose stored in reserve. This means it's essential to have a regular intake in the right amounts. The slow-acting carbohydrates in pasta and pulses gradually release energy into the bloodstream, making it possible for the brain to operate all day long.

Today's resolutions!
– To choose more wholegrain foods.
– To eat legumes at least twice a week.
– To include nuts in dishes or eat them as a snack.

The glycaemic index

Foods that contain slow-acting carbohydrates are said to have a low glycaemic index (GI), because they cause only a slow rise in blood glucose level. They are absorbed slowly by the body all through the digestive process, so they release their energy content gradually, avoiding sudden hunger pangs and moments of sluggishness. Your brain can then function smoothly, because it has a stable supply of energy.

In practice, a diet containing low-GI food ensures better long-term efficiency, whether physical or mental, and will also help you to maintain a steady weight, as it may keep you feeling full for longer. So a low-GI diet has plenty of things to recommend it!

Increasing slow-acting carbohydrates

Low-GI carbohydrates – those that are absorbed slowly – are found in foods such as pasta, legumes, fresh and dried fruit, nuts and grains. In contrast, sugar, sweetened soft drinks and sweets contain simple carbohydrates. These release energy rapidly, but the body then uses that energy up very quickly. Here are some tips to help you to obtain sustained energy from the food you eat by increasing your intake of slow-acting carbohydrates.

● Choose wholegrain foods, because the fibre they contain slows down the absorption of carbohydrates. As a result, wholegrain bread has a lower GI than soft wholemeal or white breads that don't contain any whole grains. Similarly, most processed breakfast cereals and cereal bars have a high GI: better choices include muesli and porridge, which contain whole rolled-oats grains.

● Eat fruit: most fruit has a low GI because it contains fructose, a natural form of sugar that is absorbed more slowly by the body's tissues. Dried fruit (such as apricots, prunes, figs, sultanas and raisins) is an ideal snack if you are feeling peckish or need to stay alert – for example, when walking in the country or driving.

● Eat legumes regularly. Their very low GI can help reduce the GI value of the entire meal.

● Cook your pasta al dente – so that it's still a bit firm. This way, it has a lower GI than soft pasta. And try the wholemeal varieties of pasta, which have even lower GI.

● Small new potatoes and sweet potato have a lower GI than most other types. The method you use to cook potatoes can also make quite a difference. Potatoes that are diced and then steamed, or served cold as potato salad, provide a longer-lasting supply of energy than roasted or mashed potatoes.

● Try grains such as oats and barley, which have a lower GI than rice or wheat. Some foods can be deceptive: because fat slows digestion, some very high-fat foods actually have quite a low GI – this doesn't mean that they are good overall choices for health.

Food	Glycaemic index (GI)
Sugar	100
Plain sweet biscuits	80
White bread, white rice	75
Wholegrain bread or cereals	60
Pasta	50
Lentils, dried beans	40
Apples, plums	40
Dark chocolate	40
Fruit yogurt	30

Curried bean soup

Preparation time: 25 minutes   **Cooking time:** 35 minutes   **Serves 4**

2 cans (400 g each) white
beans or lentils
1 tablespoon olive oil
1 carrot
1 tomato
1 stick celery

1 onion
3 cloves garlic
2 tablespoons mild curry
powder
375 ml light evaporated milk
Freshly ground black pepper

1 Rinse the beans or lentils and drain them carefully.

2 Wash the carrot, tomato and celery. Peel the carrot, onion
and garlic. Dice the carrot and tomato. Finely chop the
onion and garlic. Remove strings from the celery and slice.

3 In a large saucepan, fry the onion in the olive oil until
it begins to soften. Add the garlic and fry for a further
1–2 minutes, stirring frequently.

4 Add the curry powder and pepper to taste, stir and
fry until fragrant. Add the other vegetables, then
cover and simmer over low heat for 35 minutes.

5 When the beans or lentils are tender, add
the evaporated milk and process the
soup in a blender until smooth. Season
to taste and reheat. Serve immediately
while still hot.

Spicy tomato pasta

Preparation time:
15 minutes
Cooking time:
15 minutes
Serves 4

3 tomatoes
2 cloves garlic
2 anchovy fillets
1 small bunch chives
2 tablespoons olive oil
1 small dried red chilli
240 g wholemeal or white
spaghetti
Freshly ground black
pepper

1 Wash the tomatoes and
dice. Peel and finely
chop the garlic. Chop
the anchovies into small
pieces. Chop the chives.

2 Heat the oil in frying pan.
Fry the garlic, tomatoes
and chilli. Season to
taste. Leave to simmer
uncovered for 10 minutes
over a medium heat.
Remove the chilli.

3 At the same time, cook
the spaghetti in boiling
water for 7 to 8 minutes
until al dente and then
drain quickly.

4 Add the spaghetti to the
mixture in the frying pan.
Add the anchovies and
chives. Mix together over
high heat for 2 minutes.
Transfer to a serving dish
and serve immediately.

Tip This spicy tomato
sauce is also good with
other types of pasta, such
as farfalle and tagliatelle.

Summer menu

Breakfast
Wholegrain cereal or muesli
Sliced pear and blueberries
Tea or coffee

Lunch or light meal
Brown rice salad with tomato,
tuna and sweet corn
Wholegrain bread
Cottage cheese with honey
Plum

Afternoon snack
Black tea with lemon
Low-fat fruit yogurt

Dinner or main meal
Pan-fried chicken breast
• Spicy tomato pasta
Green salad with avocado
Strawberries

Winter menu

Breakfast
Porridge cooked with chopped
dried apricots and raisins
Kiwi fruit
Black tea with lemon

Lunch or light meal
• Curried bean or lentil soup
Green salad
Linseed bread
Vanilla-flavoured fromage frais
or yogurt

Afternoon snack
Wholegrain crackers with
cheese and sliced tomato
1 mandarin

Dinner or main meal
Grilled pork or lamb
Burghul salad
Braised witlof
Soy yogurt
Stewed apples and prunes

Improve neuronal connections: the benefits of omega-3

Some types of fat are essential for health; omega-3 fatty acids are an important example. These fatty acids form part of the structure of membranes in the brain and nerve cells and help to ensure optimal communication between the nerves. This is a vital function, yet omega-3 fatty acids can't be produced by the body, so they have to be obtained from food. And as the body stores only tiny quantities, it is essential to eat foods rich in omega-3 every day.

Today's resolution!
To meet my daily omega-3 requirements by eating:
– two tablespoons of canola oil or walnut oil a day
– one or two walnuts a day
– oily fish once or twice a week.

Where are omega-3 fatty acids found?

Food contains two kinds of omega-3 fatty acids, which have complementary roles. Alpha-linolenic acid (ALA) is sourced from plants, while animal foods provide docosahexaenoic acid (DHA) and eicosapentaenoic acid (EPA). Recommended intakes are around 500 mg for ALA and 1000 mg total for DHA and EPA together. To increase your omega-3 intake and ensure optimal brain health, make sure that you eat foods containing both types regularly, even if it means that you have to change your dietary habits.

The main plant sources of omega-3 are nuts and seeds such as walnuts, canola, chia seeds and linseeds. Soybeans are also a moderate source. To meet your requirements, nibble walnuts as a snack, make salad dressing with canola oil or add linseeds or chia seeds to breakfast cereal, porridge, and homemade bread and biscuits. Leafy vegetables are also relatively good sources of omega-3, provided you eat them regularly and in sufficient quantities: mache (lamb's lettuce), purslane, fennel and cress are very rich sources. The main animal source of omega-3 fatty acids is oily fish, so include salmon, mackerel, sardines, trout and tuna in your menus regularly. Some of these are available canned, and the canning process doesn't alter the omega-3 content. Canned fish is inexpensive, easy to store and provides an excellent alternative to fresh fish, as long as you choose plain fish, without any added sauces or flavours. Some meats, such as chicken, rabbit, kangaroo and grass-fed beef, also contain small quantities of omega-3. And dairy products have a reasonable omega-3 content too, which is why you shouldn't completely cut out all butter, milk and cheese from your diet.

Keeping omega-3 and omega-6 in balance

Omega-3 fatty acids help to reduce inflammation, but most omega-6 fatty acids (found particularly in sunflower and vegetable oils) tend to do the opposite. These days most of us have too much omega-6 and not enough omega-3 in our diet. To keep your cardiovascular system healthy and make sure that your brain is well supplied with blood, it's essential to restore the balance between the two. You can easily do this by cutting down on vegetable oils and margarine made with corn oil or sunflower oil, and increasing your intake of walnut or canola oil, oil-containing nuts (walnuts) and seeds (linseeds, chia seeds), and oily fish (salmon, tuna, mackerel, trout, sardines).

Food	Omega-3 content	Percentage AI*
100 g sardines	2.8 g	140%
1 piece grilled salmon (100 g)	2 g	100%
1 tablespoon (14 g) canola oil	1.4 g	70%
1 teaspoon omega-3-enriched margarine	0.6 g	30%
2 whole walnuts	0.5 g	25%
1 omega-3-enriched egg (60 g)	0.3 g	15%
Chicken breast (100 g)	0.3 g	15%

* AI refers to the total adequate intake for all types of omega-3 fats combined, as defined by the Australian National Health and Medical Research Council.

Salmon tartare

Preparation time: 25 minutes **Serves 4**

200 g fresh salmon
80 g smoked salmon
1 white onion
1 bunch chives

1 pinch hot paprika
1 tablespoon walnut oil
Juice of 1 lime
Freshly ground black pepper

1 Remove the skin from the fresh salmon, rinse quickly in cold water and pat dry with a paper towel. Peel the onion and chop finely. Chop the chives.

2 Coarsely chop the fresh and smoked salmon and place in a mixing bowl.

3 Add onion, chives, hot paprika and walnut oil. Sprinkle with lime juice and season to taste. Mix gently and serve in 4 small glass dishes.

4 Serve chilled, with thin slices of lightly toasted walnut bread.

Tip Provide lime segments to squeeze over the dish to taste.

Walnut cake

Preparation time:
25 minutes
Cooking time:
30 minutes
Serves 6 to 8

3 eggs
30 g soft butter
1½ tablespoons canola oil
70 g raw sugar
180 g self-raising flour
120 g shelled walnuts

1 Preheat the oven to 150°C. Separate the eggs. Combine the yolks, butter and sugar in a mixing bowl and beat until the sugar has dissolved.

2 Add the flour and mix well. Chop the walnuts coarsely and add to the mixture.

3 Beat the egg whites until stiff; gently cut and fold into the mixture.

4 Pour into a 22 cm springform cake tin and bake for approximately

30 minutes or until a skewer inserted in the centre comes out clean. Cool slightly before removing from the tin. Serve cold.

Tip Never chop nuts in a blender or food processor, as you will end up with an oily paste that is difficult to blend into the mixture.

Summer menu

Breakfast
Half a grapefruit
2 slices linseed bread with omega-3-enriched margarine
Soy yogurt
Coffee or tea

Lunch or light meal
Mache (lamb's lettuce), or watercress, and pine-nut salad, canola dressing
Goat's cheese
Wholegrain bread
Nectarine

Afternoon snack
Green tea
Handful of dried fruit, nuts and seeds

Dinner or main meal
Chilled tomato and capsicum soup
• Salmon tartare with walnut bread
Apricots

Winter menu

Breakfast
Freshly squeezed orange juice
Boiled omega-3-enriched egg
Walnut bread and omega-3-enriched margarine
Tea or coffee with soy milk

Lunch or light meal
Tuna, chicory and purslane salad with canola dressing
Wholegrain or linseed bread
Soy yogurt with diced pear and orange

Afternoon snack
Green tea
• 1 slice walnut cake

Dinner or main meal
Grilled grass-fed beef steak
Boiled potatoes with omega-3-enriched margarine
Braised carrots and fennel
Apple crumble with linseeds

Protect your brain: phytochemicals

We are learning more and more about the important roles that phytochemicals play in the body. These plant-based compounds are potent antioxidants that protect the body's cells from the harmful effects of time. They act naturally to slow down the ageing of cells, and some of them also improve circulation in the delicate blood vessels of the eyes, kidneys and brain. So, to keep your brain youthful and well supplied with oxygen, eat plenty of plant foods every day.

Today's resolutions!
– To drink a cup of green tea every day to increase my phytochemical intake.
– To add plenty of herbs and spices when cooking.
– To eat a variety of colourful, ripe fruit and vegetables in season.

What do phytochemicals do?

Since these compounds are not absolutely essential (unlike vitamins), it was believed for a long time that they had no effect on health. Now, after many studies, we know about their powerful antioxidant action – that they fight the effects of free radicals, which, when produced in excess, cause our cells to age faster. This makes phytochemicals genuinely protective against degenerative diseases such as cancer, cardiovascular disease, diabetes and dementia. Not only do these compounds have antioxidant effects, but they also help to neutralise substances that are toxic to the body. And some of them help to improve blood circulation in the brain, which in turn allows it to function efficiently.

There are many different types of phytochemicals, and they can be found in a variety of plant foods such as fruit, vegetables, pulses, grains, aromatic herbs, tea, coffee, cocoa and spices. The accompanying chart lists different types of phytochemicals with their food sources.

Getting the right intake

If you like fruit and vegetables, eat dark chocolate (containing at least 50 per cent cocoa) and spicy foods often, and drink tea regularly, there is every chance that you are already getting enough phytochemicals. But if you prefer preserved meats to raw vegetables or if you end your meals with cheese rather than fruit, your intake may not be sufficient. Here are some tips to help to increase it.

● Try to have at least seven servings of fruit and vegetables a day, as recommended by current nutritional guidelines.
● Eat a variety of fruit and vegetables to gain the special benefits of each kind.
● Whenever possible, start your meal with a salad or raw vegetables.

● Limit processed meats (such as ham and salami) to only once or twice a week.
● Make sure that your serves of vegetables are larger than your serve of meat or fish.
● Tea and/or coffee drinkers can have one or two cups a day.
● Season dishes with plenty of herbs (such as parsley, basil, chives) and spices (such as turmeric, cinnamon or curry). Many of the common spices are excellent sources of a variety of antioxidants, adding good health as well as flavour.
● Red wine is renowned for its antioxidant content, but be careful: alcohol has a toxic effect on the brain, undoing the benefits, so stick to about one glass per day.

Phytochemicals and their food sources

Carotenoids: carrots, mango, apricots, melon, capsicum, parsley, broccoli, green cabbage, spinach, tomato, pawpaw, passionfruit and all orange, red or green fruit and vegetables

Phenolic acids: coffee

Anthocyanins: red cabbage, beetroot, dark grapes, plums, blackcurrants and berries

Catechins: green or black tea, cocoa, red wine, olive oil

Flavonoids: potato, onion, apples, citrus fruit, grapes, soy foods, tea, cocoa

Lignans: linseeds, sesame seeds, pumpkin seeds, whole grains, legumes

Tannins: coffee, tea, red wine, beer, pomegranates, persimmons, nuts, spices

Red cabbage and apple salad

Preparation time: 15 minutes **Cooking time:** 2 minutes **Serves 4**

350 g red cabbage
1 apple
1 French (red) shallot
1 tablespoon cider vinegar
2 tablespoons canola oil
20 g raisins
20 g pine nuts
Freshly ground black pepper

1 Wash the cabbage, remove its core and shred finely in a food processor. Wash and core the apple and cut into fine strips without peeling. Peel the shallot and chop finely. Place all the ingredients in a salad bowl.

2 In a small bowl, combine the vinegar and the oil, whisking until well combined. Season to taste. Add the dressing to the salad together with the raisins and toss gently. Cover with plastic wrap and chill until ready to serve.

3 Immediately before serving, fry pine nuts in a non-stick pan for 2 minutes until golden brown. Sprinkle them on the salad and serve chilled.

Tip Preferably choose an apple with a tart flavour, such as a Braeburn or Granny Smith.

Red fruit soup

Preparation time: 20 minutes **Cooking time:** 20 minutes **Serves 4**

250 g cherries
200 g strawberries
200 g raspberries
1 organic lemon
Juice of 1 orange

40 g caster sugar
1 cinnamon stick
1 vanilla bean
Fresh mint leaves

1 Rinse the cherries and strawberries and dry carefully with a paper towel. Stone the cherries and hull the strawberries. Cut any large strawberries or cherries into smaller pieces. Place all the fruit in a stainless steel saucepan.

2 Cut 2 strips of lemon rind and add, together with the orange juice, sugar, cinnamon and a vanilla bean split in half.

3 Cook for 20 minutes over a medium heat. Remove the cinnamon. Scrape the seeds out of the vanilla bean and mix into the soup. Serve warm or cold, garnished with mint leaves.

Tip Frozen berries, either individual varieties or a berry mix, work well in this recipe. Use them without thawing.

Summer menu

Breakfast
Grapefruit juice
Wholegrain or linseed bread with berry jam
Cottage cheese
Tea with lemon

Lunch or light meal
Capsicum and tomato pizza
Soy yogurt
Deep purple plums

Afternoon snack
Black grapes
Homemade lemonade made with freshly squeezed lemon juice

Dinner or main meal
Thai fish curry with coriander, Thai basil, mint and plenty of colourful vegetables
Thai red rice
• Red fruit soup

Winter menu

Breakfast
Muesli with dried fruit, nuts and seeds
Plain reduced-fat yogurt
Chopped pear and cinnamon
Coffee or hot chocolate with milk

Lunch or light meal
Pumpkin soup
Toasted rye bread with sardines and sliced tomato
Pawpaw

Afternoon snack
Mandarin
Black tea

Dinner or main meal
Braised beef in red wine
Mashed potato
• Red cabbage and apple salad
Apple crumble

Lift your mood and sleep well: tryptophan

Tryptophan is an amino acid, one of the building blocks that form protein in our bodies. Tryptophan is special because it is used by the body to produce serotonin, which is a neurotransmitter – it carries messages from one neuron to another in the brain. Serotonin is often referred to as the 'happiness hormone', as it also plays a key role in regulating mood and sleep. It would be a pity to go without this tiny molecule!

Today's resolutions!
– To eat three serves of dairy products each day.
– To go back to traditional milky desserts such as semolina and rice pudding.
– To drink a glass of milk before bedtime.

What is tryptophan?

Tryptophan is defined as an essential amino acid – that is, an amino acid that your body needs but can't make for itself. It has to be supplied in sufficient quantities by your diet and must then be properly absorbed and transported to the brain to be effective. There are many factors that can interfere with this process. For example, some other proteins in food can prevent tryptophan from being absorbed by the brain, whereas carbohydrates help the process.

What is its purpose?

One of tryptophan's key roles is its involvement in the production of serotonin. Serotonin is a hormone that helps to control mood, appetite and sleep patterns, as well as the function of organs such as the gut. It is thought to be very important for mood stability: for example, people who suffer from depression are often lacking in serotonin, and a large number of antidepressants act mainly by increasing the level of serotonin in the brain. In addition, seasonal affective disorder, which makes sufferers feel miserable as the days turn cold and dark in autumn, is thought to be a result of altered serotonin levels. In general, serotonin is now recognised as a mood regulator – its soothing effect reduces anxiety and helps people to cope with stressful situations.

Serotonin is itself a precursor of melatonin, which is a genuine sleep hormone that is produced in the brain to regulate the body clock. Melatonin helps you to fall asleep and improves the quality of your sleep. Some mild cases of insomnia can be relieved by the simple measure of increasing the amount of tryptophan-rich food that is included in the diet – an easy solution with no side effects.

Lastly, tryptophan also controls the appetite naturally, because serotonin produces a cosy well-fed feeling: binge eating and gorging on sweets are often related to low serotonin levels. This compulsive urge to eat sweet, carbohydrate-rich food really does produce a momentary feeling of wellbeing, because it helps to optimise how the brain absorbs tryptophan.

Even though tryptophan is relatively scarce in our diet compared with other amino acids, there are some good sources. Turkey and duck meat, nuts, seeds and dairy foods are all sources of tryptophan that the body can absorb easily. Having too much protein at a meal may interfere with tryptophan absorption, so to help the action of tryptophan in the brain these foods are best consumed with carbohydrates – for example, a baked jacket potato with cheese, or a rice pudding (which combines the tryptophan in the milk with sugar and starch). In contrast, while steak with salad provides many different amino acids, it has no carbohydrates and so is less effective in optimising tryptophan supplies. Something else to bear in mind is that tryptophan is a very fragile amino acid that is destroyed by extended exposure to heat, so quick cooking methods are best. And to take full advantage of its sleep-promoting property, it's advisable to eat tryptophan-rich food from 5 pm onwards.

Like Grandma used to do

There is some measure of good sense in the custom of giving children (and adults) a glass of warm milk at bedtime. When the tryptophan in milk is combined with a little sugar, it helps to produce serotonin and, in turn, melatonin. This remedy is quite safe, so why not give it a try and see if it gives you a good night's sleep?

Vanilla and caramel eggnog

Preparation time:
10 minutes
Infusion time:
5 minutes
Cooking time:
10 minutes
Serves 4

1 litre low-fat milk
1 vanilla bean
40 g caster sugar
4 egg yolks

1 Pour the milk into a saucepan and add the vanilla bean split in two. Bring to the boil, and then set aside to infuse for 5 minutes.

2 Put the sugar in a small saucepan with 3 tablespoons water; bring to the boil over a high heat and cook for approximately 4 minutes without stirring, until golden brown. Remove from the heat and carefully add 3 tablespoons boiling water (caution: it will sizzle), stirring gently to make a caramel syrup.

3 Scrape out the inside of the vanilla bean and add its seeds to the hot milk.

4 In a mixing bowl, lightly beat the egg yolks. Gradually pour in the hot milk, beating constantly. Add the caramel syrup and beat until frothy.

5 Pour into 4 glasses and serve hot.

Summer menu

Breakfast
Apricot nectar
Wholegrain breakfast cereal with low-fat milk
Tea or coffee with milk

Lunch or light meal
Zucchini and basil frittata
Baby spinach salad
Sourdough bread
Fruit yogurt
Banana

Afternoon snack
Cold chocolate milk

Dinner or main meal
Chinese barbecued duck
Steamed brown rice
Steamed Asian greens with chives and pumpkin seeds (pepitas)
● Yogurt blancmange

Winter menu

Breakfast
Tropical fruit juice
Toast with avocado and tomato
Hot chocolate with milk

Lunch or light meal
Vegetable soup
Wholegrain crackers and cheese
Winter fruit salad

Afternoon snack
● Vanilla and caramel eggnog

Dinner or main meal
Sliced roast turkey
Baked jacket potato
Roasted carrots
Stewed apple with cinnamon
Baked custard

Yogurt blancmange

Preparation time: 15 minutes **Refrigeration time:** at least 3 hours **Serves 4**

1 sachet (10 g) gelatine powder
500 g full-fat plain yogurt
30 g raw sugar

8 g vanilla sugar
1 small mango
1 kiwi fruit

1 Sprinkle the gelatine powder into half a cup of boiling water and stir until dissolved. Let cool, then add a little of the yogurt and stir until smooth. Pour the gelatine mixture into the rest of the yogurt, stirring briskly.

2 Add the raw sugar and vanilla sugar, and beat until the sugar is fully dissolved.

3 Peel and dice the mango and kiwi fruit. Fold into the yogurt mixture.

4 Pour into 4 ramekins and refrigerate until set (at least 3 hours). Remove from the ramekins and serve immediately.

Protect your nervous system: vitamin B₁

Vitamin B₁, also known as thiamine, is needed whenever the brain uses glucose for energy. This vitamin also helps to transmit nerve impulses and plays a role in getting rid of metabolic waste, which can damage the nervous system if it accumulates. In other words, vitamin B₁ is extremely important for brain function. Deficiencies of this vitamin can cause nerve and brain disorders, but are very rare in Western countries.

Today's resolutions!
– To choose wholegrain breads and cereals.
– To have fruit, nuts and seeds instead of processed snacks.
– To include legumes in my meals twice a week.

Thiamine deficiency

Beri beri, which was first reported in Asia in the nineteenth century, is the final stage of vitamin B₁ deficiency and leads to extreme fatigue, heart failure and neurological disorders. Today, only mild thiamine deficiency is found in Western countries. This occurs mainly in people who consume excessive amounts of alcohol, because alcohol interferes with the body's absorption and use of thiamine, and because heavy drinkers tend to have a reduced thiamine intake as a result of unhealthy eating habits.

A varied diet will usually provide your daily requirement of vitamin B₁, which is an average of 1.5 milligrams. The best sources of vitamin B₁ are offal, pork, eggs, wholegrain cereals, seeds and legumes.

Food	Vitamin B₁ content
100 g pork fillet	800 µg
1 tablespoon (15 g) brewer's yeast	790 µg
1 tablespoon (15 g) wheat germ	210 µg
180 g cooked white haricot beans	200 µg
8 chestnuts (100 g)	200 µg
3 slices (60 g) wholegrain bread	180 µg
100 g calf's liver	160 µg
Handful hazelnuts (35 g)	150 µg
180 g cooked brown rice	150 µg
1 egg (60 g)	60 µg
3 slices (60 g) white bread	50 µg
180 g cooked white rice	30 µg

How to increase your vitamin B₁ intake

The following foods will help you to meet your thiamine requirements:
- Beef or veal offal (liver or heart) two to three times a month; pork, preferably lean cuts (fillet or trimmed chops) once a week.
- Legumes (beans, lentils, split peas); for variety, add them to soup or serve them as a side dish (lentil salad, red bean and tuna salad).
- Nuts and seeds, such as almonds, pine nuts, hazelnuts and sunflower seeds; add them to your meals every day or eat them as snacks.
- Grain products (rice, pasta, bread, breakfast cereals), preferably unrefined, as refining removes much of the vitamin B₁ content – white rice, for example, has virtually no vitamin B₁.
- Fruit and vegetables: these are secondary sources of vitamin B₁.
- Brewer's yeast or wheat germ: the easiest way to cover your requirements is to sprinkle one of these on salads, soups, breakfast cereal and yogurt, as they contain more vitamin B₁ than any other food.

With vitamin B₁ there is no danger of having too much, because any excess thiamine is excreted in urine. And the vitamin B₁ found in meat and grains is virtually unchanged by exposure to oxygen or heat, which means that these foods can be well cooked without destroying any of their vitamin B₁ value.

Chilli pork tortillas

Preparation time: 15 minutes **Marinating time:** 30 minutes
Cooking time: 20 minutes **Serves 4**

500 g pork fillet or boned loin
1 teaspoon ground coriander
1 small fresh red chilli, seeded and chopped
1 clove garlic, crushed
3 tablespoons lime juice
2 teaspoons sunflower oil
75 g onions, thinly sliced

400 g can red kidney beans, rinsed and drained
150 g large tomatoes, skinned, seeded and diced
Freshly ground black pepper
8 soft wholemeal tortillas
Low-fat natural yogurt, chopped fresh mint, lime wedges, to serve

1 Trim any fat from the pork, cut the meat into thin strips and place in a bowl with the coriander, chilli, garlic and lime juice. Toss well, cover and leave for 30 minutes.

2 Heat the oil in a heavy-based frying pan or wok and fry the onions for 3–4 minutes, stirring frequently. Add the drained pork and stir well for 10 minutes to brown.

3 Add the kidney beans and tomatoes and simmer for 3–4 minutes until the tomatoes have softened.

4 Warm the tortillas in the oven or under the grill.

5 Divide the pork mixture between the tortillas. Top each one with yogurt and mint, and fold the tortillas. Serve with lime wedges.

Lentils with coriander

Preparation time:
20 minutes
Cooking time:
40 minutes
Serves 4

1 large carrot
1 large onion
50 g lean bacon (optional)
2 tablespoons olive oil
300 g French-style (Puy) green lentils
1 sprig thyme
1 bay leaf
1 teaspoon coriander seeds
5 sprigs fresh coriander, picked
Freshly ground black pepper

1 Peel and chop the carrot and onion. If using bacon, cut into fine strips.

2 Heat the oil in a heavy-bottomed saucepan. Fry the carrot, onion and bacon (if using) over a low heat for 10 minutes, stirring continuously.

3 Add the lentils, thyme, bay leaf and coriander seeds. Add 1 litre water and pepper. Leave to simmer over a low heat for 30 minutes.

4 Add the coriander leaves to the lentils. Season to taste and serve very hot.

Tip This dish goes well with pan-fried salmon or fillet steak.

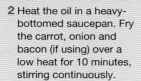

Summer menu

Breakfast
Wholegrain crispbread, spread with cottage cheese and drizzled with honey
Nectarine
Tea with milk

Lunch or light meal
Toasted sandwich with ham, cheese and baby spinach
Pear

Afternoon snack
Cherries
Flavoured soy milk

Dinner or main meal
Grilled salmon
• Lentils with coriander
Soy yogurt
Raspberries

Winter menu

Breakfast
Mango and pineapple smoothie
Porridge with hazelnuts and dates, served with soy milk
Tea or coffee

Lunch or light meal
Cauliflower soup
Liver paté
Sourdough bread
Mandarin

Afternoon snack
Handful of cashew nuts
Hot chocolate made with soy milk

Dinner or main meal
• Chilli pork tortillas
Burghul with almonds, tomatoes and parsley
Brown rice pudding with baked pear

A tonic for your neurons: vitamin C

Vitamin C is known for its stimulating effects; it's the vitamin we need to stay healthy all through the year and particularly in winter. But this is not its only benefit: it's also an antioxidant that is needed for the immune system to operate efficiently. While vitamin C is found in many foods, it is very fragile and can be destroyed by just a few minutes of contact with the oxygen in the air.

Today's resolutions!
– To eat one piece of fruit or one raw vegetable at every meal.
– In winter, to eat an orange or a kiwi fruit every day.
– To add fresh parsley regularly to my cooking.

An anti-ageing vitamin

Like vitamin E and phytochemicals, vitamin C is a powerful antioxidant. It helps to neutralise free radicals – compounds that are produced naturally by the body but which, when produced in excess, accelerate the ageing of cells. Vitamin C also helps to keep your immune system healthy, and its role in protecting against winter ills is unequalled. While there is no scientific evidence that it improves alertness, most of us notice a boost after eating an orange or a kiwi fruit, which is why it's better to eat citrus fruit at breakfast than at dinnertime.

These days, vitamin C deficiency is found only in people whose diet is extremely limited, but you still need to make sure you have your daily requirement. Pollution and smoking, for example, can increase daily requirements considerably. What's more, vitamin C is found only in fruit and vegetables, preferably eaten raw for maximum benefit. A diet that consists solely of processed foods (pizzas, biscuits and the like), starchy food, dairy products and meat doesn't contain sufficient vitamin C to meet daily requirements. And because your body stores virtually no vitamin C, it's essential to eat foods rich in vitamin C every day, and even several times a day.

How to increase your vitamin C intake

To cover your nutritional needs, follow these tips:
● Eat food rich in vitamin C regularly: kiwi fruit, orange, strawberries and other berries, mango, capsicum, cabbage, broccoli, spinach, fennel and cauliflower.
● Eat at least one raw vegetable or one piece of fruit with every meal.

● Cooking partially destroys vitamin C. To minimise losses, steaming and microwaving are the best cooking methods, and it's best to cook vegetables lightly and eat them while they are still slightly crunchy.
● Fresh herbs (such as parsley, chervil, basil, coriander and chives) and lemon juice are rich in vitamin C, so get into the habit of adding them to meals at least once a day.
● Potato is the only starchy food that contains vitamin C. It's fine to eat potatoes regularly, if possible steamed in their jackets to preserve this precious nutrient.

Food	Vitamin C content
1 cup (150 g) raw red capsicum, chopped	220 mg
1 cup (150 g) broccoli, cooked	85 mg
1 orange (140 g)	70 mg
1 kiwi fruit (70 g)	50 mg
1 cup (70 g) raw red cabbage, shredded	48 mg
1 slice rockmelon (100 g)	40 mg
200 g steamed potatoes	30 mg
1 tablespoon (15 g) parsley	20 mg
1 banana (120 g)	12 mg
150 g grated carrot	9 mg
150 g cooked carrot	6 mg

Spicy pomelo and orange salad

Preparation time: 20 minutes **Refrigeration time:** 2 hours **Serves 4**

4 sweet oranges
1 pomelo (or large pink or red grapefruit)
1 pinch hot paprika

1 pinch cinnamon
1 pinch ground cumin
2 tablespoons olive oil
Freshly ground black pepper

1 Refrigerate the oranges and the pomelo (or grapefruit) for at least 2 hours before starting. Working over a bowl to collect any juice that accumulates, remove the peel, pith and membrane from the outside of the fruit.

2 Cut the oranges and pomelo (or grapefruit) into thin rounds and arrange on a large plate. Sprinkle with their juice.

3 Sprinkle the fruit with the hot paprika, cinnamon and cumin. Season to taste with plenty of pepper. Drizzle with oil and chill before serving.

Tip To minimise the loss of vitamin C, cover the prepared dish with plastic wrap and chill as soon as possible until you are ready to serve.

Summer salad

Preparation time:
20 minutes
Cooking time:
2 minutes
Serves 4

60 g baby spinach
1 rockmelon
80 g fetta
1 clove garlic
1 tablespoon balsamic vinegar
2 tablespoons olive oil
20 g pine nuts
Freshly ground black pepper

1 Wash and dry the spinach. Place in salad bowl.

2 Peel the melon, cut it in half, remove its seeds and dice. Dice the fetta. Place the melon and fetta in a salad bowl.

3 Peel and crush the garlic. To make the dressing, mix the vinegar, pepper and garlic in a small bowl; then add the oil and whisk until

well combined. Pour the dressing over the salad.

4 Fry the pine nuts without oil in a non-stick frying pan until golden. Sprinkle over the salad. Toss gently and serve.

Tip To vary this salad recipe, try a honeydew or champagne melon with sweet, pale green flesh.

Summer menu

Breakfast
Citrus juice
Wholegrain breakfast cereal and low-fat milk
Soy yogurt with strawberries
Coffee

Lunch or light meal
Wholegrain bread roll with goat's cheese, avocado, tomato, rocket and grilled capsicum
Peach

Afternoon snack
Apricots
Yogurt

Dinner or main meal
• Summer salad
Grilled beef or lamb kebab
Grilled corn on the cob
Homemade berry sorbet

Winter menu

Breakfast
Raisin toast with fruit spread
Fruit yogurt
Kiwi fruit
Tea or coffee

Lunch or light meal
Carrot soup
Wholegrain crackers
Green salad
Mandarin

Afternoon snack
Banana and kiwi fruit soy milk smoothie

Dinner or main meal
• Spicy pomelo and orange salad
Moroccan-style chicken casserole with dried apricots and prunes
Wholemeal couscous
Greek-style yogurt

Keep your brain youthful: vitamin E

Working in synergy with its partner vitamin C, vitamin E provides an effective shield that guards the body's cells against attack by other substances. Specifically, it protects the unsaturated fatty acids that are found in cell membranes, particularly in the brain and nervous system. By keeping these precious fats intact, vitamin E helps to maintain good brain and nerve function.

Today's resolutions!
– To add nuts and seeds to all my salads and stir-fries.
– To use one tablespoon of vitamin E-rich oil every day.
– To add wheat germ to pastry and cake recipes.

Lipids and the brain

The brain is the organ with the highest concentration of fats, especially very fragile unsaturated fatty acids such as omega-3 and omega-6. When these fats break down, the cells are weakened, and this causes brain tissue to age prematurely and reduces communication between cells. Vitamin E helps to protect brain tissue by shielding these fats from damage, and also contributes to keeping the cardiovascular system healthy. It prevents cholesterol-rich plaque from blocking arteries and helps to reduce the level of blood cholesterol. In this way it optimises the blood supply to the brain and ensures its efficient operation.

The recommended intake of vitamin E is approximately 15 to 20 milligrams, and deficiency is rare in Western countries. To enable vitamin E to contribute to the health of the brain, daily intake must be combined with a diet rich in unsaturated fats.

How to meet your vitamin E requirements

In food, vitamin E is associated with fats – high levels are found, for example, in oils and nuts. Animal fats (such as butter and cream) contain far less of the vitamin than do vegetable fats, and this is why it's important to make sure you have one to two tablespoons of nuts, seeds or vegetable oils every day.

In practice, it's best to choose from the following foods:
● Nut, seed and cereal oils, such as wheat germ oil, corn oil and sunflower oil, are among the richest sources of vitamin E.
● Nuts (in particular, almonds and hazelnuts) and seeds (such as sunflower seeds) are good substitutes for chips and pretzels to serve with drinks.
● Avocado is a good source and can be used in salads and as a spread on bread. Some vegetables and fruits, such as green vegetables, fennel, cabbage and kiwi fruit, can also help to meet requirements.
● Wheat germ is rich in vitamin E and can easily be added to cereals and homemade desserts (to flan pastry or cake batter, for example).
● Oily fish (such as salmon, tuna and mackerel) contain about 1 milligram of vitamin E for every 100 grams of fish.

Food	Vitamin E content
¼ cup (65 g) tahini (sesame paste)	130 mg
1 tablespoon (10 g) wheat germ oil	15 mg
¼ cup (35 g) sunflower seeds	14 mg
1 tablespoon (10 g) corn oil	10 mg
Small handful (30 g) almonds or hazelnuts	8 mg
1 tablespoon almond or sunflower oil	6 mg
1 small avocado (200 g)	3 mg
1 cup (180 g) cooked cabbage or spinach	3 mg
1 tablespoon (10 g) wheat germ	2 mg

Avocado, kiwi fruit and sprouts salad

Preparation time: 15 minutes **Serves 4**

15 cherry tomatoes
2 small avocados
2 kiwi fruits
1 generous handful alfalfa sprouts

Juice of 1 lemon
1 tablespoon olive oil
1 tablespoon corn oil
20 g pecan nuts
Freshly ground black pepper

1 Wash and dry the cherry tomatoes. Stone, peel and slice the avocados. Peel the kiwi fruits and slice finely. Arrange tomato, avocado and kiwi fruit slices on a serving dish with the sprouts.

2 Mix the lemon juice and pepper in a bowl. Whisk in both oils gradually until well combined. Pour the dressing over the salad and toss gently.

3 Break pecan nuts into pieces with your fingers. Sprinkle over the salad and serve.

Tip Alfalfa sprouts can be found in containers in the salad section of your supermarket.

Hazelnut-crumbed chicken

Preparation time:
25 minutes
Cooking time:
10 minutes
Serves 4

60 g hazelnuts
30 g cornflakes or dry breadcrumbs
1 egg
30 g flour
4 chicken schnitzels (or chicken breast fillets, flattened with a meat mallet)
2 tablespoons sunflower oil
1 lemon
Freshly ground black pepper

1 Coarsely crush the hazelnuts with a knife. If using cornflakes, crush them to crumbs (see tip). Combine the nuts and crumbs in a shallow dish.

2 Break the egg into another shallow dish and beat with a fork. Put the flour into a third shallow dish.

3 Dip each chicken schnitzel first in the flour, next in the beaten egg and then in the hazelnut crumb mixture.

4 Heat the oil in a large, non-stick frying pan. Cook the crumbed schnitzels over a low heat until golden brown (about 5 minutes each side). Serve hot with the lemon cut into quarters.

Tip To crush the cornflakes easily, place them in a food-quality plastic bag and run a rolling pin over them.

Summer menu

Breakfast
Melon of your choice
Reduced-fat Greek-style yogurt, drizzled with honey and chopped hazelnuts
Sunflower-seed bread, toasted, with margarine
Tea or coffee

Lunch or light meal
Slice of spinach quiche
Green salad
Mango

Afternoon snack
Fromage frais with berries
Iced tea

Dinner or main meal
Smoked trout
Steamed kipfler potatoes (or other waxy potatoes)
• Avocado, kiwi fruit and sprouts salad
Peach

Winter menu

Breakfast
Grape juice
Corn fritters with avocado and tomato salsa
Soy yogurt
Tea or coffee

Lunch or light meal
Lentil soup
Mache (lamb's lettuce) or watercress salad with corn oil
Linseed bread

Afternoon snack
2 hazelnut biscuits
1 glass milk

Dinner or main meal
• Hazelnut-crumbed chicken
Fried potato
Steamed carrots
Braised cabbage with currants
Baked semolina and almond-meal custard with poached pear

Protecting the brain's energy supply: copper

Copper, a trace element found in tiny quantities in the human body, is beneficial in many ways. It's involved in producing red blood cells, improves the condition of blood vessels, helps to counter free radicals and plays a role in producing dopamine, a chemical messenger in the brain. Copper is a multipurpose nutrient, but should be treated with caution, as too much copper has toxic effects.

Today's resolutions!
– To eat legumes twice a week.
– To include liver, if I like it, once or twice a month.
– To try to include seven serves of fruit and vegetables a day.

What does copper do?

Copper is stored in the liver. It operates in synergy with iron, helping it to be absorbed into the body. To do this, it plays a role in the production of red blood cells and the supply of oxygen to brain tissue. Copper also carries oxygen to the centre of cells, so that energy and oxygen can be used by all the body's tissues.

Copper has several other important roles in the body. Like zinc and vitamin C, it is an antioxidant, which protects the body's cells from attack by excess free radicals and so helps to slow down the ageing of cells, allowing tissue, in particular brain tissue, to stay young. In the brain itself, copper is involved in the production of dopamine, which is a neurotransmitter that conveys information from neuron to neuron.

Lastly, copper is essential for the maintenance of membranes and the cell lining of blood vessels. It improves the elasticity and longevity of vessels – a role that is extremely important for ensuring efficient circulation of blood to the brain and reducing the risk of cerebral aneurism or haemorrhage.

Copper, a two-faceted nutrient

The average daily requirement for copper is around 1.2 to 2 milligrams, and in theory this is supplied by a balanced and varied diet. Copper is an element readily found in animal products (such as offal and seafood) and only vegetarians need to give special attention to their copper intake by ensuring that they eat plenty of legumes, nuts, and fresh fruit and vegetables.

But take care, for while dietary doses for nutrition are harmless, any excess of copper is neurotoxic and causes vomiting and muscular paralysis. It is therefore not advisable to take copper supplements.

To meet your daily requirements, simply use common sense. Copper-rich food such as liver and crustaceans are reliable sources, but should be eaten in moderation, no more than once a week. Other dietary sources have much lower concentrations and can provide a lower and steadier supply of copper: nuts (30 grams a day), pork or poultry (a few times a week), and fresh fruit and vegetables, which contain small quantities of copper and can provide an additional source without any risk of toxicity.

Food	Copper content
100 g calf's liver or lamb's fry	14 mg
6 oysters (100 g)	2 mg
Small handful (30 g) hazelnuts or walnuts	0.5 mg
1 cup (180 g) cooked dried lentils or beans	0.5 mg
100 g dried fruit (prunes, sultanas etc.)	0.4 mg
5 squares (50 g) dark chocolate (at least 50% cocoa)	0.4 mg
6 mussels or clams (100 g) or 0.5 litre mussels	0.3 mg
100 g cooked kangaroo meat	0.2 mg
1 heaped tablespoon (6 g) cocoa powder	0.2 mg
1 cup (180 g) cooked spinach or carrots	0.1 mg
100 g cooked meat (beef, lamb or pork)	0.1 mg

Chicken liver salad

Preparation time: 20 minutes **Cooking time:** 5 minutes **Serves 4**

150 g chicken livers, trimmed
60 g mixed salad greens
1 tomato
¼ daikon radish

3 tablespoons olive oil
1 tablespoon sherry vinegar
Freshly ground black pepper

1 Dice the chicken livers. Wash and dry the salad greens. Wash and dice the tomato. Peel the radish and cut into strips.

2 Arrange the salad greens, tomato and radish in a salad bowl.

3 Add 2 tablespoons oil and the vinegar. Season to taste and toss well.

4 Heat the remaining oil in a frying pan. Sauté the diced chicken livers, stirring over a high heat for 5 minutes. Season to taste. Arrange the chicken livers on a bed of salad and serve immediately.

Sicilian lentils with potatoes

Preparation time:
15 minutes
Cooking time:
20 minutes
Serves 4

1 kg boiling (waxy) potatoes
3 tablespoons olive oil
2 tablespoons red wine vinegar
410 g can brown lentils, rinsed and drained
150 g pitted black olives
1 tablespoon capers
2 cloves garlic
1 tablespoon lemon juice
3 tablespoons fresh flat-leaf parsley
6 spring onions
Freshly ground black pepper

1 Peel the potatoes, cut into large chunks and cook in a saucepan of boiling water for 15–20 minutes or until tender. Drain and transfer to a large bowl.

2 While the potatoes are still hot, add the olive oil and vinegar and stir through.

3 Rinse and chop the capers. Chop the garlic. Chop the parsley roughly and slice the spring onions diagonally.

4 Add the lentils, olives, capers, garlic, lemon juice, parsley and spring onions to the potatoes. Season with a pinch of salt and a good grind of black pepper and toss well to combine. Serve warm.

Summer menu

Breakfast
Carrot and apple juice
Muesli with hazelnuts, prunes and yogurt
Tea or coffee

Lunch or light meal
• Chicken liver salad
Fresh raspberries
Walnut bread

Afternoon snack
2 apricots
Tea or coffee

Dinner or main meal
Mussels steamed in white wine with leeks and tomatoes
Goat's milk curd drizzled with honey
Cherries

Winter menu

Breakfast
Orange juice
French toast with stewed plums
Hot milk with honey and wheat germ

Lunch or light meal
Wholemeal roll with hard-boiled egg, spinach and grated carrot
Apple with a handful of raisins

Afternoon snack
Vanilla yogurt
Fruit juice

Dinner or main meal
Pan-fried turkey breast
Baked jacket potato
• Sicilian lentils with potatoes
Chocolate soufflé

Ensure a good supply of oxygen to the brain: iron

Iron is essential for the formation of red blood cells and is needed to carry oxygen to all body tissues, including the brain. If the oxygen supply is inadequate or irregular, the brain will not work at full efficiency; it's as though it 'runs out of breath' at the slightest effort. Iron requirements are not always met, and women and vegetarians need to be especially careful.

How much iron do you need?

Anaemia (an abnormally low number of red blood cells) causes hypoxia – poor oxygen supply to body tissue. Without oxygen, cells cannot function properly. When mountaineers climb at higher altitudes where the air contains less oxygen, they need considerable energy to make the slightest effort. The same thing happens with an iron deficiency.

Our iron requirements are relatively low (an average of 10 to 18 milligrams a day), as the body uses it sparingly and tries to recycle it whenever possible. That said, our daily intake still needs to be quite high, as only a tiny proportion of the iron in food (5 to 20 per cent) is absorbed. In particular, women between adolescence and menopause need to replenish their reserves of red blood cells every month and so are more prone to anaemia than men. Similarly, because vegetarians rely on plant sources of iron, they are more likely to be anaemic than meat eaters.

Animal and vegetable sources of iron

Iron is found in our diet in two different forms: haem iron from animal sources (meat, offal, eggs, fish and seafood) and non-haem iron from plants (vegetables, legumes, dried fruit and nuts). Iron is absorbed from animal sources more easily than from plant sources, unless the latter are eaten at the same time as an animal source or with a large quantity of vitamin C, both of which help the absorption process. To improve the bioavailability of iron from plant sources, eat them with vitamin-C-containing vegetables or fruits, sprinkle your salads and cooked vegetables with lemon juice, or eat dishes that combine animal and plant sources of iron (pork with lentils, or tuna and haricot bean salad, for example).

Make sure you are getting enough iron to provide a good supply of oxygen to your brain by following these tips:
- Meat eaters should include lean red meat in their diet once or twice a week. Liver, kidneys, blood sausage and tongue are also rich in iron and could be included once or twice a month.
- White meat, eggs and fish have only 30 to 50 per cent of the concentration of haem iron found in red meat, but are still quite good sources.
- Excellent alternatives to red meat are shellfish and seafood (such as mussels, oysters, clams, cockles, prawns and crab).
- While iron from plant sources is assimilated less efficiently than from animal sources, it is still a good source. Legumes such as dried beans, peas and lentils are very rich in iron.

Food: animal sources	Iron content
100 g kidney or blood sausage	18 mg
100 g chicken liver	11 mg
6 mussels (100 g)	9 mg
100 g minced kangaroo meat	3 mg
6 oysters (100 g)	3 mg
2 eggs	2.5 mg
100 g lean beef or lamb	2 mg
1 fish fillet (100 g)	1 mg
Food: plant sources	**Iron content**
1 cup (180 g) cooked spinach	7 mg
1 cup (180 g) cooked lentils	4 mg
1 cup (180 g) soybeans, kidney beans, split peas	3 mg
¼ cup (35 g) pumpkin seeds	3 mg
Small handful (30 g) hazelnuts	1 mg
30 g prunes or raisins	0.8 mg

Iron-rich cottage pie

Preparation time: 15 minutes **Cooking time:** 45 minutes
Serves 4

4 large potatoes (about 600 g), peeled and chopped

¼ cup (60 ml) milk

½ cup (60 g) grated low-fat cheddar cheese

100 g small red lentils

410 g can diced tomatoes

1 tablespoon olive oil

500 g kangaroo, lamb or beef mince

1 small onion, finely chopped

2 large cloves garlic, crushed

1 large carrot, finely diced

1 large zucchini, finely diced

2 tablespoons salt-free tomato paste

145 g peas, fresh or frozen

2 tablespoons fresh parsley, chopped

Freshly ground black pepper

1 Preheat the oven to 180°C. Boil the potatoes until very tender. Drain, place in a large bowl and mash well. Stir in the milk and cheese, season to taste, and beat until creamy.

2 Simmer the lentils and tomatoes gently in a saucepan, stirring occasionally, until the lentils are soft.

3 Heat the olive oil in a large non-stick frying pan over a medium heat. Add the mince and cook for 5 minutes, breaking up any lumps. Add the onion and garlic, and cook for a further 3 minutes, or until the onion is soft. Add the carrot and zucchini and cook for a further 3 minutes,

stirring. Add the lentil mixture, tomato paste and peas, and then reduce the heat and simmer, uncovered, for 5 minutes. Stir in the parsley.

4 Spoon the mixture into a baking dish. Spread the mash topping on top of the mixture to cover completely. Bake, uncovered, for 30 minutes, or until heated through and golden brown on top.

Mandarin and lamb stir-fry

Preparation time:
25 minutes
Cooking time:
10 minutes
Serves 4

500 g boneless leg of lamb

1½ tablespoons reduced-salt soy sauce

1 teaspoon ground coriander

2 teaspoons grated mandarin zest

2 teaspoons vegetable oil

1 red capsicum, cut into 1 cm squares

3 cloves garlic, crushed

4 spring onions, thinly sliced

½ cup chicken stock

2 teaspoons cornflour

4 mandarins

Coriander leaves and spring onion, to serve

1 Trim the lamb and cut into 1 cm strips.

2 Combine the soy sauce, ground coriander and mandarin zest in a bowl. Add the lamb, tossing well.

3 Peel the mandarins, separate into segments; halve and seed each segment.

4 Heat 1 teaspoon oil in a large non-stick frying pan over a moderately high heat. Add the lamb and stir-fry for 2 minutes or until lightly browned. Transfer to a plate.

5 Reduce the heat to moderate, add the remaining oil, the capsicum, garlic and spring onions, and stir-fry for 4 minutes, or until the capsicum is crisp-tender.

6 Whisk the stock into the cornflour in a small bowl. Add to the pan and bring to the boil.

7 Return the lamb to the pan, add the mandarins and cook for 1 minute, or until the sauce is slightly thickened. Garnish with coriander leaves and shreds of spring onion.

Summer menu

Breakfast
Orange juice
Iron-fortified wholegrain cereal with sliced strawberries and low-fat milk
Tea or coffee

Lunch or light meal
Tuna and baby spinach sandwich on wholegrain bread
Peach

Afternoon snack
2 fresh figs
Handful of hazelnuts
Iced herb tea

Dinner or main meal
• Mandarin and lamb stir-fry
Steamed brown rice
Raspberry crumble

Winter menu

Breakfast
Mandarin juice
Porridge with nuts and dried fruit
Plain yogurt
Tea or coffee

Lunch or light meal
Avocado, pomelo (or grapefruit) and fennel salad
Goat's cheese with ash
Banana
Walnut bread

Afternoon snack
Raisin toast with margarine
Herb tea

Dinner or main meal
• Iron-rich cottage pie
Broccoli
Prunes and custard

Ensure sound and restorative sleep: magnesium

Magnesium is an essential mineral for nerve and muscle function and helps us to relax and sleep soundly. Because our magnesium requirements are high and our food intake of this mineral is not always adequate, deficiencies are quite common in Western countries. Today's objective is to learn how to increase your magnesium intake, relax deeply and get a good night's sleep.

Today's resolutions!
– To have a handful of dried fruit and nuts two to three times a week.
– To make sure I eat magnesium-rich vegetables.
– If I drink bottled water, to choose mineral water for extra magnesium.

What does magnesium do?

Magnesium is an important mineral that is essential for the body to function efficiently. It plays many different roles in metabolism at the cellular level and helps to control the function of the nervous system. While it is needed to both store and use the energy neurons require to work, it is also involved in transmitting nerve impulses. Magnesium is a natural sedative, helping muscles relax and making a major contribution to the quality of our sleep.

Our average daily requirement is about 300 to 400 milligrams, and this is not easy to meet because magnesium-rich food tends to be high-energy food. This means that people who are trying to lose weight will often find that by restricting their kilojoules they have also reduced their magnesium intake. When we are under stress, more magnesium is excreted in urine, increasing our requirements even further. All these factors can lead to a deficiency of this essential mineral.

Food	Magnesium content
1 cup (180 g) spinach, cooked	149 mg
1 cup (180 g) soybeans, cooked	128 mg
1 litre magnesium-rich mineral water	110 mg
1 cup (180 g) cooked brown rice	88 mg
Small handful (30 g) almonds	75 mg
1 tablespoon (15 g) wheat germ	60 mg
1 cup (180 g) cooked beans, peas or lentils	54 mg
2 squares (20 g) dark chocolate (at least 50% cocoa)	45 mg
Small handful (30 g) peanuts	39 mg
2 slices (60 g) wholegrain bread	38 mg

How to deal with magnesium deficiency

Sleep that is disturbed and not restorative, cramps, pins and needles, headaches and overwhelming fatigue are all signs that your magnesium supply may be insufficient. Supplements, in either tablet or liquid form, may be an acceptable temporary solution when taken on medical advice. But if you have a tendency to be short of magnesium, try to increase your daily intake of magnesium-rich food and so avoid suffering a deficiency. Be sure to include the following foods in your diet:
● Dried fruit and nuts contain high levels of magnesium, so eat them regularly.
● Whenever you can, choose wholegrain bread and cereal foods, which contain more magnesium than the refined versions (like white bread and white rice).
● Cocoa and dark chocolate (with at least 50 per cent cocoa) are known to contain magnesium, but we eat only relatively small quantities. Nevertheless, it's still a source that shouldn't be overlooked and is an added benefit for regular dark-chocolate eaters.
● Green vegetables also provide magnesium, so there is yet another reason for eating at least three servings of vegetables each day.
● Wheat germ is an excellent supplement to boost your daily intake of magnesium.
● Some brands of mineral water are rich in magnesium and are a perfect way of increasing your intake without putting on weight – check the labels of different brands to compare their magnesium content.

Tuna and red kidney bean salad

Preparation time:
20 minutes

Serves 4

400 g red kidney beans (canned)

1 tomato

2 spring onions

100 g tuna (canned in brine)

1 tablespoon balsamic vinegar

1 pinch paprika

1 tablespoon olive oil

1 tablespoon canola oil

¼ cup basil leaves, chopped finely

Freshly ground black pepper

1 Rinse and drain the kidney beans. Wash and dice the tomato. Peel the onions and slice finely. Drain the tuna and separate with a fork.

2 Place the beans, tomato, onion and tuna in a salad bowl. Mix gently to avoid crushing the beans.

3 To make the dressing, in a small bowl mix the vinegar, pepper and paprika. Gradually whisk in the oil until well combined.

4 Pour the dressing over the salad, sprinkle with the basil, toss gently and serve immediately at room temperature.

Summer menu

Breakfast
Hazelnut muesli
Low-fat yogurt
Nectarine
Tea with lemon

Lunch or light meal
• Tuna and red kidney bean salad
Wholemeal bread
Cherries

Afternoon snack
Small handful of nuts and raisins
Tea or coffee

Dinner or main meal
Grilled pork or lamb chop
Oven-baked potato wedges
Silverbeet in tomato sauce
Baked plums and custard

Winter menu

Breakfast
Wholemeal ricotta pancakes
Mandarins
White coffee

Lunch or light meal
Country-style soup (mixed vegetables, white haricot beans)
Wholemeal toast
Orange

Afternoon snack
Winter fruit salad
Tea

Dinner or main meal
Baked fillet of salmon
Quinoa and zucchini
• Banana parcels with chocolate sauce

Banana parcels with chocolate sauce

Preparation time: 20 minutes **Cooking time:** 15 minutes **Serves 4**

4 small bananas
20 g butter
8 sheets filo pastry
15 g white sesame seeds

30 g dark chocolate (minimum 50% cocoa)
3 tablespoons low-fat milk

1 Preheat the oven to 180°C. Peel the bananas and slice them crosswise. Melt the butter in a microwave oven for 30 seconds.

2 Spread out one filo sheet and brush with melted butter. Top with a second sheet. Place some slices of banana in the centre. Fold over the top 3 cm, then fold in the sides and roll up to form a parcel. Repeat with the remaining filo and bananas to make four parcels.

3 Place the parcels on a baking sheet, sprinkle with sesame seeds and bake for 10 minutes.

4 Break the chocolate into a small heatproof dish and add the milk. Melt in a microwave oven for 30 seconds and stir until smooth. Serve the parcels hot with the chocolate sauce.

Fighting the effects of ageing: selenium

Like all antioxidants, selenium has been the subject of much discussion for a number of years. Thanks to its ability to protect against excess free radicals, it is actually classified as an anti-ageing compound. Studies have also found that selenium plays a role in cancer prevention. But, like copper, selenium is also toxic if levels are too high. So once again, let commonsense prevail when making decisions about what you eat.

Today's resolutions!
– To eat selenium-rich vegetables once or twice a week.
– If I don't eat meat, to have eggs and dairy products and plenty of nuts and seeds.
– To choose wholegrain cereals.

What does selenium do?

Only the tiniest quantities of selenium are found in the body, but it is still an extremely important nutrient for good health. It is a major antioxidant and part of the defence system that our cells use to counter the aggressive effects of free radicals – substances that the body produces naturally but which damage healthy cells when present in excessive amounts. Selenium, then, together with the other antioxidants, helps to protect our cells from premature ageing and degenerative conditions. It also plays a role in the production of prostaglandins (which are particularly needed by blood platelets) and has a stimulating effect on the immune system.

When selenium is in short supply, the body automatically redirects it to the brain and to the endocrine glands, such as the thyroid, as it is crucial that these vital organs function efficiently. Selenium also helps to neutralise toxic substances and heavy metals (such as lead and mercury), which can impair brain function.

How to meet your selenium requirements

As levels of trace elements in food have declined over recent decades, our selenium intake has dropped by almost 30 per cent. This is mainly because of changes made to manufactured food, such as refined flour and the pre-prepared products that people often choose in preference to home-cooked dishes. As plants grow, they absorb selenium from the soil and, depending on their region of origin, grains and vegetables contain different levels of the nutrient: Australian, New Zealand and South African soils, for example, have much less selenium than soils in the United States and parts of Asia.

Our average daily selenium requirement is around 60 to 70 micrograms (µg), which, while a tiny amount, is not always covered by our dietary intake. But, as with most trace elements, excessive consumption of selenium is dangerous, because it becomes toxic in high doses. This is why it's best to target micronutrient requirements by eating a sensible diet rather than by taking pharmaceutical supplements.

The main sources of selenium are seafood and offal, the same as for zinc and copper, so the advice is the same: one or two portions a month should provide safe amounts. In practice, you'll find sufficient quantities of selenium in meat, fish, eggs and dairy products, wholegrain cereals (rather than refined products), some nuts, legumes and fresh vegetables. In general, unprocessed foods have higher concentrations of selenium than refined products or pre-prepared foods.

Food	Selenium content
6 brazil nuts	240 µg
100 g chicken liver	80 µg
100 g tuna, canned	75 µg
100 g swordfish, cooked	60 µg
6 oysters, mussels or scallops	60 µg
100 g prawns, cooked and peeled	45 µg
100 g sardines or mackerel	37 µg
2 eggs (120 g)	30 µg
100 g mushrooms	15 µg
100 g lean beef or lamb	15 µg
100 g cheese	10 µg
3 slices (60 g) wholegrain bread	9 µg
100 g cooked lentils	6 µg
Small handful (30 g) peanuts	1 µg

Spinach and mushroom omelette

Preparation time:
15 minutes
Cooking time:
15 minutes

Serves 4

150 g mushrooms

50 g baby spinach

1 clove garlic

1 tablespoon olive oil

1 pinch turmeric

1 pinch nutmeg

8 eggs

Freshly ground black pepper

1 Quickly rinse the mushrooms, wipe dry and trim the ends of the stems. Slice finely. Rinse, dry and shred the spinach. Peel and slice the garlic.

2 Heat the oil in a large, non-stick frying pan. Fry the mushrooms, spinach and garlic for 5 minutes, stirring over a medium heat. Add the pepper, turmeric and nutmeg. Place on a plate and set aside.

3 Beat the eggs in a bowl.

4 Heat the frying pan and pour in the beaten eggs. Cook the omelette over a medium heat for 10 minutes, using a wooden spoon to push the set egg mixture from the edge to the centre of pan. When all the egg mixture is starting to look just set but is still moist on the top, add the mushrooms and spinach and continue to cook over a gentle heat. Serve hot.

Summer menu

Breakfast
Grapefruit juice
Sheep's cheese
Wholegrain bread and fig jam
Tea with milk

Lunch or light meal
• Spinach and mushroom omelette
Salad of mixed greens
Goat's cheese
Sourdough bread
Plums

Afternoon snack
Watermelon
Flavoured milk

Dinner or main meal
Barbecued sardines
Baked jacket potatoes
Barbecued capsicum, corn and eggplant
Apricot sorbet

Winter menu

Breakfast
Swedish crispbread with omega-3-enriched margarine
Cottage cheese
Kiwi fruit
Coffee

Lunch or light meal
French onion soup
Lamb's lettuce and walnut salad
Wholegrain bread
Plain yogurt
Stewed pears

Afternoon snack
Hot chocolate
Wholegrain bread

Dinner or main meal
Half pomelo or pink grapefruit
• Scallops in saffron cream
Brown rice
Steamed broccoli florets
Provolone cheese
Mandarin

Scallops in saffron cream

Preparation time: 20 minutes **Cooking time:** 20 minutes **Serves 4**

400 g scallops

Chives

1 witlof

10 g canola oil

150 ml reduced-fat evaporated milk or light cream

2 units saffron threads

Freshly ground black pepper

1 Rinse the scallops and wipe dry. Wash, dry and chop the chives.

2 Wash the witlof, remove the core and slice finely.

3 Heat the oil in a frying pan. Fry the witlof and scallops for 5 minutes, stirring over a high heat. Lower the heat and cook for a further 10 minutes.

4 Add the evaporated milk, saffron and pepper. Stir gently and leave to simmer over a low heat for 5 minutes. Sprinkle with chives and serve immediately, very hot, with brown rice and steamed vegetables.

Tip Instead of the witlof you can use half a cup of any shredded greens of your choice – try rocket, spinach, watercress or even radicchio for a stronger taste. This recipe can also be made with mussels.

Boosting the learning process: zinc

Zinc is a trace element that has many different functions, and views on its importance for the body are constantly being updated. The brain needs zinc to function properly; this is clear from cases of zinc deficiency observed in patients suffering from psychiatric disorders, and in people with dyslexia or language learning difficulties. It is also an extremely important antioxidant – an adequate supply of zinc is essential to keep your brain youthful and lively.

Today's resolutions!
– To eat seafood regularly.
– To have dried fruit and nuts instead of processed snacks.
– If I eat meat, to make sure I choose lean red meat regularly, because it is a good source of zinc.

What does zinc do?

Zinc is found in tiny quantities in the human body, yet plays a crucial role, as it is essential for growth, reproduction and the immune system. It also contributes to the activity of a large number of enzymes, defending the body against attacks from excess free radicals and in so doing preventing premature ageing of body tissue.

Zinc is concentrated in the hippocampus, which is an extremely active part of the brain. This may explain why a deficiency can lead to serious depression, loss of the sense of taste or smell, or delayed brain development in children. A shortage of zinc also seems to be associated with learning difficulties, especially with regard to language acquisition. This shows that the few milligrams of zinc that we obtain from our diet are vitally important for keeping the brain functioning efficiently.

How to meet your zinc requirements

A varied diet containing animal products will, in theory, meet average daily zinc requirements which are estimated to be between 8 and 14 milligrams. The best dietary sources of zinc are seafood (such as oysters and clams), meat, offal (such as brains and kidneys), eggs and fish. Wholegrain bread, legumes and nuts contain zinc, too, but fresh fruit and vegetables are only secondary sources. Wheat germ, a natural food supplement with a number of benefits, is also a good source of zinc, so it's a good idea to get into the habit of sprinkling wheat germ flakes on your cereal, salad or yogurt every day.

Zinc is not destroyed by heat, but it does seep out into cooking water if food is boiled. Instead of boiling, try the following cooking methods:
- For offal, fry in a non-stick pan, grill or braise.
- Meat can be quickly grilled or pan-fried.
- Fish can be pan-fried, baked, steamed or cooked en papillote (in a parcel).
- Vegetables retain both flavour and minerals when microwaved, steamed or braised.

Keep the liquid from cooking shellfish such as mussels and clams, and use it to make a sauce. If you are opening your own oysters, don't wash away the brine inside them – it has a high concentration of beneficial minerals, as well as being prized for its flavour. Simply brush away any loose fragments of shell and serve the oysters with their delicious juices intact.

Food	Zinc content
6 oysters	40 mg
3 slices (60 g) wholegrain bread	5 mg
½ cup pumpkin seeds	5 mg
100 g lean beef, lamb or kangaroo	4 mg
100 g kidney or liver	3 mg
100 g prawns or mussels	3 mg
2 eggs (120 g)	2 mg
1 cup (150 g) lentils or beans	2 mg
1 plateful (200 g) of vegetables	1 mg
Small handful (35 g) of almonds or hazelnuts	0.5 mg

Meatballs with basil

Preparation time: 25 minutes **Cooking time:** 25 minutes **Serves 4**

1 bunch basil
1 clove garlic
400 g lean beef (10% fat) or kangaroo mince
1 slice wholemeal bread

20 g pine nuts
1 egg
2 tablespoons olive oil
100 ml tomato purée
Freshly ground black pepper

1 Wash and dry the basil, and shred the leaves finely. Peel and crush the garlic.

2 Place the beef or kangaroo mince in a mixing bowl. Add the crumbled bread, basil, garlic, pine nuts and egg. Mix well and season to taste. Shape the mixture into walnut-sized balls, rolling them with damp hands.

3 Heat the oil in a frying pan and fry the meatballs over a high heat for 5 minutes, turning to brown on all sides.

4 Add the tomato purée and simmer over a low heat for 20 minutes. Serve hot with rice.

Almond and bean dip

Preparation time: 20 minutes
Cooking time: 10 minutes
Serves 4

400 g white haricot or butter beans (canned)
1 tablespoon olive oil
1 pinch ground cumin
1 onion
Chives
50 g blanched almonds
Pepper

1 Rinse and drain the beans and place in a saucepan. Add oil, cumin and pepper. Cover and simmer over a low heat for 10 minutes.

2 Peel and chop the onion. Wash, dry and chop the chives.

3 In a non-stick frying pan with no added oil, fry the almonds over a low heat for 5 minutes, tossing continually to prevent

burning. Crush the almonds using a wide-bladed knife.

4 Place the beans and onion in a food processor and process until puréed. Transfer to a serving dish, stir in the chives and adjust the seasoning.

5 Sprinkle the crushed almonds over the dip and serve with raw vegetable sticks or wholegrain crackers.

Tip Served warm, this dish is also good as an accompaniment for a slice of calf's liver or a grilled lamb chop.

Summer menu

Breakfast
Muesli with plenty of nuts and seeds
Plain yogurt
Apricots
Iced lemon tea

Lunch or light meal
Prawn and tomato salad
Wholegrain crispbread
Mango or grapes

Afternoon snack
Sesame or pumpkin-seed biscuits
Tea or coffee

Dinner or main meal
6 oysters with lemon wedges
• Meatballs with basil
Wholemeal spaghetti
Fruit salad and low-fat ice cream

Winter menu

Breakfast
Orange juice
Baked beans on wholegrain toast
Tea or coffee

Lunch or light meal
Carrot soup
Wholegrain toast with blue cheese
Green salad
Apple

Afternoon snack
Raw vegetable sticks
• Almond and bean dip
Earl Grey tea

Dinner or main meal
Pan-fried kidneys with parsley and mushrooms
Steamed baby potatoes
Grilled tomatoes
Steamed green beans
Apple, raisin and almond crumble

10 days
to put some brawn in your brain

It is well known that physical activity has beneficial effects on the heart, muscles, bones and other parts of the body, but the brain can benefit too. Doing exercises daily, even simple ones, improves the capacity of your grey cells. Do you lack flexibility? Do you want to strengthen your visual acuity? Does your sense of balance leave a lot to be desired? The following exercise plan, covering a period of 10 days, consists of easy movements to stimulate your brain and doesn't require any sophisticated equipment. The exercises are specially targeted – some encourage coordination between the two hemispheres, while others make your memory work. You'll also learn relaxation and massage techniques to release stress and tension.

Put together a program that focuses on your personal needs by combining exercises that suit you: for example, start by warming up, then do a few stretches and continue with flexibility and muscle-strengthening exercises, and then finish with a relaxation session. Some exercises need two people, so ask your partner,

your children or your friends to join you. Make the most of what you have learned as soon as you get the opportunity or whenever you feel the need – at home, at work or on holiday.

The level of difficulty of the exercises is identified by the following symbols:

Easy

Medium

Hard

Some exercises have several levels of difficulty: when you can do a movement easily, move to the next level to get increased benefits from the exercise.

Keep your brain alert: sharpen your proprioception

Breaking with routine is good for the brain! In fact, by changing your habits you send new information to the nerve cells that are involved in situating the body in space and these cells must then adapt. Introducing a few simple exercises into your daily life will allow your brain to be stimulated in a different way. This will help it to stay alert and make sure your proprioception is working to full capacity.

Today's goals!
– To be able to shower with my eyes closed.
– To go to work a different way or do my shopping in a different place.
– To juggle with two or three balls.

What is proprioception?

Proprioception is an awareness of the relative position of different parts of the body in space. It's a notion that is close to kinaesthetics, but is different because it also includes the sense of balance.

The brain is constantly kept informed about the position of the limbs and their movement in space by a network of specialised nerve cells called proprioceptors, which are located among the neuromuscular fibres of the muscles, tendons and joints. Depending on where the message originates, the information collected is processed by different parts of the cerebral cortex, the centre of higher nervous functions and particularly of voluntary movement. After analysis by the cortex, responses are sent to the muscles, tendons and joints.

Proprioception is a kind of sixth sense that allows the body to keep its balance and prevents us from falling over when we move from a steady position to an unsteady position. Walking, for example, consists of a succession of unsteady positions; as we walk, the impulses from the proprioceptors as well as muscle tone are perpetually activated to ensure that the body remains balanced.

Stimulate your proprioception

As we age, our sensory and proprioceptive capacities become less sharp. All the parts of the body involved in controlling posture and, consequently, proprioception are affected – from the central control of posture and movement, to the muscles, tendons and joints that are responsible for physical control of posture and balance, as well as the proprioceptors. This decline in our proprioceptive capacities means that it becomes more difficult for us to judge how we move about in our environment and can lead to accidents, particularly to falls among elderly people. But this decrease in capacities is not inevitable. By adopting different postures in your everyday

activities, you'll stimulate your proprioception, which will make your neurons work harder, even though you're not aware of it. What's more, the simple exercises suggested on the opposite page will improve the flexibility of your joints and help you to acquire a better sense of balance, both of which will in turn help to minimise your risk of falling. And with a little practice, you'll even be able to do these movements with your eyes closed, which will increase the level of difficulty.

Neurobics or 'brain gymnastics'

When you go about your daily activities, only a small number of neurons are activated, because the brain doesn't have to pay attention to the tasks that it's used to doing. So to stimulate it, you need to change the way you do things. This is the aim of neurobics, or brain gymnastics. Neurobics consists of very simple cerebral exercises that allow the brain to function differently and prevent it from lapsing into a routine. For example, you could try reversing the roles that you normally give to your hands when you do the washing up. You could brush your teeth while balancing on one foot, then the other. You could use your left hand to operate the mouse on your computer if you are right-handed, or vice versa if you are left-handed. You could also reverse your knife and fork at meal times or put the key in the lock with your eyes closed. By making each day different and new for your brain, you'll keep it performing at maximum capacity.

⭐ The swimmer

This exercise entails staying as still as possible, while trying to extend the opposing arm and leg as far as you can.

1. Kneel on all fours, with your knees on a cushion and your hands flat on the ground.

2. As you breathe in, extend your left arm in front of you and your right leg behind you, stretching in both directions. Breathe out. Hold this position.

3. Once you are steady in this position, raise your left foot from the ground and point your toe.

4. Repeat with the opposite arm and leg. Do this movement 10 to 15 times on each side.

The correct position To help you to hold the position (step 2), contract your abdominal muscles and your buttocks. Not only will this help you to keep your balance, it will also prevent you from arching your back.

⭐⭐ The dancer

This is a perfect exercise for toning the tendons in your ankles and preventing sprains.

1. Stand with your hands on your hips, and with your legs shoulder-width apart. Bend your knees at a 90-degree angle.

2. Stand on your toes. Hold this position for 15 seconds and repeat the exercise 10 times consecutively, for 3 minutes. Use your arms to keep your balance, if necessary.

⭐⭐ The acrobat

If you do this exercise at the beach, you won't need the towel: the sand and the waves will take its place and you'll be obliged to make a much greater effort.

1. Stand on one foot, with knees slightly bent, arms extended in front of you and looking straight ahead. The foot that you're standing on must be completely flat; you can make the exercise more difficult by placing a rolled towel under your foot.

2. Hold this position for 2 or 3 minutes.

3. Repeat with the other foot.

Tip Do this exercise with bare feet to avoid falling.

Make it more challenging
Once you have mastered the exercise, you can try looking in other directions: up, to the left, down, to the right.

⭐⭐ The puppet

In this exercise you stand on one leg, with your foot placed firmly on the ground. Keep your back and head straight, looking straight ahead. Your aim is to hold the position for 30 seconds.

1. Stand with your legs shoulder-width apart and raise one knee to a 90-degree angle.

2. Move your arms up and down alternately, and then in a scissor movement from left to right.

3. Repeat with the other knee raised.

Make it more challenging
Start with small arm movements, keeping your eyes open. Then increase the difficulty by closing your eyes. Lastly, still with your eyes closed, make bigger movements, and gradually increase the speed.

⭐ The giant

This stretch calls on your proprioceptive sensors as well as your sense of balance.

1. Stand with your chest and back straight and your arms by your sides, fixing your gaze on a point far out in front of you.

2. Stand on your toes and raise your arms. Stretch up, pressing down with your toes.

3. Hold this position and when you are steady move your arms in a scissor movement above your head.

Make it more challenging Take a few steps while still on your toes, keeping a nice straight silhouette.

Improve your coordination: synchronise your laterality

The brain is divided into two hemispheres that are linked by a bundle of nerve fibres. It processes information preferentially, depending on which hemisphere the information comes from. But for maximum efficiency, the brain must call on both hemispheres at the same time. When we perform everyday physical tasks, the two hemispheres work together. This daily lifelong stimulation improves coordination, making what are in essence complex movements seem simple.

Today's goal!
To be able to tap my head with one hand and make circles on my stomach with the other. These simple movements exercise functional laterality and coordination.

One brain, two hemispheres

The brain consists of two symmetrical hemispheres, the right and the left, and each of them is responsible for carrying out very specific tasks. Certain kinds of information are in fact processed by neurons that work exclusively with either one or the other hemisphere. This specialisation of the brain is called 'functional laterality'.

The left hemisphere is logical and analytical: it processes information associated with language. The right hemisphere is responsible for emotional and instinctive aspects: it gives priority to processing visual information. However, the two hemispheres are not independent of each other: they are connected by a set of nerve fibres called the corpus callosum. To ensure that the brain functions to the best of its capacity, the two hemispheres must be well coordinated; this is very important for the exchange and processing of information, particularly with regard to visual information.

Dancing and tai chi improve coordination

Dancing and tai chi are physical learning activities that trigger a rush of blood simultaneously to each of the brain's two hemispheres, where they also activate functional laterality. When it comes to movement, each hemisphere mainly controls the opposite side of the body. By alternating movements first to one side and then to the other, dancing and tai chi allow all parts of the body to be coordinated in a symmetrical way.

Studies carried out during practice sessions of these activities have shown that there is significant stimulation in the bilateral motor areas when people visualise the movements they are to perform – in other words, the brains of the people studied reacted in part as though they themselves were carrying out the movements. By making both hemispheres in your brain work at the same time, you optimise the cooperation between them and exercise your functional laterality. In tai chi, for example, when you learn the movements and postures by heart, you put your memory to work, as well as developing other motor and intellectual skills. And you also reduce your risk of suffering from a neurodegenerative disease such as Alzheimer's.

Coordinating the two hemispheres: the Brain Gym®

The Brain Gym® is a program perfected by the American educator Dr Paul Dennison. It's a technique based on the relationship between movement and the parts of the brain that play a role in learning. It involves doing exercises and movements that stimulate the brain's two hemispheres at the same time in order to improve their coordination.

The cross crawl is a simple exercise based on an exaggeration of the principle of walking. Either seated or standing, touch your left knee with your right hand, and then repeat the operation with your right knee and your left hand. If you do this for two minutes a day, this exercise will help you to coordinate the two hemispheres of your brain by stimulating the circulation of information between them.

The Brain Gym® technique has been shown to be beneficial for intellectual activities such as spelling, writing, reading and comprehension.

★ The pendulum

This movement using an arm and the opposite leg works on the coordination between the lower limbs and the upper limbs. It also calls on your sense of balance.

1. Stand with your feet together. At the same time, raise your left arm (without lifting your shoulder) and your right leg to one side.

2. Repeat the same movement on the other side using your right arm and your left leg. Alternate 20 times in a row.

Make it more challenging
Pass a water bottle from one hand to the other with each movement.

★ The lateral wave

This exercise is a tai chi movement that should be executed smoothly without jerking and keeping your back very straight. It will also improve joint flexibility.

1. Stand with your knees bent and your feet flat on the floor, with your legs shoulder-width apart. Raise your arms horizontally in front of you while moving the upper part of your body to the right. Keep your pelvis facing forward.

2. Do the same movement to the left and then return to your starting position, lowering your arms. Repeat the exercise about 20 times.

Tips
– Breathe in deeply and expand your stomach when you lift your arms.
– Breathe out when you return to your starting position.
– Stretch your neck and hold your head up straight, as if a magnet were pulling you towards the ceiling.

★★ The majorette

For this exercise you need to execute two different arm movements simultaneously towards the front and the side, without moving your pelvis.

1. Stand with your legs shoulder-width apart. Raise your left arm in front of you and your right arm out to the side, and then alternate: left arm to the side and right arm in front. Aim to do this exercise without hesitation, making sure that your arms move precisely out to the side or to the front, without any diagonal movements.

2. Do the exercise 15 to 20 times.

Make it more challenging
Hold a water bottle or a 1 kilogram weight in each hand. You can also add movements, as in the pendulum exercise.

★★★ The alphabet

The aim of this exercise is to disassociate the upper and lower parts of the body by combining simple leg movements with more complex arm movements.

1. Stand and take one step to the right, and then one step to the left, while at the same time miming the letters of the alphabet with your arms in the air. For example, for A form a pointed hat with your arms, and have your elbows bent (as in the illustration).

2. Try making just a few letters to begin with. If you can do this without making a mistake, that's already very good.

Tip
The whole family will enjoy doing this. Ask your children and grandchildren to join in.

★★ The robot

This cross-over exercise improves your intellectual ability by involving the two hemispheres of the brain.

1. Stretch your arms out in front of you, with palms facing downwards. Cross the right arm over the left arm, then cross the left over the right. Do this movement as many times as you wish.

2. Still crossing and uncrossing your arms, lift your knees to synchronise with your arms: lift your left knee when your right arm is on top of the left, and your right knee when your left arm is on top. Repeat this 10 times.

Variation Cross your legs one in front of the other, in opposition to your arm movements.

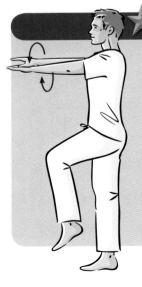

For better concentration: keep your balance

The vertical position is naturally unstable. In order to hold this posture, the body implements complex procedures ordered by the cerebellum, which is the control centre of balance. Even though some loss of the sense of balance with age is inevitable, it's possible to slow down this process by acquiring new reflexes for keeping your balance. This will also help to improve your memory and your attention.

Today's goal!
To walk in a straight line with my eyes closed for 2 or 3 metres, as though I'm on a tightrope. I can make this more difficult by placing small objects in the way so that I must step over them.

The inner ear and the cerebellum

In addition to the organ of hearing (the cochlea), the inner ear contains the vestibular organ, or the vestibule, which keeps the brain permanently informed about the position of the head and its movements. This cavity, then, is responsible for the sense of balance.

Using the information received from the vestibular organ, the cerebellum controls head and eye movements, as well as adjustments in the position of the body. It coordinates all muscle movements, both conscious and unconscious, and controls balance by sending regulating signals to the motor neurons (which enable movements) and to the spinal cord. The cerebellum also receives messages from the brainstem (central nervous system) indicating the status of some receptors on the tendons, muscles and joints. Every ten years, the volume of the cerebellum reduces by 2 per cent, and this is accompanied over time by an increased risk of falling.

Balance for a better memory

Physical activities such as gentle gymnastics, yoga and tai chi include a series of balancing movements. For this reason, they make the cerebellum work and exercise the reflex behaviours of balance. And what's more, because these activities involve both balance and coordination, they also improve the cognitive functions related to concentration and memory and, to a lesser extent, those associated with reasoning and vision.

Although balance exercises are natural, they should be practised consciously. When you turn around abruptly, it's thanks to your centres of unconscious balance, in other words to a reflex movement, that you don't fall over. It is this unconscious reflex function that mainly declines with age, while the conscious maintenance of balance is scarcely affected. This means that, paradoxically, you should be conscious of your balance and deliberately put yourself in unbalanced positions in order to improve, through new learning, the reflex movements of balance.

The following exercise stimulates the blood flow to your internal ear. Sit on a table with your legs hanging over the edge. Stretch your arms out on either side at shoulder height and tilt your body to the right using all your weight, until you feel you are on the point of falling. Then return to your starting point, and do the same movement to the left.

Tango therapy, or how to mix balance with pleasure

The tango is a very rhythmical dance; the constant twirling and turning will allow you to develop your sense of balance and movement, if you concentrate on it. In addition, repeating a movement and having to position yourself in relation to your partner also exercises your memory. But the benefits of tango don't stop there. By requiring you to pound the floor with your feet, the tango involves all your muscles and your bones, which helps to make them stronger, and it also slows the development of osteoporosis (loss of bone mass). The muscular effort that you have to make – which is progressive, slow and regular – strengthens the heart muscle and lowers blood pressure. Apart from the pleasure that dancing itself brings, practising tango therapy allows you to rediscover your self-confidence and reduces the risk of falling.

★★ The board

Hold this posture for about ten seconds on each leg. To perfect the exercise, don't bend the leg you're standing on.

1. Stand up straight and extend your arms out in front of you at shoulder height.

2. Breathing in, lift your one leg up behind you to a 45-degree angle. Breathing out, bend forward and lift your leg to 90 degrees to form a straight line with your arms, chest and leg. Bend the leg you're standing on

slightly, so as to use the stabilising muscles.

3. Throughout the exercise, breathe deeply and regularly.

4. Repeat on the other leg.

★ The swing

Ten minutes is all you need for this exercise, which is an effective way to maintain your sense of balance. Do it regularly (about 3 times a week) and your efforts will be rewarded in a few months.

1. Stand with your legs shoulder-width apart and your knees bent. Place your hands on your thighs.

2. Gently tip the upper part of your body towards the left, slightly bending the knee on that same side a little more. Then tilt your body to the right, bending your right knee.

3. Repeat this sequence 10 times, slowly and without jerking movements.

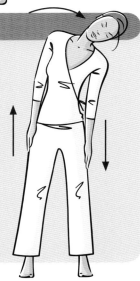

★★ The flamingo

The flamingo posture is ideal for testing your balance. To make it more difficult, do the same exercise with your eyes closed (blind flamingo). By eliminating visual reference points, you will make your sense of balance work even harder.

1. Stand with your legs slightly apart, with bare feet planted firmly on the ground.

2. Bend the right knee, and with the help of your hand, place the sole of your right foot on the inside of your left thigh.

3. Join your hands above your head by interlocking the fingers, except for the thumb and index finger, which point upwards.

4. Stretch your index fingers up as far as possible while trying to retain your balance. Keep your back and head perfectly straight.

5. Hold the position for 15 to 20 seconds and then change legs.

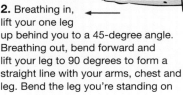

★★ Heels and toes

This exercise consists of standing on your toes (or your heels) while trying to keep your back straight, without losing your balance. To achieve this, press down on your toes (or your heels).

1. Stand with your back straight and go up on your toes.

2. Hold this position while stretching your spine up as much as possible.

3. When you have got your balance, stretch your hands above your head and then move your arms down and up in circular movements from above your head down to your sides.

4. Do this exercise for 1 to 2 minutes.

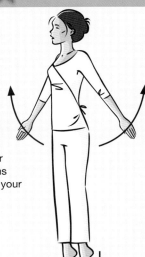

Make it more challenging

The exercise is more effective if you work with your eyes closed. When you feel comfortable with the exercise, you can try to walk with a beautiful straight silhouette, first with your eyes open and then with your eyes closed, while progressively adding the arm movements. Move at your own pace, gradually increasing the difficulty according to your ability.

Variation Do the same exercise with the weight of your body transferred onto your heels (see illustration on the right).

DAY 4

To combat stress, improve your flexibility

The stress that you experience each day causes muscle tissues to contract, making your muscles tight and reducing your freedom of movement. But if you do some flexibility exercises each day, this stress, and all the muscular tension that accompanies it, can be eliminated quite simply and very effectively. And, as a bonus, improving your flexibility will limit the risk of sustaining bone, joint and muscular injuries.

Today's goal!
Lying on my back with knees bent and soles of the feet together, to bring my knees down towards the ground, without forcing, for 20 or 30 seconds, then raise them, repeating 10 times.

Relaxed muscles, greater joint mobility

Flexibility is the physical ability to achieve an optimal range of movement in the joints by stretching the muscles. Flexibility exercises contribute to keeping your muscles relaxed and your joints more mobile. If you do them every day, they will help to maintain a good quality of life and ensure that you retain autonomy as you age.

Warm-up exercises are an indispensable prelude to any physical activity and they are also beneficial for the brain. By rotating the joints and stretching the muscles, we call on many muscle cells that are normally inactive. In turn, these muscle cells stimulate a large number of brain cells that are also usually inactive, in this way improving cognitive function.

In summary, warm-up exercises improve blood circulation in these underused parts of the body and, by so doing, stimulate the brain functions dedicated to these areas.

Reduce stress

Stress is harmful for the brain. In response to a stressful event (whether physical or psychological), the body releases a glucocorticoid called cortisol, which helps us to cope with the stressful situation. Circulating throughout the body, cortisol alters memory functions and leads to a decline in cognitive performance. The greater our levels of stress, then, the more likely we are to experience these effects.

Flexibility exercises such as stretching, gentle gymnastics or acquarobics (exercises in water) reduce stress and the level of cortisol in the blood, and this produces a feeling of general wellbeing. These exercises also improve neuromuscular coordination and increase the speed of nerve impulses, as well as the rapidity of reflexes. By making the joints and the muscles more flexible, they also protect against the risks of joint and muscle injuries. The limbering-up movements given here should be practised a minimum of twice a week for at least ten minutes.

If you don't have time to devote to this kind of exercise, remember that some daily tasks, such as gardening, washing the floor or using the vacuum cleaner, are also good for stretching and bending the body.

Mudras, or finger yoga

Most stretching exercises don't involve the hands and the fingers, but the wrist and fingers tend to become less flexible over the years. The mudras (seals or signs in Sanskrit) are an ideal remedy. These are ritual and symbolic positions of the hands practised by Hindus and Buddhists, and are also used by traditional dancers in India. The complex movements of the mudras stretch the muscles of the hands and fingers. They're also beneficial for the whole body and various organs. They promote better blood circulation and reduce the symptoms of arthritis or carpal tunnel syndrome (compression of the median nerve in the wrist).

⭐ Cat and dog

This exercise imitates the way a cat arches its back and a dog stretches. It involves moving the vertebrae one after the other, from the neck down to the kidneys, and it makes your spine more supple.

1. Get down on your hands and knees, with your hands on the floor directly below your shoulders. Make sure your body weight is evenly distributed between the hands and the knees.

Tip Pull in your stomach when you arch your back and release it when you make your back hollow.

2. Breathing in, roll up, gently arching your back and bringing your head down, while pushing down on your hands to open up the shoulder blades, until you are supporting yourself on your fingertips.

3. Breathe out deeply and lower your back gently. Stretch forward, moving your head and torso together. Tip your pelvis forward. Repeat 6 to 8 times, pausing between each repeat.

⭐⭐ The siren

This movement stretches the abdominal and dorsal muscles at the side of the body, as well as the chest.

1. Sit on the floor with your right leg bent behind you and your left leg bent in front of you.

2. Breathing in, place your right hand flat on the ground beside you and at the same time stretch the left hand above your head as high as you can to form an arc. Breathe out and do the same thing to the other side: left hand on the ground and right arm above your head.

3. Do this 8 times on each side.

Tip Place a cushion under your buttocks if the posture is difficult.

⭐ The salute

This exercise stretches the back and the pectoral muscles. It allows you to relax while developing your flexibility.

1. On your knees, bring your buttocks close to your heels and try to stretch your arms as far as possible out in front of you. Place your hands on the ground and make your back round.

2. Relax your head (no tension in the neck). As you stretch, make sure you stay in a straight line, without leaning to the side.

3. Hold the position for at least 40 seconds and try to stretch a little more with each new exhalation.

⭐⭐ One leg up

This exercise stretches the hamstrings. These muscles are very stiff in many sedentary people because they remain seated for a long time.

1. Lie on your back with your legs straight and your feet pointed. Bring your left leg up towards your chest at a 45-degree angle and take hold of it with your hands at calf level.

2. Breathe in and out deeply and regularly. With each breath, try to move your leg towards your chest a little more until you feel a pull at the back of the leg.

Tip If you have trouble doing this exercise, don't panic! Start more gently by keeping your legs bent, and then go to the next level by stretching the leg that is on the ground. With a little practice you will be able to do the movement without bending your knees.

Chase away all tension: learn to relax

It goes without saying that the brain can't function correctly when we have tension. Stress is the body's natural response when we are faced with a difficult situation that we have trouble controlling (such as danger, conflict or worry). In fact, our modern lifestyle is often stressful. That's why it's important to learn how to relax. Relaxation allows us to manage stress and has positive effects on the brain.

Today's goal!

To stand and breathe calmly and deeply, then stretch my arm up as high as possible, and then let it fall down loosely beside my body; and then to do the same with the other arm.

Relaxation leads to a modified state of consciousness

The stress and anxiety that are engendered by daily life make us secrete cortisol, a hormone that alters memory and harms the brain's capacities. The aim of practising relaxation techniques is to induce a state of muscular relaxation and to reduce stress and anxiety.

When the thousands of neurons in the brain exchange information, they produce a nerve impulse that is coherent and rhythmical – in other words, they become activated more or less at the same time, then they return to rest and are then reactivated. This process produces very weak electrical currents called brain waves, which can be measured with an electroencephalogram (EEG).

The rhythm of the brain waves varies according to what we are doing – whether we are awake, learning, resting, relaxing, or sleeping lightly or deeply. During a relaxation session, brain waves adopt a slow rhythm called alpha. This rhythm corresponds to a level of heightened consciousness and results in the synchronisation of the brain's two hemispheres. It is a transitional rhythm between waking and sleeping, and generates a modified state of consciousness, which reduces the degree of attention to certain sensory stimuli so as to concentrate on one single point.

The benefits of relaxation for the brain

Relaxation practices such as yoga, tai chi or qi gong have many beneficial effects on the brain. Some scientific studies have shown that the left prefrontal part of the cerebral cortex, which constitutes the centre of positive emotions, is more activated during a relaxation session.

On the other hand, the right prefrontal part of the cortex, which is the seat of negative emotions and anxiety, is less involved during this type of exercise. This shows that

relaxation techniques encourage positive feelings and inhibit activation of the areas of the brain associated with anxiety and negative thoughts.

People who know how to relax manage their stress better. Their cortisol level is lower during relaxation sessions, and this effect tends to persist after the session and to slow memory losses. Relaxation also improves cognitive functions and allows us to be more effective than average during tests focusing on fast reactions to visual stimuli.

Learning to breathe

It may be surprising, but most of us don't know how to breathe naturally, in other words, from the abdomen. Normally our breathing is controlled by the instinctive primitive, or reptilian, brain. But it can also be managed by the cerebral cortex and become conscious. Here is a very simple exercise to teach you how to breathe properly. To put this technique into practice you must be in a quiet place – at least for the first few times.

To begin, breathe out through your mouth as much as possible. Then breathe in through your nose, inflating your stomach and counting for 2 to 4 seconds. Hold your breath for 4 to 6 seconds. Then breathe out through your mouth while deflating your stomach and counting for 2 to 4 seconds. Repeat the sequence about 10 times. When you breathe in, you shouldn't take in more air than normal, but you should breathe more slowly. Slowing down your breathing – and therefore your heart rate – will lead to a decrease in stress.

⭐ Escape

This exercise will help you to focus your attention on the present using an autosuggestion method. It will improve your concentration and memory, while at the same time chasing away negative thoughts!

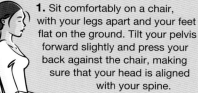

1. Sit comfortably on a chair, with your legs apart and your feet flat on the ground. Tilt your pelvis forward slightly and press your back against the chair, making sure that your head is aligned with your spine. Place your hands on your thighs with your palms facing upward.

2. Look around you and then close your eyes. Visualise the room. Try to locate any tensions in your body and be aware of the rhythm of your breathing.

3. Pay attention to the points at which your body is in contact with the chair (thighs, buttocks, back) and with the floor (the soles of your feet). Let your body feel heavy on the chair. Release your muscles and relax.

4. Breathe more deeply and more slowly. Follow the instructions given in step 2 of the exercise on the right (Breathe!) 6 or 7 times. Now visualise a calm scene.

5. This image will gradually fade. Visualise the room around you. Speed up your breathing, slowly move your feet, hands, head and other muscles. Stretch and, lastly, open your eyes.

⭐ Breathe!

This breathing method is used in the exercise on the left (Escape). You must be fully relaxed before you start, so that you can focus all your attention on your brain.

1. Follow the instructions for the 'Escape' exercise up to step 3.

2. Imagine that as you breathe in fresh air is entering through your right nostril, moving through the brain's right hemisphere, becoming warm as it passes into the left hemisphere, and then leaving as you breathe out through your left nostril.

3. Breathe in this way 3 or 4 times and then reverse the practice, beginning with the left nostril. Return to normal breathing and open your eyes.

⭐ Shake yourself!

Do this exercise for 5 minutes to rid yourself of any tension that has accumulated during the day.

1. Stand up straight and bend your knees a little. Your shoulders, arms and head should be completely relaxed.

2. Shake your whole body and then move your feet, legs, hands and arms.

3. Shrug your shoulders up and down and bend your head backwards and then forwards.

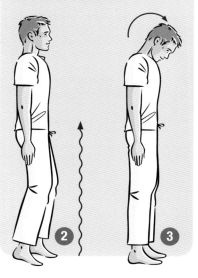

⭐ Let yourself be rocked

This exercise is for two people. It is based on the confidence you have in your partner and allows you to release tension.

1. Stand up straight and close your eyes. Let your partner tilt you backwards and forwards and from left to right, and don't resist. Be totally confident that your partner is holding you and will not let you fall. Do this exercise for 2 or 3 minutes.

2. This time your partner will gently push you forward. Resist and return to your starting point. Then repeat the movement for 2 to 3 minutes.

With several people Form a circle of five people. A sixth person stands in the middle and lets himself or herself be pushed gently from one person to the next in all directions.

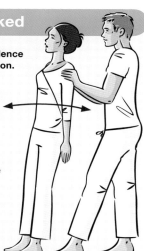

Stress relief Yoga is an excellent way to relieve tension. Meditation and relaxation techniques, as well as poses that focus on slow, steady movements and gentle stretching, promote mental peace and re-energise the body.

A natural antidepressant: take up a cardio activity

Cardio activities can be practised at any age and are a true rejuvenating treatment for the body. They strengthen the heart, breathing, muscles and bones, but they are just as beneficial for the brain. And by involving a large muscle mass, they stimulate a larger area of the brain as well. The result: relaxation and a brain that is in better shape.

Today's goal!
To say no to lifts and use the stairs whenever possible! Easy to do, this simple effort considerably increases both heart rate and lung capacity.

Take care of your cardiovascular system

Endurance is an athletic quality that is essential in many physical activities. It is the capacity to maintain a certain level of intensity during a prolonged effort. The purpose of cardio activities is to improve the function of the cardiovascular and respiratory systems. The heart and the breathing work to supply sufficient oxygen to regulate the intensity that is needed to make the effort.

Cardiovascular exercise encourages the development of aerobic metabolism: the energy used by the muscles during the effort is for the most part supplied by the oxidation of carbohydrates and fats that are available in the body. People are said to be in a state of aerobic metabolism if, during an endurance effort, they breathe quickly but are not out of breath. Of course, with age, the capacity for effort decreases, but it is possible to retrieve part of this through regular cardiovascular exercise. The physiological benefits of such training are undeniable. Practising cardio activities to an advanced age also strengthens the muscles and consolidates bone structure. The increased cardiovascular work during these activities reduces the risk of arteriosclerosis (ageing of the arteries) and high blood pressure. It also improves blood supply to the brain and so contributes to better brain function.

A younger brain

Physical endurance activities – such as long-distance walking, jogging, swimming and cycling – are undoubtedly the most beneficial for keeping your brain healthy. If you practise them for a minimum of ten minutes per day, they involve a large muscle mass, particularly in the lower limbs, and so stimulate a larger area of the brain.

From the neurophysiological point of view, cardiovascular exercise triggers the secretion of endorphins – hormones that are in the same family as morphine. Endorphins have a euphoric effect similar to that of antidepressants and they improve the mood. What's more, cardiovascular exercise delays the atrophy of the brain associated with ageing by reducing the progressive disappearance of neurons, such as those associated with learning, memory and the cognitive functions. They also protect against neurodegenerative diseases of non-genetic origin, including Alzheimer's disease.

Bushwalking improves your mood

Bushwalking, also variously known as tramping, trekking or hiking, calls for greater endurance than walking short distances, but it is nevertheless an activity that involves practically no danger and which has the advantage of gently working all the muscles of the body. Its benefits for the brain have been demonstrated by research: walkers see their depressive symptoms decrease, while their mood and self-esteem improve.

On the health side, bushwalking is a good way of fighting the risk factors of cardiovascular disease, while at the same time improving muscle tone and joint flexibility. In short, it's an activity that's appropriate for everyone, but you still need to be careful! If you suffer from arthritis, coronary insufficiency or some other heart condition, serious respiratory problems or severe arterial hypertension, respiratory insufficiency or angina that occurs during effort despite treatment, you should avoid bushwalking or consult your doctor before you start.

Make cardiovascular exercise part of your routine

There are many sports and physical activities that will give your cardiovascular system a workout. How much is enough, or too much, depends very much on an individual's current fitness level, and the advice given here is intended only as a general guide. Activities that are rated easy and medium can be done on most days and harder activities less frequently, say every second day, with a day of lighter exercise in-between. It's a good idea to check with your doctor before starting any new physical activity.

Choose one of the sports or activities listed here, or any other that uses large muscles rhythmically. It doesn't matter whether it's indoors, at home, at the gym or outside. As a rough guide to level of difficulty we've rated them as easy, medium or hard. If you're currently inactive, start by doing your chosen activity for up to 10 minutes. If you are already exercising regularly, you could start with up to 60 minutes. Take care not to do too much too soon. Starting slowly is the key, as it takes time for the body to adjust, and then gradually progress by applying the rule of 10 – that is, add no more than 10 per cent per week. However long you exercise, make sure you warm up gently for the first 5 to 10 minutes.

Indoors	Effort rating
Aerobics	Medium
Climbing stairs	Hard
Dancing (ballroom, rock, tap)	Medium
Exercise bike	Easy
Ice skating	Medium
Jazzercise	Medium
Rope skipping	Hard
Rowing machine	Medium
Step trainer	Medium
Swimming laps	Medium

Outdoors	Effort rating
Bushwalking	Hard
Cycling	Medium
Jogging	Hard
Roller skating	Medium
Tennis	Medium
Walking	Easy

Cardio activities Ballroom dancing, swimming and cycling are just some of the many activities that give your cardiovascular system a good work-out, while also improving mood and keeping your brain healthy.

Taking action:
improve your reaction time

In our daily lives the speed with which we react is very important. Letting one extra second pass before we act can have serious consequences – for example, when driving. With age, the reaction time increases because it takes longer for the brain to process the information. Practising fast ball sports such as tennis helps to improve reaction time by reducing decision-making time.

Today's goal!
– To stretch one arm out in front of me and place a coin on the back of my hand, then quickly remove my hand and catch the coin before it reaches the floor.
– To repeat with my other hand.

Reaction speed: detection, processing and action

The reaction time is the time it takes to react to external stimuli. In daily life, these stimuli are mainly visual or aural. The reaction speed can be broken down into three phases: detection, processing and action.

Detection is the period of time that the brain requires to perceive the external stimuli. This includes the stimulation of visual or sound sensors and the transmission of nerve impulses to the central nervous system. Next comes the processing phase: the central nervous system analyses the information it receives, develops an appropriate motor response and sends the order to stimulate a muscle using a nerve impulse. Lastly, the action corresponds to the initiation of the actual motor activity.

Reaction speed is variable and ranges between 0.15 and 0.25 seconds for sound stimuli, and between 0.2 and 0.35 seconds for light stimuli. Your reaction speed depends on your concentration: if the brain has to manage several tasks at the same time – for example, driving while listening to music – it will react more slowly if you suddenly have to respond to an unexpected event. Speed of reaction also depends on how old you are: it begins to decrease after 30 years of age, mainly because the brain takes longer to process the information.

Improving your decision-making speed

Tennis, table tennis and badminton are sports that involve very rapid exchanges. The movements that the body must make to send back a ball that has been struck at great speed occur before the conscious identification of the position of the ball in space and its trajectory. Practice allows the decision-making time, and so the reaction time, to be reduced. Playing these sports also strengthens the synaptic junctions (contact areas between the nerve cells) of the circuits involved in processing information. Seniors who regularly practise a sporting activity have a reaction time that is equivalent to that of young adults who don't play. Such sports also activate mirror neurons, which are stimulated both when you do a movement yourself and when you watch someone else doing it. So when you play a backhand shot in tennis, your mirror neurons are activated. The same is true when you watch someone else play this shot: in this case you are practising without moving, which helps you to process the information more quickly.

Sleep to improve your reaction time

The idea is not new: in order to be in top intellectual shape, you mustn't be tired or sleepy. As well as resting the body, sleep improves the faculties of judgment, helps to consolidate memory, stimulates your mood, allows you to solve problems – and it improves your reaction time as well. A study of swimmers has shown that they reduced their reaction time by almost 0.1 of a second when they had sufficient sleep. Try to sleep between seven and eight hours per night, and go to bed and get up at regular times. The need for sleep doesn't change with age, but it often takes a more fragmented form. If you can't manage to sleep for seven hours at night, it's a good idea to have an afternoon nap to compensate for the shorter night's sleep. The best time to have an afternoon nap is between midday and 3 pm, and it should last between 30 and 60 minutes.

⭐⭐ The mirror game

This game requires two people. It consists of imitating the other person's movements, as if you were their reflection, and matching your timing to theirs. If you are the person leading the exercise, follow your inspiration and do anything that comes to mind. If you don't have any ideas, here are a few examples.

1. Stretch your arms out in front of you and lift one knee. If you raise your right knee, for example, the other person must raise the left knee.

2. With your arms beside your body, bend your knees. Complete this movement by raising one arm in front

of you, raising the other out to the side, and so on.

Make it more challenging
Begin with leg or arm movements on the spot, and then combine these with moving backwards, forwards or to the side.

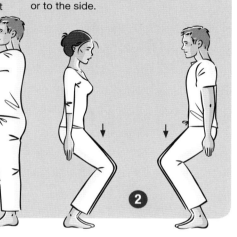

⭐⭐⭐ Reflex ball

This little exercise is easier than it seems and is ideal for working on your reaction time.

1. Throw a table tennis ball (or a tennis ball) above your head.

2. Spin around and try to catch the ball as it comes down before it touches the ground.

Variation Do the same exercise, but throw the ball against a wall. Spin around and try to catch it before the second bounce.

Make it more challenging
Throw the ball against the wall with your eyes closed. Spin around, open your eyes when you hear the ball bounce and catch it. You can also throw the ball with your right hand and catch it with your left, and vice versa.

⭐⭐⭐ Aerobics

Aerobic movements promote blood circulation to the brain, so bringing it the oxygen it needs to function correctly. Aerobics improve short-term memory, cognitive functions and reaction time. This simple LIA (low-impact aerobic) routine is a variation of aerobics that requires no equipment and doesn't involve any jumping or impact, so it is not demanding on your joints and back. What's more, this sequence of steps will promote your coordination, sense of balance and flexibility. Wear appropriate shoes to support your feet and protect your ankles.

1. Take a big step to the side with the right leg. Place the left leg behind, crossing over. Take another step to the right and bring the two feet close together. Repeat this once to the right and then once to the left.

2. Take 3 steps forward, beginning with the left foot. Bring your right foot forward, pointing your toe and lifting

your right knee. Move backwards in the same way, reversing the feet: start with the right foot and finish by raising the left knee. Accompany your steps with arm movements: raised in a V above your head, crossed in front of you at waist height and then out to the sides.

3. Extend your arms laterally and raise your right knee to the side. At the

same time, bend your left elbow, and then repeat on the other side. Do this movement alternately, twice on each side.

4. Stretch your right leg to the side while opening your arms. Then touch your buttock with your heel while lowering your arms. Do this movement once to the right, once to the left, twice to the right, and finally once to the left.

Preserving your neurons: strengthen your muscles

Muscle strength, which decreases with age, needs to be maintained if you want to remain independent for as long as possible. Doing exercises to strengthen your muscles not only helps to keep your bones strong and reduces the risk of diabetes or cardiovascular disease, it's also an excellent way of retaining your cognitive functions so that your brain remains at the peak of its capacities.

Today's goals!
– To carry shopping bags with my arms fully extended.
– To move small items of furniture when vacuuming.
– To dig or rake my garden.

Stimulate your metabolism

Muscle strength is the capacity of the muscles to exert force against resistance. The exercises that call on muscle strength have a major effect on the body, and this generates increased pressure in the blood system, particularly in the brain. Muscle-strengthening exercises stimulate the metabolism and the body's capacity to burn kilojoules. They increase physical capacity and improve muscle tone.

From the neurological point of view, the order to contract a muscle is firstly given by the brain, or more precisely by the frontal lobe, which is the starting point for the motor system (muscle coordination and control of movements in the head and neck). This order is then carried by motor neurons to the muscles in the form of electrical signals. There are two types of motor neurons: the central motor neurons, which go from the brain to the spinal cord, and the peripheral motor neurons, which link the spinal cord to the muscles.

Prepare yourself well for strengthening exercises

Exercises that develop muscle strength are intense activities that require a few precautions to avoid injuring yourself. Resuming a sporting activity is not without risk. First consult your doctor, who can assess your state of health and will be able to tell you which of the activities you should avoid.

Before beginning a series of push-ups, abdominal exercises or other muscle-strengthening exercises, do a brief warm-up exercise: walk on the spot or go up and down stairs. Then do your strengthening exercises. If you find it difficult to repeat the movement, reduce the repetitions; if you can do it easily, increase the number of repetitions in each series. Rest for two or three minutes after each exercise. Above all, breathe while you are working out. At the end of the session, do some stretching. Lastly, don't practise these exercises two days in a row and limit yourself to two or three sessions per week.

The strength of muscles depends on their condition and mass. As the years go by, we tend to move about less and do less lifting, so our strength decreases. After 50 years of age, our muscles are likely to be smaller than they were before the age of 40. Working on your muscle strength prevents the loss of muscle mass caused by ageing. And that's not all: you'll have better posture, and you'll increase your bone density and reduce the risk of diseases like osteoporosis (in which the bones become fragile).

Give your brain some brawn

Combining endurance and strengthening activities (such as push-ups and abdominal exercises) makes them more effective and increases their beneficial action on the brain. Scientific studies of muscle-strengthening exercises show that regular practice improves self-esteem and morale, while anxiety and the incidence of depression decrease among people who are prone to these conditions. In addition, this type of activity preserves neurons, especially those that are associated with cognitive functions (such as memory and acquisition of new knowledge), and has a neuroprotective effect against Alzheimer's disease. For best results, muscle-strengthening exercises should be done twice a week in the form of exercises that use the main muscle groups, with 8 to 12 repetitions of each of the movements. By toning your muscles, you will retain your functional autonomy for longer and be less prone to falls.

⭐⭐ The chair

This exercise is excellent for strengthening the thighs and the knee joints.

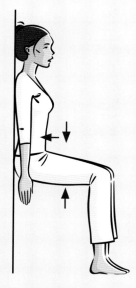

1. Stand with your back against the wall and bend your legs so that your buttocks are a little higher than your knees.

2. Hold this position for at least 30 seconds, while trying to keep the lower part of your back, your shoulders and your head pressed against the wall, without arching your back. Make sure you keep your knees in line with your heels.

Make it more challenging
Keep your buttocks at the same level as your knees and hold this position for 1 minute.

⭐ – ⭐⭐⭐ Push-ups

This basic movement is excellent for toning the pectorals, the deltoids (the front part of the shoulder) and the triceps. Suggestion: to avoid arching the lower part of your back, contract your abdominal muscles. The simple version of this exercise is recommended for beginners, women and seniors.

1. Kneel on all fours with your knees on a cushion, arms extended, hands directly below your shoulders and feet crossed.

2. Breathe in and bend your arms as you lower your ribcage towards the floor, letting your elbows go out to the sides. Keep your back straight.

3. Exhale at the end of the movement. Return to the starting position. Repeat the exercise as many times as you can, without any time limit.

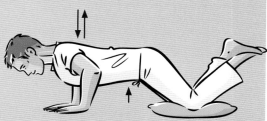

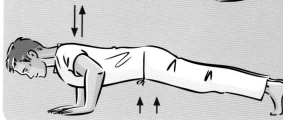

Make it more callenging Do the exercise without putting your knees on the floor (traditional push-ups). Make sure you keep your back straight.

⭐⭐ The crunch

This exercise is excellent for strengthening your abdominal muscles and improving trunk stability.

Tip For maximum benefit, make sure you keep your lower back pressed firmly into the floor while you do this exercise.

1. Lie on your back with knees bent and feet flat on the floor. Place one hand behind your head to support it and the other hand on your stomach.

2. While exhaling slowly, contract your abdominal muscles and raise your shoulder blades about 5 to 10 cm off the floor. Count to 4 as you do so to help you to control the movement. Then slowly lower your shoulders down to the floor, again counting to 4.

3. Start with 5 to 10 repetitions, and then increase up to 20 to 30 repetitions as you improve.

⭐⭐ The pedal boat

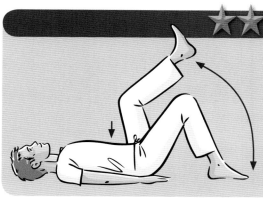

This exercise strengthens the abdominal muscles. Make sure that you pull your stomach in so that your lower back is pressed into the floor. Move slowly and evenly.

1. Lie down with your back flat against the floor, arms by your sides and knees bent.

2. Lift your right leg towards your chest, and then the left leg, moving your legs up and down as though you are pedalling.

3. Repeat the exercise 10 to 30 times on each side (2 to 4 sets).

Make it more challenging
Support yourself on your forearms.

Give your memory a boost: strengthen your visual acuity

Visual acuity is essential for perceiving external stimuli and for understanding the world around us. With age, it tends to diminish, but it's possible to make it sharper by regularly practising a kind of gymnastics for the eyes. The exercises given here are also beneficial for your brain and will facilitate the intellectual activities of memorising and reading.

Today's goal!
With head straight and still, and arm extended, to trace the infinity symbol (∞) and the figure 8 in the air several times with my index finger, following it with my eyes; then repeat daily for 1 minute.

Visual acuity: the power of the retina

The ability of the retina to distinguish details at a distance is called visual acuity. An important part of the eye, the retina is a network of nerves connected to more than 100 million photoreceptors located at the back of the eye and is a key interface between the physical world and the body's nervous system. It is responsible for the clarity of the visual images supplied to our brain.

Without visual acuity, you wouldn't be able to read this text. But you would still be able to see, because the eyes also have peripheral vision, which allows you to check what's happening to each side and to grasp the whole situation, even though it is blurred. The eye is capable of moving in its socket using the six oculomotor muscles.

As with any organ, the performance of the eye declines with age: there is a decrease in both the number of signals it perceives and the speed with which it can process information. The details perceived are not drawn as clearly or as quickly on the retina. The eye gradually loses its sensitivity as well as its mobility.

Video games sharpen vision

When you are tired of hitting a ball on a court, you can continue to exercise your visual acuity while you are sitting comfortably in your living room. According to the authoritative American journal *Psychological Science*, playing action video games significantly improves visual acuity. A one-month study showed that people who played for one hour a day improved their visual acuity by more than 20 per cent, not only in the visual field involved but also in the peripheral field of vision. The reason for this phenomenon is quite simple. There are many more visual stimuli in action video games than in daily life, and this forces the brain to adapt. Video games modify how the brain interprets visual information and train it to analyse the information more quickly.

Racquet sports are the best stimulant

Tennis, table tennis and badminton are sports that oblige the eyes to follow a ball moving at speeds that can reach 170 kilometres per hour. Focusing the eyes on this specific moving point develops visual acuity, increases the strength and flexibility of the six oculomotor muscles, and improves the coordination between hands and eyes. Studies show that playing racquet games leads to better than average ocular mobility, greater sensitivity to contrast and an improved capacity to see images clearly when distances vary quickly. These sports stimulate the brain and are extremely beneficial. This is because the brain is constructed like a huge network: when one region is activated regularly, the effects are felt in other parts of the brain, so that the whole brain benefits.

It's for this reason that the exercise these sports give to the ocular muscles has the added benefit of improving memorisation and reading skills. Racquet sports also help to improve peripheral vision, because while you are following the ball with your eyes you need to have a general view of the whole court as well. Similarly, ocular gymnastic exercises also aim to maintain and sharpen visual acuity.

★ Circles

The aim of this exercise is to move your eyes while keeping your head still. To make it even more effective, sit in a comfortable position facing a white wall.

1. Keep your head straight and focus on a spot in front of you. Look as far as you can up, and then down, to the right and to the left. Bring your gaze back to the centre.

2. Alternate the movements, moving your gaze from a point in the upper left to the lower right, and then from the upper right to the lower left, forming an X with your eyes. Bring your gaze back to the centre.

3. Now trace large circles in a clockwise direction trying to look as far as possible to the sides. Bring your gaze back to the centre. Finish the exercise by closing your eyes for a few minutes.

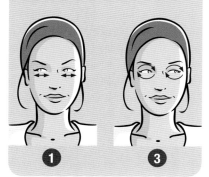

★★ The pencil

Binocular vision is indispensable for perceiving depth and estimating distances. Without it, it would be difficult to move around or easily pick up an object. The following exercise needs two people and helps your eyes to work well together.

1. Both people should hold a pencil as shown in the illustration. Move your pencil vertically at chest level, while your partner tries to touch the top of your pencil with his pencil. Now reverse roles.

2. Simply trying this exercise is enough to help you to understand how important it is for both eyes to work perfectly together. Also try to do this exercise with one eye closed.

★ Relaxing your neck

You should do this exercise regularly to eliminate tensions in the neck and increase your visual acuity.

1. Sit up straight and slowly lower your head until your chin is touching your chest. Hold this position for a few seconds, and then tilt your head backwards. Bring your chin to your chest again. Repeat this 5 to 10 times.

2. Turn your head gently to the right. Stay there for a moment, then turn your head to the left. Repeat this 5 to 10 times.

3. Slowly bend your head towards your shoulder on your right side, without letting your head move forward. Don't force it: the purpose is not to tilt your head as far as possible, but to relax. Repeat this 5 to 10 times on each side.

4. Tilt your head forward. Slowly and without jerking, roll your head to the left, backwards, to the right and then forwards again. If you can manage it, make large circles. Don't force the movement; it must be done smoothly. Do the exercise 3 to 5 times in each direction.

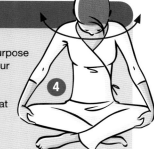

★ Focus on a point

This exercise is perfect for improving your eyes' capacity to adapt – that is, their ability to change focus depending on how far away objects are, so as to always see with the greatest clarity.

Suggestion Follow this exercise with the palming exercise (see page 293).

1. Cover your right eye with your right hand. Extend your left hand out some distance in front of your left eye, with palm facing you.

2. Focus on a specific point on your left palm, then move your palm closer to your left eye. Stop moving your hand as soon as your vision becomes blurry. Slowly return your hand to its starting position and concentrate once more on the point chosen above.

3. Repeat this exercise 5 to 10 times, then change sides. Don't forget to breathe properly during the whole exercise.

★★ Letters

This exercise is recommended for people who have been wearing glasses for years, because the eyes become lazy behind corrective lenses.

1. Without moving your head 'write' the letters of the alphabet with your eyes, without straining. Don't try to write the whole alphabet in one go. Start with 5 to 10 letters.

2. Have a break or do a palming sequence (see page 293) after each letter. Take a breath in and out and then continue. Do this exercise for 5 to 15 minutes.

Improve your ability to pay attention: try some massage

After a session of physical activity or a stressful day, there is nothing like having a good massage to relax you. In fact, by exerting a warming effect on muscle fibres and stimulating blood circulation, massage promotes the elimination of metabolic waste products that have accumulated in the muscles. But massage is not just good for the body; it's also good for the mind. It has the effect of reducing stress, anxiety and the symptoms of depression, while at the same time reinforcing your capacity for paying attention.

Today's goal!
To massage my palms for 3 to 4 minutes, using a hairbrush. This exercise is relaxing because the skin of the palm has many sensory receptors.

Massage releases muscle tension

Massage is a set of manual techniques – pressure, friction, kneading – that are applied to the soft tissues: the skin, muscles, tendons and ligaments. How does massage work? In our skin we have thousands of sensory receptors that react to the external stimuli of temperature, pain and pressure, and which send the information they have gathered through the spine to the brain. The whole body can be massaged, or only one part of the body. Massage has a warming effect on the skin and muscle fibres and it also stimulates blood circulation, so that more oxygen reaches the body's tissues.

After a prolonged physical effort, massage encourages muscle fibres to eliminate the lactic acid that may have been produced. Massage also stimulates the nerve endings in the tendons and joints that have been overused during physical exercise and allows them to relax.

Increased attention

Massage acts on the brain in several ways. Studies have shown that it reduces the activity in the right frontal lobe of the brain, which is normally more active when negative emotions are experienced, and increases the activity in the left frontal lobe, which is associated with positive feelings. The brain's production of cortisol – a hormone linked to stress and to decline of memory – decreases, while its production of endorphins increases. Endorphins possess analgesic properties and are also natural antidepressants that create a sensation of euphoria.

Massage helps to eliminate stress, anxiety and the symptoms of depression. Electroencephalograms taken after a massage session have revealed that massage also increases alertness and encourages a more open attitude. What's more, massage has been shown to improve speed and precision in performing mathematical calculations. Lastly, it stimulates the skin, the mucous membranes and their secretions, which form the first line of defence in our immune system, and so helps us to combat infectious diseases.

Are you stressed? Try reflexology!

Reflexology is an ancient technique in traditional Chinese medicine. It involves massaging certain areas, called reflexes, on the soles of the feet or the palm of the hands. Treatment consists of applying pressure to these reflex zones or massaging them. In traditional Chinese medicine, the foot is seen as a miniature representation of the human body. Certain areas on the foot are said to be linked to organs, glands or parts of the body. This makes it possible to affect the whole body indirectly and to bring immediate relaxation to the mind by stimulating the foot.

Like acupuncture, reflexology is considered to be preventive. It reduces stress and muscle tension and promotes blood and lymphatic circulation. According to reflexology enthusiasts, it releases the body's faculties of self-healing and so brings relief for various conditions.

★ Foot massage

This reflexology massage of the foot concentrates on the end of the big toe, where the reflex point for the brain is located.

1. Support the right foot with your left hand and press lightly on the upper part of the big toe with the fleshy part of your right thumb, while bending it at the joint. Make sure you don't touch the part you are massaging with your fingernail.

2. Release the pressure and slide your thumb towards the tip of your toe. Repeat this several times, making sure you never lose contact with the skin. This technique is called the caterpillar and it effectively enables you to activate the reflex area for the brain.

3. Reverse the position of the hands and repeat the movement on the big toe of the left foot.

Suggestion Use a little moisturising cream if your feet are very dry, but don't use massage oil! Slippery skin makes massaging difficult and reduces its effectiveness.

★ Self-massage of the hands

Hand reflexology is not as effective as foot reflexology. The hands are less sensitive and also they are smaller, which makes it more difficult to reach the reflex points. But this type of massage is ideal for self-treatment: you can do it at any time during the day.

1. Stimulate your brain by pressing firmly on the top of your right thumb with your left thumb. Repeat about 10 times.

2. Repeat the self-massage on the thumb of the left hand.

★ Mental clarity

In just 5 minutes, this massage technique releases any tensions that have accumulated in the neck, shoulders and head, which can cause mental fatigue and confusion. Do this self-massage at home or at work during your breaks at least twice a day.

1. Sit with your back and head straight. Close your eyes. Using the tips of your fingers, massage your temples slowly, making small circles, for about 1 minute. Then repeat in the reverse direction.

2. Intertwine your fingers and place your hands on the back of your neck, elbows apart. Press your fingers firmly together, bringing your palms closer. Starting from the base of your skull, repeat the movement down to your shoulders, for about 1 minute.

3. With the tips of your fingers, massage your neck, concentrating on the muscles on either side of your spine. Start from the base of your skull and work down to your shoulders. Do this massage for 1 to 2 minutes.

4. Put your right hand on your left shoulder, supporting your right elbow with your left hand. Knead your shoulder in a circular motion for 2 minutes. Release the knots with your fingers. Repeat with the opposite hand and shoulder.

★ Palming

This exercise allows you to rest your eyes. When we overuse our eyes, they can become painful, irritated by poor light or light that is too bright (computer and television screens). Don't forget to take a break several times a day by stopping what you are looking at. Use this time for a palming session.

1. Sit comfortably, with a straight back and shoulders relaxed.

2. Lightly place your cupped hands (without tensing them) over your eyes: your hands should not touch your eyelids.

Place your fingers on your forehead, with the little fingers touching.

3. Close your eyes. Breathe regularly and try to empty your mind for 2 to 3 minutes.

Suggestion This exercise can also be done in a standing position: this will release your back if you have been sitting for a long time.

35 days
of exercises
for your brain

This 35-day program has been developed to give your brain a work-out in sessions lasting about 20 minutes each. It consists of puzzles and exercises that call on six major skills:

logic

memory

language

observation

calculation

spatial perception

The level of difficulty gradually increases day by day, so that each new session requires a little more attention and concentration than the last.

This section is not about testing your knowledge. You have all the keys you need to be able to solve each puzzle. You just need to learn how to make better use of them.

If you have a mental block while you are trying to solve a puzzle, do one that looks easier and come back to the one you found difficult at the end of the session. If you still can't solve it, don't panic! You can always try it again later. Sometimes it's just a question of changing your approach slightly and you can find the solution to a problem that you thought would take you hours!

Of course, all the answers are given at the end of the section, starting on page 337. Check them often, as this will help you to familiarise yourself with the methods used, and then you'll be able to solve other puzzles in the same way.

After mental effort, you need to unwind! At the end of each 10-day period, you'll find a two-page 'Just for fun' section, so that you can relax and recover a little before the next session.

DAY 1

Language

1. Replace the two blanks with the same letter to find the name of an animal:

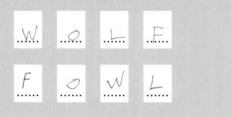

E G R E T

2. Use the letters in the word FLOW to form two other four-letter animal names.

W O L F

F O W L

3. With 5 and then 6 of the 7 letters in the phrase SAW EELS find words that mean:

a. carnivorous marine mammals

S E A L S

b. a small, slender-bodied, carnivorous land mammal.

W E A S E L

Logic

Which of the two figures suggested below logically completes this series?

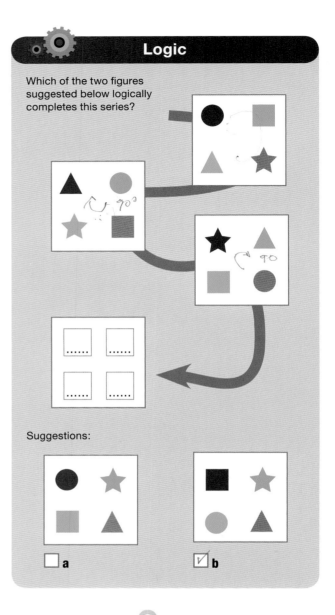

Suggestions:

☐ **a**   ☑ **b**

Logic

In each series, find the place where the logical sequence is broken. Which term has been omitted?

1.

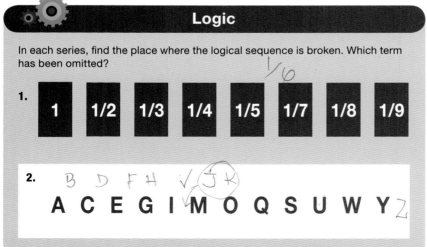

| 1 | 1/2 | 1/3 | 1/4 | 1/5 | 1/7 | 1/8 | 1/9 |

1/6

2. B D F H √ (J K)

A C E G I M O Q S U W Y Z

Calculation

Try to reach the total given at the end of each line by using each of the numbers below only once and by using the basic operations (+, −, ×, ÷) in any way you choose.

5   3   4

3 + 4 + 5 = **12**

5 × 3 + 4 = **19**

3 × 4 − 5 = **7**

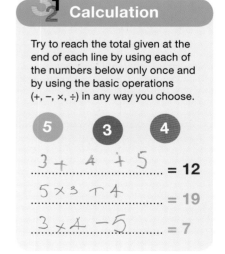

3 Calculation

Find two ways of reaching the total 37 by using each of the numbers below only once and by using the basic operations (+, −, ×, ÷) in any way you choose.

 5 7 6

5×6＋7 .... = 37

6×7−5 .... = 37

Logic

Five years ago, my brother was exactly twice the age I was then. And in eight years' time, the combined age of the two of us will be 50. How old do you think I am?

.... 13 ....

X−5 = 2(Y−5) X=2Y−5
X+Y+16=50
3Y+11=50
Y = 13   X=21

Memory

1. Look carefully at these envelopes for 30 seconds, and then cover them.

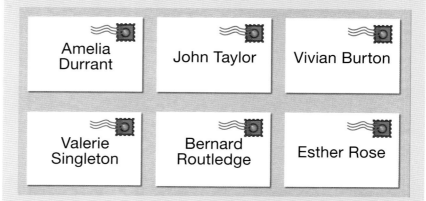

Amelia Durrant | John Taylor | Vivian Burton

Valerie Singleton | Bernard Routledge | Esther Rose

2. From memory, write the names of the addressees on the envelopes below, in the order in which they appear above.

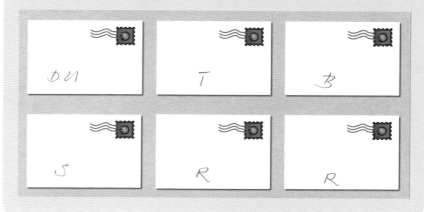

DU | T | B

S | R | R

Language

Find the animals hiding in the following anagrams.

a. SHORE _HORSE_

b. BRAZE _ZEBRA_

c. DOING _DINGO_

d. TOGA _GOAT_

e. PRESENT _SERPENT_

f. PRIDES

g. AUNT _TUNA_

h. PAROLED _LEOPARD_

i. TOAST _STOAT_

j. CORONA

k. TORTE

l. GARBED

DAY 3

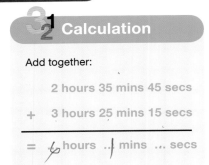

Calculation

Add together:

```
  2 hours 35 mins 45 secs
+ 3 hours 25 mins 15 secs
─────────────────────────
= 6 hours ... mins ... secs
```

Language

Which pair of the same colour must start and finish this sentence in order for it to make sense?

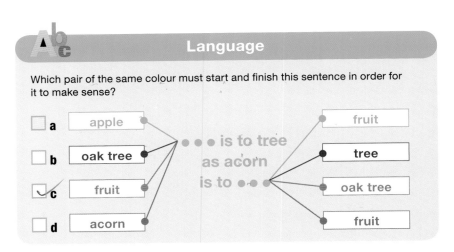

- ☐ a   apple
- ☐ b   oak tree
- ☑ c   fruit
- ☐ d   acorn

• • • is to tree
as acorn
is to • • •

fruit
tree
oak tree
fruit

Observation

Which two images below are identical?

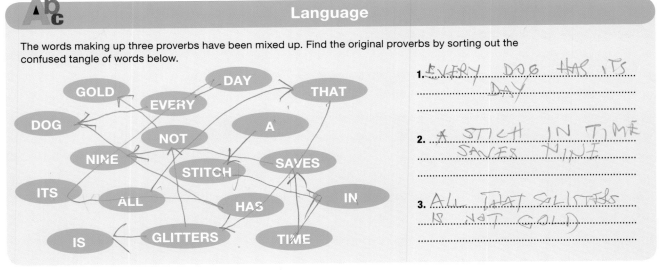

☑ a   ☐ b   ☐ c   ☑ d   ☐ e

Language

The words making up three proverbs have been mixed up. Find the original proverbs by sorting out the confused tangle of words below.

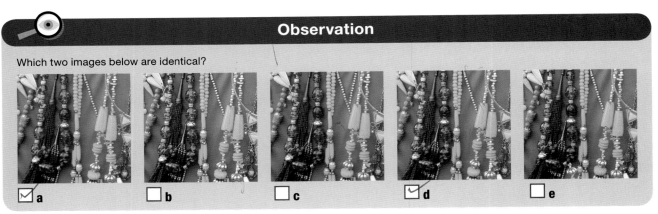

GOLD, DAY, THAT, EVERY, DOG, A, NOT, NINE, SAVES, STITCH, ITS, ALL, HAS, IN, IS, GLITTERS, TIME

1. EVERY DOG HAS ITS DAY

2. A STICH IN TIME SAVES NINE

3. ALL THAT GLISTERS IS NOT GOLD

Logic

What number must go in the blank space to complete the logical sequence?

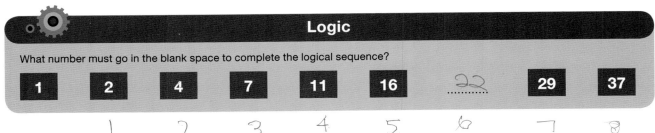

| 1 | 2 | 4 | 7 | 11 | 16 | 22 | 29 | 37 |

1 2 3 4 5 6 7 8

Memory

1. Take two minutes to study the position of the animals at the zoo.

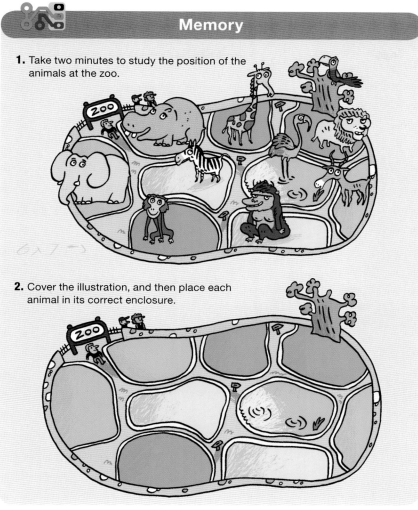

2. Cover the illustration, and then place each animal in its correct enclosure.

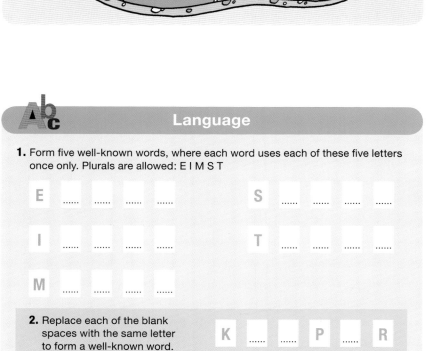

Logic

Which of the suggested figures below must be placed in the third position to complete this logical sequence?

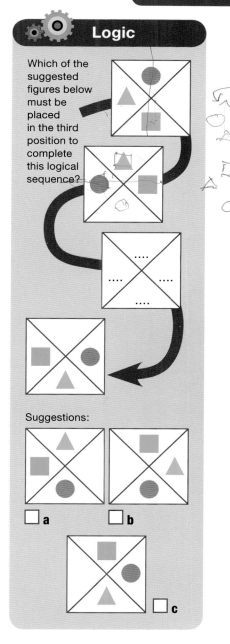

Suggestions:

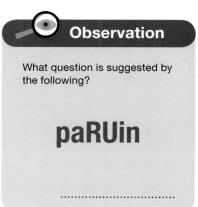

☐ a   ☐ b

☐ c

Language

1. Form five well-known words, where each word uses each of these five letters once only. Plurals are allowed: E I M S T

E ....   S ....

I ....   T ....

M ....

2. Replace each of the blank spaces with the same letter to form a well-known word.

K .... P ..... R

Observation

What question is suggested by the following?

paRUin

....

Calculation

Sam has invested all his savings, $10,000, in the stock exchange. On the first day there is a rise of 10%, and then on the next day it drops by 10%. The day after that, it increases again by 10%, and then drops again by 10% on the following day. This yo-yo effect has now been going on for a year. Sam has had enough and has decided to withdraw his $10,000 from the bank. Will he get a pleasant surprise, an unpleasant surprise, or no surprise at all?

Logic

What is the value of the domino that is needed in the third set to continue this logical sequence?

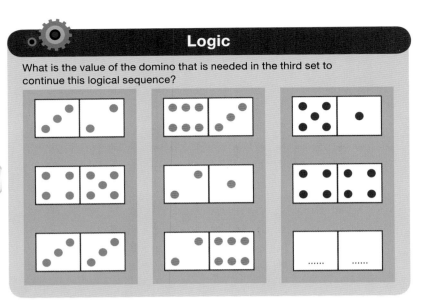

Observation

Replace each of the symbols with the letter it represents to make a common expression. Get going straight away!

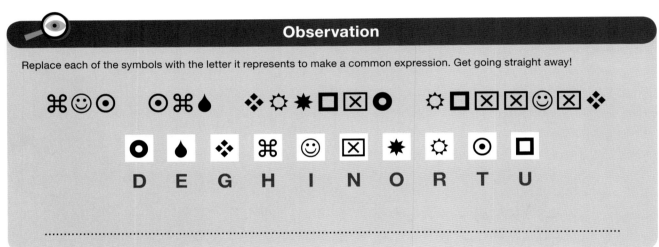

Language

1. Find the odd one out in each of these rows.

a.	goblet	bowl	knife	straw	bottle
b.	Columbia	Africa	Mexico	France	Peru
c.	swamp	stream	lake	pond	mare
d.	fir	elm	oak	birch	plain tree
e.					
f.	plum	cherry	currant	nectarine	apricot

2. Join pairs of syllables together to form five words that have something in common.

bia   mur   ra   fe   ti

dius   ster   cyx   num   coc

Memory

Study the table below for a few minutes. Try to memorise all the names, as well as their positions in the table. To help you to remember them, try noting which first or last letters they have in common, the geographical areas to which they belong and so on. When you think you have memorised them all, go to the bottom of the page and try to reproduce the original table.

Senegal	Thailand	Uruguay	Venezuela
Sweden	Finland	Norway	Denmark
Switzerland	Ireland	Japan	Kenya
Syria	Zambia	Zimbabwe	France

Language

1. Put these bricks in the correct order to form a proverb.

when   is   the   play   away

will   mice   the   cat

....

2. Study the groups of three letters in each of the bubbles to work out the two letters missing from the last one.

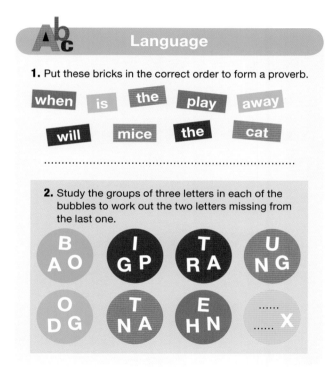

Logic

Carefully study the flags in the first column to work out the composition of the flag that should complete the second column.

Memory

S...................	T...................	....	V...................
Sweden	....	....	....
....	I...................	J...................	....
S...................	....	Z...................	....

Observation

Which two of the fragments labelled a, b, c and d can be superimposed on the large figure below without rotating them?

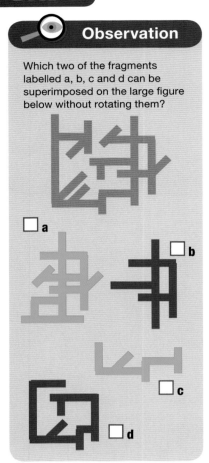

☐ a

☐ b

☐ c

☐ d

Language

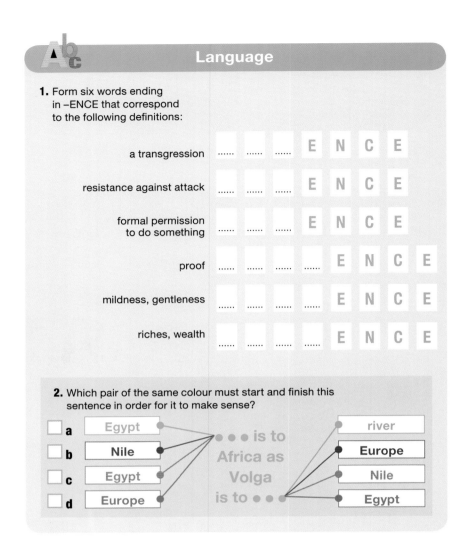

1. Form six words ending in –ENCE that correspond to the following definitions:

				E	N	C	E
a transgression

resistance against attack .... E N C E

formal permission to do something .... E N C E

proof .... E N C E

mildness, gentleness .... E N C E

riches, wealth .... E N C E

2. Which pair of the same colour must start and finish this sentence in order for it to make sense?

☐ a Egypt
☐ b Nile
☐ c Egypt
☐ d Europe

• • • is to
Africa as
Volga
is to • • •

river
Europe
Nile
Egypt

Observation

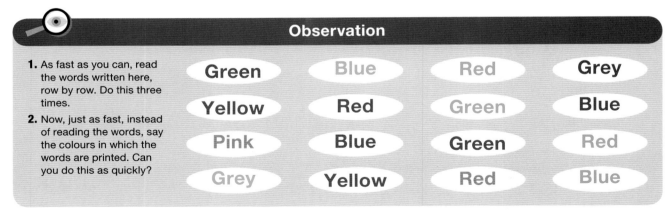

1. As fast as you can, read the words written here, row by row. Do this three times.
2. Now, just as fast, instead of reading the words, say the colours in which the words are printed. Can you do this as quickly?

Green	Blue	Red	Grey
Yellow	Red	Green	Blue
Pink	Blue	Green	Red
Grey	Yellow	Red	Blue

Logic

Find the point where the logical sequence is broken. Which term has been omitted?

| 1 | 0.5 | 0.333333 | 0.25 | 0.166666 | 0.142857 | 0.125 | 0.111111 | 0.1 |

Calculation

Without using a pen and paper, add up the following numbers in your head and write your answer at the bottom.

```
    1000
+     40
+   1000
+     30
+   1000
+     20
+   1000
+     10
```

= ....

 ## Logic

Look at the words that appear in the first five boxes. Which word must appear at the bottom of the sixth one?

Fill
Sender
Mired

More
Meat
Fake

Sired
Feat
Mender

Sake
Fired
Sore

Seat
Mill
Sill

Fender
Fore
....

 ## Memory

Carefully read and memorise the following statement:

A red circle in a blue square.

You'll come across it again later but you won't be allowed to turn back to check it.

Observation

Look carefully at each of these 15 patterns. Only one of them is shown once. Which one is it?

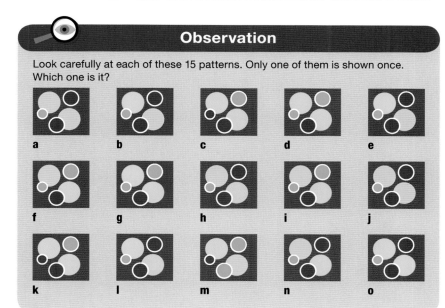

Language

Which of the four suggestions offered below best explains the saying 'All roads lead to Rome'?

- a. **Road signs indicating direction are useless.**
- b. **All eyes turn towards those who are the most powerful.**
- c. **There are several ways to get to the same result.**
- d. **We can't deny our past.**

 ## Memory

Without looking back at the sentence at the top of the page, which of the following images matches the statement you were asked to memorise?

 a   b   c   d

Calculation

1. Which colour has to be removed for each column to add up to the same total?

....

2. Which geometric shape must be removed for each column to add up to the same total?

....

Spatial perception

All sides of this dice are shown from four different viewpoints. Using only the information supplied, can you work out the number that should appear on the blank side as seen from the last viewpoint?

a

b

c

d

Language

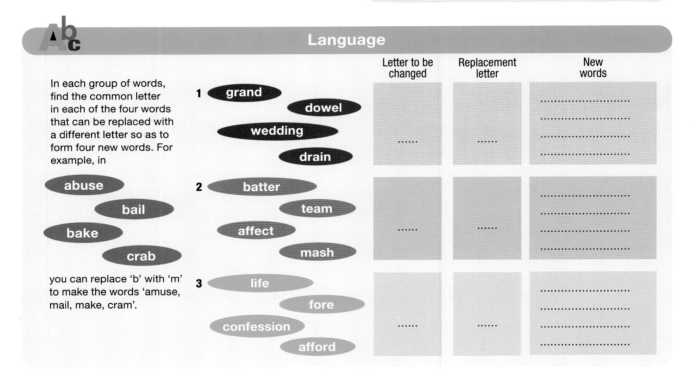

In each group of words, find the common letter in each of the four words that can be replaced with a different letter so as to form four new words. For example, in

abuse

bail

bake

crab

you can replace 'b' with 'm' to make the words 'amuse, mail, make, cram'.

1. grand / dowel / wedding / drain

2. batter / team / affect / mash

3. life / fore / confession / afford

Letter to be changed	Replacement letter	New words
......	......	....
......	......	....
......	......	....

Memory

1. Read aloud the following lines from *The Song of Hiawatha* by HW Longfellow three times, and then cover them.

Pleasant was the journey homeward,
Through the interminable forests,
Over meadow, over mountain,
Over river, hill and hollow.

2. Now fill in the missing words:

Pleasant was the ...... homeward,
Through the .... forests,
Over ......, over mountain,
Over ......, hill and ....

Logic

Complete the four sentences below using the numbers given.

1.6 4 7.5 50
80 112.5 190
220 400
118,750,000

1. A blue whale can weigh up to ..... tonnes; this is the equivalent of ..... Cuban hummingbirds which weigh only ...... grams each.

2. An ant is capable of lifting more than ...... times its own weight. Can you imagine a human weighing ..... kilos lifting more than ...... tonnes?

3. A squid can swim up to ..... km/h. This is 15 times faster than a human swimming champion, who must be content with ...... km/h.

4. A flea doesn't seem to jump very high. However, a flea can jump ..... times its own height. A human high-jumper would need to jump a height of .... metres to match it!

Observation

1. Replace the symbols by one of the letters they represent to reveal an expression connected with good or bad luck.

G	E	C	M	U	F	L	O	D
A	N	J	V	H	I	S	K	R

2. Put the letters in each line in the right order to spell the names of two well-known female singers. The name on the top line will read in the traditional way, from left to right, the name on the bottom line will read from right to left.

P	I	F	I	T	H	E	A	D
R	O	D	I	S	A	S	A	N

Logic

Which number replaces the question mark in the following series?

3	18	90	360	1080	2160	?

☐ a. 3240   ☐ b. 2160   ☐ c. 3680   ☐ d. 0

Language

1. Each of the following words contains an anagram and each anagram begins with the same letter. What are the anagrams?

ULCER ....

NECTAR ....

MEDICAL ....

TROUNCES ....

2. Find the consonants that will enable you to complete the following words.

a. ...... E ...... E .... I ....

b. ...... A ...... A ...... A ...... I A

c. ...... O ...... O ...... E ...... E O U ......

d. ...... I .... I .... E

e. ...... A I .... A ...... E

f. .... I ...... E ...... I O ......

JUST FOR FUN

True or false?

Try to work out if the following claims about famous paintings and artists are true or false. Circle the letters beneath 'True' or 'False' that correspond to your answers, and then reorder the letters you have circled to spell the name of an artist.

	TRUE	FALSE

1. You would need 87 copies of the *Mona Lisa*, by Leonardo da Vinci, to cover *The Raft of the Medusa,* by Géricault.

R   S

2. The *Mona Lisa* was stolen in 1911 and found again in 1913.

I   E

3. Picasso would have been 100 years old in 2004.

G   N

4. *Poppy Fields near Argenteuil* is one of the best-known paintings by Édouard Manet.

P   E

5. Marc Chagall was born Moishe Shagal in Russia.

O   T

6. Rembrandt, in contrast to Van Gogh, died an enormously wealthy man in 1669.

I   R

___ ___ ___ ___ ___ ___

Zigzag words

The names of 30 composers have been hidden in this grid. They can be read in all directions: horizontally, vertically, up and down, from right to left and from left to right. The names are arranged in zigzag patterns – one is shown to get you started. They never cross, and each letter can be used only once. Cross the names off the list as you find them. When you have found them all, use the nine remaining letters to spell the name of a composer born in Cologne, Germany, who subsequently acquired French nationality.

```
M I R E I S Y K H O V E N N T O A H
O S C H L A T S T H C A F O E D Y S
Z A R U B E R N E E B B P M V N U S
B I T E B H C I V E C R U R E R A R
F Z G R N A A M A L L S S O D D E T
L E T Y E U P N R T S I A M E I B S
A L O L O T E R G Z I N H U B I E R
R L U L H C S L O O I E L S V D L G
E N B I T T A E S I L R Y S I V A S
A G A W S C L O R C R E B Z T A H M
M U H C S A R K P R E L I S L R B H
A N N V E I F O N I P U O C E V A R
```

Bach ✓	~~Mozart~~
Beethoven ✓	Pergolesi
Berg ✓	Prokofiev
Berlioz	Purcell
Bizet	Ravel
Brahms ✓	Rossini
Couperin	Salieri
Debussy ✓	Scarlatti
Haydn	Schoenberg
Lalo ✓	Schubert
Liszt ✓	Schumann
Lully	Strauss ✓
Machaut	Stravinsky
Mahler	Vivaldi ✓
Monteverdi	Wagner

Spot the differences

There are seven differences between these two pictures. Can you find them?

 A little anatomy

1. What is the arachnoid membrane?

☐ **a.** One of the three meninges that cover the brain and spinal cord.

☐ **b.** A tendon in the centre of the hand.

☐ **c.** An imaginary muscle in Spiderman.

2. What is the anvil bone?

☐ **a.** A bone in the heel.

☐ **b.** One of the three small bones in the ear.

☐ **c.** A frontal bone which sometimes makes the head heavy.

3. The calyx is:

☐ **a.** A part of the kidney carrying the urine.

☐ **b.** The wall of the nasal cavity.

☐ **c.** A gland that secretes tears.

4. The hamstring is:

☐ **a.** The space between the fingers and toes.

☐ **b.** A group of three muscles in the thigh.

☐ **c.** The division of blood vessels at the base of the liver.

5. What is horripilation?

☐ **a.** A sudden nervous attack.

☐ **b.** The deterioration of a bone in the back of the skull.

☐ **c.** The reflex that produces a temporary change in the skin commonly known as 'goose bumps'.

6. Fundus refers to:

☐ **a.** An organ that is particularly resistant to cold.

☐ **b.** The upper part of the stomach.

☐ **c.** A bone in the skull.

 Letter switch

Change only one letter in each of the following words to make a new word. For example, by replacing an S with a T, you can change PASS to PAST.

a. REVERE

....

b. HALLOW

....

c. SCARF

....

d. GULLET

....

e. GROSS

....

f. PURE

....

g. TURNER

....

h. SUITE

....

i. OOZE

....

j. FLOWER

....

Language

Pair up these words to form six compound words.

under   skate   heart   peace

break   maker   stand   table

green   spoon   house   cheap

Calculation

By changing the numbers 1, 2 and 3 into the operational signs +, − and =, give a logical meaning to the following sets of figures and work out the value of the last two figures.

44146290 ....

47147294 ....

85340245 ....

49258137346 ....

461462551.... ....

Spatial perception

Which of these figures is not identical to the others?

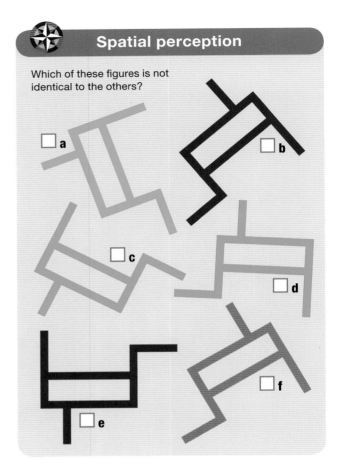

☐ a   ☐ b   ☐ c   ☐ d   ☐ e   ☐ f

Memory

Below are the first lines of some popular songs. Can you supply the title and the name of the original artist who performed them?

a. I am just a poor boy, though my story's seldom told ....

b. Come gather 'round people/Wherever you roam ....

c. Train whistle blowing, makes a sleepy noise ....

d. Day-o, day-ay-ay-o, daylight come and me wan' go home ....

e. Oh, give me land, lots of land under starry skies above ....

Observation

Which two images are exactly the same?

☐ a   ☐ b   ☐ c   ☐ d   ☐ e

Calculation

Use the numbers shown on the right, and the basic operations (×, ÷, +, −), to reach the total shown below. You can use each number once only.

6

4

5 **2**

....

.... = 37

Observation

What phrase is suggested by the following?

CLAP CLAP CLAP CLAP CLAP CLAP CLAP CLAP CLAP

....

....

Spatial perception

Person A takes the second on the left and keeps going until he reaches the wall, then turns right and goes straight ahead until he reaches the next wall. He then turns left and keeps going until he reaches the next wall, then turns left and keeps going until he reaches the next wall.

Person B takes the second on the left, then takes the second on the right and continues until he reaches the next wall. He then turns left twice and keeps going until he reaches the next wall.

Where is each person at the end of his walk?

Language

1. In a faraway land the only inhabitants are trolls, gnomes and elves. Given that all the trolls are red, all the gnomes have only one eye and all the elves have two eyes, are the following propositions true or false?

	True	False
a. In this faraway land, there are no inhabitants who are red and have only one eye.	☐	☐
b. Elves can be red.	☐	☐
c. I see an inhabitant with only one eye: it is neither an elf nor a troll.	☐	☐
d. I see a red inhabitant with only one eye: it is either a gnome or an elf.	☐	☐
e. I see a red inhabitant with two eyes: it is perhaps an elf.	☐	☐

2. Which word does not follow the same rule as the others?

floppy   caftan   almost

chintz   biopsy

chills

effort   hippy

3. What are the three anagrams of ALLERGY?

ALLERGY

a. ....

b. ....

c. ....

Language

Build the stairs by adding the letter given to the word appearing in the previous line to form a new word. The order of the letters can be changed.

TRUE

+ N ....

+ E ....

+ I ....

+ D ....

+ L ....

Calculation

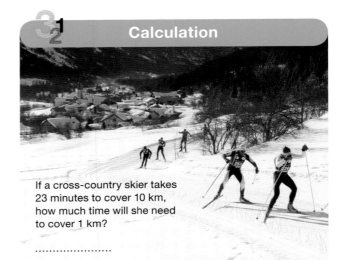

If a cross-country skier takes 23 minutes to cover 10 km, how much time will she need to cover 1 km?

....

Observation

Look at these bottles for 30 seconds, and then cover the picture.

Which one has been added?

Logic

1. Look at the words in the first line and the colours in which they are written to work out the logic that leads to the second line.
Which of the following is the last word: gale, male, pale, sale, tale?

wing	brave	fawn	mirth	crew	sale
ring	grave	yawn	girth	brew	....

2. Draw the figure that logically completes this series.

 ....

³₂¹ Calculation

The same number completes the logical sequence in both of the following arrangements. What is it?

4	2	4	6
8	4	0	5
9	5	4	6
6	1	....	3

5	3	5	7
2	1	8	9
7	4	9	7
6	4	....	8

Language

1. Take out one letter from each of the words in the grid so that the remaining letters still spell an existing word. Put each deleted letter in the box at the end of the line. When you have finished, you will be able to read vertically the name of a famous twentieth-century painter.

P	A	D	D	L	E	D	
B	A	I	L	I	N	G	
C	H	A	R	M	E	D	
M	A	I	M	I	N	G	
S	H	A	V	I	N	G	
D	E	S	C	E	N	T	
C	O	R	O	N	E	R	

2. Which couple of the same colour must you use in order for this sentence to make sense?

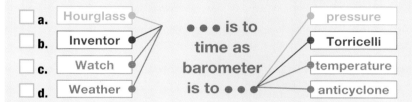

- ☐ a. Hourglass
- ☐ b. Inventor
- ☐ c. Watch
- ☐ d. Weather

● ● ● is to time as barometer is to ● ● ●

- pressure
- Torricelli
- temperature
- anticyclone

Observation

How many circles can you see?

....

Memory

Study the fish in this aquarium for three minutes. Cover the picture, wait one complete minute, and then identify the colours of the ten fish.

Calculation

1. Garry plays Spider Solitaire on his computer. He has won **15** matches and lost **20** since he discovered this game. The table of statistics indicates the percentage of his wins: **15** out of **35**, i.e. **42.85%**. How many games does he need to win in a row to increase this score to **50%**?

....

2. Now work through the same process for Gyan, who so far has won **1025** games out of **2290**.

....

Spatial perception

In this grid there are 15 houses. Your goal is to find the position of the garden belonging to each of the houses, which can be located in a neighbouring square either horizontally or vertically. The numbers appearing at the beginning of each row indicate the number of gardens located there. Shade in the squares that do not have a garden (as we have started to do) to gradually recreate the plan of the area.

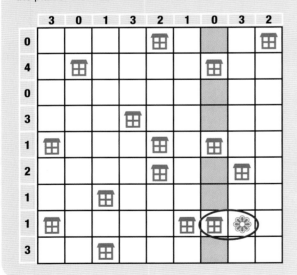

Logic

Replace the two blank spaces with a letter and number that continue the logical progression of the sequence.

| A | 3 | D | 2 | F | 5 | K | 3 | N | 5 | .... | .... | Z |

Observation

ARTICHOKE and SPINACH have been coded with the following colours. Another five vegetables have been coded below in the same way. What are they?

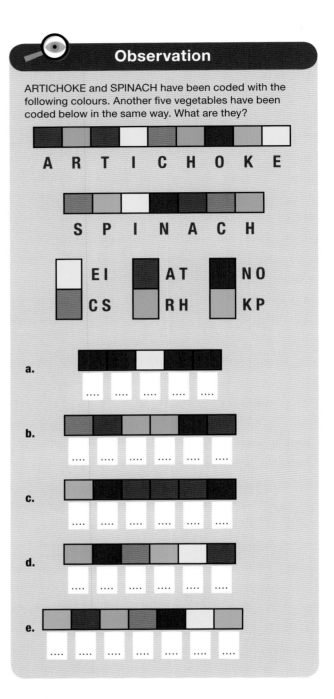

a. ....

b. ....

c. ....

d. ....

e. ....

Language

What four-letter word can be inserted between the brackets to complete the first word and start the second?

STAGE(.... ....)SOME

Calculation

Complete the following addition:

	2 hours	42 mins	51 secs
+	5 hours	53 mins	27 secs
+	8 hours	41 mins	44 secs
=	... hours	... mins	... secs

Logic

Five friends, Stan, Fred, Christopher, Omar and Uri have just started their own rock group. They are called FOCUS

F O C U S

Their sisters – Olivia, Christine, Sandi, Asha and Hannah – prefer rap music. They decide to start their own group as well. What will their stage name be?

☐ **a.** HADES

☐ **b.** CHAOS

☐ **c.** HAVOC

Logic

What card should fill the empty space to complete this logical sequence, both horizontally and vertically?

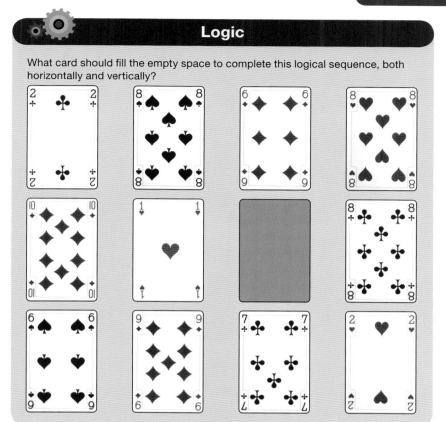

Language

Which is the odd word out in this group?

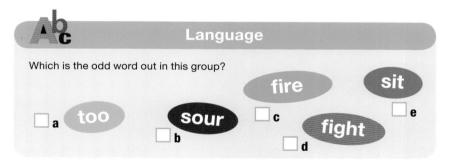

☐ a **too**
☐ b **sour**
☐ c **fire**
☐ d **fight**
☐ e **sit**

Observation

Look carefully at each of these patterns. Only one is shown once. Which one is it?

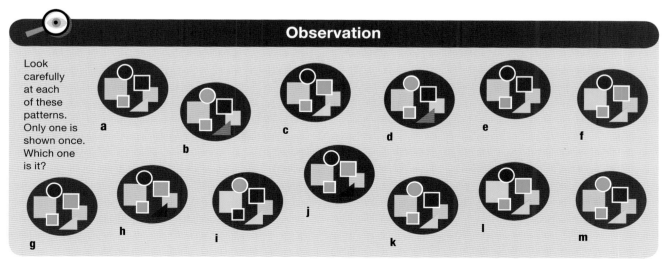

Observation

Look at each of the paired expressions of letters and numbers and decide whether they are exactly reversed or not, then tick the box for Yes or No. For example, 45RT18LM is the reverse of ML81TR54. Allow yourself a maximum of 2 minutes to complete this exercise.

			Yes	No
a.	AZERTYUIOP	PIOUYTREZA	☐	☐
b.	124554512	2154554521	☐	☐
c.	NAO0OANO	ONA0O0AN	☐	☐
d.	CCC3C3CC3	3CC3C3CCC	☐	☐
e.	ERREURRE	ERREURRE	☐	☐
f.	MALAYALAM	MALAYALAM	☐	☐
g.	NAO0ONAO0OAN	NAO0OANO0ONA	☐	☐
h.	s1drl21sir1	1ris12ldr1s	☐	☐
i.	WMWWVMMVM	MVMMVWMWM	☐	☐
j.	1§5(25(==+)u%	%u(+==)52)5§1	☐	☐

Logic

It is midday. My friend has just left and has arranged to meet me at the cinema when the small hand on my watch has gone around 10 times. What time will it be when I meet him?

....

3¹⁄₂ Calculation

Find the two ways of obtaining 24,337 by using each of the numbers below only once and by using the basic operations (×, ÷, +, −) in any way you choose.

155   **156**   **157**

....
.... = 24,337

....
.... = 24,337

Language

	A	N						
+ T	......	......	......					
+ U	......	......	......	......				
+ D	......	......	......	......	......			
+ T	......	......	......	......	......	......		
+ E	......	......	......	......	......	......	......	
+ T	......	......	......	......	......	......	......	......

1. Build the stairs by adding the letter given to the word appearing in the previous line to form a new word. The order of the letters can be changed.

2. If all the cats in the world are blue, all trees are cats and no chicken is a tree:

	Yes	No
a. Can a chicken be a cat?	☐	☐
b. Can a tree be red?	☐	☐
c. Can a cat be something other than a tree?	☐	☐

Observation

1. Study the numbers below. Which digit recurs most frequently?

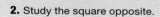

Memory

Look at each image, together with the word that accompanies it. After two minutes, hide the original drawings and try to reproduce them below.

STOP GO ENTRY EXIT

....

2. Study the square opposite.

Can you work out in one minute which one of the squares below does not contain any of the letters shown in the square on the right?

```
    R  D
A    E
  G    T
```

a
```
    M
D  K  E
  I  Z
```
b
```
  T    J
  D  E
  H    T
```
c
```
    O
U    P  D
  H    Y
```
d
```
  S   C
Q  B
 N   F
```
e
```
    R  D
  N  H
  G    S
```
f
```
      O
E    P   I
  Z   T
```

Calculation

A bag that is closed and opaque contains nine balls: three green ones, three red ones and three purple ones. What is the minimum number of balls you need to take out of the bag (without checking as you go) to be certain that you have at least one ball of each colour?

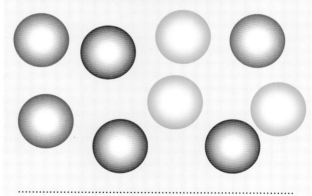

....

Spatial perception

This cube is shown from four different viewpoints. Using only the information supplied, can you work out what should appear on the blank side of the last image?

a **b** **c** **d**

Calculation

Try to reach the total given at the end of each line by using each of the numbers below only once and by using the basic operations (×, ÷, +, −) in any way you choose.

3   **5**   **7**   **11**

.... = **67**

.... = **92**

.... = **168**

.... = **388**

Observation

There are seven differences between these two images. Can you find them?

Language

1. Using the six letters of the word TINSEL, form four new words. Plurals are allowed.

S ....

.... S ....

.... S .....

.... S

2. Fill in the blanks to make four six-letter words, each made up of two consonants, shown in place for you, and four vowels (A, E, I, O , U). Vowels can be used more than once in a word.

.... D .... S

.... C .... C ....

.... R L

.... T .... P ....

3. Which of the four words below logically completes the sequence opposite?

HAMPER
ROUTE
HIJACK
SCISSORS

CRABCAKE

DEFINE

AFGHAN

WEIGHING

....

MONOPOLY

SUPERSTAR

ASTUTE

Logic

Which of the following numbers should be placed in the blank below to logically complete this sequence: 00, 41, 53 or 87?

00   **10**   **11**   **21**   **31**   **23**   **60**   **34** **45**   **82**

Clue: there are nine different numbers, apart from those suggested, that could logically be entered in the blank space.

Memory

Study the table below. Try to memorise all the words, as well as their position in the table. Use your imagination to create associations. You could try making up sentences using the different elements, or look for words that are similar in sound. When you think you have remembered them all, go to the table at the bottom of the page and try to reproduce them.

Dog	Wet	Grass	Rug	Vert
Paul	White	John	Winter	Snow
Pole	Layer	Ozone	Zone	Stick
Cat	Dry	Verb	Grandpa	Light
Hat	Second	Proverb	Papyrus	Lightning

Calculation

A person betting on horse races notices that he has won exactly one time out of two since he started betting: 50 of his horses have won, but 50 have let him down! How many times does he need to win in succession if he wants to increase his success rate to 75%?

Language

Take out one letter from each of the words in the grid so that the remaining letters still spell an existing word. Put each deleted letter in the box at the end of the line. When you have finished, you will be able to read vertically the name of a web that first made its appearance in 1974 and has been spreading ever since. In some lines more than one letter can be removed; the mystery word will help you decide which is the correct letter to choose.

W	A	I	V	I	N	G	
D	I	N	N	E	R	S	
S	T	A	Y	I	N	G	
A	P	P	E	A	L	S	
R	A	M	B	L	E	D	
B	A	N	K	E	R	S	
C	R	E	A	T	E	D	
T	A	N	G	L	E	D	

Memory

....	....	G.....................	....	V.....................
....	W.....................	....	....	S.....................
Pole	....	....	Z.....................	....
....	....	....	G.....................	L.....................
....	....	....	....	....

Jigsaw puzzle

Nine of the ten scattered pieces are sufficient to recreate the original image. Which is the unused piece? Can you put the other pieces back in the right places?

Dates and numbers

1. In what year were Herculaneum and Pompeii destroyed by a volcanic eruption?

☐ **a.** 179 BC

☐ **b.** 79 BC

☐ **c.** 79 AD

☐ **d.** 179 AD

2. What was the estimated population of the world in the year 1000?

☐ **a.** 100 million

☐ **b.** 300 million

☐ **c.** 400 million

☐ **d.** 600 million

3. How many years did the Hundred Years War actually last?

☐ **a.** 60

☐ **b.** 90

☐ **c.** 100

☐ **d.** 116

4. How many of the six wives of Henry VIII were beheaded?

☐ **a.** One

☐ **b.** Two

☐ **c.** Three

☐ **d.** Four

Crack the code

Replace each of the symbols by the letter that it represents to decode this quote from Leonardo da Vinci.

_ H _ _ _   _

T _ _ _ _ _ _

_ _ A _ _   _ _ _

L _ _ _ _ _ _ _   W _ _ _ _ _ _ _ ,

_ _ _ _ _ V _   _ _ N _   _ _ _ R _ _ _ _ _

_ _ _ _ _ _ _ _ .

✿	❀	✤	✿	❀
A	D	L	H	T
B	E	N	R	U
W	I	O	S	V
		G		

Fakes

Which of the ten details shown on the left belong to the image below?

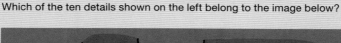

Logic

Which of the following words is the odd one out? Take into account the letters that make up each word, and any possible additions or substitutions.

ACTOR

APPLE

EVER

LAWLESS

LOPPED

RIGHT

Memory

Look at the top target for three minutes to try to memorise the distribution of the shaded areas. Cover it, and then try to fill in the same shaded areas on the bottom target.

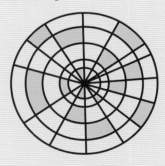

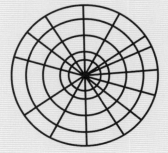

 Language

1. Replace each blank space with a letter to make six words that start with the letter 'I'. Some letters have been placed to help you.

a. I .... G

b. I .... Q .... L .... Y

c. I .... S .... L ....

d. I .... E .... M

e. I .... L .... M

f. I .... Y ....

2. Six words have had two or more syllables removed. Piece them together again, using the syllables provided. Note that there are sometimes several possible solutions, but only one combination will enable you to complete all the words.

a. .... TRI ....

b. .... TY

c. .... QUA ....

d. .... DI ....

e. DIA ....

f. .... ER ....

LI   CAP   IN   HAN   MET   CIOUS   RIC   ET   NI   BER   GUING   LO   TY

Calculation

Using addition, how do you reach a total of 34 in all directions (horizontally, vertically and diagonally) using the 12 coloured tiles? Place each of them in a square of the same colour.

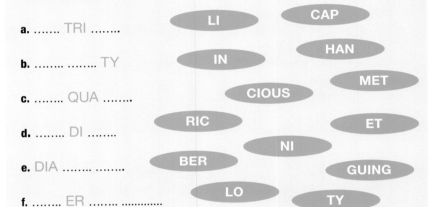

Observation

Which of the six silhouettes below exactly matches the drawing on the right?

☐ a
☐ b
☐ c
☐ d
☐ e
☐ f

Language

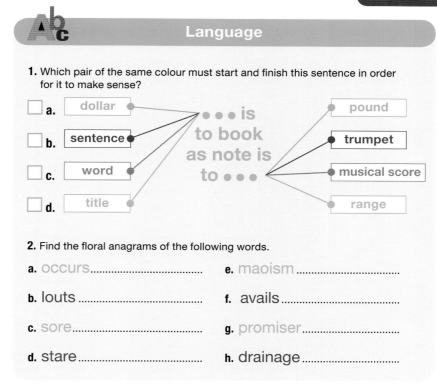

1. Which pair of the same colour must start and finish this sentence in order for it to make sense?

☐ **a.** dollar
☐ **b.** sentence
☐ **c.** word
☐ **d.** title

• • • is
to book
as note is
to • • •

pound
trumpet
musical score
range

2. Find the floral anagrams of the following words.

a. occurs ....

b. louts ....

c. sore ....

d. stare ....

e. maoism ....

f. avails ....

g. promiser ....

h. drainage ....

Logic

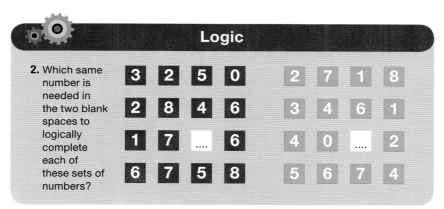

2. Which same number is needed in the two blank spaces to logically complete each of these sets of numbers?

3	2	5	0
2	8	4	6
1	7	....	6
6	7	5	8

2	7	1	8
3	4	6	1
4	0	....	2
5	6	7	4

Memory

Look at these beads for a few minutes and then cover them.

Now try to draw them in the right order on the string.

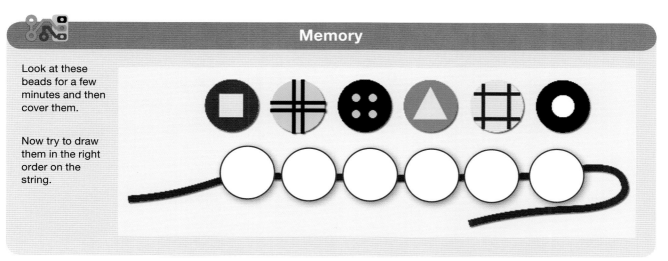

Observation

There are seven differences between these two pictures. Can you find them?

Spatial perception

Mark the garden for each house. Each garden is located in a neighbouring square, horizontally or vertically. Each black number indicates the number of gardens in that row or column. Shade in the squares without a garden.

Language

1.

	A	T
+ R	.....	.....	.....
+ E	.....	.....	.....	.....
+ I	.....	.....	.....	.....
+ P	.....	.....	.....	.....	.....
+ S	.....	.....	.....	.....	.....
+ A	.....	.....	.....	.....	.....	.....	.....

Build the stairs by adding the letter given on the left to the word appearing in the previous line to spell out a new word. The order of the letters can be changed.

2. The following lines are the result of intermingling the letters that make up words for: **a.** two colours, **b.** three animals and **c.** three flowers. The order of the letters in each word has not been changed. What are the eight words?

a. BRVOIOLEWNT

.... / ....

b. RACHINONCTELEROPATOSE

.... / .... / ....

c. TANGUELERAMINIPOUMNE

.... / .... / ....

Calculation

At the end of today's trading, the stock market index closed at 2882 points.

This number is a palindrome. It reads the same from left to right as from right to left.

By how many points must the index rise tomorrow to achieve the same unusual effect?

Observation

1. Draw the interlocking circles below in one go, without lifting your hand. First establish where you must begin and end, and then trace the path with your finger before using a pencil.

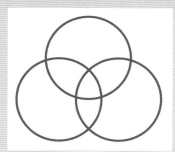

2. Look at each of the paired groups of letters and numbers and decide if they are exactly reversed or not, then tick the box for Yes or No. For example 3#PO$ is the reverse of $OP#3. Allow yourself a maximum of two minutes to complete this exercise.

Yes No

a. ♣♦♦♠♣♣♥♥♣♣   ♣♣♥♥♣♣♠♦♦♣ ☐ ☐

b. ▲▶▼◀▼▲▶▶▲   ▲◀◀▲▼▶▼◀▲ ☐ ☐

c. 🎵♪♪🎵←↑→   →↑←🎵♪♪🎵 ☐ ☐

d. ¼½¾½¼¾¾½¼   ¼½¾¾¾¼¼½¾½¼ ☐ ☐

Language

The word SERPENTS has two anagrams that both start with the same consonant. What are they?

Spatial perception

This cube is shown in full from three different viewpoints. Using only the information supplied, can you complete the blank side of the last cube?

  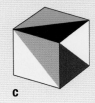 
a b c d

 Calculation

A farmer grazes his **herd** in a **rectangular** field. The long side (length) measures **500 metres** more than the short side (width). In order to go around the entire perimeter of the field, the farmer must walk **4 kilometres**. What is the width of the field?

 Memory

Look at the left column for three minutes to try to memorise the drawings. Cover it, and then try to reproduce them identically in the right column.

Language

Six words have had two or more syllables removed. Piece them together again, using the syllables provided. Note that there are sometimes several possible solutions, but only one combination will enable you to complete all the words.

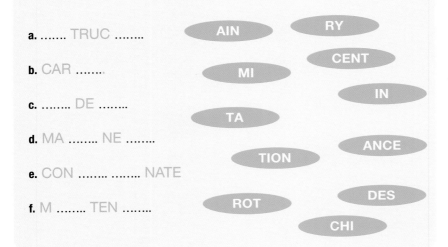

a. .... TRUC ....

b. CAR ....

c. .... DE ....

d. MA .... NE ....

e. CON .... NATE

f. M .... TEN ....

AIN   RY

CENT

MI

IN

TA

ANCE

TION

DES

ROT

CHI

Memory

Study the five figures below, on the top row, for three minutes and try to memorise their shapes and colours. Cover the top row, wait one full minute and then try to colour in the white figures in the second row, reversing the colours as has been done for you in the first one.

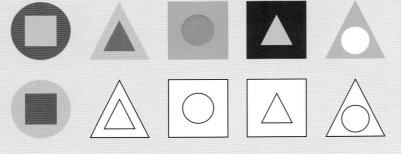

Spatial perception

Imagine that the cut-out shapes below are made of cardboard. Find the three that you need to superimpose to create the figure A (left), and work out the order in which they must be superimposed.

A

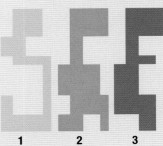

1   2   3

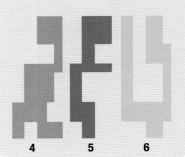

4   5   6

Calculation

If **6** saws saw **6** planks in **6** minutes, how many planks can **12** saws saw in **12** minutes?

....

Logic

What two numbers are needed to complete the following sequence?

| 18 | 5 | 15 | 7 | 12 | 9 | .... | .... | 6 | 13 | 3 | 15 |

Language

1. Replace the blanks with letters to change these 'numbers' into words. To help you, the 23 missing letters are listed below. Cross each letter out as you use it.

A A A
B C
E E E
F G H
L L N
O O P
R R R
S V Y

a. T H ... R E ... ... E

b. F ... ... O U R

c. F ... ... I V ... ... E

d. S ... ... I ... X

e. S E V E ... ... N ... ...

f. E ... ... I G H T

2. Take out one letter from each of the words in the grid, so that the remaining letters still spell out an existing word. Put each deleted letter in the box at the end of the line. When you have finished, you will be able to read vertically the name of someone who lives on the banks of the Nile. In some lines more than one letter can be removed; the mystery word will help you decide which is the correct letter to choose.

E	N	T	E	R	I	N	G	
E	S	C	A	R	G	O	T	
Y	E	A	R	N	I	N	G	
S	P	I	N	N	E	R	S	
T	E	R	M	I	N	A	L	
S	T	E	A	L	I	N	G	
H	E	A	V	I	E	S	T	
M	E	R	C	H	A	N	T	

Logic

Which of the following words is the odd one out? Take into account the letters that make up each word, and any possible additions or substitutions.

CIVIC **RADAR**

KAYAK **SNOWFLAKE**

RACECAR **LEVEL**

Calculation

1. Place the numbers from 1 to 10 in this square so that each row, each column and each large diagonal adds up to the same total of 65. There are two solutions.

12	21	20	.....	.....
.....	13	22	16	.....
.....	.....	14	23	17
18	.....	.....	15	24
25	19	.....	.....	11

2. In order to calculate the volume of a parallelepiped (such as a cube), we multiply the width by the length by the height. But in the case of a sphere, it is up to you to work out a method. Look at the two spheres shown below. If a sphere S1 has a radius which is double that of another sphere S2, how many times greater is the volume of S1 compared to S2?

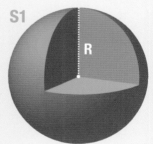

☐ **a.** 2 times
☐ **b.** 4 times
☐ **c.** 6 times
☐ **d.** 8 times

Observation

How many squares can you count?

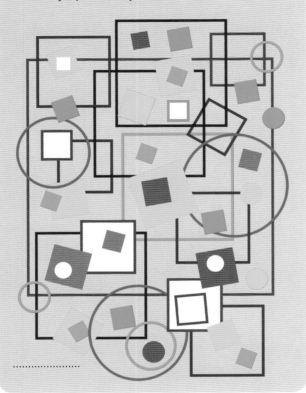

....

Language

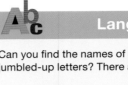

Can you find the names of eight fruits in these jumbled-up letters? There are two fruits in each line.

a. PEHACREPA

.... / ....

b. GORNAMOGANE

.... / ....

c. BELNAPANAPA

.... / ....

d. WAPTIROCAPWAP

.... / ....

Memory

Read the following groups of three words several times and then cover them before looking at the second part.

1. large, stupid, muscular

2. intelligent, small, noisy

3. scrawny, quiet, stupid

Of the following four groups of words, which one is not a perfect opposite to one of the groups of three words given above?

a. noisy, muscular, stupid

b. small, intelligent, scrawny

c. muscular, noisy, intelligent

d. stupid, large, quiet

Logic

Study the column of dominos on the left. Now look at the column on the right. To continue this logical sequence, what is the value of the blank domino and the order of its colours?

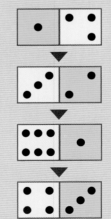

Observation

There are seven differences between these two images. Can you find them?

Calculation

1. Which geometric shape must be removed so that each of the columns adds up to the same total?

....

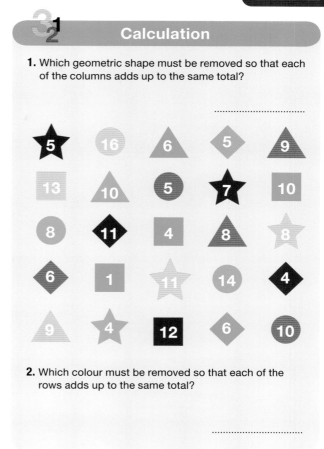

2. Which colour must be removed so that each of the rows adds up to the same total?

....

Language

1. Use the clues supplied to fill in the blanks and find 10 words ending with –INE.

a. put together   .... I N E

b. to give the exact meaning of   .... I N E

c. cow-like   .... I N E

d. to form a mental image   .... I N E

e. a mechanical device   .... I N E

f. a periodic publication   .... I N E

g. a butter substitute   .... I N E

h. the backbone   .... I N E

i. relating to a deity   .... I N E

2. What three-letter word can be inserted between the brackets to complete the first word and start the second?

BUTTER(.... ....)CAKE

DAY 29

Language

1. The following lines are the result of intermingling the letters that make up words for: **a.** two spices, **b.** three herbs and **c.** three nuts. The order of the letters in each word has not been changed. What are the eight words? Don't take any notice of the different colours; only the letters are important.

a. CLTUROMEVRICES

.... / ....

b. ROPSCHAERSIMAVERSLYEY

.... / .... / ....

c. PEACALCAMNSHONEDW

.... / .... / ....

2. Each of these proverbs and expressions has been slightly changed. What is the correct version?

He who hesitates is last.

A rolling stone is no great loss.

One good term expects another.

Dead men have no tails.

Every crowd has a gold edge.

Beggars can't be fussy.

Calculation

A **square** has a side with the length L. By increasing this side by **6** cm, the area of the square is increased by **216** cm². It so happens that **216 = 6 x 6 x 6**. What was the original length of the side of the square?

....

Spatial perception

Imagine that the disks below are made of glass. Find the three disks that must be superimposed on one another to recreate the original rainbow disk. You don't need to rotate any of the disks.

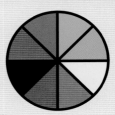

☐ a ☐ b ☐ c

  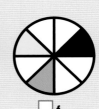

☐ d ☐ e ☐ f

Memory

Look at the grid on the left for four minutes and try to memorise the positions of the various symbols.

Cover it and then try to put each symbol in the same place in the blank grid on the right.

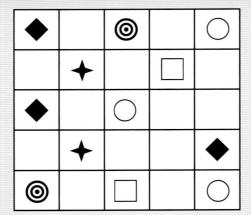

Calculation

Each brick in this pyramid of numbers represents the total of the numbers in the two bricks immediately below it. In addition, of the two numbers missing from the base, the second has twice the value of the first. Use this information to recreate the whole of the pyramid.

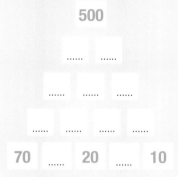

500

....

....

....

70 ...... 20 10

Logic

1. Work out the logical principle determining the sequence of the following geometric figures and then draw in the missing figures.

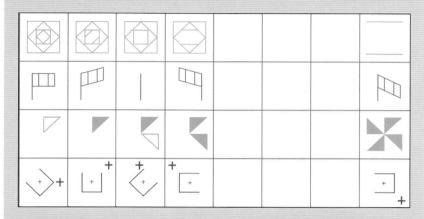

2. Work out the logical principle determining the sequence of these numbers and then find the seventh.

11   17   25   35   47   61   □ ....

Language

Form three words of nine letters by adding an 'I' to the letters in GARMENTS.

G A R M E N T S + I

a. ....

b. ....

c. ....

Observation

There are seven differences between these two images. Can you find them?

Observation

Look carefully at each of these seven shapes. Ignoring the colours, which have been varied on purpose to ensure that you concentrate on the shapes, identify the figure that appears only once.

a   b   c   d   e   f   g

Anagram crossword

Each clue is an anagram that needs to be unscrambled to solve this crossword.

Across

1. Aim into it.
6. No bud.
7. Debar.
9. Deaf.
10. Sent it.
12. I dream.
14. Rats.
17. Ten of.
18. Anger.
19. Nip thy gal.

Down

2. No mud.
3. Diet.
4. Be last.
5. Canoe.
6. UFO flab.
8. Severed.
11. Dry ban.
13. To Mel.
15. No net.
16. Char.

Matching up

Pair each writer with his or her own quotation.

Dorothy Parker	A	A	1. Time you enjoy wasting was not wasted.
Samuel Coleridge	B	B	2. Memory is the treasury and guardian of all things.
Mark Twain	C	C	3. All the world's a stage.
Sophocles	D	D	4. Of all noises, I think music is the least disagreeable.
Groucho Marx	E	E	5. Wise-cracking is simply callisthenics with words.
William Shakespeare	F	F	6. Poetry: the best words in the best order.
Samuel Johnson	G	G	7. Golf is a good walk spoiled.
Clive James	H	H	8. I intend to live forever, or die trying.
Cicero	I	I	9. A short saying often contains much wisdom.
John Lennon	J	J	10. Fiction is life with the dull bits left out.

Whose call is that?

Draw on your memory and your knowledge to find the term normally used to describe the call of the following animals. Sometimes there may be more than one term.

a. crows ....

b. owls ....

c. chicks ....

d. monkeys............

e. ducks ....

f. hens ....

g. roosters.............

h. frogs..................

i. wolves...............

j. elephants ....

k. snakes...............

l. lions ....

m. bears..................

n. turkeys ....

o. geese ....

p. pigs ....

q. hyenas................

r. mice ....

s. dogs..................

t. horses ....

u. donkeys.............

v. sheep ....

w. cows ....

Animal figures

1. What is the approximate length of the tail of a hippopotamus?
- ☐ **a.** 5 cm
- ☐ **c.** 1 m
- ☐ **b.** 50 cm
- ☐ **d.** 2 m

2. How tall can a male giraffe grow?
- ☐ **a.** 3 m
- ☐ **c.** 12 m
- ☐ **b.** 6 m
- ☐ **d.** 18 m

3. What is the weight of an adult male African elephant?
- ☐ **a.** 1.5 t
- ☐ **c.** 7 t
- ☐ **b.** 3.5 t
- ☐ **d.** 15 t

4. How fast can an emu run?
- ☐ **a.** 12 km/h
- ☐ **c.** 60 km/h
- ☐ **b.** 30 km/h
- ☐ **d.** 90 km/h

Sudoku puzzle

Solve this puzzle – a classic Sudoku grid – by placing the nine squares of numbers, below right, into the large grid on the left. Each row and each column must contain the numbers from 1 to 9 only once. To help you, two numbers have already been placed in the grid.

	4							
					3			

4	7	5	7	6	9	4	2	5
3	1	6	4	8	5	3	7	1
8	9	2	2	1	3	8	6	9
9	5	8	1	8	3	6	9	1
3	7	6	2	6	9	8	2	4
1	4	2	7	5	4	5	3	7
6	2	1	2	8	3	7	3	4
5	4	8	5	9	7	9	1	2
9	3	7	1	4	6	6	5	8

Logic

What is on the hidden card?

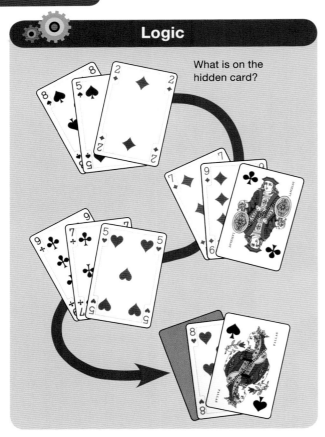

Observation

Seven of the eight picture fragments below (**a–h**) are sufficient to recreate the original picture. Which piece is not used?

Memory

What place is this? Try to use as few clues as possible by covering them and then uncovering one at a time.

a. I am the land of the Red Dragon and the daffodil...............................

b. Some claim Lewis Carroll met Alice in one of my seaside resorts. ....

c. The locals call me Cymru. ....

d. I am part of the United Kingdom. ....

e. My capital is Cardiff. ....

Language

Build the stairs by adding the letter given on the left to the word appearing in the previous line to form a new word. The order of the letters can be changed.

	I	N						
+S	.....	.....	.....					
+E	.....	.....	.....	.....				
+M	.....	.....	.....	.....	.....			
+O	.....	.....	.....	.....	.....	.....		
+T	.....	.....	.....	.....	.....	.....	.....	
+O	.....	.....	.....	.....	.....	.....	.....	.....
+C	.....	.....	.....	.....	.....	.....	.....	.....

Language

Change one letter only in each of the following words to make a new word. For example, by replacing 'S' with 'T', you can change PASS to PAST.

a. QUITE

....

b. DOTAGE

....

c. INFECT

....

d. SLOPE

....

e. BREAK

....

f. ALTITUDE

....

3½ Calculation

How much is half of a third of a quarter of **24** multiplied **100** times by itself?

....

 Language

The letters of the following words – all synonyms of words meaning 'to talk' or 'to communicate' – have been jumbled up. Can you put them back in the correct order?

Example: A T B E D E = D E B A T E

a. S O G S I P ....

b. T R A C T H E ....

c. T R U T E ....

d. O T I G A N T E E ....

e. T U R T E M ....

f. S I C S U D S ....

g. V O R C E N E S ....

h. P E X S E R S ....

i. M I S T A R N T ....

j. F R O N C E ....

k. L A Y P E R ....

Observation

Which one is the odd one out?

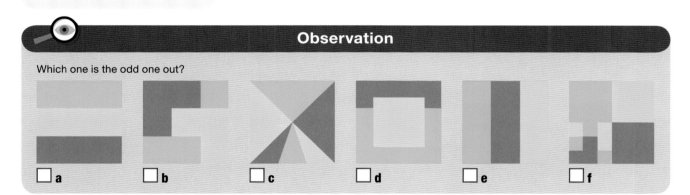

☐ a   ☐ b   ☐ c   ☐ d   ☐ e   ☐ f

Logic

In each of the following series of words, there is one word that doesn't share a particular property with the others. Take into account the letters that make up each word, as well as any possible additions or substitutions to decide which word is the odd one out in each line.

a.	SYMBOL	REACHING	SIGHTED	FLUNG	FETCHED	OUT
b.	APPLE	BOTTLE	MINT	OLIVE	BRICK	MOSS
c.	BLOWER	BRACKET	BLAST	BORDER	BOOT	BALLOT

Calculation

Place the numbers from 1 to 19 in the hexagons. By adding the numbers in each line either vertically or diagonally (each made up of three, four or five cells), you should always reach the same total. Each number must be placed in a cell of the same colour as itself. In order to find the total that must be reached in each line, start by adding all the numbers together from 1 to 19 and then reason logically.

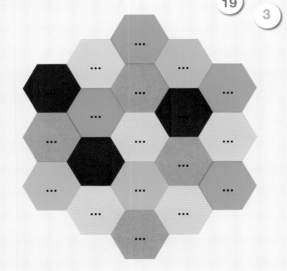

Language

Replace the blanks with letters to change these 'cities' into words. To help you, the 23 missing letters are listed below. Cross each letter out as you use it.

A C C
E E F
G I M
N N N
O O O
P P
R R R
T T V

a. T U __ N I __ S

b. __ __ P A R I S __ __

c. __ O __ S __ L __ __ __ O __

d. __ __ R __ I __ O

e. __ __ R __ O __ M E __

Spatial perception

Look at this figure.

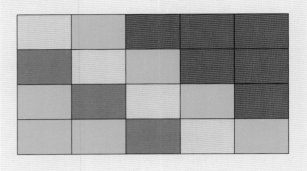

Which three of the numbered pieces below should you put together to make the above figure? (Don't superimpose or modify the shape of the pieces.)

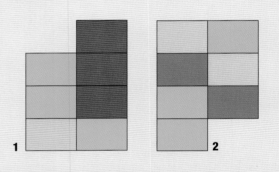

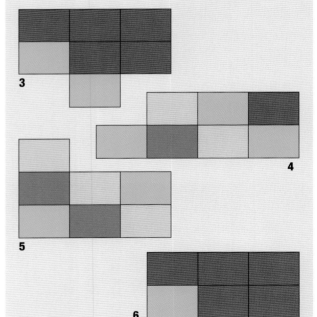

Memory

Study the table below. Try to memorise all the names as well as the position of each in the table. Use your imagination to create associations. When you think you have remembered them all, go to the table at the bottom of the page and try to reproduce them.

Saratoga	Indiana	Manitoba	Oklahoma	Nebraska
Denver	Austin	Vermont	Idaho	Delaware
Florida	Rhode Island	Atlanta	Nashville	Kansas
Missouri	Augusta	California	Hawaii	Albany
Louisiana	Ohio	Utah	Indianapolis	Seattle

Language

1. Which same letter needs to be inserted into the blank spaces to form an existing word?

a. C A .... I E ....

b. .... I .... L E

2. What four-letter word can be inserted between the brackets to complete the first word and start the second?

FOOT(.... ....)PAD

Logic

What numbers should appear on the four blank circles on the snake.

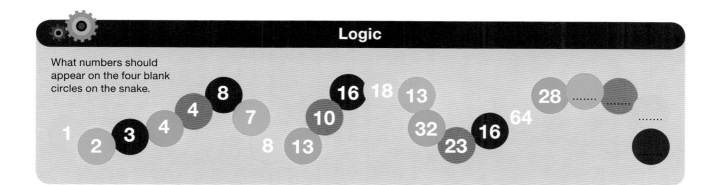

1 2 3 4 4 8 7 8 13 10 16 18 13 32 23 16 64 28 ....

Memory

				N......................
....	....	....	I......................	....
....	....	A......................	....	....
....	A......................	....	....	....
....	....	....	....	....

Logic

1. In the current configuration, the left column adds up to 22 and the right column adds up to 23. Find the tricks that allow you to move three blocks in order to obtain two columns that have the same total.

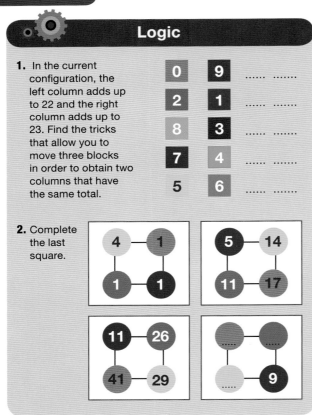

0   9 ....
2   1 ....
8   3 ....
7   4 ....
5   6 ....

2. Complete the last square.

| 4 — 1 | 5 — 14 |
| 1 — 1 | 11 — 17 |

| 11 — 26 | ..... — ..... |
| 41 — 29 | ..... — 9 |

Spatial perception

Mark the garden belonging to each house. The gardens are located in a neighbouring square, either horizontally or vertically, and the black numbers indicate the number of gardens in that row or column. Shade in the squares that do not have a garden to recreate the plan of the area.

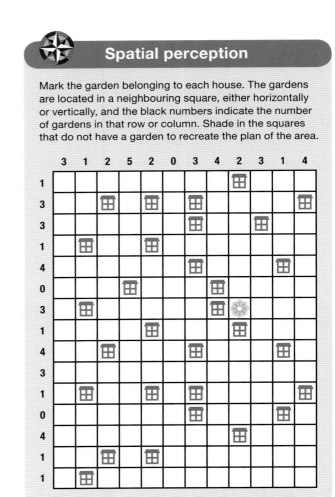

Language

Find the single one-word anagram for each of these six words.

REACTIVE = ...

CARTHORSE = ...

ANCESTRIES = ...

ENUMERATION = ...

REASSORTMENT = ...

DEMAGNETISER = ...

Answers

DAY 1

Language
1. egret.
2. fowl, wolf.
3. a. seals. b. weasel.

Logic
b. The shapes all move clockwise, while the colours keep their same position.

Logic
1. It is a series of inverted whole numbers. 1/6 is missing.
2. Every second letter of the alphabet is given. The sequence is broken between I and M. K is missing.

Calculation
For example:
3 + 4 + 5 = 12
(3 × 5) + 4 = 19
(3 × 4) − 5 = 7

DAY 2

Calculation
(5 × 6) + 7 = 37
(6 × 7) − 5 = 37

Logic
If *x* is the age of the younger brother five years ago, the older brother was then 2*x*. Today, they are respectively *x* + 5 and 2*x* + 5. In eight years' time they will be *x* + 13 and 2*x* + 13. This makes a total of 3*x* + 26. For 3*x* + 26 to equal 50, *x* must equal 8. So the child who is speaking is 13 today (8 + 5).

Language
a. horse. b. zebra. c. dingo. d. goat.
e. serpent. f. spider. g. tuna.
h. leopard. i. stoat. j. racoon.
k. otter. l. badger.

DAY 3

Calculation
6 hours 01 min 00 secs.
45 secs + 15 secs make 1 min. Don't forget to carry over the conversion of 35 mins + 25 mins into 1 hr.

Language
c. Fruit is to tree as acorn is to oak tree.

Observation
Images **a** and **d** are identical.

Language
1. Every dog has its day.
2. A stitch in time saves nine.
3. All that glitters is not gold.

Logic
The number is 22. You move from the first to the second number by adding 1, then from the second to the third by adding 2, then 3, then 4 etc. You therefore need to add 6 to 16 to continue this logical progression. After 22 comes 22 + 7 = 29, then 29 + 8 = 37 and so on.

DAY 4

Logic
The figure **b**. The yellow circle and the blue square move a quarter of a turn anticlockwise and therefore always remain facing each other. The green triangle moves a quarter of a turn in a clockwise direction.

Language
1. emits, items, mites, smite, times.
2. E (keeper).

Observation
Are you in pain? (RU in pain)

DAY 5

Calculation
A very unpleasant surprise. On the first day Sam's credit of $10,000 increases to $11,000 (10,000 + 10% of 10,000). The next day, the 10% drop reduces his savings (11,000 − 1100, 10% of 11,000) to $9,900! In two days, Sam has lost 1% of his capital. Gaining 1% is like multiplying by 1.1; losing 10% is like multiplying by 0.9. So, 364 days after he started investing, Sam will have 10,000 × 1.1182 × 0.9182 = 10,000 × 0.99182 = 1,605.48. Multiplying this factor of 0.99 by itself 182 times has reduced Sam's savings to about $1600!

Logic
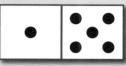

In each set, you obtain a total of 10 by adding up the dots on the left sides of the three dominos. This same total is reached by adding up the dots on the right sides. The final domino in the third set will therefore be 1/5.

Observation
The expression is 'Hit the ground running'.

Language
1. a. The knife is not used for drinking, unlike the other objects. b. Africa is a continent; the others are all countries. c. The stream is the only one in which the water is moving. d. The fir is the only conifer. e. A currant is the only one that does not contain a stone.
2. There were five bones to be discovered: coccyx, femur, radius, sternum, tibia.

DAY 6

Language
1. When the cat is away, the mice will play.
2. Each of the groups of three letters can form the name of an animal: boa, pig, rat, gnu, dog, ant, hen. The letters needed to form the name of an animal in the last bubble are F and O (FOX).

Logic

The missing flag is obtained by adding the colours of the other two in the second column.
In the first column: blue + yellow gives green, white + yellow gives yellow and red + yellow gives orange. Black remains black and covers the other colours.
In the second column: blue + blue remains blue, yellow + red gives orange and pink + white remains pink. The black stars are superimposed on the pink.

Memory

There are several mnemonic strategies to help you to memorise this table. The countries in the first column all start with an S and those in the first line start with the alphabetical series S-T-U-V. The same applies to the last three words in the third line: I-J-K. The K of Denmark suggests the K of Kenya in the line below it. Three countries ending in –AND appear in column 2. The countries in the second line are all Scandinavian countries.

DAY 7

Observation

b and **c**.

Language

1. offence, defence, licence, evidence, lenience, opulence.
2. **b**: Nile is to Africa as Volga is to Europe.

Observation

It is very unusual to say the colours as quickly as we can read the words. This phenomenon is called the Stroop effect, after John Ridley Stroop, who published a study on it in 1935. Reaction time is slowed because the brain is processing conflicting information.

Logic

0.2. The exercise should remind you of the series on page 296: 1 1/2 1/3 1/4 1/5 1/7 1/8 1/9. This is the same series, but expressed in decimal form. Here, 1/6 is present and it is 1/5 that has been omitted. The missing number is therefore 0.2, located between 0.25 and 0.166666.

DAY 8

Calculation

The correct total is 4100. When the brain is confronted with the task of retaining numbers moving from tens to hundreds and at the same time of independently adding thousands, it has a tendency to mix the two operations, and many people will have answered 5000.

Logic

Make. There are three first letters used (F, M and S) and six different endings (-ake, -eat, -ender, -ill, -ired, -ore). There is only one combination of these that is missing, M-ake.

Observation

Pattern **h** is shown once only.

Language

The saying is best explained by **c**.

Memory

The image that matches the statement at the top of the page is **b**.

DAY 9

Calculation

1. Red. When the red numbers are removed, each column adds up to 15.
2. The triangle. When the triangles are removed, each column adds up to 9.

Spatial perception

The number is 3. View **d** is identical to view **c** but has been pivoted a quarter of a turn clockwise. The missing number is therefore the one that appears on the side opposite 2. All the numbers from 1 to 6 are visible. The one you are seeking is not 1, or 2, or 4 (present in views **c** and **d**), or 5, or 6 (because these last two are on a side adjacent to the side where 2 appears, according to view **b**). Therefore 3 is the number on the blank side.

Language

1. T replaces D (grant, towel, wetting, train).
2. E replaces A (better, teem, effect, mesh).
3. C replaces F (lice, core, concession, accord).

DAY 10

Logic

1. A blue whale can weigh up to 190 tonnes; this is the equivalent of 118,750,000 Cuban hummingbirds which weigh only 1.6 grams each.
2. An ant is capable of lifting more than 50 times its own weight. Can you imagine a human weighing 80 kilos lifting more than 4 tonnes?
3. A squid can swim up to 112.5 km/h. This is 15 times faster than a human swimming champion, who must be content with 7.5 km/h.

4. A flea doesn't seem to jump very high. However, a flea can jump 220 times its own height. A human high-jumper would need to jump a height of 400 metres to match it!

Observation

1. Four-leaf clover.
2.

Logic

The question mark is replaced by **b**, 2160. You move from the first to the second number by multiplying by 6 (3 × 6 = 18), then to the next number by multiplying by 5 (18 x 5 = 90), then by 4 (90 × 4 = 360), then by 3 (360 × 3 = 1080), and lastly by 2 (1080 × 2 = 2160). You therefore need to multiply 2160 by 1 to complete the series. The next number would be 0 and would end the series.

Language

1. cruel, canter, claimed, construe.
2. **a.** serendipity. **b.** macadamia.
   c. homogeneous. **d.** discipline.
   e. fairytale. **f.** criterion.

JUST FOR FUN

True or false?

1. True. (R)
2. True, it was stolen by an Italian named Peruggia. (I)
3. False, he was born in 1881. (N)
4. False, the painting is by Claude Monet. (E)
5. True. (O)
6. False, he died bankrupt. (R)

With these six letters you can spell the name of RENOIR.

Zigzag words

The remaining letters spell Offenbach.

Spot the differences

A little anatomy

1. a. **2.** b. **3.** a. **4.** b. **5.** c. **6.** b.

Letter switch

Other answers may be possible. **a.** revert. **b.** callow. **c.** scare. **d.** mullet. **e.** cross. **f.** pare. **g.** burner. **h.** smite. **i.** doze. **j.** blower.

DAY 11

Language

Cheapskate, greenhouse, heartbreak, peacemaker, tablespoon, understand.

Spatial perception

The odd one out is **d**. The small bar on the two parallel segments has been moved.

Calculation

Replacing 1 with +, 2 with =, and 3 with – gives the following:
$44 + 46 = 90$
$47 + 47 = 94$
$85 – 40 = 45$
$49 = 58 + 37 – 46$
The last one is $46 + 46 = 55 + ??$ To reach a total of 92 on each side of the equals sign, the missing number is 37.

Memory

a. *The Boxer*: Simon and Garfunkel.
b. *The Times They Are A-changing*: Bob Dylan
c. *Morningtown Ride*: The Seekers
d. *Banana Boat Song (Day-o)*: Harry Belafonte
e. *Don't Fence Me In*: Roy Rogers, but popularised by Bing Crosby (both of them recorded the song in 1944).

Observation

Images **a** and **c** are identical.

DAY 12

Calculation

$2 + 6 = 8$
$4 \times 8 = 32$
$32 + 5 = 37$

Observation

A round of applause.

Spatial perception

Person A is at point 10; person B is at point 7.

Language

1. a. False. A troll, who is red, can have only one eye. **b.** True. Just because the trolls are red, it doesn't mean that the elves can't be red. **c.** False. Of course it can't be an elf, because all elves have two eyes, but there can be trolls who only have one eye. **d.** False. Being either a gnome or an elf means not being a troll. A red inhabitant with only one eye can be a troll. **e.** True. Elves have two eyes and there is nothing stopping them from being red.
2. caftan. In all the other words the letters appear in alphabetical order.
3. gallery, largely, regally.

DAY 13

Language

tuner, tureen, retinue, reunited, interlude.

Calculation

2 minutes and 18 seconds. To find the solution, you need to convert minutes into seconds. 23 minutes is the equivalent of $23 \times 60 = 1380$ seconds. If the skier covers 10 km in 1380 seconds, she will need 10 times less, i.e. 138 seconds, to cover 1 km. You therefore reconvert the seconds into minutes: 2 minutes and 18 seconds. Doing the division too quickly may produce the answer 2 minutes 30 seconds. This is because calculations of time are made in base 60 and are not as immediate as in base 10, which we use for our everyday calculations.

Logic

1. Pale. Only the first letter of each word in the second line is different from the first line. The initial of the colour used in the first line is taken as the first letter of the word in the second line. For example, the colour of the first word 'wing' is red, so 'r' is used as the first letter of the second line. By this logic, the colour pink of the last word 'sale' gives the missing word 'pale'.
2.

Turn your book a quarter of a turn to the left and hide the right half of the series shown. You will read in capital letters: E F G H I J. The next figure will therefore be a K to which its mirror image has been attached.

DAY 14

Calculation

The number is 8. The number formed by the two numbers in the middle of each line is the result of multiplying the other two numbers on this same line.
Thus, in the first line: $24 = 4 \times 6$; $40 = 8 \times 5$; $54 = 9 \times 6$. Therefore, the number missing on the last line is 8, to give $18 = 6 \times 3$.
The same applies to the second square: $35 = 5 \times 7$; $18 = 2 \times 9$; $49 = 7 \times 7$ and $48 = 6 \times 8$.

Language

1. You could take out: P (addled), I (baling), C (harmed), A (miming), S (having), S (decent) and O (corner). The name of the painter is Picasso.
2. a. Hourglass is to time as barometer is to pressure.

Observation

38 circles.

DAY 15

Calculation

1. The first question can be solved by trial and error. Garry must win 5 games to reach a score of 20 out of 40 and 50%. But this 5 can be found more 'scientifically': in order to reach 50%, the number of victories must be equal to the number of defeats. It is therefore the difference between 15 and 20.

2. Gyan won 1025 games and lost 2290 – 1025 = 1265. He therefore needs to win 1265 – 1025 = 240 in a row to move directly to a 50% success rate.

Spatial perception

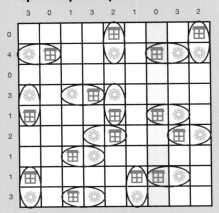

Observation

a. onion. **b.** carrot. **c.** potato. **d.** rocket. **e.** parsnip.

Logic

S then 7. The number indicates the number of places you need to move through the alphabet to read the letter that follows: there are 3 places between A and D, 2 between D and F, 5 between F and K and 3 between K and N. By moving forward another 5 places we reach S, and to reach Z we need to move another 7 places (T, U, V, W, X, Y, Z).

Language

Stage(hand)some.

DAY 16

Calculation

17 hours 18 mins 2 secs.

Logic

The five of spades. Each line will then add up to a total of 24 and contain a card of each suit. Each column will add up to a total of 18.

Logic

b. CHAOS. To form the name of their group, the artists have taken the initials of their first names.

Language

c. Fire. By changing just one letter in each of the others, you spell out a sequence of even numbers: two, four, six, eight. Five, produced when you change a letter in 'fire', is an odd number, and therefore out of place in the sequence.

Observation

Pattern **i** is the only one shown once.

DAY 17

Observation

a. No. I and O are reversed.
b. No. There is an extra 5 in the second column.
c. No. O0O and 0O0.
d. Yes.
e. No. E and U are reversed.
f. Yes. This is a real word; it is the name of a language spoken in India. Words that read the same backwards as forwards are called 'palindromes'.
g. No. The last NA in the right column should be AN.
h. No. The letters 'dr' have not been reversed.
i. No. The end should be WMW and not MWM.
j. No. This last case is harder to understand. Everything has been reproduced correctly except for the parentheses, which have been reversed. The brain integrates this information without finding it strange, because it is concentrating on the other inversions.

Logic

Midday. It will be midday again, but five days later, because the little hand tracing the hours completes two revolutions per day.

Calculation

155 × 156 + 157 = 24,337
156 × 157 – 155 = 24,337

Language

1. ant, aunt/tuna, daunt, tundra, unrated, truanted.
2. a. Yes. The statement 'all trees are cats' does not also mean that 'all cats are trees'. A chicken cannot be a tree, but it can be a cat or anything else other than a tree. **b.** No. All trees are cats and all cats are blue, therefore all trees are blue. **c.** Of course. A cat can be any number of things, including a tree. Or not. If you made a mistake in your answers, it is because you add to the suggestions given in the statement elements of knowledge from your own world, where trees, chickens and cats are completely different from what this exercise imposes.

DAY 18

Observation

1. The number 6.
2. Square **d**.

Calculation

Seven. You simply have to envisage the worst case scenario, i.e. taking out three balls of the same colour, then three of a second colour. The seventh one will necessarily be of the third colour. If your answer was four, it is because you supposed that you would take out three balls of different colours on the first three attempts.

Spatial perception

From views **b** and **c**, you can deduce that the blue crosses (+ and ×) are on two opposing sides. On the four other sides, the following patterns occur in order: yellow stripes, red stripes, red stripes, and yellow cross. There are two sides with red stripes and one with yellow stripes. View **d** must therefore correspond to view **a**, after being pivoted a quarter of a turn towards the back. The missing side is therefore the blue cross, +.

DAY 19

Calculation
For example: 3 + 5 = 8; 8 × 7 = 56;
56 + 11 = 67
3 × 5 = 15; 7 × 11 = 77; 15 + 77 = 92
3 + 11 = 14; 5 + 7 = 12; 14 × 12 = 168
5 × 7 = 35; 35 × 11 = 385;
385 + 3 = 388.

Observation

Language
1. silent, listen, enlist, inlets.
2. odious, acacia, aerial, utopia.
3. hijack; each word in the sequence contains three consecutive letters in alphabetical order. 'Hijack' is the only one of the four suggested words that follows this rule.

Logic
53. The sequence progresses regularly by one unit if we examine the sum of the numbers making up each number.
00 (0 + 0 = 0); 10 (1 + 0 = 1)
11 (1 + 1 = 2); 21 (2 + 1 = 3)
31 (3 + 1 = 4); 23 (2 + 3 = 5)
60 (6 + 0 = 6); 34 (3 + 4 = 7)
45 (4 + 5 = 9); 82 (8 + 2 = 10)
You therefore must include a number where the total of the digits is 8. 53 is the only acceptable candidate but, as suggested in the clue, 08, 17, 26, 35, 44, 62, 71 and 80 would also have been acceptable.

DAY 20

Calculation
Be careful not to answer 25. It is true that the person betting would have then won 75 times, but from 100 + 25 = 125 attempts. And 75 out of 125 represents 60%, not 75%. If this punter wants to have won three times out of four (75%), his losing bets must represent only a quarter of his races. By winning several times in a row, his failures will remain blocked on 50. 50 is a quarter of 200 (100 bets more than at present). In order to move from a 50% to a 75% success rate, our betting man must therefore come up with a winning horse 100 times in a row! His success rate would then be 150 out of 200 = 75%.

Language
You could take out: I (waving), N (diners), T (saying), E (appals), R (ambled), N (bakers), E (crated), T (tangled). The name of the web is internet.

Memory
You can start by thinking that a wet dog who was rolling around in the grass is resting on a green rug. The second line has white, winter and snow. The fourth line gives the opposite of the first line (dry cat), and there are also close associations in sound between some of words in this line and those immediately below them in the fifth line (cat/hat, verb/proverb, grandpa/papyrus).

JUST FOR FUN

Jigsaw puzzle
Piece number **7** does not belong to the puzzle.

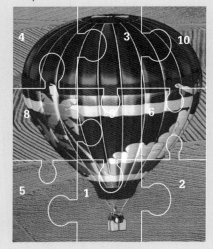

Dates and numbers
1. c. 79 AD, with the eruption of Vesuvius. **2. b.** 300 million. **3. d.** 116 years, from 1337 to 1453. **4. b.** two, Anne Boleyn and Catherine Howard.

Crack the code
While I thought that I was learning how to live, I have been learning how to die.

Fakes
Only the details 1, 5, 6, 7 and 10 belong to the image.

DAY 21

Logic
Apple. All the other words can be preceded by F to create a new word: factor, fever, flawless, flopped, fright.

Language
1. a. iceberg. **b.** inequality. **c.** insular. **d.** interim. **e.** Islam. **f.** idyll.
2. a. intriguing. **b.** liberty. **c.** loquacious. **d.** handicap. **e.** diametric. **f.** eternity.

Calculation

1	16	11	6
13	4	7	10
8	9	14	3
12	5	2	15

DAY 22

Observation
Silhouette **f.**

Language
1. c. Word is to book as note is to musical score.
2. a. crocus. **b.** lotus. **c.** rose. **d.** aster. **e.** mimosa. **f.** salvia. **g.** primrose. **h.** gardenia.

Logic
In each line of each square, the sum of the first two numbers is equal to the sum of the last two numbers.
3 + 2 = 5 + 0; 2 + 8 = 4 + 6;
6 + 7 = 5 + 8.
2 + 7 = 8 + 1; 3 + 4 = 6 + 1;
5 + 6 = 7 + 4.
Therefore, 2 is needed in the blank space of each square to find the same balance in the third lines of each square: 1 + 7 = 2 + 6; 4 + 0 = 2 + 2.

DAY 23

Observation

Language
1. rat, tear, irate, pirate, traipse, parasite.
2. **a.** brown, violet. **b.** rhinoceros, antelope, cat. **c.** tulip, anemone, geranium.

Spatial perception

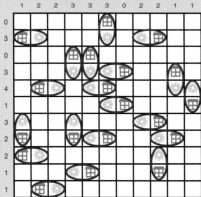

Calculation
The next palindrome number is 2992. The stock market index must therefore rise by 110 points.

DAY 24

Observation

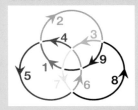

2. **a.** No. A sequence ♣ ♠ ♣ (clubs/spades/clubs) has replaced the original sequence ♠ ♣ ♠ (spades/clubs/spades).
b. No. The second term is symmetrical, but not reversed, as asked for in the instructions. The correct response would have been:
.
c. Yes. Each term is transferred correctly, but in the reverse position. The position of the arrows is admittedly disconcerting.
d. No. There is one ¾ too many.

Calculation
In order to go around the field, the farmer covers twice the length and twice the width. Since the length is 500 metres more than the width, he therefore covers four times the width plus twice 500 metres. Therefore, 4 widths + 1000 metres = 4 kilometres. Four widths therefore equal 3 kilometres, and consequently one width equals 750 metres. The field is therefore 750 metres wide and 1250 metres long.

Language
The two anagrams are pertness and presents.

Spatial perception

The first three cubes show all six sides: two yellow/blue, one blue/black, one red/green, one green/yellow and one red/yellow. Figure **d** therefore corresponds to figure **c** after it has been pivoted half a turn, leaving the red/green side on the top of the cube.
Figures **b** and **c** establish (by pivoting and turning over the green/yellow side) that the blue/black side is opposite the side with blue above/yellow below, as seen in figures **c** and **d**.
The four sides touching the red/green side are the two sides yellow/blue (figure **a**), the yellow/green side (figure **c**) and the blue/black side (since it is opposite a yellow/blue).
The missing side is therefore the blue/black side.

DAY 25

Language
a. destruction. **b.** carrot. **c.** indecent.
d. machinery. **e.** contaminate.
f. maintenance.

Spatial perception
The three shapes to superimpose are shape 6 (the first), then shape 2 (in the middle), and shape 5 (on top).

Calculation
24 planks. If the 6 saws have sawn their first 6 planks in 6 minutes, they will saw 6 more for the following 6 minutes. That will make 12 sawn planks. And 6 similar saws will also saw 6 planks in the same time. Therefore a total of 24 planks will be sawn.

Logic
9 then 11. Two separate sequences are interwoven here. One decreases by 3 each time (18, 15, 12, 9, 6, 3), and the other increases by 2 (5, 7, 9, 11, 13, 15).

DAY 26

Language

1. **a.** therefore. **b.** flavour. **c.** forgivable. **d.** sphinx. **e.** severance. **f.** eyesight.
2. You could take out: E (renting), G (coaster), Y (earning), P (sinners), T (mineral), I (tangles), A (thieves), N (rematch). Someone who lives on the banks of the Nile is an Egyptian.

Logic

Snowflake. All the other words are palindromes: that is, they read the same from left to right as from right to left.

Calculation

1. First possibility:

Alternative solution:

2. d. Sphere S1 is 8 times greater than sphere S2. Each of the three dimensions in space is doubled, and since these dimensions multiply between themselves, the volume is $2 \times 2 \times 2 = 8$ times greater. The volume of sphere S1 is $4/3\pi R^3$. The volume of the second one will therefore be equal to $4/3\pi(R \times 2)^3$, i.e. $8 \times 4/3\pi R^3$.

DAY 27

Observation

The figure contains 40 squares.

Language

a. peach, pear. **b.** mango, orange. **c.** apple, banana. **d.** apricot, pawpaw.

Memory

Group **a** is not the opposite of any of the three groups of words above. Group **b** is the opposite of group **1**, **c** is the opposite of **3**, and **d** is the opposite of **2**.

Logic

In the left column, in order to go from the first domino to the fourth, you need to proceed as follows:
On the left side of the domino, add 2, then multiply by 2, and then finally subtract 2 ($1 + 2 = 3$; $3 \times 2 = 6$; $6 - 2 = 4$).
On the right side of the domino, subtract 2, then divide by 2 and lastly add 2 ($4 - 2 = 2$; $2 \div 2 = 1$; $1 + 2 = 3$). Therefore, in the right column, on the left side of the domino:
$0 + 2 = 2$; $2 \times 2 = 4$; $4 - 2 = 2$; and on the right side of the domino: $6 - 2 = 4$; $4 \div 2 = 2$; $2 + 2 = 4$.
For the colours, the smaller number on each domino has a yellow background and the larger number has a blue background.

DAY 28

Observation

Calculation

1. The triangle. The total of each column will then add up to 32.
2. Blue. The total of each line will then add up to 35.

Language

1. **a.** combine. **b.** define. **c.** bovine. **d.** imagine. **e.** machine. **f.** magazine. **g.** margarine. **h.** spine. **i.** divine.
2. Butter(cup)cake.

DAY 29

Language

1. **a.** cloves, turmeric. **b.** rosemary, parsley, chives. **c.** pecan, almond, cashew.
2. **a.** He who hesitates is lost. **b.** A rolling stone gathers no moss. **c.** One good turn deserves another. **d.** Dead men tell no tales. **e.** Every cloud has a silver lining. **f.** Beggars can't be choosers.

Calculation

The fact that 216 is the cube of 6 is pure chance. The area of the first square is L^2. The new one, which is larger, has an area of $(L + 6)^2$. We want $(L + 6)^2 - L^2$ to equal 216. By developing this, $12L + 36 = 216$, i.e. $12L = 180$ and $L = 15$. The initial square had a side measuring 15 cm (and an area of 225 cm^2); the new one has a side measuring 21 cm and an area of $21 \times 21 = 441$ cm^2, i.e. 216 cm^2 more than the old one.

Spatial perception

Disks **a**, **d** and **f**.

Calculation

500

255 245

140 115 130

95 45 70 60

70 25 20 50 10

Logic

1.

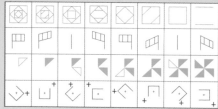

2. The first two numbers, 11 and 17, are separated by a gap of six. The gaps that follow are, in succession, 8 (6 + 2), 10 (8 + 2), 12 (10 + 2), 14 (12+ 2), so the next gap number will be 16 (14 + 2), making the seventh number 77.

Language

a. emigrants. b. mastering.
c. streaming.

Observation

Observation

Figure **e** appears only once.

Anagram crossword

Matching up

A5, B6, C7, D9, E8, F3, G4, H10, I2, J1.

Whose call is that?

Your answers should include:
a. crows caw. **b.** owls hoot/screech.
c. chicks cheep. **d.** monkeys chatter.
e. ducks quack. **f.** hens cluck/cackle.
g. roosters crow. **h.** frogs croak.
i. wolves howl. **j.** elephants trumpet.
k. snakes hiss. **l.** lions roar. **m.** bears growl. **n.** turkeys gobble. **o.** geese cackle/hiss. **p.** pigs oink/grunt.
q. hyenas laugh. **r.** mice squeak.
s. dogs bark/yelp/yap. **t.** horses neigh/whinny. **u.** donkeys bray.
v. sheep bleat/baa. **w.** cows moo/low.

Animal figures

1. b. **2.** b. **3.** c. **4.** c.

Sudoku puzzle

9	5	8	6	2	1	7	3	4
3	7	6	5	4	8	9	1	2
1	4	2	9	3	7	6	5	8
7	6	9	1	8	3	4	2	5
4	8	5	2	6	9	3	7	1
2	1	3	7	5	4	8	6	9
6	9	1	4	7	5	2	8	3
8	2	4	3	1	6	5	9	7
5	3	7	8	9	2	1	4	6

Logic

The four of hearts. The first two cards are always the same suit, and as a heart has been revealed, the hidden card must also be a heart. The value of the middle card is midway between the values of the cards on either side: five is midway between two and eight, nine is midway between seven and the jack, and seven is midway between five and nine. This means that the hidden card must be a four, because eight falls midway between four and the queen.

Observation

Piece **d** is unused.

Language

Sin, sine, mines, monies, moisten, emotions, economist.

Memory

Wales.

Language

Other answers may be possible:
a. quote. **b.** dosage. **c.** insect.
d. elope. **e.** creak. **f.** aptitude.

Calculation

A quarter of 24 is 6, a third of 6 is 2 and half of 2 is 1. You can multiply 1 by itself as many times as you want, the result will always be 1.

Language

a. gossip. **b.** chatter. **c.** utter.
d. negotiate. **e.** mutter. **f.** discuss.
g. converse. **h.** express. **i.** transmit.
j. confer. **k.** parley.

Observation

The odd one out is **d**. It is the only figure in which the surface area occupied by each of the colours is not identical.

Logic

a. symbol. All the other words can be preceded by the prefix 'far': far-reaching, far-sighted, far-flung, far-out. **b.** brick. All the other words are a shade of green, except for brick, which is a shade of red. **c.** boot. With all the other words, you can remove the first letter, 'b', and still have a word: lower, racket, last, order, allot.

DAY 33

Calculation

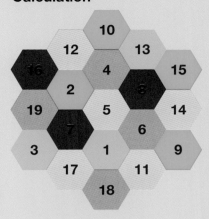

The sum of the numbers 1 to 19 is 190. To divide this total equally between five rows, the total of each row must be 190 ÷ 5 = 38. Starting off with the two sides, each of which has 3 elements, two of which are blue, the sequences 10 13 15 and 15 14 9 are easily placed. The remaining placements are obvious.

Spatial perception

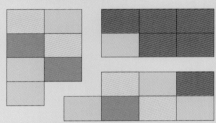

Language

a. turnips. **b.** comparison.
c. consolation. **d.** vertigo.
e. performer.

DAY 34

Language

1. a. R (carrier). **b.** G (giggle).
2. foot(note)pad.

Logic

The numbers on the rings should be 19, 128, 33, 22. Three different sequences are interwoven here. The first adds 3 to each new element (1, 4, 7, 10, 13, 16), the second doubles each time (2, 4, 8, 16, 32, 64), and the third adds 5 (3, 8, 13, 18, 23, 28). The missing numbers are therefore 19 (first sequence, 16 + 3); 128 (second sequence, twice 64); 33 (third sequence, 28 + 5); 22 (return to the first series, 19 + 3).

Memory

Each line contains three states and two cities in the USA; the same applies to each column. The first letters of the words on four of the lines form first names: Simon, David, Frank and Louis. All the words in the first line end in A. The most difficult part is to memorise the positions of the names starting or ending in A. Concentrate on this point, and then the rest can be found by deduction.

DAY 35

Logic

1. The sum of the numbers from 1 to 9 will always be 45, and it is impossible to obtain 22.5 on each side. But certain tricks will allow you make the two columns the same: for example, by inverting the 9 to make a 6. You then swap the 2 and the 1 so that each side adds up to 21. Other tricks include inverting the 6 to make a 9, or exchanging other blocks.

2.

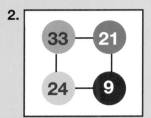

In order to find the yellow ball, you add 3 to the blue. By adding the blue and the yellow, then dividing by 5, you obtain the pink.
By multiplying the blue by 2 and subtracting the pink, you find the value of the orange ball.
To reach the pink 9, blue + yellow must = 45. Knowing that yellow = blue + 3, that implies that yellow = 24 and blue = 21.
Pink is therefore (24 + 21) ÷ 5 = 9 and orange = 2 × 21 − 9 = 33.

Spatial perception

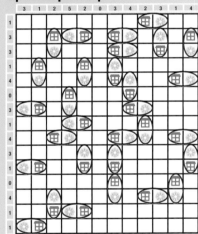

Language

a. creative. **b.** orchestra. **c.** resistance
d. mountaineer. **e.** remonstrates.
f. disagreement.

Index

Recipes (see pages 232–71)

Credits

Abbreviations: t = top, c = centre, b = bottom, l = left, r = right

Photographs

10 cb BSIP, **10** bl, br BSIP/Collection Photo Researchers; **11** b BSIP; **14** Akg-Images, Paris/Cameraphoto, **14** l, r Jupiter Images; **17** l BSIP, br Lookatsciences/Patrice Latron; **18** t Cosmos/Quest/SPL, br Andia.FR/E. Soudan/Alpaca, bc Cosmos/David Nicholls/SPL; **20** Cosmos/SPL/Gusto; **21** l Shutterstock.com/Bedolaga; **28** bl Michael Maconachie/Auscape, cl Graeme S Chapman; **29** t Corbis/Bettmann; **30** t Jupiter Images, b *wine, copper pot, cup and saucer* Brand X Pictures, *bread* iStockimages.com/ivanmateev, *napkins* Dreamstime. com/Rozhenyuk, *salt and pepper* Shutterstock.com/Mr. Klein, *water* Shutterstock.com/V R Photos, *butter* Shutterstock.com/Smit, *apples* RD; **34** t Corbis/Atlantide Phototravel, b Jupiter Images; **35** P. Thompson (1980), Margaret Thatcher: a new illusion. Perception, 9, 383-384; **40** b Corbis/Patrick Guis/Kipa; **48** t, b Jupiter Images; **49** t Jupiter Images, **49** b Corbis/Bettmann; **50** Jupiter Images; **51** t Corbis/Roland Schlager/ EPA, b Getty Images/Photonica/Richard Kolker; **54–55** Akg-Images, Paris; **54** bl Corbis/© Philadelphia Museum of Art, cr Corbis/Gallo Images, bc Jupiter Images; **55** br Cyril Ruoso/Dominique Fontenat, c Getty Images/Co Rentmeester/Time & Life Pictures; **56** b Corbis Saba/Claudio Edinger © Louise Bourgeois/Adagp, Paris, 2009, c Rue Des Archives/Pablo Picasso avec Faune en céramique © Succession Picasso 2009, t Rue Des Archives/Lebrecht; **57** BSIP James Cavallini, BSIP/Collection Photo Researchers, Phanie; **58** Jupiter Images; **59** Phanie; **61** t Jupiter Images, b Rue Des Archives/The Granger Collection NYC; **62** l Jupiter Images; **63** l Allarts/Camera 1/Cinea/The Kobal Collection, br Getty Images/Digital Vision; **64** Getty Images/Iconica/ Michael Brinson; **65** Corbis; **68** Photolibrary; **71** Corbis/Bettmann; **77** t Jupiter Images, b Brand X Pictures; **78** t Dreamstime.com/Tdmartin, c Shutterstock.com/Eastimages, b iStockphoto.com/FrankvandenBergh; **79** t iStockphoto.com/JochenScheffl, b AFP Photo/Jim Watson; **80** t, b Jupiter Images; **81** bl, bc, br Jupiter Images, t © 2009 King Features Syndicate, Inc.™ Hearst Holdings, Inc.; **90** t Food Collection, b Hemis.fr/Emilio Suetone; **94** Photolibrary; **96** b Jupiter Images; **97** t Jupiter Images, b Shutterstock.com/Monkey Business Images; **100** RD; **103** Christian Adam; **107** *4* Shutterstock.com/Loskutnikov, *6* Shutterstock.com/Pius Lee, *10* Shutterstock.com/ilFede; **112** tl iStockphoto.com/bo1982; **114** b Collection Christophe L; **115** t iStockphoto. com/petrograd99, c, b Jupiter Images; **117** t iStockphoto.com/studio9; **119** All Jupiter Images except bl Photodisc, cl Stockdisc; **122** Jupiter Images; **123** AFP Photo/Rob O'Neal/Florida Keys News Bureau via Getty Images; **127** bl BSIP/Photo Researchers; **127** cl Corbis/Hulton-Deutsch Collection; **129** iStockphoto.com/ JamesBrey; **131** Corbis/Hulton-Deutsch Collection; **132** Corbis/Layne Kennedy; **136** iStockphoto.com; **139** Jupiter Images; **141** r Reuters; **142** Jupiter Images; **146** Signatures/ZIR; **147** Collection Christophe L; **150** b Hemis.fr/Mattes; **157** t Shutterstock.com/Jacqui Martin; **166** BSIP/Jacopin; **167** b The Kobal Collection; **168** Presse Sports/Prévost; **181** Jupiter Images; **183** Getty Images; **184** Photolibrary; **185** t REA/Itay Barshadski/ Israel Sun, b Getty Images; **188** l Reuters/Aung Hla Tun, r Reuters/Finbarr O'Reilly; **190** Jupiter Images; **191** cr Didier Pavois, bl Figaro Photo/Sébastien Soriano; **194** l, c Jupiter Images, r Oredia/Alexandre Jacques; **195** Corbis/Kipa/Catherine Cabrol; **198** Getty Images; **199** Photolibrary; **201** t, b Jupiter Images; **202** Presse Sports/UweSpeck/Witters; **205** Photolibrary; **207** Sipa Press/Fayolle; **208** t Emmanuelle Thiercelin/fedephoto. com, b Getty Images; **213** REA/Pierre Bessard; **218** b Pascal Goetgheluck; **219** Jupiter Images; **220** tl Cosmos/ Alfred Pasieka/SPL, cl Dreamstime.com/Newlight, br Jupiter Images; **222** t Jupiter Images, c, b Photolibrary; **225** bl Jupiter images; **235** t Christian Adam, b Food Collection; **237** t Christian Adam, b Food Collection; **239** t Christian Adam, b Food Collection; **241** t Christian Adam, b Food Collection; **243** t Christian Adam, b Food Collection; **244** Brand X Pictures; **245** RD; **247** t Christian Adam, b Shutterstock.com/motorolka; **249** t Christian Adam, b iStockimages.com/Floortje; **251** t Christian Adam, b Food Collection; **253** t Shutterstock.com/romvo, b Christian Adam; **255** t Shutterstock.com/Jozsef Szasz-Fabian, b Christian Adam; **257** t RD, b Shutterstock. com/Jane Rix; **259** t Christian Adam, b Shutterstock.com/Joe Belanger; **261** t Christian Adam, b Food Collection; **263** t Christian Adam, b Shutterstock.com/Peter zijlstra; **265** RD; **267** t Shutterstock.com/Olga Miltsova, b Christian Adam; **269** t Shutterstock.com/Norman Chan, b Christian Adam; **271** t Christian Adam, b Food Collection; **278** Shutterstock.com/Simon Krzic; **280** Shutterstock.com/Yuri Arcurs; **283** b Shutterstock. com/Phil Date; **284** Shutterstock.com/Goodluz; **285** l Shutterstock.com, c Shutterstock.com/EpicStock, r Shutterstock.com/Supri Suharjoto; **290** Shutterstock.com/Galina Barskaya; **292** Shutterstock.com/ wormdog51; **307** Getty/Photodisc; **317** Getty Images/Allsports Concepts/Chris Cole; **318** Corbis/Royalty Free; **327** Jupiter Images; **331** RD.

Illustrations

Laurent Audouin 29, 31, 72, 74, 98, 149, 154, 299, 311, 319, 321, 322, 332; **Delphine Bailly** 21 r, 26–27, 32–33, 39, 44, 45, 46, 47 b, 196; **Grégoire Cirade** 73, 148 t; **Colman Cohen** 153; **Bernard Courtois** 12 t, 93, 151, 152, 156, 223; **Sylvie Dessert** 10, 11 t, 13, 15, 16 b, 19, 47 t, 92, 128, 161; **Hélène Lafaix** 275, 277, 279, 281, 283, 287, 289, 291, 293; **Hélène Perdereau** 12 b, 16–17, 22, 28, 38, 40, 42, 60, 62 r, 69, 70, 76, 84, 89, 95, 96, 101, 102, 108, 116, 127, 141 l, 146–147, 150 t, 154, 160, 165, 167 t, 170, 180, 186, 189, 197, 200, 204, 206, 210, 216, 218 t, 221, 226, 228, 231.

Concept code: GR 1258/G
Product code: 041 4261